Hands-On Microsoft® Windows® Server 2003

Michael J. Palmer

THOMSON

COURSE TECHNOLOGY

Australia • Canada • Mexico • Singapore • Spain • United Kingdom • United States

THOMSON

COURSE TECHNOLOGY

Hands-On Microsoft® Windows® Server 2003

is published by Course Technology

Senior Editor:
William Pitkin III

Product Manager:
Charles G. Blum

Production Editor:
Elena Montillo

Manufacturing Coordinator:
Trevor Kallop

MQA Technical Leader:
Nicole Ashton

Product Marketing Manager:
Jason Sakos

Associate Product Manager:
Tim Gleeson

Associate Product Manager:
Nick Lombardi

Cover Design:
Julie Malone

Text Designer:
GEX Publishing Services

Compositor:
GEX Publishing Services

Disclaimer
Course Technology reserves the right to revise this publication and make changes from time to time in its content without notice.

ISBN 0-619-18608-9

BRIEF

Contents

TABLE OF

Contents

Introduction

Hands-On Microsoft® Windows® Server 2003 is your opportunity to explore and learn Microsoft's newest server operating system. This book is designed to provide you with a broad understanding of Windows Server 2003 from installation to configuration, to management and monitoring. If you are new to server administration, this book can give you the knowledge you need to manage servers and server resources on small to large networks. If you are an experienced server administrator, this book provides a fast way to get up to speed in Windows Server 2003.

Each chapter is filled with all types of aids to help you quickly learn and retain what you have learned, including extensive screen reproductions and illustrations. The objectives at the start of every chapter give you an overview of what you will be able to accomplish and can be used for a fast review of the chapter contents. At the end of each chapter, there are chapter summaries for more in-depth point-by-point review. Throughout each chapter, you'll find many hands-on activities, so that you can immediately practice and apply what you are learning. This approach not only makes learning more interesting, but it helps prepare you for real-life administration activities. Besides the hands-on activities, each chapter gives you experience through realistic case studies that put you in the shoes of a Windows Server 2003 consultant who works in all kinds of situations fulfilling the needs of clients. Other learning tools include a list of key terms that you have encountered in the chapter and a set of review questions.

Intended Audience

Hands-On Microsoft® Windows® Server 2003 is intended for anyone who wants to learn and practice using Windows Server 2003. The computer concepts that you need to know are typically explained as you encounter them. However, for best understanding (although not required) it is helpful to have some prior experience with a Windows operating system, such as Windows 2000 or Windows XP, and a very basic knowledge of the purpose of network servers.

Chapter Descriptions

There are twelve chapters and one appendix in this book. The beginning chapters provide an introduction to the Windows Server 2003 operating system, and show how to install and configure Windows Server 2003, and how to use Active Directory. The middle chapters address how to configure vital services, such as file and folder services, printing, data storage, network services, and remote access. The chapters at the end of the book focus on configuring security, server and network monitoring, and ensuring server reliability. The appendix provides supplementary information about server installation options.

Chapter 1, "Introduction to Windows Server 2003, Standard Edition" discusses each of the Windows Server 2003 operating systems: Standard Edition, Web Edition, Enterprise Edition, and Datacenter Edition. The chapter also provides more detailed information about specific features of Windows Server 2003 and discusses Windows Server 2003 networking.

Chapter 2 "Installing Windows Server 2003, Standard Edition" explains how to prepare for an installation, describes different installation methods, and steps through an installation. The chapter additionally discusses using service packs, creating an Automated System Recovery set, and how to troubleshoot installation problems.

Chapter 3, "Configuring the Windows Server 2003 Environment" shows you how to install and configure hardware and how to begin configuring the operating system for everyday performance, including how to configure protocols. You also learn how to configure the Windows 2003 registry.

Chapter 4, "Introduction to Active Directory and Account Management" explains beginning use of Active Directory and how to install Active Directory. You also learn how to manage user accounts and security groups.

Chapter 5, "Configuring, Managing, and Troubleshooting Resource Access" teaches you how to manage folders and files, particularly in relation to setting up security. You learn how to create shared objects, such as folders, and how to publish them in Active Directory. You additionally learn how to implement the Distributed File System and how to establish disk quotas.

Chapter 6 "Configuring Windows Server 2003 Printing" provides information about the inner workings of Windows Server 2003 printing, including how to install local, network, and Internet printers. You learn how to manage print jobs and how to troubleshoot printing problems.

Chapter 7 "Configuring and Managing Data Storage" shows you how to configure basic and dynamic disks, plus how to manage disks and troubleshoot problems. You learn how to use disk fault tolerance and how to perform disk backups and restores.

Chapter 8 "Managing Windows Server 2003 Network Services" focuses on how to configure the essential services needed for a smooth functioning network, including DHCP, DNS, WINS, Internet Information Services, and Telnet.

Chapter 9 "Configuring Remote Access Services" enables you to learn how to set up Windows Server 2003 as a Remote Access Server and to how to configure a virtual private network. This chapter also focuses on how to configure Terminal Services for running applications directly on a server.

Chapter 10 "Securing Windows Server 2003" discusses the use of group and security policies for fine tuning security at a server and on clients that access a server. The Encrypting File System is additionally discussed as a means of securing information in folders and files.

Chapter 11 "Server and Network Monitoring" teaches you how to monitor a server and a network for troubleshooting and to prevent problems. You learn how to use tools such as Task Manager, System Monitor, Network Monitor, and the SMNP Service.

Chapter 12 "Managing System Reliability and Availability" enables you to develop problem-solving strategies for handling server difficulties. Specifically, you learn how to resolve boot problems, protect critical system files, use server logs to diagnose or prevent a problem, troubleshoot security and connectivity, and remotely manage a server.

Appendix A "Winnt and Winnt32 Installation Switches" provides information on the large number of switches that can be used to customize a server installation.

Features and Approach

Hands-On Microsoft® Windows® Server 2003 is one in a series of Course Technology Hands-On books that differ from other server and networking books by offering a unique hands-on approach and orientation to real-world situations and problem solving. To help you comprehend how Microsoft Windows Server 2003 and network management concepts and techniques are applied in real-world organizations, this book incorporates the following features:

- **Chapter Objectives**—Each chapter begins with a detailed list of the concepts to be mastered. This list gives you a quick reference to the chapter's contents and is a useful study aid.

- **Hands-On Activities**—Hands-on activities are incorporated throughout the text, giving you practice in setting up, managing, and troubleshooting a network system. The activities give you a strong foundation for carrying out network administration tasks in the real world.

- **Chapter Summary**—Each chapter's text is followed by a summary of the concepts introduced in that chapter. These summaries provide a helpful way to recap and revisit the ideas covered in each chapter.

- **Key Terms**—All of the terms within the chapter that were introduced with boldfaced text are gathered together in the Key Terms list at the end of the chapter. This provides you with a method of checking your understanding of all the terms introduced.

- **Review Questions**—The end-of-chapter assessment begins with a set of review questions that reinforce the ideas introduced in each chapter. Answering these questions will ensure that you have mastered the important concepts.

- **Case Projects**—Each chapter closes with a multipart case project. In this realistic case example, as a consultant at Bayside IT Services, you implement the skills and knowledge gained in the chapter through real-world setup and administration scenarios.

- **On the CD ROM**—On the CD-ROM you will find a free 180-day evaluation copy of Microsoft Windows Server 2003, Enterprise Edition.

Text and Graphic Conventions

Additional information and exercises have been added to this book to help you better understand what's being discussed in the chapter. Icons throughout the text alert you to these additional materials. The icons used in this book are described below.

Tips offer extra information on resources, how to attack problems, and time-saving shortcuts.

Notes present additional helpful material related to the subject being discussed.

The Caution icon identifies important information about potential mistakes or hazards.

Each Hands-on Activity in this book is preceded by the hands-on icon.

Case project icons mark the end-of-chapter case projects, which are scenario-based assignments that ask you to independently apply what you have learned in the chapter.

Instructor's Resources

The following supplemental materials are available when this book is used in a classroom setting. All of the supplements available with this book are provided to the instructor on a single CD-ROM.

Electronic Instructor's Manual. The Instructor's Manual that accompanies this textbook includes additional instructional material to assist in class preparation, including suggestions for classroom activities, discussion topics, and additional activities.

Solutions. The instructor's resources include solutions to all end-of-chapter material, including the Review Questions, Hands-on Activities, and Case Projects.

ExamView®. This textbook is accompanied by ExamView, a powerful testing software package that allows instructors to create and administer printed, computer (LAN-based), and Internet exams. ExamView includes hundreds of questions that correspond to the topics covered in this text, enabling students to generate detailed study guides that include page references for further review. The computer-based and Internet testing components allow students to take exams at their computers and also save the instructor time by grading each exam automatically.

PowerPoint presentations. This book comes with Microsoft PowerPoint slides for each chapter. These are included as a teaching aid for classroom presentation, to make available to students on the network for chapter review, or to be printed for classroom distribution. Instructors, please feel at liberty to add your own slides for additional topics you introduce to the class.

Figure files. All of the figures and tables in the book are reproduced on the Instructor's Resource CD, in bitmap format. Similar to the PowerPoint presentations, these are included as a teaching aid for classroom presentation, to make available to students for review, or to be printed for classroom distribution

System Requirements

Hardware:

- Listed in Microsoft's Hardware Compatibility List
- Pentium 550 MHz processor
- 256 RAM
- 2 GB disk space (or more depending on how many services you want to install)
- VGA monitor
- Mouse or pointing device
- Network interface card connected to the classroom, lab, or school network
- 3.5 inch high-density floppy disk drive
- CD-ROM drive (recommended but not required)
- Tape or CD-R drive (recommended but not required)
- Modem (recommended but not required)
- Printer (to practice setting up a network printer)

Software:

- Windows Server 2003, Standard or Enterprise Edition. This book was written using Windows Server 2003, Standard Edition. However, it also can be used with Windows Server 2003, Enterprise Edition because the differences are minimal in terms of configuring and managing a server. Further, the activities in the book use the classic desktop theme that is installed by default.

ACKNOWLEDGMENTS

Many fine people have made this book possible. I want to thank Will Pitkin of Course Technology and Rick Kennedy of Digital Content Factory for the opportunity to work on this book. Charlie Blum has skillfully and patiently managed and directed this project along with the coordinating and supportive efforts of Moirag Haddad.

I am also indebted to Elena Montillo for her dedicated work as production editor and to Mark Goodin who has copyedited the entire manuscript. Scott Schnoll has provided important assistance as the technical editor. Nicole Ashton's quality assurance team has given comprehensive support by carefully checking the accuracy of the text and testing each hands-on activity.

DEDICATION

In memory of Earl F. Michael

1

INTRODUCTION TO WINDOWS SERVER 2003, STANDARD EDITION

After reading this chapter and completing the exercises, you will be able to:

♦ Identify the key features of each platform that makes up the Windows Server 2003 family

♦ Understand the advantages of using Windows XP Professional on a Windows Server 2003 network

♦ Understand the features of Windows Server 2003 that make it an ideal server operating system

♦ Plan a Windows Server 2003 networking model

♦ Understand the protocols best suited for Windows Server 2003

♦ Implement TCP/IP in Windows Server 2003

Servers and networks provide the life blood for information handling in businesses and organizations all over the world. When you use the Internet to check stock quotes, purchase a music CD, or access your favorite news Web site, chances are that you are linking into a Microsoft Windows 2000 Server or a Windows Server 2003 computer. On-call physicians are paged for emergencies, organ donors are located, and new medical procedures are taught through the help of Microsoft Windows servers. The next time you apply for a job, send an e-mail, develop a budget, or take a class, the facilitator in the background may be a Microsoft Windows server.

As a Microsoft Windows Server 2003 professional, you have a ground-floor opportunity to participate in a technology that continues to push the boundaries of information sharing. This chapter provides a beginning by introducing you to the different Windows Server 2003 platforms and discusses the advantages of using Windows XP Professional with Windows Server 2003 for a lower total cost of operations. You'll also learn some of the capabilities of Windows Server 2003 that make it ideal as a server operating system. The last portion of the chapter will offer a discussion of the peer-to-peer and server-based network connectivity models, as well as the fundamentals of the TCP/IP protocol suite.

WINDOWS SERVER 2003 PLATFORMS

Businesses today have a wide variety of needs, making it difficult for a single operating system to include all the necessary features. Windows Server 2003 is divided into four different operating system platforms. Each of the platforms has similar capabilities while also containing unique features that make each platform suitable for different server environments—allowing businesses to choose the platform that best meets their needs.

The Windows Server 2003 operating system comes in the following platforms, which are discussed in the next sections:

- Windows Server 2003, Standard Edition
- Windows Server 2003, Web Edition
- Windows Server 2003, Enterprise Edition
- Windows Server 2003, Datacenter Edition

Windows Server 2003, Standard Edition

Windows Server 2003, Standard Edition, provides the foundation for the Windows Server 2003 operating system platforms and is designed to meet the everyday needs of small to large businesses. It provides file and print services, secure Internet connectivity, and centralized management of network resources. This platform is built on Windows 2000 Server and is the upgrade path from that operating system.

Windows Server 2003, Standard Edition, provides basic operating system elements that enable file and printer sharing over a network and secure management of these assets. It supports up to two processors in a **symmetric multiprocessor (SMP) computer**, which is a computer that uses more than one processor. The maximum RAM this platform can use is 4 GB. For companies that develop their own software, Windows Server 2003 is compatible with the Common Runtime Language used in Microsoft .NET Framework and Microsoft Visual Studio .NET; and Windows Server 2003 enables computer programmers to develop and use program code in several different languages. Windows Server 2003, Standard Edition, also makes it easier for server administrators to manage access to server resources, such as files.

A small company or a department in a larger company might use Windows Server 2003, Standard Edition, to manage its accounting and payroll software, for example. A medium-sized or large company might use it to manage e-mail or to manage network resources. Small to large companies might use Windows Server 2003 to manage users' access to application software, such as Microsoft Office.

Windows Server 2003, Web Edition

Windows Server 2003, Web Edition, is designed for hosting and deploying Web services and applications. This platform also supports up to two processors and as much as 2 GB of RAM. It is particularly optimized to run Microsoft Internet Information Services (IIS) 6.0.

Small to large companies, or departments within an organization that develop and deploy a single Web site, are examples of the intended users of this platform. They can employ it to develop a Web site that takes advantage of the .NET Framework tools and XML Web services. One limitation of Windows Server 2003, Web Edition, is that it cannot be used to manage network resources via hosting Active Directory, a function that is available to all other Windows Server 2003 platforms. You'll learn more about Active Directory later in this chapter.

Windows Server 2003, Enterprise Edition

Windows Server 2003, Enterprise Edition, is designed to meet the needs of networks with applications and Web services requiring high-end servers and a high level of productivity. Windows Server 2003, Enterprise Edition, supports up to eight processors in SMP computers and comes in versions for 32-bit x86 processors and 64-bit Itanium processors. In addition to these features, this platform has the following advantages:

- Supports up to 32 GB for x86 processor computers and up to 64 GB for Itanium processor computers

- Enables **clustering** up to eight computer nodes. Clustering is the ability to increase the access to server resources and provide fail-safe services by linking two or more discrete computer systems so they appear to function as though they are one.

- Supports **hot-add memory**, in which RAM is added without shutting down the computer or operating system

- Provides Non-Uniform Memory Access (NUMA) support for SMP computers that enable a processor to access memory designated for other processors; and in the case of the Enterprise Edition, applications can be written so that they take advantage of NUMA capabilities, including faster memory access

- Provides Microsoft Metadirectory Services to facilitate networks that use multiple directory services to track and manage access to such resources as user accounts, shared folders, and shared printers

Medium-sized to large organizations might use this platform to host large-scale accounting, manufacturing, or inventory systems. A college might use this platform for a student information or registration system. A bank might take advantage of this platform because if its reliability and availability.

Windows Server 2003, Datacenter Edition

Windows Server 2003, Datacenter Edition, is designed for environments with mission critical applications, very large databases, and information access requiring high availability. This platform offers support for eight to 32 processors in an SMP computer, plus eight-node clustering capacity. Like the Enterprise Edition, the Datacenter Edition enables hot-add memory for increased server availability. The RAM capabilities for the Datacenter Edition are the most robust at 64 GB for x86 processor computers and 128 GB for Itanium processor computers. Windows Server 2003, Datacenter Edition, is the most industrial-strength platform designed for large database applications in any organization. A university alumni association might use it to house a database that tracks information on thousands of alumni all over the world. A large company might use it for an integrated accounting system that stores information in a complex database. A national investment firm might use it to track and manage the investment holdings of its customers.

Table 1-1 summarizes the minimum recommended hardware requirements for each of the Windows Server 2003 platforms.

Table 1-1   Windows Server 2003 minimum recommended hardware requirements

Hardware	Standard Edition	Web Edition	Enterprise Edition	Datacenter Edition
CPU	Recommend at least 550 MHz	Recommend at least 550 MHz	Recommend at least 733 MHz	Recommend at least 733 MHz
Disk space	A minimum of 1.5 GB for the operating system	A minimum of 1.5 GB for the operating system	A minimum of 1.5 GB for the operating system (2 GB for Itanium computers)	A minimum of 1.5 GB for the operating system (2 GB for Itanium computers)
Processor support	Up to 2; determine the number of processors based on the application	Up to 2; determine the number of processors based on the application	Up to 8; determine the number of processors based on the application	8 to 32; determine the number of processors based on the application
RAM	Recommend at least 256 MB	Recommend at least 256 MB	Recommend at least 256 MB	Recommend at least 1 GB

Activity 1-1: Determining the Windows Server 2003 Operating System Edition

Time Required: Approximately 5 minutes

Objective: Use My Computer to determine which edition of Windows Server 2003 is running on your computer.

Description: In medium-sized and large organizations a computer room may have tens or hundreds of servers. Sometimes it is important for a server administrator to verify which edition of Windows Server 2003 is running on a particular server. In this activity, you learn how to make a quick determination. You will need a server account provided by your instructor or server administrator.

1. Log onto your Windows Server 2003 computer using your account name and password.
2. Click **Start** and then right-click **My Computer**.
3. Click **Properties**.
4. Notice the operating system type that is listed under the System: section of the General tab. What operating system is in use?
5. Close the **System Properties** window.

Activity 1-2: Comparing the Windows Server 2003 Platform Features

Time Required: Approximately 15 minutes

Objective: Compare Windows Server 2003 Standard Edition, Web Edition, Enterprise Edition, and Datacenter Edition.

Description: One of the best ways to learn about the similarities and differences of the Windows Server 2003 platforms is to view information about them that is published on Microsoft's Web site. In this activity, you access *www.microsoft.com* and learn more about each of the platforms.

1. Start a Web browser, such as **Internet Explorer** or **Netscape Communicator**, in Windows Server 2003, Windows 2000, or Windows XP.
2. Type the Web site address **www.microsoft.com**, and press **Enter**.
3. Select the link **All Products**, and then select the link **Servers**. (Note that these links may change. If they do, look for a Windows link and select to view product information for Windows Server 2003, or search for Windows Server 2003.)
4. Select the link for **Windows Server 2003**.
5. Select the link for **Product overview** and read the information presented about each edition of Windows Server 2003.

6. Return to the Web page for Windows Server 2003 (the page displayed in Step 4), by clicking the link **Windows Server 2003 Home**.

7. Click the link for **Compare the editions** and read the comparison information.

8. Close **Internet Explorer** or **Netscape Communicator**.

WINDOWS XP PROFESSIONAL AND WINDOWS SERVER 2003

The client workstation operating system most compatible with Windows Server 2003 is Windows XP Professional. A **client** is a computer that accesses resources on another computer via a network or direct cable connection; a **workstation** is a computer that has its own central processing unit (CPU) and may be used as a stand-alone or network computer (often used for a combination of word processing, spreadsheet, scientific, and other individual applications).

The overall goal of Microsoft is to use the Windows Server 2003 platforms and Windows XP Professional on the same network to achieve a lower **total cost of ownership (TCO)**. The TCO is the total cost of owning a network, including hardware, software, training, maintenance, and user support costs. Windows XP Professional is intended as a reliable, easy-to-configure workstation operating system to be used in a business environment in a peer-to-peer network or as a member of a domain. A **domain** is a grouping of network objects, such as computers, servers, and user accounts that provides for easier management. Recognizing that professionals are highly mobile, Windows XP Professional is designed to work equally well on a desktop computer or on a mobile computer.

 To learn more about Windows XP Professional and its relationship to TCO read the article, "Higher Yields: The Financial Benefits of Windows XP Professional" published by Microsoft at *www.microsoft.com/windowsxp/pro/evaluation/whyupgrade/bizval/default.asp*.

Windows Server 2003, Standard Edition, is intended to play a key management role on the network by hosting **Active Directory**—a database of computers, users, groups, shared printers, shared folders, and other network resources—and by offering a multitude of network services. Windows XP Professional (and Windows 2000 Professional) offers the best compatibility with Active Directory. By combining Windows XP Professional client workstations and Windows Server 2003, Standard Edition, under the management of Active Directory, it is possible to centralize security, applications, application updates, and automated client configuration via a server, thus reducing the TCO.

Another of the long-term objectives of Microsoft is to encourage users to convert all workstation operating systems on a network to Windows XP Professional, because the TCO for Windows XP Professional is less than for other workstation operating systems such as Windows 95 and Windows 98. The TCO is less because Windows XP Professional is able to use automated installation, configuration, desktop, and management policy features controlled through Windows Server 2003, Standard Edition. Many desktop configuration settings (including software deployment) can be automated from Windows Server 2003, Standard Edition, to Windows XP Professional, so that the user can set up a client workstation with practically no technical knowledge or assistance.

WINDOWS SERVER 2003 FEATURES

Like its Windows NT Server and Windows 2000 Server predecessors, Microsoft Windows Server 2003 (all editions) includes many features that make it a versatile server **network operating system (NOS)**:

- Centralized administration and management of resources
- Security
- Scalability and compatibility

- Reliability
- Distributability
- Fault tolerance and recovery

Each of these features is discussed in the following sections.

Centralized Administration and Management of Resources

Active Directory is implemented as a service that allows network **resources** such as users, computers, printers, applications, policies, and data to be centrally organized. This provides centralized administration and gives administrators the ability to remotely manage network resources. Objects that are stored in Active Directory are accessible to users throughout an organization making network resources easier to locate. Users do not need to know the physical location of the objects because they are logically grouped into a central location. The specific structure of Active Directory is easily adapted, so it can be customized to meet the needs of almost all business environments.

A server-based network consists of resources that can be centrally managed. Windows Server 2003 offers a way to centralize management of network resources in order to simplify network management tasks.

One way in which Windows Server 2003 makes a network easier to manage is through Active Directory and the grouping of objects into organizational units, domains, trees, forests, and sites. These objects are explained in Chapter 4. Active Directory offers a way to manage resources, workstations, software, and the network from one central location. For the network administrator, this means that the network resources can be managed with minimum confusion and time expenditure.

 Remember that all editions of Windows Server 2003, except the Web Edition, can host Active Directory. However, the Web Edition can still be managed through Active Directory.

Security

At one time, computer security was given little attention. Today, security is an essential issue. Network servers house sensitive data that must be protected from intruders who may try to access it through a local network or via the Internet. Windows Server 2003 provides many levels of security through the following features that are discussed in Chapters 5 and 10.

- File and folder permissions
- Security policies
- Encryption of data
- Event auditing
- Various authentication methods
- Server management and monitoring tools

Scalability and Compatibility

Most companies want a system that can grow as their organization's needs grow. **Scalability** is the ability of a computer operating system to continue to meet the demands of a growing business; for example, it is the ability of an operating system to scale to multiple processors. Windows Server 2003, Standard Edition, for instance, can be scaled to handle substantial growth. The operating system can support from 1 to 15,000 user connections. It works on single-processor computers and can be scaled to dual-processor SMP computers. Windows Server 2003, Datacenter Edition, can run on computers that have up to 32 processors, depending on the capability of the hardware. Both Windows Server 2003, Enterprise Edition, and Windows Server 2003, Datacenter Edition, can run on Itanium computers with 64-bit capabilities.

Windows Server 2003 (all editions) is also compatible with many different operating systems, making it an ideal choice for a network environment running a variety of different platforms. Windows Server 2003 can coexist with IBM, Novell, UNIX, Banyan, DEC, and other network operating systems. It can be accessed by workstations with any of the following operating systems:

- MS-DOS
- Windows 3.x
- Windows 95 and Windows 98
- Windows Me
- Windows NT (Server and Workstation)
- Windows 2000 (all editions)
- Windows XP (Professional and Home)
- Macintosh
- UNIX
- Linux

Activity 1-3: Sample Features for Non-Microsoft Systems

Time Required: Approximately 10 minutes

Objective: View sample services that can be installed for compatibility with UNIX and Macintosh clients.

Description: Some networks do not take full advantage of the Windows Server 2003 connectivity options for computers running UNIX and Macintosh, such as file or print services. In this activity you get a glimpse of some of those features, and in Chapter 3 you learn how to install them.

1. Log on to the Windows Server 2003, Standard Edition.

2. Click **Start**, point to **Control Panel**, and click **Add or Remove Programs** as shown in Figure 1-1.

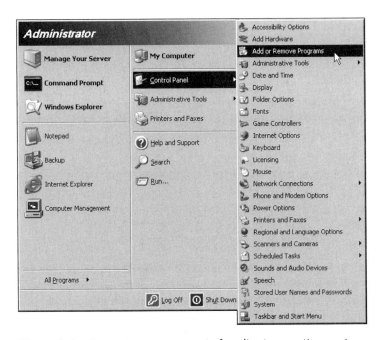

Figure 1-1   Accessing components for client operating systems

3. Click **Add/Remove Windows Components**.

4. In the Components: box, scroll to **Other Network File and Print Services**, and click that option. Click the **Details** button. What services are shown for Macintosh and for Unix?

5. Click **Cancel** in the Other Network File and Print Services dialog box.

6. Click **Cancel** in the Windows Components Wizard dialog box.

7. Close the **Add or Remove Programs** dialog box.

Reliability

Several features make Windows Server 2003 reliable and powerful. One feature is that the operating system kernel runs in **privileged mode**, which protects it from problems created by a malfunctioning program or process. The **kernel** consists of the core programs and the computer code of the operating system. The privileged mode gives the operating system kernel an extra level of security from intruders and prevents system crashes due to poorly written applications.

Legacy applications, such as MS-DOS programs or any 16-bit applications, are run within a virtual DOS machine to protect the operating system. The virtual DOS machine tricks the MS-DOS application into responding as though it were the only application running. Each virtual DOS machine session runs in a separate memory space, and several MS-DOS programs and 16-bit programs can be running at once. If a program attempts to make a direct call to memory or to a hardware component, and the operating system detects an error condition or an exception to security, the program may be stopped without affecting the operating system or any other programs that may be running.

Activity 1-4: Determining When the Virtual DOS Machine is in Use

Time Required: Approximately 5 minutes

Objective: Learn how to monitor a 16-bit Windows or an MS-DOS application that is running via the virtual DOS machine.

Description: Server administrators frequently monitor one or more servers to determine what is being run so that they have a better idea of how to manage specific applications. Even though it is not the recommended best use of a server's resources, sometimes it is necessary for an organization to run an older specialized MS-DOS application, or more likely, a 16-bit Windows application, because a newer version has not been developed. In this project, you learn how to determine when an MS-DOS or 16-bit Windows program is running. The virtual DOS machine runs through a Windows Server 2003 program called ntvdm.exe (ntvdm stands for NT virtual DOS machine) and its program process is called wowexec.exe (wowexec stands for Windows on Windows executive). An MS-DOS or 16-bit Windows program should already be installed for your use. Ask your instructor for its location.

1. Log on to Windows Server 2003, Standard Edition, using an account provided by your instructor or an account that has Administrator privileges.

2. Click **Start** and then click **Run**.

3. In the Open box, enter the path to the MS-DOS or 16-bit Windows program, such as C:\Program Files\myprogram.exe. Click **OK**.

4. Right-click the **taskbar** at the bottom of the screen, and click **Task Manager**.

5. Click the **Applications** tab if it is not already selected.

6. Find the program you started in Step 3 and right-click it. Click **Go To Process**. The Processes tab is now displayed and the program you started is highlighted, such as myprogram.exe. Just below the program is wowexec.exe, which is the virtual DOS machine program process within which your DOS program is running. Notice that both wowexec.exe and the program you started are indented to show that they are considered by the system as 16-bit Windows or MS-DOS programs.

7. Close **Task Manager** and close the program that you started.

Another powerful feature of Windows Server 2003 is that it takes full advantage of the multitasking and multithreading capabilities of modern Pentium and Itanium computers. **Multitasking** is the ability to run two or more programs at the same time. For example, Microsoft Word can print a document at the same time that a Microsoft Excel spreadsheet can calculate the sum of a column of numbers. **Multithreading** is the capability of programs written in 32-bit code to run several program code blocks, or "threads," at the same time. For instance, a Microsoft Access database query runs a thread to pull data out of the database, while another thread generates a subtotal of data already obtained.

The multitasking in Windows Server 2003 is called **preemptive multitasking**. That means each program runs in an area of memory separate from areas used by other programs. Early versions of Windows used cooperative multitasking, in which programs shared the same memory area. The advantage of preemptive multitasking is that it reduces the risk of one program interfering with the smooth running of another program.

Distributability

There are many software applications written to distribute functions among computers. For example, a sales analysis program might use programs at one computer, databases from two other computers, and special information display screens at a user's computer. The process of dividing computer functions across many computers is called **distributability**.

Windows Server 2003 handles software distributability through the **Distributed Component Object Model (DCOM)**, an option designed for client/server networks so that software components can communicate over a network and software applications can be integrated across several computers. For example, DCOM makes it possible for a payroll system program on one server to make a remote procedure call over a network to a specific bank's server to transmit automatic deposit data.

Fault Tolerance and Recovery

Windows Server 2003 employs many technologies to aid in the recovery of hardware and software failure. These recovery and fault-tolerance capabilities include:

- Recovery from hard disk failure through software RAID
- Protection from data loss through backup
- Recovery from system configuration errors
- Protection from power outages
- Advanced warning about system and hardware problems

You'll learn more about these features in Chapters 3, 7, and 12.

PLANNING A WINDOWS SERVER 2003 NETWORKING MODEL

In its simplest form, a network is two or more computers linked together. This provides users with the ability to share devices, applications, exchange files, and communicate via e-mail or video conferencing. The following sections will introduce you to the two basic networking models used with Windows Server 2003 and its workstation clients (such as Windows XP Professional): the peer-to-peer model and the server-based model.

Microsoft Windows Server 2003 is a server NOS. It is used to coordinate the ways computers access resources available to them on the network. A **network** is a communications system enabling computer users to share computer equipment, application software, and data, voice, and video transmissions. Physically, a network contains computers joined by communications cabling or sometimes by wireless devices. Networks can link users who are in the same office or building, in a different state, or anywhere in the world (see Figure 1-2).

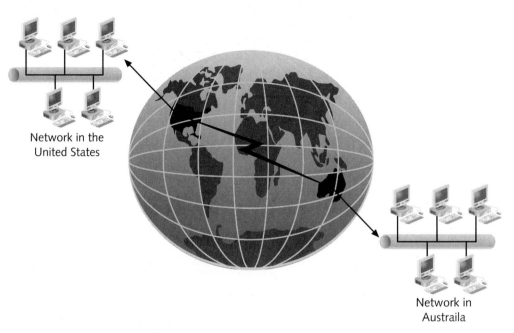

Figure 1-2   Networking across continents

A workstation or client NOS is one that enables individual computers to access a network, and in some cases to share resources on a limited basis. As you learned earlier, a workstation is a computer that has its own central processing unit (CPU) and may be used as a stand-alone or network computer for word processing, spreadsheet creation, or other software applications. A client is a computer that accesses resources on another computer through a network or by a direct connection.

Microsoft Windows Server 2003 can be implemented using either peer-to-peer networking, server-based networking, or a combination of both. **Peer-to-peer networking** focuses on spreading network resource administration among server and nonserver members of a network, while **server-based networking** centralizes the network administration on one or more servers. Often small organizations use the peer-to-peer networking model, while medium-sized and large networks use the server-based model.

Peer-to-Peer Networking

A peer-to-peer network is one of the simplest ways to configure a network, and is often used for home offices and small businesses. On a peer-to-peer network, workstations are used to share resources such as files and printers and to connect to resources on other computers. Windows XP Professional is an example of an operating system that can be used for peer-to-peer network communication. Files, folders, printers, applications, and devices on one computer can be shared and made available for others to access. No special computer, such as a mainframe computer or server, is needed to enable workstations to communicate and share resources, although in some cases a server can be used as a powerful workstation (see Figure 1-3).

Peer-to-peer networking can be effective for very small networks, but there are some disadvantages to this model that must be considered. With this model, management of network resources is decentralized. As the network increases in size and the number of shared network resources increases, administration becomes more and more difficult.

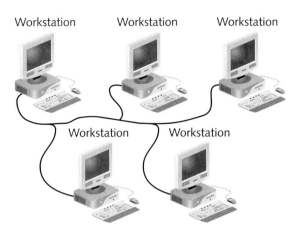

Figure 1-3   A simple peer-to-peer network without a server

The security of the resources is another important issue. Each of the users is responsible for the security of their own resources and must know how to set the proper permissions. Also, a client operating system is not designed to handle a growing load of clients in the same way as a server operating system.

Peer-to-peer networks are generally designed for about 10 workstations or less. As the number of work-stations surpass this number this model becomes less effective for the following reasons:

- Peer-to-peer networking offers only moderate network security, as user account information must be managed on each workstation.

- There is no centralized storage of information for account management. As the number of net-work users grows, so does the need to have a central place to store and manage information. It is much easier to manage files by locating them on a central file server.

- Network management becomes more difficult because there is no point of centralized administrative control from which to manage users and critical files, including backing up important files.

- Peer-to-peer networks can often experience slow response times because this model is not optimized for multiple users accessing one computer. If many workgroup members decide to access one shared drive or some other shared resource at the same time, all members are likely to experience slow response. On Microsoft networks, a **workgroup** is a number of users who share drive and printer resources, and it represents an alternative (generally for small networks) to organizing resources in a domain.

Activity 1-5: How to Determine if a Computer is in a Domain or Workgroup

Time Required: Approximately 5 minutes

Objective: Discover if a particular computer is a member of a domain or a workgroup.

Description: Some networks combine the use of domains and workgroups. Often workgroups are less secure and less tightly managed than a domain, leaving workgroup resources more susceptible to intrud-ers and more likely to have problems with reliable access to shared resources, such as files. In this activity, you learn how to determine if a computer is a member of a domain or workgroup. Use Windows XP Professional or Windows Server 2003 for this activity.

1. With your computer logged on, click **Start**, and then right-click **My Computer**.

2. Click **Properties**.

3. Click the **Computer Name** tab from within the System Properties window.

4. Examine the information on the tab to determine if this computer is part of a domain or workgroup and note your findings. Also, by what name is the computer known to the network? (Keep the computer's name in mind as computer names are discussed later in this chapter.)

5. Close the **System Properties** window.

Server-based Networking

Microsoft Windows Server 2003 is a more scalable network operating system than Windows XP Professional, and unlike Windows XP Professional, it has features that make it a true server operating system. A **server** is a single computer that provides extensive multiuser access to network resources. For example, a single server can act as a file and print server, a Web server, a network administration server, a database server, an e-mail server, or a combination of any of these. Depending on the hardware capabilities, the server may be able to handle hundreds of users at once, providing fast response when delivering the shared resource, and less network congestion when multiple workstations access that resource. Figure 1-4 illustrates a Windows Server 2003 server-based network.

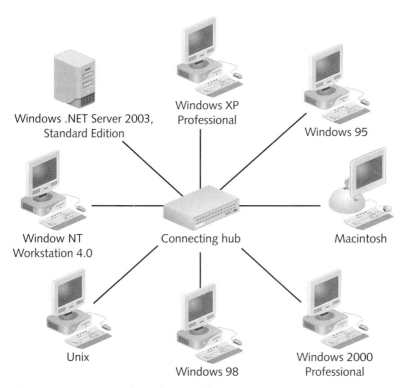

Figure 1-4   A server-based network

The server-based model offers a wide array of options for networking. For instance, implementing this model can provide the following advantages:

- Users only need to log on once to gain access to network resources.

- Security is stronger because access to shared resources can be intentionally managed from one place—the server—rather than randomly managed on many independent peer-to-peer computers.

- All members can share computer files.

- Printers and other resources can be shared; they can also be located in a central place for convenience.

- All members can have electronic mail (e-mail) and send messages to other office members through an e-mail server such as Microsoft Exchange Server.

1

- Software applications, such as an accounting package or word-processing software, can be stored and shared in a central location.

- All computers can be backed up more easily. With a network and server, the backups can be performed from one location and regularly scheduled to run from the server.

- The sharing of computer resources can be arranged to reflect the work patterns of groups within an organization. For example, managing partners in a legal firm can be one group for the purpose of sharing management and financial information on the server.

- The server administrator can save time when installing software upgrades. For example, to implement the latest version of Microsoft Word, the administrator upgrades the software installation files on the server. Then Microsoft Word users on the network can upgrade their versions from the server.

Protocols for the Windows Server 2003 Networking Model

Servers and clients on a Windows Server 2003 network communicate through a set of communications guidelines that are similar to using a language, but the language used by computers is in a binary format of zeros and ones that is sent through network communications cable. The communication languages of computers are called **protocols**. A protocol consists of guidelines for the following:

- How data is formatted into discrete units called packets and frames

- How packets and frames are transmitted across one or more networks

- How packets and frames are interpreted at the receiving end

Packets and **frames** are units of data transmitted from a sending computer to a receiving computer. These units might be compared to words in a language. In a language, people communicate by using words to compose sentences and paragraphs in order to convey a thought. The words by themselves do not convey the full thought until they are placed in the context of a sentence or paragraph. Like words, packets and frames usually do not convey full meaning until the complete stream of information is received; and just as words must be properly placed in sentences and paragraphs, packets and frames must be received in the proper order to be understood.

 Sometimes the terms "packet" and "frame" are used as if they have the same meaning. However, there is a difference between these terms, which is that a packet operates at a higher level of communication than a frame. The higher level of communication associated with a packet enables it to contain routing information so that it can be forwarded from one network to another.

Windows Server 2003 and its clients primarily use the **Transmission Control Protocol/Internet Protocol (TCP/IP)** which is really a suite of protocols and utilities that support communication across **local area networks (LANs)** and the Internet. A LAN is a network of computers in relatively close proximity, such as on the same floor or in the same building. TCP/IP has become the worldwide protocol of choice. One reason for this is that TCP/IP is the protocol used for Internet communication. As companies continue to utilize the Internet as an essential component of their businesses, it makes sense to use TCP/IP as the internal protocol, rather than dedicating additional network resources to use another one. TCP/IP is also popular because it is designed as an open standard, that is, no one owns TCP/IP. It can also be used to connect computers running almost any operating system. In addition, many people around the world are working on improving the standards on which TCP/IP is based.

Transmission Control Protocol

The **Transmission Control Protocol (TCP)** portion of TCP/IP provides for reliable end-to-end delivery of data by controlling data flow. Computers or network stations agree upon a "window" for data transmission that includes the number of bytes to be sent. The transmission window is constantly adjusted to account for existing network traffic. TCP/IP monitors for requests to start a communications session, establishes sessions with other TCP stations, handles transmitting and receiving data, and closes transmission sessions when they are finished. TCP is also considered a **connection-oriented communication** because it ensures that packets are delivered, that they are delivered in the right sequence, and that their contents are accurate.

 Some applications use the **User Datagram Protocol (UDP)** with IP instead of using TCP. These are typically applications in which the reliability of the communication is not a major concern, such as for information used to boot diskless workstations over a network. UDP is a **connectionless communication** because it does not provide checking to make sure that a connection is reliable and that data is sent accurately. The advantage of UDP is that it has less overhead than TCP.

Internet Protocol

The **Internet Protocol (IP)** portion of the TCP/IP protocol provides network addressing to ensure data packets quickly reach the correct destination. It uses a system of addressing that consists of four numbers separated by a period, such as 129.77.15.182. IP also provides for routing data over different networks, so that data sent from one network only goes to the appropriate destination network instead of to all networks that are linked together. Routing is accomplished through a device called a **router**, which connects networks, is able to read IP addresses (see the next section), and can route or forward packets of data to designated networks as shown in Figure 1-5. IP also handles fragmenting packets, because the packet sizes may vary from one network to another. IP is a connectionless communication because it relies on TCP to provide connection-oriented communications.

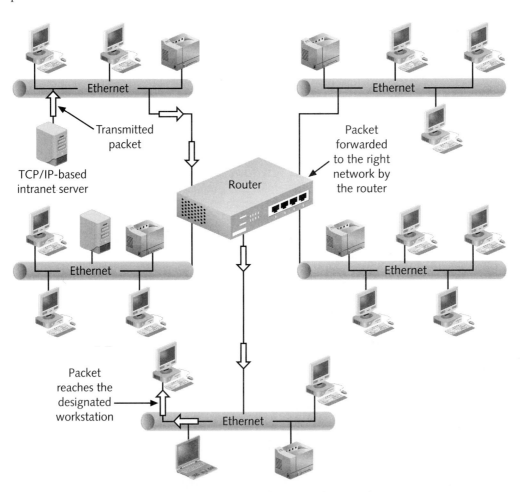

Figure 1-5   A router forwarding packets to a designated network

The combined TCP/IP protocol is particularly well suited for medium-sized and large networks, but it becomes important on any enterprise network or on a local area network that connects to a wide area network.

IP Addressing

The **IP address** format is called the **dotted decimal notation** address. It is 32 bits long and contains four fields of decimal values representing eight-bit binary octets. An IP address in binary octet format looks like this: 10000001.00000101.00001010.1100100, which converts to 129.5.10.100 in decimal format. Part of the address is the network identifier (NET_ID), and another part is the host identifier (HOST_ID), depending on the size of the LAN, how the LAN is divided into smaller networks, and if the packet is unicast or multicast. A **unicast** is a transmission in which one packet is sent from a server to each client that requests a file or application, such as a video presentation. If five clients request the video presentation, the server sends five packets per each transmission to the five clients. In the same example, a **multicast** means that the server is able to treat all five clients as a group and send one packet per transmission that reaches all five clients (see Figure 1-6). Multicasts can be used to significantly reduce network traffic when transmitting multimedia applications. A third type of communication is called a **broadcast**, which sends a communication to all points on a specific network (routers are often configured so that they do not forward broadcasts to other networks).

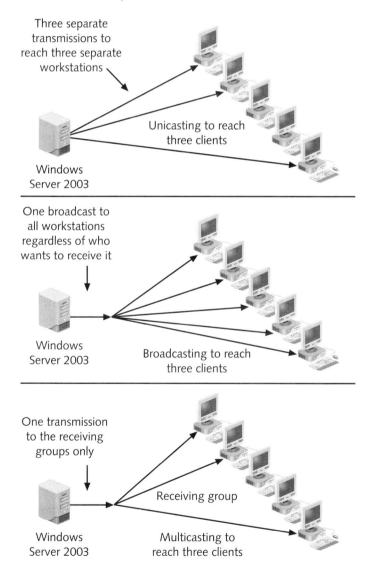

Figure 1-6   Unicasting, broadcasting, and multicasting

In a unicast on a typical medium-sized LAN (with up to 65,536 connections), the first two octets are normally the network ID and the last two are the host ID. In a multicast transmission on the same network, the four octets are used to specify a group of nodes to receive the multicast. Such a group usually consists of nodes that are multicast subscription members.

Another special-purpose form of addressing is the **subnet mask**. A subnet mask is used for two purposes: to show the class of addressing used, and to divide a network into subnetworks to control network traffic. In the first instance, the subnet mask enables an application to determine which part of the address is for the network ID and which is for the host ID. For example, a subnet mask for a Class A network is all binary ones in the first octet and all binary 0s in remaining octets: 11111111.00000000.00000000.00000000 (255.0.0.0 in decimal).

To divide the network into subnetworks, the subnet mask consists of a subnet ID within the network and host IDs, which is determined by the network administrator. For example, the entire third octet in a Class B address could be designated to indicate the subnet ID, which would be an octet of 11111111.11111111.11111111.00000000 (255.255.255.0). Another option would be to designate only the first five bits in the third octet as the subnet ID and the last three bits (and last octet as well) for the host ID, which would be 11111111.11111111.11111000.00000000 (255.255.248.0). This approach might be used to reduce the number of unused IP addresses, so that they are not wasted.

 Many server administrators use TCP/IP because the ability to create subnets provides important versatility in controlling network congestion and in setting up security so that only authorized users can reach specific parts of a network or specific intranets.

IP Address Considerations

When planning your TCP/IP implementation, you will need to consider a few specific rules.

The network number 127.0.0.0 cannot be assigned to any network. It is used for diagnostic purposes. For example, the address 127.0.0.1 is known as the loopback address, and it is used for diagnostic testing of the local TCP/IP installation. For instance, you might use the TCP/IP-based utility, pathping, as shown in Figure 1-7 to test connectivity using the loopback address.

```
Command Prompt

Microsoft Windows [Version 5.2.3790]
(C) Copyright 1985-2003 Microsoft Corp.

C:\Documents and Settings\Administrator>pathping 127.0.0.1

Tracing route to banker.jpcompany.com [127.0.0.1]
over a maximum of 30 hops:
  0  banker.jpcompany.com [127.0.0.1]
  1  banker.jpcompany.com [127.0.0.1]

Computing statistics for 25 seconds...
            Source to Here   This Node/Link
Hop  RTT    Lost/Sent = Pct  Lost/Sent = Pct  Address
  0                                            banker.jpcompany.com [127.0.0.1]
                                0/ 100 =  0%   |
  1    0ms     0/ 100 =  0%    0/ 100 =  0%   banker.jpcompany.com [127.0.0.1]

Trace complete.

C:\Documents and Settings\Administrator>_
```

Figure 1-7   Testing a local TCP/IP installation using the loopback address

The standard implementation of TCP/IP also reserves a series of addresses known as private addresses. Table 1-2 shows the IP network numbers that have been reserved for such purposes.

Table 1-2   Reserved IP network numbers

Network Number	Subnet Mask	IP Address Range
10.0.0.0	255.0.0.0	10.0.0.1 to 10.255.255.254
172.16.0.0 to 172.32.0.0	255.255.0.0	172.16.0.1 to 172.32.255.254
192.168.0.0	255.255.255.0	192.168.0.1 to 192.168.255.254

No one can use these IP addresses on the Internet. They are designed for use on a private network behind a network address translation (NAT) device, such as a firewall or proxy server. If you do have a NAT device, you can use any of these addresses on your own private network.

You cannot assign a network number to a computer or any other host on the network. For example, your network number might be 198.92.4.0 (subnet mask 255.255.255.0). You cannot assign this number to a computer on the network.

You also cannot assign the highest number on a network to a host. In the example above, you cannot assign 198.92.4.255 to a host on the network. This address is interpreted as a broadcast message for the subnet and all of the computers on the subnet would receive the packet. On the network referred to here, any numbers from 198.92.4.1 to 198.92.1.254 are valid numbers for hosts.

Activity 1-6: Sample Utilities for IP Address and Connectivity Testing

Time Required: Approximately 10 minutes

Objective: Practice using the Windows Server 2003 Command Prompt window and pathping and tracert commands.

Description: Two tools that enable you to test IP-addressing issues and connectivity on a network are pathping and tracert. Pathping is used to test connectivity to another network by using IP address information. Pathping can also calculate the number of IP packets returned from each router through which pathping passes. Tracert simply determines the number of routers, called hops, through which it passes. Because both utilities report IP addressing for the hops, you can use them not only to determine connectivity, but to identify malfunctioning routers by IP address. This activity enables you to practice both commands from the Windows Server 2003 Command Prompt window. Before you start, obtain from your instructor an off-site network address or name that you can use, or use a name from a favorite Web site in the form of myfavoritesitename.com.

1. Click **Start**, point to **All Programs**, point to **Accessories**, and click **Command Prompt**.

2. At the prompt, type **pathping** plus the name or address of the computer you are contacting, such as pathping myfavoritesitename.com. What results do you see?

3. Next, type **tracert** plus the name or address of the computer you are contacting, such as tracert myfavoritesitename.com. What are the results?

4. Close the **Command Prompt** window.

Static and Dynamic Addressing

Each server and workstation needs a unique IP address, either specified at the computer or obtained from a server that assigns temporary IP addresses. Before setting up TCP/IP, you need to make some decisions about how to set up IP addressing on the network. The options are to use what Microsoft calls static addressing or dynamic addressing. **Static addressing** involves assigning a dotted decimal address that becomes each workstation's permanent, unique IP address. This method is used on many networks, large and small, where the network administrator wants direct control over the assigned addresses. Direct control may be necessary where network management software is used to track all network nodes and the software depends on each node having a permanent, known IP address. Permanent addresses give consistency to monitoring network statistics and to keeping historical network performance information. The disadvantage is that IP address administration can be a laborious task on a large network. Most network administrators have an IP database to keep track of currently assigned addresses and unused addresses to assign as new people are connected to the network.

Dynamic addressing automatically assigns an IP address to a computer each time it is logged on. An IP address is leased to a particular computer for a defined period of time. This addressing method uses the **Dynamic Host Configuration Protocol (DHCP)**, which is supported by Windows Server 2003 for dynamic addressing. The protocol is used to enable a Windows Server 2003 server with DHCP services to detect the presence of a new workstation and assign an IP address to that workstation. On your network, this would require you to load DHCP services onto a Windows Server 2003 server and configure it to be a DHCP server. It would still act as a regular server for other activities, but with the added ability to automatically assign IP addresses to workstations. A Windows 2000 DHCP server leases IP addresses for a specified period of time, which might be one week, one month, one year, or a permanent lease. When the lease is up, the IP address is returned to a pool of available IP addresses maintained by the server.

 When you use DHCP, plan to apply it to client workstations and not to servers, or to make each server's IP address permanent. It is important for server IP addresses to always remain the same so there is no doubt about how to access a server. For example, consider how hard a Web server would be to find on the Internet if its IP address changed periodically.

Default Gateway

In Windows Server 2003, if you statically configure the IP address, plan to supply the subnet mask information as well as the default gateway. The **default gateway** is the IP address of the router that has a connection to other networks. The default gateway address is used when the host computer you are trying to contact exists on another network. This could be compared to a room with only one door. If you are in the room, you can talk to anyone else who is also in the room, but if you ever want to go to another room, you must use the door. The default gateway is like the door. If a computer is connecting only to local computers, it will never need the default gateway; but as soon as it needs to go outside the network, it needs to know the exit point.

For example, Table 1-3 shows the TCP/IP configuration for ComputerA and ComputerC and their default gateways.

Table 1-3   Sample TCP/IP configurations

Computer	IP Address	Subnet Mask	Default Gateway
ComputerA	133.229.143.72	255.255.0.0	133.229.1.1
ComputerC	133.225.143.92	255.255.0.0	133.225.1.1

When ComputerA tries to communicate with ComputerC, it determines that ComputerC is on a different network. ComputerA has to send the packet to a remote network, so it uses its default gateway as the exit to that network. Because the default gateway is set as the router (133.229.1.1), ComputerA sends the packet to the router, and the router forwards the packet to ComputerC. When ComputerC replies to the message, it sends the packet to its side of the router (133.225.1.1), and the router forwards the packet to ComputerA.

 Most of the time the default gateway (and the router IP address) are set as the first valid host number on a subnet. There is no technical reason to do this; it simply makes it easier to remember the configuration.

Name Resolution

Even when using the decimal notation for the IP address instead of the 32-bit number, most users still have difficulty remembering the IP addresses for their computers. Generally, computers are referred to by their names, which are NetBIOS names for older Windows-based systems and/or host names for computers on networks that use **Domain Name System (DNS)** servers. DNS is a TCP/IP application protocol that enables a DNS server to resolve (translate) domain and computer names to IP addresses, or IP addresses to domain and computer names.

Examples of names include, CORPDC1, RAMERZ, ACCOUNTANT, or any name that an organization or user chooses to uniquely identify a computer on the network. The problem with using names is that names cannot be used by TCP/IP, which can only use the IP address when contacting another computer.

Therefore, if computer names are going to be used to connect to other computers, there must be some method of determining the IP address that matches a computer name. Windows Server 2003 enables use of both NetBIOS and host names to resolve IP addresses to computer names.

NetBIOS Names

Before Windows 2000 and Windows 2003 server platforms, the primary means of locating computers on a Windows-based network was by the computer's NetBIOS name. The Browse list and mapped drives were also based on NetBIOS names.

 Windows Server 2003 still supports NetBIOS names for backwards compatibility with previous versions of Windows. Every Windows Server 2003 computer can still be accessed using the NetBIOS name.

There are a number of methods available to resolve NetBIOS names to IP addresses, but the preferred method is using a **Windows Internet Naming Service (WINS)** server. WINS is a Windows Server 2003 service that enables the server to convert NetBIOS workstation names to IP addresses. A WINS server stores a database of computer names and their corresponding IP addresses. The biggest advantage of WINS is its dynamic nature. When a WINS client computer is connected to the network and turned on, it automatically registers its name and IP address with the WINS server. Then, any other WINS client can query the WINS server for the IP address using the computer name.

NetBIOS names can also be resolved through the use of broadcasts and files called LmHosts files (Lm stands for LAN Manager, which was an early server operating system offered through Microsoft and IBM). However, these methods present two main problems. First, broadcasts can create a significant amount of network traffic, as all computers on a network have to look at the broadcast packets. Second, in most cases, broadcast messages do not cross routers. LmHosts are text files stored on each computer that list computer names and IP addresses. One problem with LmHosts files is that they are located on all computers and must be manually updated whenever computer names or IP addresses change (although it is also possible to centralize LmHosts to one file that all other LmHosts files use as a reference). In most cases, WINS is the best solution only if NetBIOS names are used.

Host Names

Using host names is the preferred method of resolving computer names to IP addresses in Windows Server 2003. In fact, you can turn off NetBIOS on a Windows Sever 2003 computer so that host name resolution is the only method of name resolution that is available.

The best method in Windows Server 2003 for resolving host names to IP addresses is to use Dynamic Domain Name System (DDNS). DDNS is a modern DNS application that enables client computers to automatically register their IP addresses in DNS without intervention by a user or network administrator.

If a DNS server is not available, broadcasts and HOSTS files can also be used to resolve IP addresses to host names. These methods, however, require much more effort to administer.

Physical Addresses and the Address Resolution Protocol

Besides the IP address, each network station also has a unique physical or device address. The **Address Resolution Protocol (ARP)** is used to acquire the physical addresses associated with other computer **network interface cards (NICs)**. Every NIC has a physical address, or media access control (MAC) address. A NIC is a card in a networked device that attaches that device to the network. The MAC address is programmed on the NIC when it is manufactured, and no two NICs have the same MAC address. In order for computers to communicate with each other, they must know the MAC addresses of each other's network interface cards. Proper communications using TCP/IP rely on both IP addresses and MAC addresses.

For example, consider a computer (ComputerA) that is trying to connect with another computer (ComputerB) with an IP address of 192.168.1.200. In making the connection, the following occurs:

1. By examining the IP address and subnet mask, ComputerA determines that the two computers are on the same network. ComputerA then checks its ARP cache to see if it already has the MAC address for the IP address of ComputerB.

2. If ComputerA does not have the address, then ARP sends out a packet to look for the address. The packet is a request for the MAC address for host 192.168.1.200.

3. All of the computers on the network examine the packet, but only the computer with the right IP address (ComputerB) responds. When ComputerB sees this request, it puts the MAC address for ComputerA into its own ARP cache and then sends back its MAC address to ComputerA.

4. ComputerA puts the MAC address into its ARP cache, and communication continues. The MAC address remains in the cache for two to 10 minutes, depending on how often the address is used. If the two computers are not on the same network and the information needs to cross a router, a similar process occurs, except that the ARP request asks for the MAC address of the router.

Every computer running Windows Server 2003 has an ARP cache that can include the recently resolved MAC addresses as well as statically assigned values in the ARP cache. To view the information in the ARP cache, open a Command Prompt window and then type arp –a.

The arp –a command shows you the MAC addresses along with the corresponding IP addresses that the local computer currently has in its ARP cache. The dynamic entries are stored in the ARP cache for two minutes, unless the entry is used during those two minutes. If the entry is used within two minutes, then the entry will be stored for 10 minutes. The static entries stay in the ARP cache until the computer is rebooted or until the entry is removed using the arp -d command.

Activity 1-7: Using the ARP command

Time Required: Approximately 10 minutes

Objective: Practice using the Windows Server 2003 Command Prompt window and ARP command.

Description: The ARP command is a great addition to your tool kit of utilities for diagnosing a network problem. In this activity you practice using the ARP tool with the -a switch to view the contents of the ARP cache, the -d switch to reset the cache, and the /? switch to view a listing of all ARP switches. You need to be logged into a computer running Windows Server 2003, Standard Edition, using an account provided by your instructor or an account with Administrator privileges.

1. Click **Start**, point to **All Programs**, point to **Accessories**, and click **Command Prompt**. (Alternatively, you can click Start, click Run, enter cmd in the Open: box, and click OK.)

2. At the prompt, type **arp –a**. Your screen should look similar to the one in Figure 1-8.

Figure 1-8   Using the ARP command

3. Type **arp −d** * at the prompt.

4. Type **arp −a** again. What information is now displayed?

5. Type **arp /?** at the prompt. What switches are displayed other than /?, −a, -d?

6. Close the **Command Prompt** window.

IMPLEMENTING TCP/IP IN WINDOWS SERVER 2003

There are two aspects to implementing TCP/IP in Windows Server 2003: installing it and then configuring it. Installing TCP/IP is the easiest part of the implementation. Configuring TCP/IP can be more complex, depending on whether your network uses static or dynamic addressing. You learn about installation and configuration in the next sections.

Installing TCP/IP

One of the most essential elements in network setup is understanding how to install TCP/IP. TCP/IP is the only protocol that is installed by default when you install Windows Server 2003. However, if you have not installed TCP/IP or if it has been removed, then you use the same process to install TCP/IP as you use to install any of the other protocols available to Windows Server 2003.

Activity 1-8: Installing TCP/IP

Time Required: Approximately 10 minutes

Objective: Install TCP/IP, if it is not already installed in Windows Server 2003.

Description: If the default network installation was not selected when Windows Server 2003 was installed or if TCP/IP has been removed, it is vital to know how to reinstall it. The following steps show you how.

1. Click **Start**, point to **Control Panel**, point to **Network Connections**, and click **Local Area Connection**.

2. Click the **Properties** button.

3. Click the **Install** button.

4. Click **Protocol**, and click **Add** as shown in Figure 1-9.

5. Click **Internet Protocol (TCP/IP)** and click **OK**.

6. Leave the Local Area Connections Properties dialog box open for the next activity.

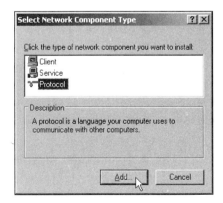

Figure 1-9   Installing a protocol

Configuring TCP/IP

As you learned earlier in this chapter, there are two basic approaches that can be used to configure the TCP/IP settings in Windows Server 2003: static addressing and dynamic addressing. In the following sections you learn how to use each approach.

Using static addressing for all computers on a network can be quite a job. However, some organizations prefer this approach to maintain the ability to track network problems by IP address. Other organizations use static addressing for servers and certain other network devices, such as routers, but use dynamic addressing for their users' computers. When you use static addressing, ensure that all of the parameters are correctly entered to avoid duplicate or conflicting entries that may result in one or more computers that cannot access the network. This is particularly true when configuring a server that must be reliably available to a large number of users.

Activity 1-9: Statically Configuring TCP/IP

Time Required: Approximately 10 minutes

Objective: Practice manually configuring TCP/IP for situations in which static addressing is used.

Description: Some organizations prefer to use a static IP address for some or all of the computers on the network. For example, servers are often given a static IP address that does not change, because if it did, there might be confusion about how to reliably access a particular server. In this activity, you learn how to configure the TCP/IP address information manually. Before you start, obtain an IP address, subnet mask, and default gateway from your instructor. Furthermore, obtain an IP address for the preferred DNS server, and if needed, an address for the alternate DNS server.

1. Make sure that the Local Area Connection Properties dialog box is still open from the previous activity. If it is not, click **Start**, point to **Control Panel**, point to **Network Connections**, and click **Local Area Connection**. Click the **Properties** button.

2. Click **Internet Protocol (TCP/IP)**, and then click **Properties**.

3. Click **Use the following IP address:** and then type the IP address, subnet mask, and default gateway for this computer (see Figure 1-10). (Enter periods after each number set to advance from box to box.)

4. Click **Use the following DNS server addresses** if necessary.

5. Type the IP address for the **Preferred DNS server:** and, if needed, type the IP address for the **Alternate DNS server**.

6. Click the **Advanced** button. What tabs are available for advanced information? Click each tab to see the specific information that you can enter. Click **Cancel**.

7. Click **OK**.

8. Click **Close** on the Local Area Connection Properties box.

9. Close the Local Area connection status box.

Automated Address Configuration

Windows Server 2003 supports two automated addressing approaches. One is **Automatic Private IP Addressing (APIPA)**, which is used to automatically configure the TCP/IP settings for a computer without using a Dynamic Host Configuration Protocol (DHCP) server. The other approach is to use dynamic addressing through the use of a DHCP server.

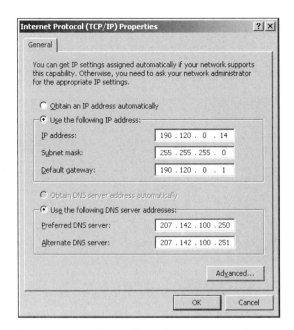

Figure 1-10   Static IP address configuration

Automated Addressing through Automatic Private IP Addressing

Notice in Figure 1-10 that you have the option to obtain an IP address automatically. When a computer that is configured to automatically obtain an IP address is switched on, it tries to find a DHCP server to obtain an IP address. As you learned earlier in this chapter, a DHCP server is a server that uses software and DHCP to automatically assign an IP address from a pool of possible addresses. If there is no DHCP server available, the computer automatically assigns itself an IP address from the reserved range of 169.254.0.1 to 169.254.255.254 and a subnet mask of 255.255.0.0. The computer is not able to assign itself a default gateway or the IP address for a Windows Internet Naming Service (WINS) or Domain Name System (DNS) server. Also as you learned earlier, WINS is a Windows Server 2003 service that enables the server to convert NetBIOS workstation names to IP addresses for Internet communication. DNS is a TCP/IP application protocol that enables a DNS server to resolve domain and computer names to IP addresses, or IP addresses to domain and computer names. The main problem with automatic configuration is that the computer can only communicate with other computers on the same network that are also automatically configured.

Automatic configuration is appropriate for small organizations that have only one network segment and where the computers do not need to use DNS or access another network. In an environment where a DHCP server is set up, but might be temporarily unavailable, automatic configuration can result in some computers having different IP addresses than the others on the network, which results in the computers not being able to communicate. In a situation like this, automatic configuration should be disabled.

Automatic configuration can be disabled through the Windows Server 2003 registry. The **registry** is a database used to store information about the configuration, program setup, devices, drivers, and other data important to the setup of Windows operating systems, such as Windows Server 2003. To disable automatic configuration you use a registry editor, such as regedt32—but always use great caution in a Registry editor to avoid inadvertently changing a value that might corrupt the operating system. The following are general steps you can follow to disable automatic configuration, but note that these are presented for your information and not as a hands-on activity. You will need access to the network using an account with Administrator privileges to modify the registry.

1. Click **Start** and then click **Run**.

2. Enter **regedt32** in the Open: box, and click **OK**. You see the regedt32 window as shown in Figure 1-11.

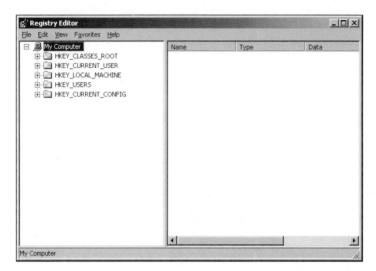

Figure 1-11   Opening the Registry editor

3. In the registry, browse to the key **HKEY_LOCAL_MACHINE\System\CurrentControlSet\ Services\Tcpip\Parameters\Interfaces***adaptername*** (the adaptername is the reference to the network interface card in your computer).

4. Click **Edit**, point to **New**, and click **DWORD Value**.

5. Create the value **IPAutoconfigurationEnabled** as a Reg_Dword value. Assign the data as **0**.

6. Close **regedt32**.

Dynamic Addressing through a DHCP Server

Dynamic addressing through a DHCP server is a very common way to configure TCP/IP on many networks, particularly medium-sized and large networks. To enable this type of configuration, you must first install and configure a DHCP server on the network (see Chapter 8). This server can be configured to dynamically assign an IP address to all the client computers that are set up to automatically obtain an IP address. In addition to assigning the IP address, the DHCP server can also assign the subnet mask, default gateway, DNS server, and other IP settings.

Using a DHCP server can save you a great deal of administrative effort. You only need to configure one server and most of your TCP/IP tasks are done. You learn how to configure a DHCP server later in this book.

To configure a Windows-based computer for dynamic configuration, you select Obtain an IP address automatically in the Internet Protocol (TCP/IP) Properties dialog box shown in Figure 1-10. After this option is configured, the computer contacts a DHCP server on its network to obtain an IP address.

CHAPTER SUMMARY

❑ The Windows Server 2003 platforms include Standard Edition, Web Edition, Enterprise Edition, and Datacenter Edition. Each platform has unique features designed to meet the needs of different network environments.

❑ Windows Server 2003 includes many features making it a scalable, efficient network operating system.

❏ The two types of networking models are peer-to-peer networks and server-based networks.

❏ Peer-to-peer networking is intended for small networks. For most networks, a server-based networking model offers increased performance, scalability, security, and centralized management.

❏ TCP/IP is the default protocol installed with Windows Server 2003 and is required by Active Directory.

❏ TCP/IP is an industry-standard suite of protocols and application utilities that enable communication across local and wide area networks.

❏ Every network device, such as a computer or router, must have a unique IP address to ensure network connectivity and the delivery of data. An IP address consists of two parts: the network identifier and the host identifier. Each IP address also has an associated subnet mask to distinguish between the network part and the host part and to enable creating subnets for traffic management.

❏ IP addresses can be manually configured using static addressing or automatically configured, using APIPA or dynamic addressing through a DHCP server.

KEY TERMS

Active Directory — A central database of computers, users, shared printers, shared folders, and other network resources, and resource groupings that is used to manage a network and enable users to quickly find a particular resource.

Address Resolution Protocol (ARP) — A protocol in the TCP/IP suite that enables a sending station to determine the MAC or physical address of another station on a network.

Automatic Private IP Addressing (APIPA) — Windows Server 2003 supports Automatic Private IP Addressing (APIPA) to automatically configure the TCP/IP settings for a computer. The computer assigns itself an IP address in the range of 169.254.0.1 to 169.254.255.254 if a DHCP server is not available.

broadcast — A message sent to all computers on a network segment (but usually blocked to other segments by a router).

client — A computer that accesses resources on another computer via a network or direct cable connection.

clustering — The ability to increase the access to server resources and provide fail-safe services by linking two or more discrete computer systems so they appear to function as though they are one.

connectionless communication — Also called a connectionless service, a communication service that provides no checks (or minimal checks) to make sure that data accurately reaches the destination node.

connection-oriented communication — Also called a connection-oriented service, this service provides several ways to ensure that data is successfully received at the destination, such as requiring an acknowledgement of receipt and using a checksum to make sure the packet or frame contents are accurate.

default gateway — The IP address of the router that has a connection to other networks. The default gateway address is used when the host computer you are trying to contact exists on another network.

distributability — Dividing complex application program tasks among two or more computers.

Distributed Component Object Model (DCOM) — A standard built upon the Component Object Model (COM) to enable object linking to take place over a network. COM is a standard that allows a software object, such as a graphic, to be linked from one software component to another (such as copying a picture from Microsoft Paint and pasting it in Microsoft Word).

domain — A grouping of resource objects—for example, servers, computers, and user accounts—to enable easier centralized management of these objects. On Windows Server 2003 networks, a domain is contained within Active Directory as a higher-level representation of how a business, school, or government agency is organized.

Domain Name System (DNS) — Also called Domain Name Service, a TCP/IP application protocol that enables a DNS server to resolve (translate) domain and computer names to IP addresses, or IP addresses to domain and computer names.

dotted decimal notation — An addressing technique that uses four octets, such as 100000110.11011110.1100101.00000101, converted to decimal (e.g., 134.22.101.005) to differentiate individual servers, workstations, and other network devices.

dynamic addressing — An IP address that is automatically assigned to a client from a general pool of available addresses and that may be assigned each time the client is started or it may be assigned for a period of days, weeks, months, or longer.

Dynamic Host Configuration Protocol (DHCP) — A network protocol that provides a way for a server to automatically assign an IP address to a workstation on its network.

frame — A unit of data that is transmitted on a network that contains control and address information, but not routing information.

hot-add memory — Memory that can be added without shutting down the computer or operating system.

Internet Protocol (IP) — Internet Protocol (IP) is the Internet layer protocol responsible for addressing packets so that they are delivered on the local network or across routers to other networks or subnets.

IP address — A logical address assigned to each host on an IP network. It is used to identify a specific host on a specific network.

kernel — An essential set of programs and computer code that allows a computer operating system to control processor, disk, memory, and other functions central to its basic operation.

local area network (LAN) — A network of computers in relatively close proximity, such as on the same floor or in the same building.

multicasting — A single message is sent from one location and received at several different locations that are subscribed to receive that message.

multitasking — The capability of a computer to run two or more programs at the same time.

multithreading — Running several program processes or parts (threads) at the same time.

network — A communications system that enables computer users to share computer equipment, software, and data, voice, and video transmissions.

network operating system (NOS) — Software that enables computers on a network to communicate and to share resources and files.

packet — A unit of data that is transmitted on a network that contains control and address information as well routing information.

peer-to-peer networking — A network on which any computer can communicate with other networked computers on an equal or peer basis without going through an intermediary, such as a server or host.

preemptive multitasking — Running two or more programs simultaneously so that each program runs in an area of memory separate from areas used by other programs.

privileged mode — A protected memory space allocated for the Windows Server 2003 kernel that cannot be directly accessed by software applications.

protocol — A strictly defined set of rules for communication across a network that specifies how networked data is formatted for transmission, how it is transmitted, and how it is interpreted at the receiving end.

Registry — A database used to store information about the configuration, program setup, devices, drivers, and other data important to the setup of Windows operating systems, such as Windows Server 2003.

resource — Has two definitions: (1) on a network, this refers to an object such as a shared printer or shared directory that can be accessed by users; and (2) on workstations as well as servers, a resource is an IRQ, I/O address, or memory that is allocated to a computer component, such as a disk drive or communications port.

router — A device that connects networks, is able to read IP addresses, and can route or forward packets of data to designated networks.

scalability — The ability of a network operating system to meet the increased demands and growth of a business.

server — A single computer that provides extensive multiuser access to network resources.

server-based networking — A model in which access to the network and resources, and the management of resources, is accomplished through one or more servers.

static addressing — An IP address that is assigned to a client and that remains in use until it is manually changed.

subnet mask — Used to distinguish between the network part and the host part of the IP address and to enable networks to be divided into subnets.

symmetric multiprocessor (SMP) computer — A type of computer with two or more CPUs that share the processing load.

total cost of ownership (TCO) — The cost of installing and maintaining computers and equipment on a network, which includes hardware, software, maintenance, and support costs.

Transmission Control Protocol (TCP) — Part of the TCP/IP suite, a protocol that is responsible for the reliable transmission of data on a TCP/IP network. TCP is a connection-oriented protocol ensuring that all packets sent using TCP are delivered successfully and in the right order.

Transmission Control Protocol/Internet Protocol (TCP/IP) — The default protocol suite installed with Windows Server 2003 that enables network communication.

unicast — A message that goes from one single computer to another single computer.

User Datagram Protocol (UDP) — A connectionless protocol that can be used with IP, instead of TCP.

Windows Internet Naming Service (WINS) — A Windows Server 2003 service that enables the server to convert NetBIOS computer names to IP addresses for network and Internet communications.

workgroup — As used in Microsoft networks, a number of users who share drive and printer resources in an independent peer-to-peer relationship.

workstation — A computer that has its own central processing unit (CPU) and may be used as a stand-alone or network computer for word processing, spreadsheet creation, or other software applications.

REVIEW QUESTIONS

1. The Biology Department at a university is interested in hosting and maintaining its own simple Web site to enable students and researchers to view information about the department and to post news about what various alumni are doing. Which of the following Windows Server 2003 platforms is the best fit for their needs?

    a. Datacenter Edition

    b. Enterprise Edition

    c. Web Edition

    d. None of the above because Windows Server 2003 no longer hosts Web services.

2. Which of the following is an example of a diagnostic IP address?

    a. 127.0.0.1

    b. 122.90.10.20

    c. 150.50.0.5

    d. 190.21.50.0

3. What feature of Windows Server 2003 allows you to run MS-DOS programs?

    a. virtual 16-bit machines

    b. virtual DOS machine

    c. Active Directory

    d. Windows Server 2003 cannot run MS-DOS programs.

4. Active Directory can be used to centrally organize which of the following?

   a. computers

   b. users

   c. printers

   d. all the above

   e. only a and c

5. You are setting up a network for a single office consisting of six workstations and one printer. Users want to occasionally share data. All users need access to the printer. What network model would best meet the requirements?

   a. user-based

   b. peer-to-peer

   c. print-based

   d. server-based

6. _____ is the ability to connect two or more servers to enable fail-safe computing and appear as one server.

   a. Server farming

   b. Processor joining

   c. Bonding

   d. Clustering

7. In Windows Server 2003, _____ contains recently resolved physical addresses.

   a. ARP cache

   b. ICMP memory

   c. network disk storage

   d. multicasting storage

8. Which of the following operating systems can connect to Windows Server 2003? (Choose all that apply.)

   a. Windows NT Workstation 4.0

   b. Windows 98

   c. Windows XP Professional

   d. Macintosh

9. Which of the following is a connection-oriented protocol that helps ensure the reliability of a data transmission?

   a. IP

   b. UDP

   c. TCP

   d. all of the above

   e. only a and b

10. Your company is planning to implement a large database to track information about 62,800 customers, and that database needs to be housed on an operating system that is scalable to 12 processors and that has high availability. Which of the following operating systems is the best match for this application?

    a. Windows Server 2003, Standard Edition

    b. Windows Server 2003, Enterprise Edition

    c. Windows Server 2003, Datacenter Edition

    d. None of the above, because the highest number of processors supported by these operating systems is eight.

11. You have been asked to develop a network upgrade plan for an accounting firm. Administrators at the firm have expressed the need to reduce the TCO over a span of a year. Which of the following recommendations would you include in your plan?

    a. Upgrade existing Windows NT 4.0 servers to Windows Server 2003, Standard Edition.

    b. Upgrade all workstations to Windows 98 or Windows Me.

    c. Upgrade all workstations to Windows XP Professional.

    d. all of the above

    e. only a and b

    f. only a and c

12. Which of the following operating systems support SMP technology? (Choose all that apply.)

    a. Windows Server 2003, Datacenter Edition

    b. Windows Server 2003, Standard Edition

    c. Windows Server 2003, Web Edition

    d. Windows Server 2003, Enterprise Edition

13. What is the default subnet mask when you use Automatic Private IP Addressing?

    a. 255.255.0.0

    b. 255.255.255.0

    c. 255.240.0.0

    d. 255.244.240.0

14. When you statically configure the IP address in Windows Server 2003, which of the following parameters do you supply? (Choose all that apply.)

    a. subnet mask

    b. DHCP address format

    c. default gateway

    d. Internet Control Message Protocol address

15. Your organization's network uses NetBIOS and host names, but one problem is that the network does not have the ability to efficiently resolve NetBIOS names to IP addresses, particularly for Internet communications. What does it need?

    a. a DHCP server

    b. a Network Neighborhood server

    c. UDP configured on the servers for NetBIOS name translation

    d. a WINS server

16. Which of the following is true about a router?

    a. It links networks together.

    b. It can read IP addresses.

    c. It forwards data packets to designated networks.

    d. all of the above

    e. only a and b

    f. only b and c

17. If a Windows-based client is configured to "Obtain an IP address automatically" and cannot lease an IP address from a DHCP server, it self-assigns itself an IP address from which of the following ranges?

    a. 10.10.0.1 to 10.10.0.254

    b. 169.254.0.1 to 169.254.255.254

    c. 254.169.0.1 to 254.169.0.254

    d. 192.168.0.1 to 192.168.0.254

18. A physical or MAC address is _____.

    a. only configured for a DNS server

    b. programmed into a network interface card

    c. the last two octets in an IP address

    d. the first two octets in an IP address

19. Dynamic IP addressing is made possible by a _____.

    a. DHCP server

    b. Workstation Management server

    c. router configured as a dynamic IP addressing server

    d. RAS IP Assignment server

20. One reason why Windows Server 2003 is reliable is because the kernel runs in _____.

    a. machine language

    b. an optimized C interpreter

    c. privileged mode

    d. .NET server machine runtime

CASE PROJECTS

Case Project Background

To make the most of what you are learning about Windows Server 2003, it is valuable to experience how it is used in different situations. Consequently, at the end of each chapter you will have the opportunity to apply your newly gained knowledge to a range of small to large fictitious organizations through the vehicle of case projects and in the role of an employee for a consulting firm. The advantage of using the role of a consultant is that you will experience situations in many different kinds of organizations with different kinds of computer users.

Your role is as a consultant for Bayside IT Services. Bayside IT Services provides consulting services throughout the United States and Canada, specializing in server operating system implementation, network design, application development, and on-going support services to clients. Bayside's clients range in size from small single offices to large enterprise networks. Its customers are businesses, corporations, schools, colleges, universities, and government agencies.

Case Project 1-1: Planning an Upgrade

Your assignment this week is to work with Lakeview Park, which is a large amusement park in Southern California that offers a variety of rides, but also includes specialty shows, restaurants, shopping areas, a small zoo, and tourist housing. The amusement park is fully networked and currently uses a combination of Windows NT Server 4.0 and basic Windows 2000 servers. They have a small overworked IT Department that needs assistance in planning for an upgrade of all servers to Windows Server 2003.

1. What networking model is Lakeview Park currently using? Should they consider using a different model?

2. Most of the servers that Lakeview Park is currently using are single processor servers. When they upgrade, they would like to consolidate their servers onto fewer computers using more powerful processors and operating systems. What Windows Server 2003 editions enable them to consolidate in this fashion, and why?

Case Project 1-2: Resolving Upgrade Issues

Lakeview Park requires help to resolve two different issues as a result of their decision to upgrade. Currently at Lakeview Park, all workstations connected to the servers are running Windows 98. In the process of upgrading the servers, the IT Department asks your advice about whether to upgrade the workstations connected to the servers. What is your advice?

The mailing office, which regularly sends mass mailings to advertise happenings at Lakeview Park, currently uses a 16-bit Windows application on a Windows NT 4.0 server to sort addresses for bulk postal rates. Can this 16-bit application work in Windows Server 2003? Explain your answer.

Case Project 1-3: Considering Static and Dynamic Addressing

Lakeview Park has hired a new inexperienced server administrator who has little background in using IP addressing. How would you explain IP addressing to him? Include in your explanation a comparison of static and dynamic addressing. Also, discuss your recommendation about which addressing method to use in this organization—static or dynamic.

Case Project 1-4: Installing TCP/IP

The new server administrator has just installed Windows Server 2003 on a test computer, but rather than taking the default configuration for TCP/IP, he performed a custom configuration for a different protocol. Is there a way to install TCP/IP without installing the entire operating system from scratch? If so, explain the steps.

2

INSTALLING WINDOWS SERVER 2003, STANDARD EDITION

After reading this chapter and completing the exercises, you will be able to:

♦ Prepare for a Windows Server 2003 installation

♦ Explain and perform the different Windows Server 2003 installation methods, such as attended, unattended, and upgrades

♦ Install and manage service packs

♦ Create an Automated System Recovery set

♦ Troubleshoot installation problems

♦ Uninstall Windows Server 2003, Standard Edition

W indows Server 2003, Standard Edition, is designed to install easily, as long as you complete some preinstallation tasks. Ignoring the preinstallation phase may lead to a failed installation or problems occurring later that could have been easily avoided. This chapter introduces you to the preinstallation tasks that should be completed and the hardware requirements that must be met before installing Windows Server 2003, Standard Edition. After you are familiar with the preinstallation tasks, you will then learn the different methods of installing Windows Server 2003, Standard Edition. These methods include an attended installation, an unattended installation, and an upgrade from Windows NT Server 4.0.

All operating systems must be maintained after they are installed, and Windows Server 2003, Standard Edition, is no exception. You'll learn how to maintain a server by installing service packs. Service packs provide operating system updates including enhanced features and repairs to reported issues. Another important part of maintaining a server is troubleshooting. This chapter will show you how to create an Automated System Recovery set for emergencies and you'll learn how to troubleshoot common installation problems. Finally, you will learn how to uninstall Windows Server 2003, such as in situations where a computer is reassigned for a different operating system or is given to another department or organization for use.

PREPARING FOR INSTALLATION

Advanced planning is one of the most important steps in preparing for a Windows Server 2003, Standard Edition, installation. Performing the preinstallation tasks outlined in this section increases the likelihood of a successful installation. Gathering information and making decisions about how you want to install the operating system before actually doing it also helps to avoid problems during and after the installation.

The following preinstallation tasks should be completed before installing Windows Server 2003, Standard Edition:

- Identify the hardware requirements and check hardware compatibility.
- Determine disk partitioning options.
- Choose a file system.
- Choose a licensing mode.
- Decide which protocols to install.
- Determine domain or workgroup membership.

Hardware Requirements and Compatibility

The first step in planning the installation of any operating system is to determine the hardware requirements. Most operating systems come with a list of bare minimum hardware requirements that must be met for the operating system to run, along with a list of recommended requirements. It is always better to exceed the bare minimum; how much to exceed the minimum is determined by what role the Windows 2003 server will play on the network.

Table 2-1 outlines the minimum requirements to install Windows Server 2003, Standard Edition.

Table 2-1   Minimum hardware requirements to install Windows Server 2003, Standard Edition

Component	Intel-type (x86) Computer Requirements
Processor	Pentium 133 MHz or faster (550 MHz recommended)
Display	VGA or better
Memory (RAM)	128 MB (256 MB recommended)
Hard disk space	1.5 GB
Floppy disk drive	High-density 3.5-inch
CD-ROM drive	Required for installations not performed over the network (12X or faster)
Network interface	**Network interface card (NIC)** required to connect to a network—a NIC is an adapter board designed to connect a workstation, server, or other network equipment to a network medium
Mouse or pointing device and keyboard	Required

Many servers today come with multiple processors to distribute the processing load. As you learned in Chapter 1, Windows Server 2003, Standard Edition, is designed to run on both single processor and dual-processor SMP systems.

Achieving Compatibility by Using the Hardware Compatibility List

Before any final decisions are made in selecting hardware, you should check the Microsoft **hardware compatibility list (HCL)** for Windows Server 2003, Standard Edition. A copy of the HCL usually can be found in the \Support folder on the Standard Edition's CD-ROM. The most up-to-date version is available on the Microsoft Web site, *www.microsoft.com/hwdq/hcl*, or if the information has moved, search *www.microsoft.com* for the Standard Edition HCL. Also, look for the "Designed for Windows Server 2003" logo on products that have been tested for the operating system. Microsoft reviews all types of hardware to determine whether they work with Windows Server 2003 editions and other Microsoft operating systems.

In many places in the book, Windows Server 2003, Standard Edition, is referred to simply as Standard Edition for the sake of brevity.

If you are upgrading a computer that has been used for a different operating system, such as one currently running Windows NT Server 4.0, that computer may already be on the HCL, but it may still be necessary that you upgrade the **basic input/output system (BIOS)**. The BIOS is a program on a read-only or flash memory chip that establishes basic communication with components such as the monitor and disk drives. Before you upgrade, contact the computer manufacturer or visit the manufacturer's Web site to determine if a BIOS upgrade is needed prior to installing Windows Server 2003. If an upgrade is needed, the manufacturer will provide an upgrade file and instructions about how to perform the upgrade.

Activity 2-1: Determining the BIOS Version of a Computer

Time Required: Approximately 10 minutes

Objective: Learn how to determine the BIOS version on a computer.

Description: Before you check with a computer manufacturer about which BIOS version on an older computer is compatible with Windows Server 2003, you need to determine the BIOS version currently used on the computer. Also, before installing a new operating system on any computer, new or old, it is always wise to have the most current BIOS installed on that computer. Some computers display the BIOS version at boot up. On nearly all computers, you can determine the BIOS version by entering the BIOS setup for the computer. This activity provides general instructions for determining the BIOS version.

1. Find out from your instructor or lab assistant how to access the computer's BIOS setup. On most computers you access the BIOS setup screen by typing a specific key right after turning on the computer's power. For example, some computers use the F1, F2, or Del keys. Also, on some computers there is a brief message flashed at boot up (before the operating system is loaded) that tells you what key sequence to use.

2. In most cases, the BIOS version number is displayed on the first setup screen. If it is not, follow the on-screen instructions to view or access the various BIOS setup menu(s) for the BIOS version information. You will most likely use the arrow keys on your keyboard to advance through the menus. *Make absolutely certain that you do not change any of the parameters in the BIOS setup.*

3. Record the BIOS version.

4. Exit the BIOS setup without making any changes. On some computers, you can exit by pressing Esc and typing No to the query about saving your changes.

Determining Disk Partitioning Options

Knowing how you plan to partition your hard disks and on which partition you plan to install the operating system can make the Standard Edition Setup program go much more smoothly. Creating a **partition** is a process in which a hard disk section or a complete hard disk is prepared for use by an operating system. A disk can be formatted after it is partitioned. When you **format** a disk, this process divides the disk into small sections called tracks and sectors for the storage of files by a particular file system. During the installation, the Setup program detects how your hard disk is currently partitioned (see Figure 2-1). Standard Edition Setup allows you to install the operating system on an existing partition or create a new one on which to install the operating system. Depending on how your hard disk is currently partitioned, you are presented with one or more of the following options by Setup:

- *Create a new partition on an unpartitioned hard disk*—If the hard disk currently contains no partitions, you need to create and size at least one partition for the operating system.

It is generally a good idea to only create and size a partition for the operating system. Once the installation is complete you can use the Microsoft Management Console (MMC) Disk Management Snap-in to create additional partitions with the remaining free hard disk space. The MMC is an administrative tool that is used for a variety of server management tasks. A snap-in is one of many specific tools, such as the Disk Management Snap-in, that can be installed in the MMC.

- *Create a new partition on a partitioned hard disk*—If the hard disk is already partitioned, you can create a new partition with any free space, keeping in mind the minimum partition size needed to install the Standard Edition.

- *Install on an existing partition*—If there is an existing partition that is large enough, you can choose to install the Standard Edition onto it.

- *Delete an existing partition*—If the hard disk is currently partitioned, you can choose to delete any existing partitions and use the new unpartitioned space to create and size a new partition.

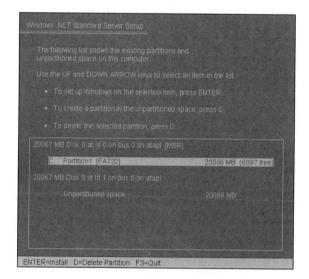

Figure 2-1   Setup detecting existing partitions

Activity 2-2: Determining How an Existing Windows 2000 Server is Partitioned

Time Required: Approximately 10 minutes

Objective: Determine the amount of space on disks in a Windows 2000 server and how the disks are partitioned.

Description: If you are upgrading a Windows 2000 server to Windows Server 2003, Standard Edition, it is wise to check the available disk space and the partitioning before you start. This check enables you to make plans about partitioning, including how to change existing partitions, before you begin the upgrade. For this activity, you need access to a computer running Windows 2000 Server, with an account that has Administrator privileges. If a Windows 2000 Server is not available, you can use the same steps in Windows Server 2003 for practice.

1. Right-click the **My Computer** icon on the desktop, and click **Manage**; or if **My Computer** is not on the desktop (in Windows Server 2003), click **Start**, then right-click **My Computer,** and click **Manage**.

2. Click the **Disk Management** option listed under Storage in the left pane.

3. Record the drive letter assignments, and the file systems in use on each partition. Also, record the size of each partition. Figure 2-2 shows an illustration of the Disk Management display in Windows 2000 Server.

4. Close the Computer Management window.

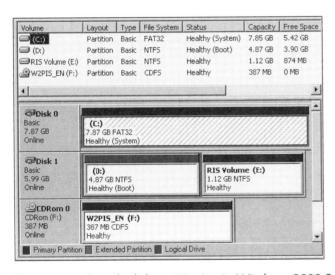

Figure 2-2 Sample disk partitioning in Windows 2000 Server

Choosing a File System

Once you have partitioned the hard disk you need to choose a file system with which to format it. Like all editions of Windows Server 2003, the Standard Edition supports file allocation table (FAT) versions 16 and 32 file systems and the NT file system (NTFS). NTFS has all the basic features of the FAT file system and also has many advanced features, such as better security, disk quotas, built-in file compression, encryption, indexing, and **portable operating system interface (POSIX)** support—making it the recommended file system for Windows Server 2003. POSIX is a set of standards designed to enable portability of applications from one computer system to another and has been used particularly for UNIX systems.

  In some configurations, NTFS is the required file system. For example, Active Directory only supports NTFS, so if you plan to configure Standard Edition to host Active Directory, at least one NTFS partition is required on the local computer.

If you are unsure about which file system to select, keep in mind that you can convert from FAT32 to NTFS while preserving all data using the convert command-line utility (see Figure 2-3). However, we strongly recommend using NTFS for all installations because the security and disk recovery features alone make it the best choice.

```
Command Prompt                                                    _ □ ×

C:\>convert f: /fs:ntfs
The type of the file system is FAT.
Volume Serial Number is 80A8-898D
Windows is verifying files and folders...
File and folder verification is complete.
Windows has checked the file system and found no problems.

2,251,096,064 bytes total disk space.
      196,608 bytes in 3 hidden files.
2,250,899,456 bytes available on disk.

       65,536 bytes in each allocation unit.
       34,349 total allocation units on disk.
       34,346 allocation units available on disk.

Determining disk space required for file system conversion...
Total disk space:              2198528 KB
Free space on volume:          2198144 KB
Space required for conversion:   15517 KB
Converting file system
Conversion complete

C:\>_
```

Figure 2-3   Converting from FAT to NTFS

Table 2-2 compares FAT16, FAT32, and NTFS.

Table 2-2   FAT16, FAT32, and NTFS compared

Feature	FAT16	FAT32	NTFS
Total volume size	4 GB	2 GB to 2 TB	2 TB
Maximum file size	2 GB	4 GB	Theoretical limit of 16 exabytes
Compatible with floppy disks	Yes	Yes	No floppy disks
Filename length	11 characters	256 characters	256 characters
Security	Limited security based on attributes and shares	Limited security based on attributes and shares	C2-compatible extensive security and auditing options
File compression	Supported with extra utilities	Supported with extra utilities	Supported as part of NTFS
File activity tracking	None	None	Tracking via a log
POSIX support	None	Limited	POSIX.1 support
Hot fix	Limited	Limited	Supports hot fix
Large database support	Limited	Yes	Yes
Multiple disk drives in one volume	No	No	Yes

Hot fix is the ability to automatically "fix" data in areas of a hard disk that have become damaged or corrupted over time, without taking down the computer or operating system. Whenever possible, the operating system moves the data to a reserved good area, without users noticing. The damaged areas of disk are then marked so they are not used again.

Choosing a Licensing Mode

When you install Standard Edition, you are prompted for a CD key. This is your license to install the operating system. Once it is installed you also need to purchase **client access licenses (CAL)**. CALs give client computers the right to connect to a computer running Windows Server 2003, Standard Edition. For example, if a client computer needs to access shares on a file server running Standard Edition, a CAL is required. There are two licensing modes to choose from, per server and per seat.

With **per server licensing**, CALs are purchased on a per server basis. For each server, you must purchase as many CALs as there are clients connecting to the server at any given time. This is the most cost effective choice for small companies that have a single server. If you have more than one server, the per seat option is the preferred licensing mode.

With **per seat licensing**, CALs are purchased on a per client basis. A license is purchased for each client computer that accesses a Standard Edition server. Once a per seat license has been purchased for a client computer, the client can connect to any Windows 2003 server on the network.

If you are unsure of what licensing mode to choose during Setup, select the per server option. Anytime after the installation of Standard Edition, you are allowed a one-time conversion from per server to per seat. This is also a one-way conversion that means you cannot convert from per seat to per server.

Making a Protocol Selection

You need to select a protocol to use for communicating on the network. Windows Server 2003, Standard Edition, supports several different protocols, as shown in Table 2-3.

Table 2-3 Protocols supported by Standard Edition

Protocol	Description
AppleTalk Protocol	Used for communications with Apple computers
NWLink (NW stands for NetWare)	Emulates the IPX/SPX protocol suite used for communications with older NetWare servers (particularly prior to version 5.x servers)
Internet Protocol (TCP/IP)	Used for TCP/IP version 4 communications (version 4 is used on most networks)
TCP/IP version 6	Used for TCP/IP version 6, which is mainly deployed on experimental or educational networks; Microsoft and other vendors are working for broader use because it solves TCP/IP version 4 IP address shortages
Network Monitor Driver	Used by Windows Server 2003 network monitoring tools
Reliable Multicast Protocol	Used primarily for reliable multimedia applications on networks that have multiple use traffic (audio, visual, data, and a combination of these)

 Windows Server 2003 does not support the NetBEUI protocol, which is an older protocol used primarily on some Windows NT servers, though it is also supported by Windows 2000 servers. If you are upgrading an older server that uses NetBEUI, plan to convert it to TCP/IP before the upgrade. Also, reconfigure any workstations that are using NetBEUI so that they communicate via TCP/IP. Note that NetBEUI is also not supported by Windows XP Professional.

Fortunately you do not need to make all of these decisions from the start. You can configure additional protocols after the server is set up. If you use the default protocol setup, Standard Edition installs TCP/IP and assumes that there is a DHCP server—which means you do not have to provide configuration information for TCP/IP. Many network administrators install Standard Edition using the default TCP/IP setup with DCHP for convenience. After the installation you can statically configure an IP address using the method outlined in Chapter 1.

Determining Domain or Workgroup Membership

During the setup process you need to determine the type of network access for which your computer should be configured. As you recall from Chapter 1, a computer running Windows Server 2003 can be configured in a workgroup model or as a member of a domain.

If you choose to configure your computer in a workgroup, during setup you are prompted to provide the name of the workgroup you wish to join or create a new one.

If you choose to add the computer to a domain the following requirements must be met:

- Provide the DNS name of the domain you wish to join, for example, northwest.widgets.com.

- A computer account in the domain you wish to join. If you have administrative privileges in the domain, you can create the computer account during Setup and you will be prompted for an administrative account and password. If you do not have administrative privileges, the computer account can be created prior to installation by a domain administrator.

- There must already be one domain controller and a DNS server online before you can join the domain.

 If the server you are configuring is the first one in a proposed domain, configure the server as in a workgroup. After the server is installed and started, you can install Active Directory and config-ure the first domain as you are installing Active Directory. Active Directory requires that there is at least one domain.

OVERVIEW OF THE WINDOWS SERVER 2003 INSTALLATION METHODS

Once you have completed all the necessary preinstallation tasks, you are ready to install the operating sys-tem. The following section outlines the different installation methods available and steps through a clean installation of Standard Edition; you just need to decide on an installation method that best meets your needs. The method you choose depends on the resources in your computer. For example, if the computer is not equipped with a CD-ROM drive, you can perform an installation over a network. The primary installation methods are as follows:

- CD-ROM installation

- Network installation

- Upgrade or installation from an existing operating system

- Unattended installation

Each of the installation methods consists of techniques to boot the computer and enable you to load the installation files. Even though the startup techniques vary, such as performing the installation from CD-ROM or over the network, in every case you start the setup by running either Winnt.exe (Winnt) or Winnt32.exe (Winnt32). Winnt and Winnt32 perform the same function, but Winnt32 runs in the 32-bit Windows environment.

Winnt is used if your computer is already running MS-DOS, Windows 3.1, or Windows 3.11, or if you start an installation directly from the CD-ROM. Use Winnt32 if the computer is already loaded with Windows 95, Windows 98, Windows Me, Windows NT with Service Pack 5 or later, Windows 2000, or Windows XP.

Both Winnt and Winnt32 support the use of switches to enable you to customize the installation. For example in Winnt, if you want to specify a location for the installation files that is different from the folder from which you start Winnt.exe, use the /s switch and specify the drive and directory after the switch, such as Winnt /s:e:\I386. Another example is using the Winnt /a switch to initiate the accessibility options for those who have visual, hearing, or movement disabilities. When using Winnt32, you may want to check the computer to make sure is it compatible with Standard Edition by using the /checkupgradeonly switch, or if you have trouble during the installation use the /debug switch to record errors in a file. See Appendix A for a complete listing of the Winnt and Winnt32 switches.

 The switches available in Winnt and Winnt32 are similar, but not identical.

Activity 2-3: Viewing the Winnt32 Command-line Help Information

Time Required: Approximately 15 minutes

Objective: Learn where you can find information about the Winnt32 command-line switches.

Description: Sometimes it is important to review the Winnt32 command-line options, particularly if you are performing special steps associated with an installation. In this activity, you learn how to view the Windows Help file for Winnt32 by using the /? switch. You can perform this activity on a computer running virtually any modern Windows-based operating system, as well as Windows Server 2003.

1. Insert the Windows Server 2003, Standard Edition, CD-ROM, if it is not already loaded in the CD-ROM drive.

2. If you see the Welcome to the Microsoft Windows Server Family screen, use the option to close it.

3. Click **Start** and click **Run**.

4. In the Open: text box, enter the drive letter for the CD-ROM drive plus \i386\winnt32 /?, such as e:\i386\winnt32 /? (see Figure 2-4). Click **OK**.

5. What are the three main sections of information in the help file?

6. Close the Windows Help window.

7. Leave the CD-ROM inserted for the next activity.

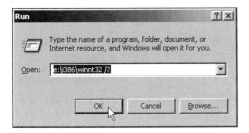

Figure 2-4   Accessing Winnt32 help information

Activity 2-4: Using a Winnt32 Switch to Assess Hardware Compatibility

Time Required: Approximately 10 minutes

Objective: Run the Winnt32 /checkupgradeonly switch to verify that a computer is compatible with Windows Server 2003.

Description: If you are not certain whether your computer hardware is compatible with Windows Server 2003, run a compatibility check. If the computer passes the check, this is a strong indication that the Windows Server 2003 installation will go smoothly. This activity shows you how to run the check. Use a computer running Windows 2000 Server or Windows Server 2003 for this activity.

1. Make sure that the Windows Server 2003, Standard Edition, CD-ROM is still inserted. If not perform Steps 1 and 2 of Activity 2-3.

2. Click **Start** and click **Run**.

3. In the Open: text box, enter the drive letter of your CD-ROM drive plus \i386\winnt32 /checkupgradeonly, such as e:\i386\winnt32 /checkupgradeonly. Click **OK**.

4. If you are connected to the Internet, click **Yes, download the updated Setup files (Recommended)**. If you do not have an Internet connection, click **No, skip this step and continue installing Windows**. Click **Next**.

5. If you selected Yes, download the updated Setup files (Recommended) in Step 4, wait a short time for the dynamic update to complete.

6. Observe the Microsoft Windows Upgrade Advisor dialog box. Did it find any problems? If so, select each listed item one at a time, and click the Details button. Figure 2-5 illustrates the dialog box with no problems listed.

7. Click **Finish**.

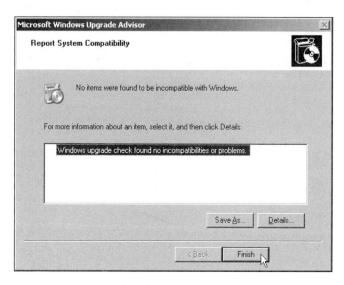

Figure 2-5   Upgrade Advisor system compatibility report

CD-ROM Installation

If your computer is capable of booting from a CD-ROM (this must be set up through the computer's BIOS), you can start the setup program directly from the Windows Server 2003, Standard Edition, CD-ROM. To start the installation from CD-ROM:

1. Make sure the computer's BIOS is set to boot first from the CD-ROM drive (see Activity 2-2 to learn how to access the BIOS setup on a computer).

2. Insert the Windows Server 2003, Standard Edition, CD-ROM in the CD-ROM drive.

3. Turn off the power to the computer.

4. Turn on the computer, and press any key to boot from the CD-ROM, if requested.

This method automatically starts the Setup program. Simply follow the instructions on the screen.

Network Installation

Network installation enables you to install the operating system from a shared network folder on another computer. This method is useful if you have a diskless computer or one that does not have a CD-ROM drive. Also, the method is useful if you operate a large network and plan to install multiple servers. The network installation can be fast (but usually not as fast as the CD-ROM installation), and you can arrange to install all of the servers in the same way.

Follow these general steps to start a network installation:

1. Copy the installation files to the host computer that offers the shared folder, such as an existing server. To copy the files, first create the folder on the host computer, calling it, for example, I386. Insert the Windows Server 2003, Standard Edition, CD-ROM in the host computer and copy the files from the I386 folder on the CD-ROM. You also have the option of just sharing the CD-ROM itself.

2. Share the host's folder, assigning Read or Change share permissions.

3. To start the installation, connect to the shared folder from the target computer.

4. Run the Winnt.exe or Winnt32.exe program (depending on the operating system you used to boot the prospective server), using the switches that match your needs. (See Appendix A.)

Follow the instructions on the screen.

Activity 2-5: Create a Shared Folder for a Network Installation

Time Required: Approximately 20 minutes

Objective: Practice creating a shared folder for a Windows Server 2003, Standard Edition, installation.

Description: If you work in an organization that generates many servers, the network installation can be a good option. It enables you to install the server operating system from nearly anywhere on a network without having to carry around the CD-ROM. In this activity, you create a shared folder and then copy the Standard Edition files to that shared folder. For this project you need a computer running Windows Server 2003, the Windows Server 2003, Standard Edition, CD-ROM, and an account from which to create the shared folder.

1. Insert the Windows Server 2003, Standard Edition, CD-ROM into your CD-ROM drive. Exit the Welcome to the Microsoft Windows Server 2003 Family screen.

2. Click **Start**, point to **All Programs**, point to **Accessories**, and click **Windows Explorer**.

3. Click **My Computer** in the left pane to view the drive information in the tree below it.

4. Create a new folder on drive C: (or another drive) called WinNET by clicking the drive in the left pane, clicking the **File** menu, pointing to **New**, and then clicking **Folder**. Type **WinNET** as the name of the new folder, and press **Enter**.

5. Click + (the plus sign) in front of the **CD-ROM drive** in the tree, such as E:, to display its subfolders.

6. Click **Local Disk C:** (or the disk on which you created the folder), if its contents are no longer displayed in the tree.

7. Click the **I386** folder under the CD-ROM drive (such as drive E:) in the left pane to display its contents. Click the cursor anywhere in the right pane. Type **Ctrl+A** to select the entire contents, and drag the contents to the **WinNET** folder.

8. After the files are copied, right-click the **WinNET** folder, and then click **Sharing and Security**.

9. Click the **Share this folder** radio button, and make sure that the default share name is WinNET.

10. Click the **Permissions** button, and make sure that the Everyone group has the **Allow** box checked for **Read**. Also, be certain there are no checks in any of the other boxes. If any are checked, remove the check marks. The dialog box should look like the one illustrated in Figure 2-6.

11. Click **OK**, and then click **OK** again.

12. Close Windows Explorer.

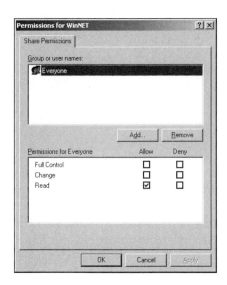

Figure 2-6   Setting the shared folder permissions

Activity 2-6: Practice Starting a Network Installation

Time Required: Approximately 10-15 minutes

Objective: Start an installation over a network.

Description: In this activity you practice the steps to run an installation over the network from the shared folder you created in Activity 2-5. Access the shared folder from a computer running Windows NT 4.0 with Service Pack 5 or later, a computer running Windows 2000, or a computer running Windows XP Professional.

1. Double-click **Network Neighborhood** from the desktop, if you are using Windows NT 4.0. Double-click **My Network Places** from the Windows 2000 or Windows XP desktop; or if **My Network Places** is not on the Windows XP Professional desktop, click **Start,** and click **My Network Places**.

2. Locate the computer containing the WinNET folder you created and then locate the folder. For example, you may need to double-click Entire Network, double-click Microsoft Windows Network, double-click a domain or workgroup, and then double-click the computer name, depending on which version of Windows you are using. (In Windows XP Professional, in the My Network Places window, select View workgroup computers under Network Tasks and then Find and double-click the computer.)

3. In Windows NT 4.0 and Windows 2000, right-click the **WinNET** folder, and then click **Map Network Drive**. In Windows XP Professional, click the **WinNET** folder, click the **Tools** menu, and then click **Map Network Drive**.

4. In Windows NT 4.0 and Windows 2000, select the letter of a drive that is not already mapped, and then click **OK** or **Finish**. In Windows XP Professional, choose a drive letter that is not already mapped, and click the **Browse** button as shown in Figure 2-7. Locate and click the **WinNET** folder in the list, and click **OK**. Click **Finish**.

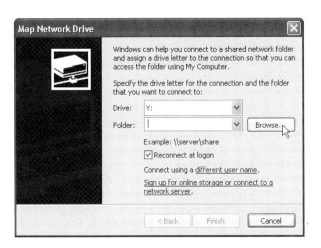

Figure 2-7 Mapping a drive in Windows XP Professional

5. Click **Start**, click **Run**, and then click the **Browse** button.

6. Find and double-click the **WinNET** shared folder under My Computer.

7. Find and double-click **Winnt32**.

8. Click **Cancel** in the Run dialog box so that you do not actually start the installation.

Installation from an Existing Operating System

If your computer is running a previous version of Windows, you can perform an upgrade instead of doing a clean install. If you perform an upgrade, Windows Server 2003, Standard Edition, is installed into the same directory as the current operating system. The benefit of performing an upgrade is that most of your settings, files, and applications are upgraded as well and do not need to be reinstalled. Standard Edition can be upgraded from any of the following operating systems. If you are running an operating system that is older than those listed below, you need to upgrade to one of the following and then upgrade to Standard Edition.

- Windows NT Server 4.0 (running Service Pack 5 or later)
- Windows 2000 Server

 If you are running Windows NT Enterprise Edition 4.0 or Windows 2000 Advanced Server you can upgrade to Windows Server 2003, Enterprise Edition, but not to Windows Server 2003, Standard Edition.

To begin an upgrade:

1. Boot the computer to use its current operating system.

2. Insert the Windows Server 2003, Standard Edition, CD-ROM.

3. When you see the What do you want to do? screen, click **Install Windows Standard Server**.

Follow the instructions on the screen. The first dialog box enables you to specify whether to perform an upgrade or to perform a new installation from scratch (see Figure 2-8). Use the Upgrade (Recommended) option to replace the current operating system, but keep your existing settings and applications. Use the New Installation (Advanced) option to perform a fresh (from scratch) installation of the operating system.

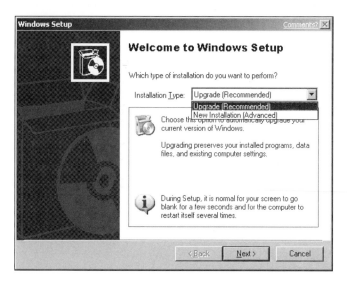

Figure 2-8   Selecting the installation type

Once the installation is underway, Setup starts by collecting information about the current system as shown in Figure 2-9.

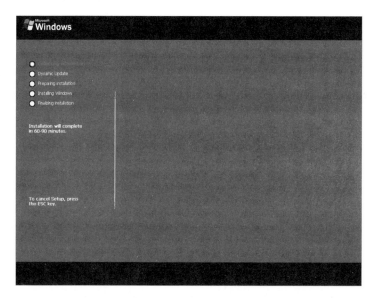

Figure 2-9   Collecting information about the system

Unattended Installation

An unattended installation is usually performed via a network installation, but you specify a set of unattended parameters before the Standard Edition installation begins. The parameters enable you to provide a script or answer file, which gives responses to questions that come up in the installation. No license agreement is presented during the unattended installation, because it is assumed that you have already read the license information and that you have the appropriate number of licenses for the total number of unattended installations. Performing an unattended installation will be discussed in more detail later in the chapter.

2

PERFORMING A CD-BASED ATTENDED INSTALLATION

Once you have gathered all your information and determined which options you want to use to install Standard Edition, you can proceed with the installation. The next sections outline an installation using the CD-ROM only method, but installations are nearly the same for all methods. The Setup program process basically consists of two parts. In the first part, text-based Setup screens are presented (these screens are graphical if you start by using Winnt32 when a 32-bit operating system is already loaded on the computer). This part primarily focuses on detecting the hardware and loading installation files onto the computer. The second part is a graphical display that uses Windows-based dialog boxes that enable you to configure information specific to the server, such as the Administrator account password, the server name, and domain or workgroup membership.

To begin the installation process, insert the Windows Server 2003, Standard Edition, CD-ROM, and restart your computer so that it boots from the CD-ROM. During the first phase of Setup, the following occurs:

- Setup inspects your current hardware configuration and loads drivers and other files.
- The License Agreement is displayed.
- Hard drives are scanned to see if any previous versions of Windows are installed.
- Hard drives are scanned to determine the partitioning scheme and file systems in use.
- Setup prompts you to choose or create a partition on which to install Standard Edition and which file system to use to format the partition.

At this point in the setup process, the partition on which you choose to install the operating system is formatted with the file system you specified. Once complete, the GUI mode portion of Setup begins. During this portion of Setup, you are prompted for the following information:

- Regional and language settings, plus the option to personalize software
- The Product Key that is located on the CD-ROM case
- The licensing mode (per server or per seat)
- A unique computer name and Administrator account password
- Date and time settings
- Network settings
- Domain or workgroup membership

Once all the steps have been completed, Setup installs the selected components, installs Start menu items, registers components, saves settings, and removes temporary files. At this point you can click Finish and restart your system.

PERFORMING AN UNATTENDED INSTALLATION

If you are installing on multiple computers it may be easier to perform an unattended installation. This means creating an answer file containing information that you would normally have to provide during the setup process. The following section discusses the different ways to automate the installation of Standard Edition and the different ways of creating an answer file.

Creating an Answer File

Unattend.txt is an actual answer file that is provided as an example, and is found in the \I386 folder on the Windows Server 2003, Standard Edition, CD-ROM (see Figure 2-10). An **answer file** is a text file that contains a complete set of instructions for automating the installation of Windows Server 2003. You can use a text editor, such as Notepad, to create or edit an answer file, or use Setup Manager, which is found in the Support\Tools\Deploy.cab file on the Windows Server 2003, Standard Edition, CD-ROM. Use the Start button Run option to start Setupmgr.exe, which initiates the Windows Server 2003 Setup Manager Wizard. Follow the steps in the Wizard to create or modify an answer file (see Figures 2-11 and 2-12).

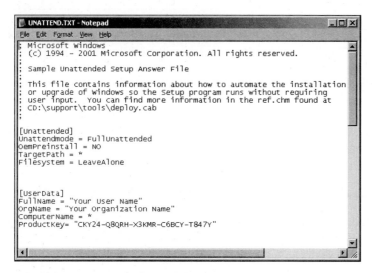

Figure 2-10   Sample Unattend.txt file

Figure 2-11   Welcome to Setup Manager window

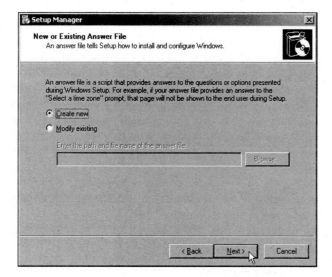

Figure 2-12   Using Setup Manager to create an answer file

The answer file contains predetermined answers to questions asked during Setup, including information about what file system to use, where to install the operating system files, and the name assigned to the server. The following is an example of several answers that can be provided in the answer file. (See the Unattend.txt file in the /I386 folder on the installation disk for more examples.):

```
[Unattended]
Unattendmode = Fullunattended
OemPreinstall = No
TargetPath = WINDOWS
Filesystem = NTFS

[UserData]
Fullname = "Sara Martin"
Orgname = "Nishida and McGuire"
Computername = "Lawyer"
```

Activity 2-7: Viewing the Sample Answer File

Time Required: Approximately 15 minutes

Objective: Study the format and contents of the sample Unattend.txt file.

Description: One of the best ways to learn how to write the contents of an answer file for an unattended installation is by examining the Unattend.txt file provided on the Windows Server 2003, Standard Edition, CD-ROM. In this activity, you open the file and study its structure.

1. Insert the Windows Server 2003, Standard Edition CD-ROM into your CD-ROM drive. (If the CD-ROM is already inserted and you do not see the Welcome to the Microsoft Windows Server 2003 Family screen, click Start, click My Computer, and double-click the CD-ROM drive.)

2. From the Welcome to the Microsoft Windows Server 2003 Family screen, click the option to **Perform additional tasks**.

3. Click the option to **Browse this CD**.

4. Double-click the **I386** folder.

5. Scroll through the contents until you locate the **UNATTEND.TXT** file. Double-click the file.

6. From within Notepad scroll through the file to view its contents.

7. What sections are provided in the file? Under which section of the answer file would you list those programs you want launched after the installation is complete and the user logs on for the first time?

8. Close Notepad. Close all open windows.

Activity 2-8: Using Setup Manager

Time Required: Approximately 20 minutes

Objective: Create a new answer file using Setup Manager.

Description: Setup Manager steps you through creating an answer file from scratch. In this activity you use Setup Manager to create an example answer file. Before you start, ask your instructor for the location of the Setupmgr.exe file (or use My Computer to find and double-click the Support\Tools\Deploy.cab file on the Windows Server 2003, Standard Edition, CD-ROM, double-click Setupmgr.exe, follow the instructions to install the program and record the location of where you installed it). You need a Product Key to complete this activity.

1. Click **Start**, click **Run**, and use the **Browse** button to locate and then double-click **Setupmgr.exe**. After the path to the program is displayed in the Open: text box, click **OK**.

2. Click **Next** (refer to Figure 2-11).

3. Be certain that **Create new** is selected, and click **Next** (refer to Figure 2-12).

4. What choices are in the Type of Setup dialog box? Click Unattended setup, if it is not already selected. Click **Next**.

5. Click **Windows Server 2003, Standard Edition**, and then click **Next**.

6. The next dialog box (see Figure 2-13) enables you to specify the type of user interaction. Select **Fully automated**, and then click **Next**.

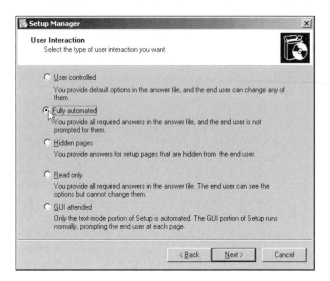

Figure 2-13   Selecting the type of user interaction

7. What distribution share options are available? Select **Set up from a CD**, and then click **Next**.

8. Accept the license agreement terms, and then click **Next**. (If you feel you cannot accept these terms, click Cancel to discontinue.)

9. Enter your name in the Name text box and enter **My Company** in the Organization text box. Click **Next**.

10. Click **Next** to accept the default Display Settings.

11. Select a time zone that applies to your area and click **Next**.

12. Enter the product key and click **Next**.

13. Use the default Per server license for 5 connections, and then click **Next**.

14. Enter your last name in the Computer name text box, click **Add**, and then click **Next**.

15. Enter a password for the Administrator account, confirm the password, and then click **Next**.

16. Select **Typical settings** on the Networking Components dialog box, and click **Next**.

17. If requested, the default Workgroup selection, and click **Next**.

18. Use the default Windows Components selections, and click **Next** (you may not see this step).

19. Click **Next** for the Telephony dialog box.

20. Click **Next** for the Regional Settings dialog box.

21. Click **Next** for the Languages dialog box.

22. Click **Next** for the Browser and Shell Settings dialog box.

23. What is the default name for the installation folder? Click **Next**.

24. Click **Next** for the Install Printers dialog box.

25. Click **Next** for the Run Once dialog box.

26. Click **Finish** for the Additional Commands dialog box.

27. Use the default path to store your answer file, but rename the file using unattend plus your initials, such as unattendrm.txt. Make a note of the path and file name for Step 29. Click **OK**.

28. Click **Cancel** to exit Setup Manager.

29. Use My Computer or Windows Explorer to browse for the file you created in Step 28 and double-click the file to view its contents.

30. Does the answer file you created in this activity have any sections that were not in the sample Unattend.txt file you viewed in Activity 2-8? Are there any sections not in the file you created, but that were in the sample file? Record your answers.

31. Close **Notepad**.

32. Close all open windows.

To further customize an unattended installation, you can create a **uniqueness database file (UDF)**. The UDF works in conjunction with the answer file, allowing you to create a unique answer set for each server set up. For example, the UDF might contain the server name. Each server would have a uniqueness ID in the database associated with its information. The uniqueness ID is specified by the /UDF<uniqueness id> command used with the Winnt or Winnt32 command.

Using an Answer File with Booting

An alternative to performing an unattended installation over the network is to use an answer file along with booting from the CD-ROM. The answer file is created in the same way as the example Unattend.txt file, but after you create the file, name it Winnt.sif (a .sif file is called an image file) and copy it to a floppy disk. Also, the contents of the Winnt.sif answer file must have a section heading that starts with [Data] and another section heading called [User Data] that specifies the product key on the Windows Server 2003, Standard Edition, CD-ROM case. Using this method, you follow these steps:

1. Set up the computer's BIOS to boot first from CD-ROM.

2. Insert the Windows Server 2003, Standard Edition, CD-ROM and turn on the computer.

3. Immediately insert the floppy disk containing the Winnt.sif file as soon as you see the first text-based setup screen.

4. The Winnt.sif file controls how the setup runs from the CD-ROM in unattended mode.

Specifying Components

Yet another unattended option is to specify which Standard Edition components, such as Management and Monitoring Tools, are to be installed during the GUI portion of setup. You specify which components to install by creating a Cmdlines.txt file, which is used in conjunction with an answer file and that contains a series of command lines to be executed. The Cmdlines.txt file must be located in a folder that you create, called \OEM that is placed on the shared network drive containing the installation files or on the floppy disk containing Winnt.sif. The command sequence in the Cmdlines.txt file begins with [Commands] and underneath that heading are placed the individual commands, one to each line, surrounded by quotes.

If you plan to duplicate multiple servers, so each is exactly like the other, Standard Edition supports the Sysprep.exe program which is used to clone the server operating system on computers that have the same hardware characteristics. Sysprep.exe is available on the Windows Server 2003 Standard Server CD-ROM in the Support\Tools\Deploy.cab file. This program is run from the Start button and Run option. Another utility, available in the Resource Kit for Windows Server 2003, is called Syspart.exe, which is intended for cloning computers that have different hardware configurations.

UPGRADING A WINDOWS NT SERVER AND DOMAIN

You can use steps similar to those described in the previous sections to upgrade Windows NT Server 4.0 to Windows Server 2003, Standard Edition, with the option of retaining security settings, account information, group information, and the domain. When upgrading a Windows NT 4.0 domain, you can begin by upgrading any member servers first or upgrading the domain controllers first. A **member server** is a server that is a member of an existing Windows 2000 domain, but that does not function as a domain controller. If you decide to upgrade your domain controllers first, the first server to be upgraded should be the **Primary Domain Controller (PDC)**. A PDC is a server that maintains the master copy of user account and other server resource information. A **Backup Domain Controller (BDC)** is a server that houses a copy of the information stored in the PDC.

Use the following guidelines to upgrade the Windows NT server and the corresponding Windows NT domain:

- To minimize downtime and the impact of the upgrade on users, coordinate a time when you can upgrade the server and domain when no one is accessing it.

- Back up each Windows NT 4.0 server that will be upgraded, including its Registry, before you start an upgrade. Also, make an emergency repair disk before you start.

- Before upgrading the PDC, synchronize it with an existing BDC and take that BDC offline. In the event that the upgrade fails you can return the network to its previous state by bringing the BDC online and promoting it to a PDC.

- If you are upgrading more than one server in a domain, start by upgrading the Windows NT 4.0 PDC to be converted to the first Windows 2003 server domain controller (DC). Next, and one at a time, upgrade each Windows NT 4.0 Backup Domain Controller (BDC) to be a Windows 2003 server domain controller (or some can be upgraded to member servers, but plan to have at least two domain controllers for redundancy).

If TCP/IP is not already implemented, consider installing TCP/IP on the servers before you upgrade; or consider setting up the first upgraded server (the former PDC) as a DHCP server and use the default TCP/IP configuration for each upgraded server. Also, configure the first upgraded domain controller with DNS, if a DNS server is not already present.

To begin the upgrade process, use the Winnt32 program on the Windows Server 2003, Standard Edition, CD-ROM making sure you select to perform an upgrade so you can retain existing settings. During the upgrade process, the Active Directory Installation Wizard launches and allows you to join an existing domain tree or forest, or create a new one (these options will be discussed further in Chapter 4).

The Active Directory Installation Wizard upgrades the PDC or BDC to have Windows Server 2003 directory services and Kerberos authentication services. Also, it converts the Security Accounts Manager (SAM) database in the Windows NT Registry to the database used by Active Directory so that accounts, groups, and security information is retained. If you are upgrading a BDC that is to be set up as a child domain, then a Kerberos transitive trust (see Chapter 4) is automatically created with the parent domain.

After you upgrade a PDC, it is still recognized by any Windows NT BDCs as the domain master and can synchronize with live BDCs until they are upgraded. Also, remember it is generally a good idea to take one BDC out of production (as a backup) until all domain controllers have been successful upgraded.

After all servers are upgraded and there are no Windows NT servers connected to the domain, convert the domain (or all domains) to either Windows 2000 native mode (for domains that have only Windows 2000 and 2003 servers) or to Windows .NET mode (for domains with only Windows servers). This allows you to take full advantage of Active Directory. Chapter 4 discusses domain levels and how to convert a domain.

INSTALLING AND MANAGING SERVICE PACKS

All vendors' operating systems usually have bugs or problems, even though vendors do their best to find and remedy them prior to shipment. Whether you install Standard Edition by using an attended or unattended method, plan to immediately check the Microsoft Web site for any updates offered through service packs. **Service packs** are designed to correct security issues as well as problems affecting stability, performance, or the operation of features included with the operating system. Once you've installed the operating system it is always a good practice to download and apply the latest service pack to fix any known issues and patch any security holes. The latest service packs for different Microsoft operating systems can be found at *www.microsoft.com/downloads*.

 Installing a service pack is considered a major upgrade and should be given serious consideration because some of the operating system files will be replaced. There is always a chance that the upgrade may fail or new problems may occur after installing the service pack. This is more of an issue for those servers that are already running on the network and being used by clients.

Use the following guidelines when installing the latest service packs for Windows Server 2003 (or any other Microsoft operating systems):

- Download the latest service pack from Microsoft's download site. The service pack is also usually available for order on CD-ROM.

- Review the documentation that comes with the service pack. This details the installation procedures and alerts you to any problems associated with installing the service pack.

- If the server is in the production environment, be sure to perform a full backup before you do the installation.

- If the server is already available to clients, publicly schedule when the service pack will be installed as the server will need to be rebooted during the installation. This alerts clients to any downtime.

- Once the service pack is installed, document any problems that occurred and how you fixed them, for future reference.

CREATING AN AUTOMATED SYSTEM RECOVERY SET

After you have installed Standard Edition, you should create an Automated System Recovery (ASR) set in the event that your system fails. The **Automated System Recovery (ASR) set** is similar to an emergency repair disk that is created under previous versions of Windows and contains the system files needed to start your system. The ASR set has two components: (1) a backup of all system files (1.5 GB or more) and a backup of system settings (about 1.44 MB). ASR does not back up application data files, which you must do separately and is discussed later in this book.

An ASR set can be created using the Backup program that comes with Standard Edition. You should create a new ASR set each time you make an important change to a server, such as adding a protocol or installing a new driver for a network interface card. A **driver** is software that enables a computer to communicate with devices such as network interface cards, printers, monitors, and hard disk drives. Each driver has a specific purpose, such as handling network communications.

 Consider making two copies of the ASR set, one to keep in the room where your server is located and another to store off site, such as where you store off-site backup media for your production data.

Activity 2-9: Creating an ASR set

Time Required: Approximately 10 minutes without media or 30–40 minutes with media

Objective: Create a backup of the system files and system settings in an ASR set.

Description: Begin backing up important system startup information as soon as possible so that you develop good habits in providing for system recovery. You may not need this backup often, but when you need it, you really need it. This activity shows you how to create an ASR set. You need two or three blank CD-Rs or a tape to hold over 1.5 GB of system files and a floppy disk for the system settings backup. Also, you need access to the Standard Edition via an account with Administrator privileges. If you do not have access to blank CD-Rs or a tape, simply click **Cancel** instead of **Finish** in Step 7.

1. Click **Start**, point to **All Programs**, point to **Accessories**, point to **System Tools**, and click **Backup**.

2. When the Backup or Restore Wizard starts, click the **Advanced Mode** link.

3. Click the **Automated System Recovery Wizard** button as shown in Figure 2-14.

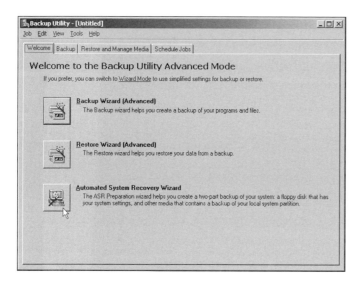

Figure 2-14   Creating an ASR set

4. Click **Next** when the Automated System Recovery Preparation Wizard starts.

5. What is shown as the default media type? What is the default file name? Change the path for the default file name to the CD-ROM or tape drive you are using. Insert the CD-ROM or tape.

6. Click **Next**.

7. Click **Finish** to write the backup files to the CD-ROM or tape. Or click **Cancel** and stop here, if you do not have these removable media available.

8. You see the Automated System Recovery information box and then the Backup Progress dialog box as the files are being copied. Figure 2-15 illustrates the Backup Progress dialog box.

9. When requested, insert a blank formatted floppy disk, and click **OK**.

10. Remove the floppy disk and CD-ROM or tape, and click **OK**.

11. Close the Backup Progress dialog box and the Backup Utility window.

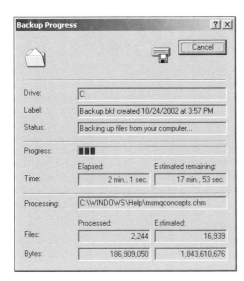

Figure 2-15   Backup Progress dialog box

TROUBLESHOOTING INSTALLATION PROBLEMS

With proper planning many installation problems can be avoided, but even the most experienced installers can still experience difficulties. Following the preinstallation tasks previously outlined in the chapter can help to ensure a successful installation. Also keep the following points in mind to avoid problems:

- Ensure that the hardware is listed on the HCL for Windows Server 2003, Standard Edition.

- Test all hardware before installing the operating system.

- Run the computer manufacturer's diagnostics before installing the operating system.

- Run a comprehensive test of the hard disk to ensure it is functioning properly.

Sometimes prevention is not enough and installation problems occur. Most problems are related to hardware drivers or to the actual hardware. For example, the computer may contain a CD-ROM drive or display adapter that is newly marketed and not contained in the installation selection list. If Windows Server 2003 Setup does not contain the driver or it is not included on a disk with the hardware, it is necessary to contact the computer vendor for a new driver. Sometimes an adapter card, such as a network interface card or hard disk adapter, becomes loose when the computer is moved and the card simply needs to be reseated. Also, a SCSI adapter cable may not be properly terminated. Table 2-4 provides a list of common problems and steps to solve the problems.

Table 2-4   Troubleshooting a Windows Server 2003 installation

Problem Description	Solution Steps
Installation fails when connecting to the domain controller	Make sure you have previously created an account in the domain or have a user account with administrative privileges and provided the right domain name. Also, make sure the computer is connected to the network, that the domain controller and DNS server are working, and that you are using the right protocol.

Table 2-4   Troubleshooting a Windows Server 2003 installation (continued)

Problem Description	Solution Steps
Setup did not find any mass storage devices on the computer. There is an Inaccessible Boot Device message.	The most common cause is that Setup does not have a driver for a SCSI device or is detecting storage devices in the wrong order, such as the CD-ROM drive first. Press F6 when Setup first starts and provide a driver for the mass storage device that will hold the operating system files. Check to make sure all adapters and controllers are working properly. Check power to all devices. Reseat adapters and controllers. For SCSI devices ensure: (1) the SCSI cabling is properly installed, (2) SCSI devices are terminated, (3) SCSI devices are correctly addressed, and (4) the BIOS correctly recognizes all SCSI adapters. Also, be sure the SCSI boot drive is addressed as 0. Check the manufacturer's recommendations for configuring SCSI adapters and hard disk drives. Try replacing the adapter before replacing the drive(s). For EIDE drives: (1) check the controller, (2) ensure file I/O and disk access are set to standard, and (3) ensure the system drive is the first device recognized by the controller. For IDE and ESDI drives: (1) check the cabling and controller, (2) check the drive setup in the BIOS for master/slave relationships, and (3) ensure the drive is properly recognized in the BIOS.
Media Errors	If you receive media errors when installing from the CD-ROM, try installing from another CD-ROM drive. If the problem still persists, use another Windows Server 2003, Standard Edition, CD-ROM.
The installation fails when installing the network components.	Go back to configure the network settings. Make sure you have installed a protocol that is appropriate for your network and that you have provided all the information needed to set up the protocol. Check the network interface card to ensure it is working. Reseat or replace the card and start Setup again. Use the diagnostic software provided with the card to test for problems. If this does not work, try a card from a different manufacturer, in case there is a hardware incompatibility.
A problem is reported with NTOSKRNL.EXE or in finding NTLDR.	The Boot.ini file needs to be changed to indicate where to find Windows Server 2003, Standard Edition, (if other than on the primary system drive) or NTLDR is not on the drive used to boot (called the system drive). If NTLDR is missing entirely from the computer, use the ASR set to restore it.
The operating system does not install or does not start after installation.	Verify that the hardware you are using is supported by Windows Server 2003, Standard Edition.
A STOP message appears during the installation.	Start the installation again. If the STOP message appears a second time, record the message and consult a Microsoft technician or use Microsoft's online TechNet or Knowledge Base information.
Computer locks up	Check the IRQ and I/O settings for conflicts among hardware components and cards (check the NIC and any specialized cards in particular).

UNINSTALLING WINDOWS SERVER 2003, STANDARD EDITION

At some point it may be necessary to uninstall Standard Edition. For example, if your server is being replaced with a newer model you may wish to install a different operating system on the old server. Uninstalling Standard Edition is a relatively straightforward process and requires you to format the partition on which it has been installed.

Before uninstalling Standard Edition, be sure to back up any important data.

2

If you are installing another operating system, such as Windows 2000 Professional or Windows 2000 Server, insert the CD-ROM into the CD-ROM drive and restart the computer (make sure the BIOS is set to boot from the CD-ROM). During the setup process choose to delete and/or format the partition on which Standard Edition is installed. You can also use the FDISK and FORMAT utilities on a startup disk (such as a Windows 98 startup disk) to delete and format the partition. Once the partition has been formatted you can install a new operating system.

 If all else fails, boot from the Windows Server 2003, Standard Edition, CD-ROM and proceed with Setup until you reach the point at which it displays the current partitions. Use the option to delete the partition with the system files (or delete all of the partitions) and then exit Setup. Install the new operating system.

CHAPTER SUMMARY

❏ The preinstallation tasks should be completed before installing Windows Server 2003, Standard Edition. Verify the hardware is on the HCL, meets the minimum requirements for the operating system, and determine how you want to configure the operating system during setup.

❏ Windows Server 2003 can be installed using any of several methods, which include: CD-ROM only, installing over a network, installing from an existing operating system, and an unattended installation. Fortunately, the installation follows a logical step-by-step process that automates many activities— detection of the disk storage and NIC, for example. Although you may need to troubleshoot a specific installation problem, the likelihood of having to deal with a problem is reduced in proportion to how well you planned in advance.

❏ Computers running Windows NT Server 4.0 (with Service Pack 5 or later) or Windows 2000 Server can be upgraded to Windows Server 2003, Standard Edition.

❏ An answer file can be used to automate the installation of Windows Server 2003. There is a sample answer file on the Windows Server 2003, Standard Edition, CD-ROM which can be modified. You can also use Setup Manager to modify an existing file or create a new one.

❏ When upgrading a Windows NT 4.0 domain, you can begin by upgrading the member servers or the domain controllers. When upgrading the domain controllers to Windows Server 2003, Standard Edition, the PDC usually should be upgraded first.

❏ Service packs should be installed to fix any known problems with the operating system.

❏ After you have completed the installation, create an Automated System Recovery set to recover your system in the event of failure.

❏ To uninstall Windows Server 2003, Standard Edition, repartition and format the hard drive and then install the operating system to replace Standard Edition.

KEY TERMS

answer file — A text file that contains a complete set of instructions for automating the installation of Windows Server 2003.

Automated System Recovery (ASR) set — Backup media, such as CD-Rs and a floppy disk, containing the system files and settings needed to start a system running Windows Server 2003 in the event of a system failure.

Backup Domain Controller (BDC) — A server that maintains a read-only copy of the user accounts database that is replicated from the PDC.

basic input/output system (BIOS) — A program on a read-only or flash memory chip that establishes basic communication with components such as the monitor and disk drives. The advantage of a flash chip is that you can update the BIOS.

client access license (CAL) — A license to enable a workstation to connect to Windows Server 2003 as a client.

driver — Software that enables a computer to communicate with such devices as network interface cards, printers, monitors, and hard disk drives. Each driver has a specific purpose, such as to handle network communications.

format — An operation that divides a disk into small sections called tracks and sectors for the storage of files.

hardware compatibility list (HCL) — A list of computer hardware tested by Microsoft and determined to be supported by a specific Microsoft operating system, such as Windows Server 2003, Standard Edition.

hot fix — Ability to automatically "fix" data in areas of a hard disk that have become damaged or corrupted over time, without taking down the computer or operating system. Whenever possible, the operating system moves the data to a reserved good area, without users noticing. The damaged areas of disk are then marked so they are not used again.

member server — A server that is a member of an existing Windows 2000 Server or Windows Server 2003 domain, but that does not function as a domain controller.

network interface card (NIC) — An adapter board designed to connect a workstation, server, or other network equipment to a network medium.

partition — A process in which a hard disk section or a complete hard disk is set up for use by an operating system. A disk can be formatted after it is partitioned.

per seat licensing — A server software license that requires that there be enough licenses for all network client workstations.

per server licensing — A server software license based on the maximum number of clients that log on to the server at one time.

portable operating system interface (POSIX) — Standards set by the Institute of Electrical and Electronics Engineers (IEEE) for portability of applications.

Primary Domain Controller (PDC) — The server that maintains the master copy of user account information.

service pack — An operating system update that provides fixes for known problems and provides product enhancements.

uniqueness database file (UDF) — A text file that contains an answer set of unique instructions for installing Windows Server 2003 in the unattended mode and that is used with an answer file.

REVIEW QUESTIONS

1. You are working on a disaster recovery document and must include information about how to back up important Windows Server 2003 system files and system settings. What utility should you discuss in the document?

   a. Automated System Recovery set

   b. System Swap and Shadowing

   c. Repair Disk

   d. Emergency System Save Backup

2. In your preinstallation preparations, you are considering the file systems to use for a Windows Server 2003, Standard Edition, installation. For this installation you want to take advantage of the best folder and file level security. Which file system should you use?

   a. FAT16

   b. FAT32

   c. NTFS

   d. CDFS

3. You have finished installing Windows Server 2003, Standard Edition. During the installation you accepted the default configuration. You now want to make the server a member of your domain. Which of the following requirements must be met? (Choose all that apply.)

   a. A WINS server must be available.

   b. A domain controller must be available.

   c. A DNS server must be available.

   d. A DHCP server must be available.

4. Which of the following operating systems can be directly upgraded to Windows Server 2003, Standard Edition? (Choose all that apply.)

   a. Windows 95

   b. Windows 98

   c. Windows 2000 Server

   d. Windows 2000 Advanced Server

   e. Windows Me

5. Which protocol(s) is (are) installed with a typical installation of Windows Server 2003, Standard Edition?

   a. NetBEUI

   b. TCP/IP

   c. IPS/SPX

   d. DLC

6. You are planning to install Windows Server 2003, Standard Edition on a computer that has a 700 MHz processor, 64 MB of RAM, and 1.2 GB of disk space. Which of the following should you consider in your preplanning?

   a. Upgrade to at least a 1 GHz processor to meet the recommended requirements.

   b. Upgrade to at least 128 MB of RAM to meet the minimum requirements.

   c. Upgrade to at least 1.5 GB of disk space to meet the minimum requirements.

   d. all of the above

   e. only a. and b.

   f. only b. and c.

7. You are installing Windows Server 2003, Standard Edition. When prompted to choose a licensing mode you are unsure as to which option to choose. How should you proceed?

   a. Choose the per network option as you can convert to per seat after the installation.

   b. Choose the per client option as you can convert to per server after the installation.

   c. Choose per server as you can convert to per seat after the installation.

   d. Choose per seat as you can convert to per computer after the installation.

8. You are performing the preinstallation tasks before installing Standard Edition. You want to verify that your computer is compatible with the operating system. What switch can you use with the Winnt command to check for system compatibility?

   a. /verifysystemonly

   b. /checkcompatibility

   c. /verifyupgradeonly

   d. /checkupgradeonly

9. What is the purpose of the HCL?

    a. It is a program supplied by Microsoft to test hardware compatibility.

    b. It is a key code to access the Microsoft customer hot line.

    c. It is a list of hardware compatible with TCP/IP developed by the IEEE.

    d. It is a list from Microsoft of hardware that is compatible with a specific Windows operating system.

10. You are configuring the network for a manufacturing firm. The network consists of twenty servers, each running Standard Edition and each supporting over 200 clients. Which licensing mode should you choose?

    a. per seat

    b. per client

    c. per server

    d. per computer

    e. per network

11. Which of the following methods is (are) used to install Windows Server 2003, Standard Edition? (Choose all that apply.)

    a. CD-ROM only

    b. over the network

    c. unattended

    d. floppy disk only

12. You are planning to upgrade your organization's Windows NT 4.0 servers and domain to Windows Server 2003, Standard Edition. Which of the following should be your first step?

    a. Upgrade the BDCs.

    b. Upgrade the PDC.

    c. Back up all Windows NT 4.0 servers and their Registries.

    d. Upgrade the member servers.

13. Which of the following folders on the Windows Server 2003, Standard Edition, CD-ROM contain the installation files you would copy to a shared drive to enable multiple computers to be installed?

    a. \Support

    b. \I386

    c. \Setup

    d. \Install

14. Two of your organization's server operators have hearing disabilities. Which of the following enables you to install Standard Edition for accessibility?

    a. winnt32 /dudisable

    b. winnt /a

    c. winnt32 /cmd:access

    d. winnt /e:enable

15. You installed Standard Edition and during Setup chose to format the partition using FAT32. To take advantage of added features, you now want to use NTFS on the partition. What command-line utility can you use?

    a. convert

    b. format

    c. switch

    d. partition

16. You are planning to install Standard Edition on a member server. The member server is running Windows NT Server 4.0 with Service Pack 3. You plan to perform an upgrade to retain your current settings. What should you do before beginning the upgrade?

   a. Format the partition with NTFS.

   b. You must first upgrade to Windows 2000 Server.

   c. Upgrade Windows NT Server 4.0 to Service Pack 5 (or higher).

   d. Windows NT Server 4.0 cannot be upgraded to Standard Edition

17. How can you obtain a service pack? (Choose all that apply.)

   a. Load it from the Windows Server 2003 installation CD-ROM.

   b. Download it from the Microsoft Web site.

   c. Order it as a CD-ROM from Microsoft.

   d. Microsoft no longer uses service packs for Windows Server 2003, it uses only interactive dynamic updates for individual problem fixes.

18. You insert the Windows Server 2003, Standard Edition, CD-ROM to install the operating system on a computer; however, when you power off the computer and reboot, the computer tries to boot from the hard drive, which has no files. Which is your best option?

   a. Set the BIOS boot order to start with the CD-ROM drive.

   b. Temporarily unplug the hard drive from its controller before starting the installation.

   c. Insert a floppy disk with the MS-DOS command files, boot to the command line, and use the winnt /drive:cd command to start the installation.

   d. Change the CD-ROM drive speed to at least 24X.

19. You are installing Standard Edition and want to make it a member server within an existing domain. Before the new server can join the domain, what requirements need to be met? (Choose all that apply.)

   a. There must be a DNS server on the network.

   b. You must have a user account in the domain with administrative privileges to create a computer account.

   c. There must be a domain controller available on the network.

   d. There must be a WINS server on the network.

20. Which of the following are protocols supported by Standard Edition? (Choose all that apply.)

   a. AppleTalk

   b. NWLink

   c. Network Monitor Driver

   d. TCP/IP version 4

   e. TCP/IP version 6

CASE PROJECTS

Case Project Background

Hard Rock Bikes employs 422 people in Victoria, British Columbia. This company manufactures and distributes mountain bikes all over the world. In Victoria, they have one building that houses the Management, Accounting, Sales, IT, Research, and Bike Testing Departments. In an adjacent building, there is a large plant that houses the Manufacturing, Inventory, and Distribution Departments. The IT Department at Hard Rock Bikes has little familiarity with Windows-based servers because they primarily support large centralized UNIX computers for the Management, Accounting, IT, and Manufacturing Departments.

However, the Sales, Research, and Inventory Departments have their own Windows-based servers for specialized applications. Support for the Windows-based servers is outsourced to your firm, Bayside IT Services, and you are the primary support person for Hard Rock Bikes.

Case Project 2-1: Upgrading the Sales Department Windows NT 3.51 Servers

The Sales Department has two Windows NT 3.51 servers that they want to upgrade to Windows Server 2003, Standard Edition. The server coordinator for the Sales Department informs you that he plans to upgrade the Windows NT 3.51 servers directly to Standard Edition. Is he correct in his assumption? If not, what must be done first?

Case Project 2-2: Assessing the Hardware Needs of the Sales Department

As you are advising the server coordinator for the Sales Department, you remember that the department is using two identical computers that have older peripherals, 133 MHz processors, four disk drives each with 750 MB of storage, and 64 MB of RAM. Also, you learn from the server coordinator that the department plans to go to new sales software and a large sales database that will need at least 4 GB of disk storage. What is your advice for the server coordinator?

Case Project 2-3: Inventory Department Server Installation

The Inventory Department has been using an aging UNIX system and software, but now wants to replace it with a dual-processor SMP server running Standard Edition. Approximately 277 people in the Management, Sales, Manufacturing, and Inventory Departments will use the information on this server. What preinstallation steps do you recommend to the Inventory Department before actually purchasing and installing the server?

Case Project 2-4: Considering Installation Options

While you are working with the Inventory Department, the Research Department contacts you because they have heard you are working with the other departments addressing their needs. The Research Department has two Windows 2000 Servers that they want to upgrade to Windows Server 2003, Standard Edition. After you talk with the Research Department, the IT director calls because she is responsible for purchasing the operating system software. She is wondering if each department needs its own CD-ROM or if there are other installation options that can be used by all of the departments. What are the options and what option or options do you recommend?

3

CONFIGURING THE WINDOWS SERVER 2003 ENVIRONMENT

After reading this chapter and completing the exercises, you will be able to:

♦ Install and configure hardware devices

♦ Configure the operating system working environment, including performance options, processor scheduling, memory usage, environment variables, startup and recovery options, power options, and protocols

♦ Understand the registry and how to use the Registry Editor

Successfully installing Windows Server 2003 provides a foundation on which to build and customize a server for your organization. The next step is to customize the operating system using the tools that are now installed and ready to use. There are hundreds of ways to customize your server to match specific hardware and software needs; successfully finding that match is a preventive step toward avoiding possible future problems such as slow server response.

This chapter will introduce you to indispensable tools for configuring your server, as well as some troubleshooting tools. You will begin by learning how to add new hardware using the Add Hardware option in Control Panel and how to configure and manage installed hardware using Device Manager. You'll learn how to configure the operating system for top performance, for specialized startup and recovery options, for computer power management, and for additional protocols. You'll learn to use the Add or Remove Programs tool to install additional operating system components. Finally, you'll explore the registry, which is a storehouse of all important configuration information, plus you will learn to use the Registry Editor.

CONFIGURING SERVER HARDWARE DEVICES

Sometimes you need to replace existing hardware in a server because of failure of a component. At other times you need to upgrade the hardware, or simply add another component, such as a second network adapter. Windows Server 2003 offers both Plug and Play services and the Add Hardware Wizard to enable the installation of hardware. Hardware devices can include the following:

- Disk drives
- Disk controllers
- Network adapters
- CD-ROM drives
- Keyboards
- Pointing devices
- Monitors

For those times when you add or replace hardware, you need to be familiar with how to install and configure new hardware on your server.

Plug and Play

One important advance in computer hardware and operating system software is the ability to automatically detect and configure newly installed hardware devices, such as a disk or tape drive. This is called **Plug and Play (PnP)**. For this capability to work, PnP must be:

- Built into the device
- Enabled in the target computer's BIOS
- Built into the computer operating system kernel

Modern hardware, including computers and peripherals, almost universally supports PnP. PnP eliminates hours of time server administrators and computer users once spent installing and configuring hardware. When you purchase a computer or a new device, make sure that it is PnP compatible and that the PnP compatibility conforms to the PnP capabilities used by the operating system.

Installing a Plug and Play device is a relatively simple process of attaching the device and then waiting for Windows Server 2003 to detect it and install the appropriate drivers. In some cases once the device is installed, you may need to configure its properties and settings. Keep in mind that you should review the manufacturer's installation instructions before attempting to connect the device to your computer.

 Depending on your computer system, it may be necessary to power down before installing some types of devices. Also, even if it is not necessary to power down to install a device (such as one connected to a universal serial bus port) you still may have to restart your computer in order for Windows to detect the new device. Further, some computer manufacturers prefer that you use the CD-ROM they have supplied to ensure the most recent driver or operating system software is installed, such as special options for configuring or troubleshooting the device.

If Windows does not automatically detect newly installed hardware or if the device you are installing is non–Plug and Play, you can use the Add Hardware Wizard to manually launch PnP or to manually install the device without PnP.

Add Hardware Wizard

The Add Hardware Wizard is used to:

- Invoke the operating system to use PnP to detect new hardware
- Install new non-PnP compatible hardware and hardware drivers
- Troubleshoot problems you may be having with existing hardware

The Add Hardware Wizard is started from Control Panel. Control Panel is similar to a control center, where you can customize Windows Server 2003 for devices, network connectivity, dial-up capabilities, and many other functions.

Activity 3-1: Adding and Troubleshooting a Device

Time Required: Approximately 15 minutes

Objective: Learn how to add a new device or troubleshoot an installed device that is having problems.

Description: You can use the Add Hardware Wizard to add a new device and to troubleshoot a device. In this activity, you first learn how to add a device and then you practice troubleshooting a device (the mouse). You do not need to attach a new device or to simulate a problem with the mouse in advance of starting the activity.

1. Click **Start**, point to **Control Panel**, and click **Add Hardware**. (Alternatively, you can click **Start**, point to **Control Panel**, click **System**, click the **Hardware** tab, and click the **Add Hardware Wizard** button.)

2. Click **Next** after the Add Hardware Wizard starts, as in Figure 3-1.

Figure 3-1   Starting the Add Hardware Wizard

3. At this point the Add Hardware Wizard searches to detect any hardware that has not yet been installed.

4. Click **Yes, I have already connected the hardware**. What other option could you select? Click **Next**.

5. Scroll through the list of hardware that is already installed. What types of devices are installed? How would you install a new device that is already attached?

6. Find the mouse in the hardware list and double-click that selection to practice troubleshooting this device.

7. If there are no problems with the mouse and its connection, you should see this reported as shown in Figure 3-2.

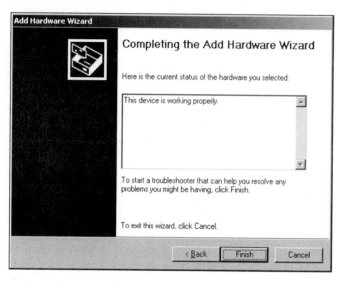

Figure 3-2   Results screen

8. Click **Finish** to see an example of the Mouse Troubleshooter. How would you continue to find out how to troubleshoot a problem with the mouse?

9. Close the Help and Support Center window.

Configuring and Managing Hardware

Windows Server 2003 provides a variety of ways to configure and manage hardware. The following sections will introduce you to key tools included with Windows Server 2003 that can be used to manage the hardware installed on your server.

Device Manager

The Add Hardware Wizard is very effective in automatically setting up hardware parameters, such as **resources**. A server's resources include the **interrupt request (IRQ) line** (which is a channel for communication with the CPU) and other elements such as the **I/O address** (the address in memory through which data is transferred between a computer component and the processor) and reserved memory range. For example, a computer contains a limited number of IRQ lines, typically 15 for Intel-based computers (lines 01 to 15). The video display, each disk drive, each serial and parallel port, and the sound card all use a dedicated IRQ to communicate with the processor. Each also needs reserved memory addresses for I/O operations. Sometimes there are resource conflicts when a network adapter, a new SCSI device adapter, or some other hardware is automatically configured.

Besides using the Add Hardware Wizard, you can use Device Manager to check for a resource conflict and to examine other properties associated with a device. Device Manager provides a graphical view of all hardware currently installed on your computer. It can also be used to:

- Verify if hardware installed on your computer is working properly.
- Update device drivers.
- Disable a device.
- Uninstall a device.
- Configure the settings for a device.

For example, consider a situation in which there is an IRQ line conflict between the NIC and a modem that you have just installed. The conflict is apparent because the NIC no longer communicates with the network and the modem cannot connect through the telephone line you attached to it. The place to go to determine the problem and resolve it is Device Manager.

Activity 3-2: Resolving a Resource Conflict

Time Required: Approximately 10 minutes

Objective: Use Device Manager to resolve a resource conflict

Description: Sometimes a resource conflict is subtle, such as a NIC locking up intermittently because it uses a portion of an I/O address range that is also used by another device. In this activity, you learn how to check for a resource conflict.

1. Click **Start**, right-click **My Computer**, and click **Manage** on the shortcut menu. (Alternatively, you can click **Start**, point to **All Programs**, point to **Administrative Tools**, and click **Computer Management**.) You see the Computer Management window. (A third way to start the Device Manager, but that does not display the Computer Management window, is to click **Start**, point to **Control Panel**, click **System**, select the **Hardware** tab, and click **Device Manager**.)

2. Click **Device Manager** in the tree under System Tools, as shown in Figure 3-3. The right pane displays the devices known to the operating system.

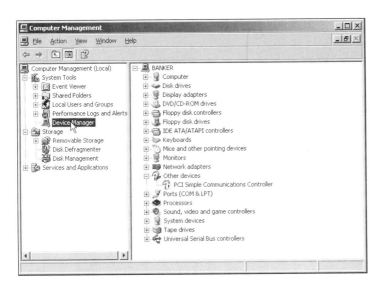

Figure 3-3   Starting Device Manager

3. Double-click **Network adapters** in the right pane.

4. Right-click the adapter installed in your computer, and then click **Properties**.

5. Notice the tabs that appear in the properties dialog box. Check out each tab to see what it is for and record your observations about the purpose of each tab.

6. Select the **Resources** tab as shown in Figure 3-4. What resource settings are used for the NIC?

7. Are there any resource conflicts reported? How would you solve a resource conflict? Record your findings.

8. Click **Cancel** on the NIC properties dialog box.

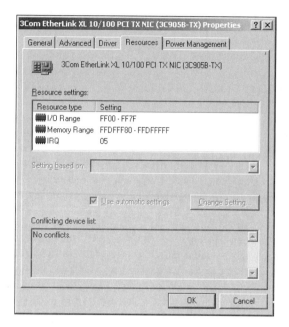

Figure 3-4   Checking for a resource conflict

9. Before you exit Device Manager, find out what resources are used by another device, such as a communications port or the display adapter.

10. Close the **Computer Management** window.

Configuring Hardware Profiles

A **hardware profile** is a set of instructions telling the operating system which devices to start or which device settings to use when your computer starts. By default, there is one hardware profile (Profile 1) created when you install Windows Server 2003 (see Figure 3-5). Every device installed on your computer is enabled in the default profile.

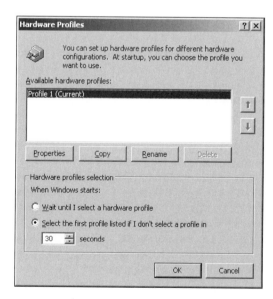

Figure 3-5   Default hardware profile

One of the most common uses for hardware profiles is with portable computers. Most portable computers are, at different times, used in the office, at home, and on the road when traveling. You can create multiple profiles and use Device Manager to enable or disable specific devices for each one. For example, you may have a hardware profile for home that disables the network card if you only use a modem. You can create a second hardware profile for the office that enables your network card and disables your modem.

Activity 3-3: Creating a Hardware Profile

Time Required: Approximately 10 minutes

Objective: Learn how to create a hardware profile.

Description: Hardware profiles are particularly useful for portable computers. You may have a special-purpose server configured on a portable computer, such as a server that is used in portable biology field research situations where lab locations frequently change. In this activity, you learn how to access hardware profiles and how to create a new profile.

1. Click **Start**, point to **Control Panel**, and click **System**. (Another way to access the System Properties dialog box is to click **Start**, right-click **My Computer**, and click **Properties**).

2. Click the **Hardware** tab.

3. Click the **Hardware Profiles** button.

4. Click **Profile 1 (Current)**, if necessary, and click the **Copy** button.

5. Enter **Profile** and your initials, such as ProfileJG. Click **OK**.

6. Click the new profile you created, if necessary, and click **Properties**. You see a dialog box similar to Figure 3-6.

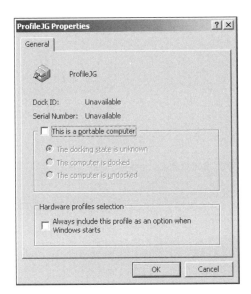

Figure 3-6 Configuring a hardware profile

7. Notice that if you are working on a portable computer you can click, This is a portable computer, and configure a profile to reflect the docking state of the computer.

8. If you want this profile to be the default profile when your computer boots, you can use the selection, Always include this profile as an option when Windows starts.

9. Click **Cancel**.

10. Click the profile you created, and click **Delete**. (Do not delete Profile 1.)

11. Click **Yes** to verify that you want to delete the profile.

12. Click **OK**, and click **OK** again.

Once a new profile is created, restart your computer with that profile as the default. You can then use Device Manager to configure or disable specific devices for that profile.

Configuring Driver Signing

When you install a device such as a pointing device or a NIC, you have the option to make sure that the driver for that device has been verified by Microsoft. When a driver is verified by Microsoft, a unique digital signature is incorporated into that driver in a process called **driver signing**. After you install Windows Server 2003, you can choose to be warned that a driver is not signed, to ignore whether or not a driver is signed, or to have the operating system prevent you from installing a driver that is not signed. The warning level is assigned by default, so that you are made aware of when a driver you are installing is unsigned, but you can still select to install or not to install that driver.

Activity 3-4: Configuring Driver Signing

Time Required: Approximately 10 minutes

Objective: Configure the Block option in driver signing

Description: Besides ensuring that you use drivers compatible with Windows Server 2003, driver signing also enables you to avoid unauthorized drivers that are out of date. Most server administrators set driver signing at the warning level or at the level to prevent unsigned drivers from being installed. In this activity, you learn how to set driver signing at the Block level, which prevents an unsigned driver from being installed.

1. Click **Start**, point to **Control Panel**, and click **System**.

2. Click the **Hardware** tab, and click **Driver Signing** (see Figure 3-7).

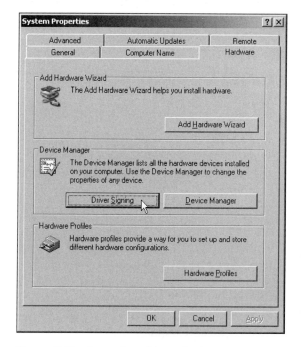

Figure 3-7   Accessing driver signing

3. Notice the three options: Ignore - Install the software anyway and don't ask for my approval; Warn - Prompt me each time to choose an action; or Block - Never install unsigned driver software.

4. Click **Block – Never install unsigned driver software**, as shown in Figure 3-8.

3.

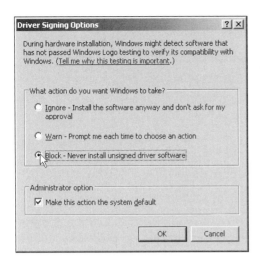

Figure 3-8 Configuring driver signing for the Block option

5. Be certain that **Make this action the system default** is checked, and if not, check it.

When you check this option, this means that Windows Server 2003 will apply signature verification to users who log on to the server and attempt to install any software (which gives you a measure of assurance that users cannot install unsigned drivers).

6. Click **OK** to save your settings in the Driver Signing Options dialog box.

7. Click **OK** to exit the System Properties dialog box.

When you configure driver signing, you configure it to apply to all new software installations, as well as device drivers, because besides drivers, many critical operating system files are also signed. Each time you install a word processor or spreadsheet application, there is a risk that an important operating system file, such as a .dll (dynamic-link library) file, may be overwritten by a file that is unsigned. If you have selected the Block option, this means that drivers and operating system files cannot be modified or overwritten by files that do not have the appropriate digital signature. No software installation can inadvertently install a driver or system file that is inappropriate for your version of Windows Server 2003.

Using the System File Checker   If you do not have the Block option set for driver signing and you copy an inappropriate file—such as one that is outdated or from a different operating system—over a system or driver file such as a .dll, .exe, or .sys file, Windows Server 2003 can be set to automatically run the System File Checker when the operating system boots. The System File Checker locates the original system file in the Windows\system32\dllcache folder and then copies it over the inappropriate file. You also have the option to manually run the System File Checker from the Command Prompt window to check files without rebooting.

Activity 3-5: Manually Running the System File Checker

Time Required: Approximately 5 minutes to learn about command switches and 30 to 40 minutes to run the test

Objective: Start the System File Checker to verify all system files.

Description: The System File Checker is an excellent tool for verifying your system, particularly if you feel it is not responding quite right or that a driver or system file has become corrupted. These problems may occur when there is a power failure on a system that is not on a battery backup or when the power filter for the system is not working properly to assure quality power. This activity shows you how to start the System File Checker. Note that the best practice is to run the System File Checker only when there are no users on the system.

1. Click **Start**, point to **All Programs**, point to **Accessories**, and click **Command Prompt**.

2. Type **sfc /?** and press **Enter** in the Command Prompt window to view the switch options you can use to check and replace files.

3. What are the switch options? Which option would you use to perform a check of the files every time the system is rebooted? Record your findings. If you don't have permission from your instructor to run the System File Checker or if there are users on your system, close the Command Prompt window at this point.

Remember that it is safest to have users off the system when you check files, and you may need to reboot before a replaced file goes into effect. In some cases, the checker may request that you insert the Windows Server 2003 CD-ROM to obtain a file.

4. At the prompt, type **sfc /scannow** and press **Enter**.

5. The checker displays an information box to show its progress (see Figure 3-9). You may need to shrink the Command Prompt window or click the Flashing Windows File Protection button on the taskbar to see the box.(Also, you may be prompted to insert the Windows Server 2003 CD-ROM.) If the System File Checker finds a file that needs to be replaced, it prompts you.

6. Close the Command Prompt Window.

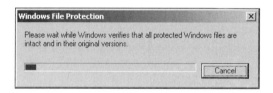

Figure 3-9   Information box for the System File Checker

Using Sigverif to Verify System and Critical Files   Windows Server 2003 includes another tool, called Sigverif, that verifies system and critical files to determine if they have a signature. This tool only scans files and does not overwrite inappropriate files, enabling you to use the tool while users are logged on. After the scan is complete, the results are written to a log file, called sigverif.txt. If the tool finds a file without a signature that you believe needs to be replaced, you can replace the file when users are off the system.

Activity 3-6: Verifying Critical Files for a Signature

Time Required: Approximately 15 minutes

Objective: Use Sigverif to find unsigned files.

Description: If you have driver signing in the Ignore or Warn modes, you may experience a situation in which you copy drivers onto the system that interfere with the normal function of the server—perhaps a file that is missed even by the System File Checker. For example, you may install a new disk drive, install the drivers from the manufacturer's CD-ROM, and then find that some other peripheral is not working right, because it shares a common .dll file. This activity shows you how to use the Sigverif tool to locate the unsigned files that may be the source of the problem and that should be replaced.

1. Click **Start** and click **Run**.

2. Type **sigverif** in the Open box, and click **OK**.

3. Click the **Advanced** button. Notice the options that you can set, as shown in Figure 3-10. Click **Notify me if any system files are not signed**, if this option is not already selected.

Figure 3-10   Configuring the Sigverif options

4. Click **OK.**

5. Click **Start**.

6. Did the scan find any unsigned files? Click **OK** when the scan is completed, and then click **Close**.

7. Open **Windows Explorer** or **My Computer** and browse to the drive on which the Windows folder is located.Open the Windows folder, and look for the Sigverif.txt file. Double-click the file to view its contents.

8. Examine the Status column to see which files are signed or not signed.

9. Close **Notepad**. Click **No** if asked to save your changes.

10. Close Windows Explorer or My Computer.

CONFIGURING THE OPERATING SYSTEM

After the operating system has been installed it can be configured to optimize performance and meet very specific requirements. Using tools included with Windows Server 2003, you can configure elements of the operating system such as performance options, environment variables, startup and recovery options, power options, and protocols. The following sections will discuss important ways in which you can configure the operating system, focusing on configuration tools that are used from Control Panel: System, Network Connectivity, and Power Options.

Configuring Performance Options

Windows Server 2003 enables you to configure and optimize your server for performance. There are three basic areas of performance that you can configure:

- Processor scheduling and memory usage

- Virtual memory

- Memory for network performance

Configuring Processor Scheduling and Memory Usage

Processor scheduling allows you to configure how processor resources are allocated to programs. The default is set to Background services, which means that all programs running receive equal amounts of processor time. Applications are programs you are likely to be running at the server console, such as a backup program. Normally you want to leave the default setting for Background services. Sometimes, though, you may need to select the Programs option to give most of the processor's resources to a particular program. For instance, if you determine that a disk drive is failing and you want to back up its contents as fast as possible using the Backup tool, you use this option to give the Backup tool more processor time and thus make it work faster.

The memory usage option is used to configure how much system memory is used to run programs versus how much is allocated for server functions. Select the Programs option if your computer is temporarily acting as a workstation mainly running programs at the console. Select the System cache option (this is the default setting) if your computer is acting as a network server or running programs that require a large amount of memory.

Activity 3-7: Configuring Processor Scheduling and Memory Usage

Time Required: Approximately 5 minutes

Objective: Learn where to set up processor scheduling and set memory usage.

Description: Sometimes it is important to temporarily reconfigure a server to function more like a workstation, so that applications in the foreground have the most resources. This is true, for example, if you need to perform an immediate backup to save vital data during a system emergency. In this activity, you learn where to set the system resources for processor scheduling and memory usage.

1. Click **Start**, point to **Control Panel**, and click **System**.

2. Click the **Advanced** tab.

3. In the Performance section, click the **Settings** button.

4. Click the **Advanced** tab to see the dialog box shown in Figure 3-11. Notice the options that can be set under Processor scheduling and under Memory usage.

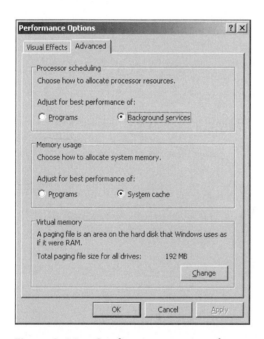

Figure 3-11   Configuring server performance

5. Click **Cancel** and click **Cancel** again.

Configuring Virtual Memory

Virtual memory is disk storage used to expand the capacity of the physical RAM installed in the computer. When the currently running programs and processes exceed the RAM, they treat disk space allocated for virtual memory just as if it is real memory. The disadvantage of this is that memory activities performed through virtual memory are not as fast as those performed in RAM (although disk access and data transfer speeds can be quite fast). Virtual memory works through a technique called **paging**, whereby blocks of information, called pages, are moved from RAM into virtual memory on disk. On a Pentium computer, data is paged in blocks of 4 KB. For example, if the system is not presently using a 7 KB block of code, it divides the code block between two pages, each 4 KB in size (part of one page will not be completely full). Next, both pages are moved to virtual memory on disk until needed. When the processor calls for that code block, the pages are moved back into RAM.

Before virtual memory can be used, it must first be allocated for this purpose by tuning the operating system. The area of the disk that is allocated for this purpose is called the **paging file**. A default amount of virtual memory is always established when Windows Server 2003 is installed, but the amount should be checked by the server administrator to ensure that it is not too large or too small.

Besides size, the location of the paging file is important. Some tips for locating the paging file are:

- Server performance is better if the paging file is not placed on the boot partition (the one with the \Windows folder) of basic disks or the boot volume of dynamic disks (you'll learn more about the types of disks later in this book).

- If there are multiple disks, performance can be improved by placing a paging file on each disk (but avoid placing the paging file on the boot partition or volume that contains the system files in the \Windows folder).

- In a mirrored set or volume, place the paging file on the main disk, and not on the mirrored (backup) disk.

- Do not place the paging file on a stripe set, striped volume, stripe set with parity, or RAID-5 volume, which are all specially set up disks to increase performance and fault tolerance.

When you tune the size of the paging file there are two parameters to set: initial size and maximum size. A general rule for configuring the initial size is to start with the size recommended when you view the default virtual memory setting, which is the amount of installed RAM times 1.5. For a server with 256 MB of RAM, the initial paging file size should be at least 384 MB (256 × 1.5). Set the maximum size so it affords plenty of room for growth—such as twice the size of your initial paging file setting. For example, if your initial setting is 384 MB, then consider setting the maximum size to 768 MB. When it is operating, Windows Server 2003 always starts using the initial size and only expands the size of the paging file as additional space is needed.

Activity 3-8: Configuring the Paging File

Time Required: Approximately 5 minutes

Objective: Learn where to configure the initial and maximum size of the paging file.

Description: One way to inexpensively improve the performance of a server is to adjust the size of the paging file. If a server seems to run a little slower than desired because the memory (RAM) is often used to the maximum, consider increasing the maximum paging file size. This activity shows you where to configure the paging file.

1. Click **Start**, point to **Control Panel**, and click **System**.

2. Make sure that the **General** tab is displayed. How much memory is in the computer, as shown under the Computer category? Record your finding.

3. Click the **Advanced** tab.

4. Click the **Settings** button in the Performance section of the tab.

5. Click the **Advanced** tab, and then click the **Change** button. See Figure 3-12. What are the current settings on your computer? Are the settings appropriate for the amount of memory in the computer?

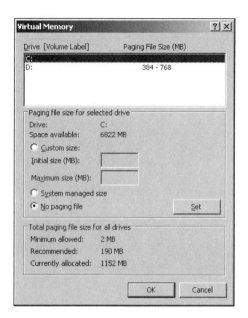

Figure 3-12   Configuring virtual memory

6. Click **Cancel** to leave the Virtual Memory dialog box, and click **Cancel** to exit the Performance Options dialog box. Close the **System Properties** dialog box.

If you change the virtual memory settings, the new settings do not go into effect until the server is rebooted. Also, in Figure 3-12 notice that drive C:, which is the boot partition for this computer, does not have a paging file. You can improve the performance of a computer by not placing the paging file on the same drive as the \Windows folder, but instead placing the paging file on other drives, such as drive D: in this example.

Configuring Memory For Network Performance

Memory can be divided between server functions and network connectivity functions. The server functions include software applications, printing, and currently running services. Network connectivity is related to the number of user connections at a given time. Server functions use RAM and paging. The network connectivity only uses RAM. If the server performance is slow because memory is busy, the network memory parameters should be checked and tuned.

Network memory is adjusted from the Network Connections option in Control Panel, by configuring the memory parameters in Figure 3-13 as properties of the Local Area Connection's File and Printer Sharing for Microsoft Networks installation.

The memory optimization settings are described in Table 3-1. For example, if a server has 120 users who regularly access word processing and spreadsheet files on the server or who regularly install software from the server, the Maximize data throughput for file sharing option should be checked; or if there are only 32 users on a small network, check the Balance option button.

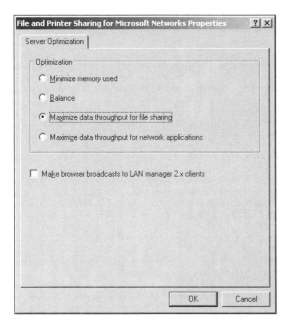

Figure 3-13   Adjusting memory allocation for network performance

Table 3-1   Configuring server RAM for network optimization

Options	Description
Minimize memory used	Optimizes the memory used on servers with 10 or fewer simultaneous network users
Balance	Optimizes memory use for a small LAN with about 64 or fewer users
Maximize data throughput for file sharing	Used for a large network with over 64 users where file and print serving resources need more memory allocation to make the server efficient
Maximize data throughput for network applications	Used in servers that primarily handle network connections and to reduce paging activity when this affects server performance, such as on a server that mainly authenticates users to the network or that handles databases that distribute functions to the client (in client/server systems)
Make browser broadcasts to LAN Manager 2.x clients	Used for networks that have both Windows Server 2003 and the Microsoft (and IBM) early server operating system, LAN Manager

If increasing the paging file size or adjusting the memory used for network performance does not improve the speed of the server, this may be a sign that you need to add more memory.

Activity 3-9: Configuring for Network Performance

Time Required: Approximately 5 minutes

Objective: Learn where to configure memory for network performance.

Description: Just after you install Windows Server 2003, you should ensure memory is configured for optimal network performance. In this activity you configure a server that is intended to mainly provide an SQL Server database (which distributes memory use to the client) and handle several hundred network connections (users).

1. Click **Start**, point to **Control Panel**, point to **Network Connections**, and click **Local Area Connection**.

2. Click the **Properties** button.

3. Click **File and Printer Sharing for Microsoft Networks**, and click **Properties**. How is Server Optimization currently configured?

4. Click **Maximize data throughput for network applications**, if this option is not already selected.

5. Click **OK**.

6. Click **Close** to exit the Local Area Connection Properties dialog box, and click **Close** on the Local Area Connection Status dialog box.

Configuring Environment Variables

Environment variables are used to tell the operating system where to find certain programs, how to allocate memory to programs and to control different programs. This is similar to using the Temp and Path commands in MS-DOS.

Environment variables can be broken down into two categories: system environment variables and user environment variables. **System environment variables** are defined by the operating system and apply to any user logged onto the computer. Administrators can add new system environment variables or change the values of existing ones. **User environment variables** can be defined on a per user basis, such as specifying the path where application files are stored.

Keep the following points in mind when you are working with environment variables:

- System environment variables are always set first.

- Variables set in the autoexec.bat startup file are set next, overwriting any system environment variables in conflict (except for path variables which are set after user environment variables).

- User environment variables are set next, overriding any conflicting system environment variables and autoexec.bat variables.

- Path variables defined in the autoexec.bat are set last.

Path variables define paths to specific folders, and enable you to run applications stored in those folders from the Start button Run option without specifying a path to an application.

Activity 3-10: Configuring Environment Variables

Time Required: Approximately 5 minutes

Objective: Learn where to configure system and user environment variables.

Description: A newly installed Windows Server 2003 operating system has several system and user environment variables that are set up by default. In this activity, you learn where to configure the system and user environment variables and at the same time determine which ones are currently configured on your system.

1. Click **Start**, point to **Control Panel**, and click **System**.

2. Click the **Advanced** tab.

3. Click **Environment Variables** to display a dialog box similar to Figure 3-14. Which user and system environment variables are already defined on your system? How would you add a new variable?

4. Click **Cancel** to close the Environment Variables dialog box.

5. Click **Cancel** to close the System Properties dialog box.

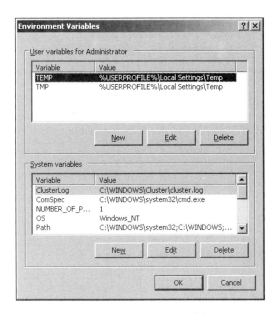

Figure 3-14 Environment variables

Configuring Startup and Recovery

Windows Server 2003 enables you to configure parameters that dictate the startup sequence and how the system recovers from errors. Check these settings after you install the operating system to ensure the default settings match your needs. The startup parameters enable you to modify the Boot.ini file for a dual-boot system in order to specify which operating system to boot by default and how long to wait in seconds before starting the operating system. You can also edit the Boot.ini file manually by using Notepad (using Windows Explorer or My Computer, find the Boot.ini file on the root of the drive that contains the \Windows folder, and double-click the file).

The startup and recovery parameters enable you to provide instructions about how to recover in the event of a system failure. For example, you can have the system create a log to help you locate the source of the failure after the computer reboots, and you can instruct the computer to reboot automatically upon failure. The options are as follows:

- Write an event to the system log.

- Send an administrative alert.

- Write debug information to the default file, \Windows\Memory.dmp, or to a file you specify.

- Have the computer automatically reboot immediately after the failure.

Activity 3-11: Configuring Startup and Recovery

Time Required: Approximately 10 minutes

Objective: Configure startup and recovery options.

Description: Soon after you install Windows Server 2003 it is important to customize the system startup and recovery options to match how your organization operates. This assignment shows you how to configure these parameters on a nondual boot system so that the system does not automatically start up after a system failure. The advantage of not automatically restarting is that the system administrator has time to examine the system before it is rebooted. This is important, for example, when there is a disk drive that is failing; not automatically rebooting allows the drive to be replaced before users resume work.

1. Click **Start**, point to **Control Panel**, and click **System**.

2. Click the **Advanced** tab.

3. Find the Startup and Recovery section on the tab, and click the **Settings** button in that section.

4. Set the **Time to display list of operating systems** parameter to **15** seconds (see Figure 3-15), so that you still have time to access recovery options when the system boots, but to reflect that you do not need time to select another operating system at boot up because this is not a dual boot system.

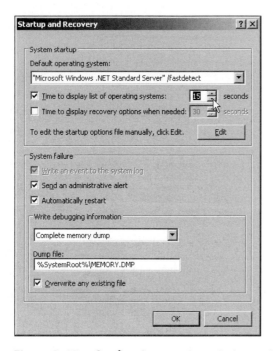

Figure 3-15   Configuring a system startup option

5. If **Automatically restart** is checked, remove the check mark (which means the system does not reboot after a failure until you manually do so).

6. Click **OK** in the Startup and Recovery dialog box.

7. Click **OK** in the System Properties dialog box.

Configuring Power Options

After you have installed Windows Server 2003, check the power management options to make sure that they are set appropriately for the computer and the way you are using the computer on the network. The default power scheme is set at Always On, which means that it turns the monitor off after 20 minutes of no activity and never turns off the hard disks. Also, the default setup is to run the shutdown procedure when you press the power off button, instead of placing the computer in standby mode. **Standby** is a mode in which the computer components are shut down and information in memory is not written to hard disk—which means if the power goes out in standby mode, information in memory is lost. The power supply and CPU remain active, waiting to start up all components when you press a key or move the mouse.

Configure the power options by clicking Start, pointing to Control Panel, and clicking Power Options. Access the Power Schemes tab first to establish the power settings, which include settings for desktop and portable computers. The settings change on the basis of the power scheme that you select, Portable/Laptop or Minimal Power Management, for example. In most situations, you will likely select Always On or Minimal Power Management, which are options that primarily involve display monitor power management. Another option is to create your own settings by specifying how soon to turn off the monitor, whether to turn off the hard disks, and whether to use standby mode.

Activity 3-12: Configuring Power Options

Time Required: Approximately 5 minutes

Objective: Create a customized power option called Server.

Description: Many server administrators set up customized power options for their servers. In this activity, you learn how to create a customized power option called Server in which the monitor is shut off after one hour, but the hard disks are never shut off for power savings.

1. Click **Start**, point to **Control Panel**, and click **Power Options**.

2. Ensure that the **Power Schemes** tab is displayed.

3. Click the **Turn off monitor** list arrow, and click **After 1 hour**.

4. Make sure that the Turn off hard disks list box displays Never.

5. Make sure that the System standby list box displays Never.

6. Click **Save As**, type **Server** in the Save Scheme dialog box, and click **OK**. Click **Apply** (see Figure 3-16).

7. Click each of the other three tabs to view the additional parameters that can be set.

8. Click **OK** to save your work.

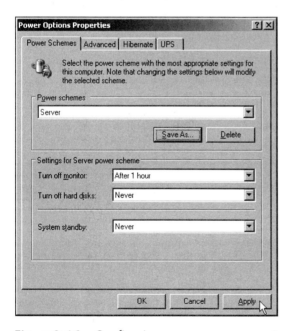

Figure 3-16   Configuring power management

When you configure the power options, also check the Advanced tab to determine whether the computer powers off or goes into standby mode, which is determined by what you enter in the "When I press the power button on my computer" box. Because you will likely be working on the computer hardware or want to perform a cold boot when you power the computer off, the default is set to Shut down as shown in Figure 3-17. If you select Stand by, consider checking the box titled, "Prompt for password when computer resumes from standby," so that only an authorized server administrator can access the server.

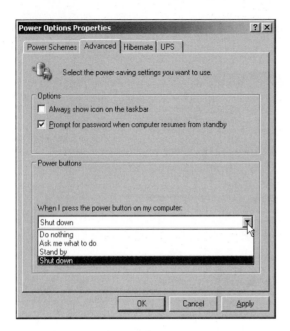

Figure 3-17   Advanced power management options

The third tab, Hibernate, enables you to set up the computer to hibernate when it is not in use. **Hibernate** mode is similar to standby, but with two important differences: the memory contents are saved before shutting down the disks, and it takes longer to restart all components to resume where you left off.

The fourth tab, UPS, enables you to configure an **uninterruptible power supply (UPS)**, which is a battery backup device that temporarily supplies power to the server when the main power goes out. You can set up communications between the UPS and Windows Server 2003 usually through a serial connection so that the UPS notifies the server when there is a power outage and the server sends you an alert.

Disk drives, memory, and other key server components can sustain damage from power outages and fluctuations, such as brownouts. Also, the server may lose valuable data when a sudden power problem causes it to shut down without the opportunity to save data. A UPS is the best fault-tolerance method to prevent power problems from causing data loss and component damage.

All UPS systems are designed to provide power for a limited time period, such as 10 to 20 minutes, so a decision can be made, based on how long the power failure will last, as to whether to shut down computers immediately. Of course, the amount of time the batteries can provide power depends on how much and what equipment is attached to the UPS. This is why most people attach only critical equipment to a UPS, such as computers and monitors, external disk arrays, and tape drives. Most UPS systems also include circuitry to guard against power surges and power brownouts.

Some manufacturers recommend against plugging laser printers into a UPS, because those printers draw excessive power when turned on, risking damage to the UPS.

The general steps for configuring a UPS connection to Windows Server 2003 are:

1. Click **Start**, point to **Control Panel**, click **Power Options**, and click the **UPS** tab.

2. Click the **Select** button and in the Select manufacturer list box, select the UPS manufacturer, such as American Power Conversion.

3. Select the specific UPS model in the Select model box, such as PowerStack.

4. In the On port box, specify the COM port to which the UPS is attached, such as COM2. Click **Finish**.

5. Click the **Configure** button in the Power Options Properties dialog box.

6. Configure the options that are appropriate to the UPS, including how to send out notifications of a power failure, when to sound a critical alarm that the UPS is almost out of power, the option to run a program just before the UPS is out of power, and if you want the computer and UPS to shut down just before the UPS is out of power. Click **OK**.

7. Click **Apply**.

8. Check the message at the bottom of the dialog box to make sure that the UPS is connected and communicating with the server. A large "X" in a red circle appears if it is not properly connected and communicating. If it is not, make sure that the serial cable is attached, ensure that you configured the same server port in Step 4 as is used for the cable, and make sure that the UPS is turned on.

9. Click **OK**.

Configuring Protocols

The Windows Server 2003, Standard Edition, installation steps in Chapter 2 illustrate how to install the default protocol configuration, and Chapter 1 discusses manual TCP/IP installation. However, you may need to add other protocols or to modify the existing configuration to customize the server for your network. Use the Network Connections option within Control Panel to set up the server to communicate using other protocols, such as IPX/SPX for NetWare clients, AppleTalk for Macintosh clients, or to reconfigure TCP/IP. For example, you might use IPX/SPX to set up Windows Server 2003 to communicate with a Novell NetWare server.

Installing NWLink IPX/SPX/NetBIOS Compatible Transport Protocol

If there are pre-NetWare version 5.x computers on your network, you can install NWLink IPX/SPX/NetBIOS Compatible Transport Protocol to enable communications between those servers and a Windows 2003 server. This protocol is installed using the Network Connections option in Control Panel.

After installing the NWLink IPX/SPX/NetBIOS Compatible Transport Protocol, make sure that the right network number and frame type are implemented to work with the NetWare server to which you will connect. Depending on the version, NetWare may be using Ethernet frame types 802.2 or 802.3, Ethernet II, or Ethernet SNAP. The Windows 2003 server should be using the same frame type as the NetWare servers already on the network. If there is only one frame type in use, you can have Windows Server 2003 automatically detect it. If two or more frame types are in use, you need to configure each frame type. In this circumstance, the best practice is to consult with the NetWare server administrator to find out what frame types are in use and how to configure for them.

To check the frame type configuration information after the protocol is installed, click Start, point to Control Panel, point to Network Connections, right-click Local Area Connection, and click Properties. Double-click NWLink IPX/SPX/NetBIOS Compatible Transport Protocol in the scroll box. Leave the internal network number as 00000000 if you only plan to connect to a NetWare server as a client. If you are connecting to a NetWare server to use File and Print Services for NetWare, IPX routing, or a NetWare service that uses **Service Advertising Protocol (SAP)**, then designate an internal network number, such as 00000001. SAP is used by NetWare clients to identify servers and the network services provided by each server. An internal network is mainly used for IPX routing to create the equivalent of a private virtual network between a NetWare server and one or more Windows 2003 servers.

If the servers to which you are connecting only use one frame type, Windows Server 2003 automatically determines which frame type is in use so that you do not need to configure it. If more than one frame type is used, Windows Server 2003 defaults to the Ethernet 802.2 frame type, and you need to manually configure the other frame types and network number.

Before configuring NWLink, coordinate your configuration activities with the NetWare server administrator in your organization.

Activity 3-13: Configuring NWLink

Time Required: Approximately 10 minutes

Objective: Learn how to install and configure NWLink for communications with older NetWare servers.

Description: Some networks have older NetWare servers, such as NetWare version 3.x or 4.x servers. To enable Windows Server 2003 to communicate with these servers, you need to install NWLink IPX/SPX/NetBIOS Compatible Transport Protocol. This activity gives you experience installing and configuring the protocol.

1. Click **Start**, point to **Control Panel**, point to **Network Connections**, right-click **Local Area Connection**, and click **Properties**.

2. Click the **Install** button, and then double-click **Protocol**.

3. Click **NWLink IPX/SPX/NetBIOS Compatible Transport Protocol**, and then click **OK** (see Figure 3-18).

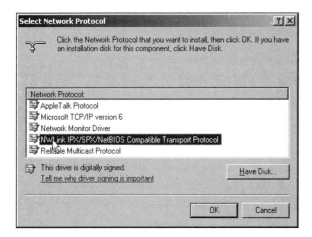

Figure 3-18   Installing NWLink

4. In the Local Area Connection Properties dialog box, click **NWLink IPX/SPX/NetBIOS Compatible Transport Protocol**, and then click **Properties**. What parameters are configured already? Would you change the Internal network number in order to use a NetWare server for File and Print Services?

5. Click **Manual frame type detection**, and then click **Add**.

6. In the **Manual Frame Detection** dialog box, click the down arrow to view the options for **Frame type**. What are the options?

7. Click **Cancel**.

8. Click **Cancel** again, and then click **Close** to exit the Local Area Connection Properties dialog box.

Installing AppleTalk

AppleTalk and other protocols are installed using the Network Connections option in Control Panel and by following similar steps as those described for installing NWLink (see Activity 3-13). However, there are no additional properties, such as frame type or internal network number, to configure for AppleTalk.

Installing Additional Windows Server 2003 Components

Additional components and software that you did not install during Windows Server 2003 Setup can be installed in one of two ways: using the Network Connections tool and using the Add or Remove Programs tool.

Installing Components Using the Network Connections Tool

The components that are installed through the Network Connections tool include:

- *QoS Packet Scheduler*—Quality of Service Packet Scheduler provides specified levels of guaranteed delivery of data packets over the network for critical or multimedia applications (your network must be first be equipped with QoS IEEE 802.1p devices).

- *Service Advertising Protocol (SAP)*—An IPX/SPX (NWLink)-compatible protocol that is used by NetWare clients to identify servers and the network services provided by each server.

- *Internet Connection Firewall*—This is used for small office environments in which multiple computers share an Internet connection; it creates a firewall that controls the type of traffic allowed into the network.

Activity 3-14: Installing Components Via the Network Connections Tool

Time Required: Approximately 5 minutes

Objective: Learn how to install the components available through the Network Connections tool.

Description: In this activity you view where to install the QoS Packet Scheduler, Service Advertising Protocol, and Internet Connection Firewall.

1. Click **Start**, point to **Control Panel**, point to **Network Connections**, right-click **Local Area Connection**, and click **Properties**.

2. Click the **Install** button.

3. Double-click **Service**. Notice that there are two services you can install: QoS Packet Scheduler and Service Advertising Protocol.

4. Click **Cancel** in the Select Network Service dialog box. Click **Cancel** in the Select Network Component Type dialog box.

5. Click the **Advanced** tab in the Local Area Connection Properties dialog box.

6. Check the box labeled **Protect my computer and network by limiting or preventing access to this computer from the Internet**.

7. Click the **Settings** button.

8. What tabs are available on which to configure settings? Click each of the tabs to see the options that you can configure.

9. Click **Cancel**. Remove the check mark from the box, **Protect my computer and network by limiting or preventing access to this computer from the Internet**.

10. Click **Cancel**.

Installing Components Using the Add or Remove Programs Tool

Most of the additional Windows Server 2003 components, such as Web Application Server, Networking Services, and Indexing Service are installed using the Add or Remove Programs tool in Control Panel. Table 3-2 presents a list of components you can install.

Table 3-2   Windows Server 2003, Standard Edition, components

Component	Description
Accessories and Utilities	Installs components that include a wizard to configure accessibility options, accessories such as Notepad, communications tools, games, and multimedia tools
Application Server	Provides a large range of Web application capabilities including ASP.NET for programming, message queuing, Internet Information Services (IIS), COM+, and other services
Certificate Services	Used for certification authority for security through certificates
E-mail Services	Installs POP3 e-mail capabilities along with the e-mail protocol of the Internet, which is Simple Mail Transfer Protocol (SMTP)
Fax Services	Enables fax capabilities
Indexing Service	Used to quickly search file contents for specific words or strings of words
Internet Explorer Enhanced Security Configuration	Used to provide additional security controlling how users access Web sites
Management and Monitoring Tools	Used to manage and monitor the server and the network
Networking Services	Installs protocols and services for DNS, DHCP, WINS, and other network services
Other Network File and Print Services	Enables print services for UNIX and file and print services for Macintosh computers
Remote Installation Services	Enables the installation of Windows 2000, Windows XP, and Windows Server 2003 on remote computers that also can be booted remotely
Remote Storage	Used to enable Windows Server 2003 to write files to remote devices, such as tape drives
Terminal Server	Enables clients to run programs located on the server, as though they were terminals
Terminal Services Licensing	Controls licensing for terminal services
UDDI Services	Provides Universal Description, Discovery, and Integration (UDDI) capabilities within an enterprise or between business partners for Web services
Update Root Certificates	Enables automatic downloads of the most recent root certificates from Windows Update as necessary
Windows Media Services	Used to "stream" multimedia from the server to the clients, so that an audio/video file starts playing before it is fully received

Activity 3-15: Installing Components Using the Add or Remove Programs Tool

Time Required: Approximately 10 minutes

Objective: Learn how to use the Add or Remove Programs tool.

Description: The Add or Remove Programs tool is vital for setting up your server with services desired by your organization, such as e-mail services, specialized network services, or Web services. In this activity you learn how to use the Add or Remove Programs tool to install Print Services for Unix.

1. Click **Start**, point to **Control Panel**, and click **Add or Remove Programs**.

2. Click the **Add/Remove Windows Components** selection on the left side of the window.

3. Scroll through the options in the Windows Components Wizard window (see Figure 3-19). To find out more about a component, click it, and then read the Description section.

4. Double-click Application Server. Notice that you can select one, several, or all of a variety of subcomponents, such as ASP.NET. Enable network COM+ access and others. To find out about a specific subcomponent, click it, and then read the Description section in the dialog box. Click Cancel to return to the list of Windows components.

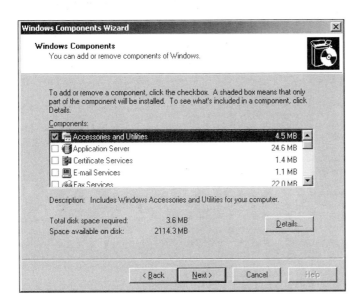

Figure 3-19   Windows Components Wizard

5. Again scroll through the list of components. If there is a check mark in front of a component and the check box is white, this means all of the subcomponents for that component are currently installed. If the box is gray and checked, some but not all of the subcomponents are installed.

6. Double-click **Other Network File and Print Services**. What subcomponents are listed?

7. Check the box for **Print Services for Unix**. Click **OK**. Notice that the check box for Other Network File and Print Services is now grey with a check mark.

To add a component or subcomponent, you place a check mark in the box in front of it and continue with the installation steps. To remove a component or subcomponent, you remove its check mark and continue.

8. Click **Next**.

9. The Windows Components Wizard takes a few moments to configure and install (or remove) your selections. It may also ask that you insert the Windows Server 2003 CD-ROM. (If you do need to insert the CD-ROM, exit out of the Welcome to Microsoft® Windows® Server 2003 screen.)

10. Click **Finish**.

If a particular component needs additional configuration after it is installed, you see a Configure button displayed in the **Add or Remove Programs** window. Click Configure to finish the configuration.

11. Close the Add or Remove Programs window.

UNDERSTANDING THE WINDOWS SERVER 2003 REGISTRY

The Windows Server 2003 registry is a very complex database containing all the information the operating system needs about the entire server. For example, the initialization files used by earlier versions of Windows operating systems, including the critical System.ini and Win.ini files, are contained in the registry. They also may exist as separate files, but this is only necessary for programs that are not designed for compatibility with the registry, such as early MS-DOS and pre-Windows 95 programs. Some examples of data contained in the registry are:

- Information about all hardware components, including the CPU, disk drives, network interface cards, CD-ROM drives, and more

- Information about Windows Server 2003 services that are installed, which services they depend on, and the order in which they are started

- Data about user profiles and Windows Server 2003 group policies

- Data on the last current and last known setup used to boot the computer

- Configuration information about all software in use

- Software licensing information

- Control Panel parameter configurations

In Windows Server 2003, the Registry Editor is launched from the Start button Run option as either Regedt32 or Regedit. The Registry Editor window is very straightforward, with common menu utilities such as File, Edit, View, Favorites, and Help (see Figure 3-20).

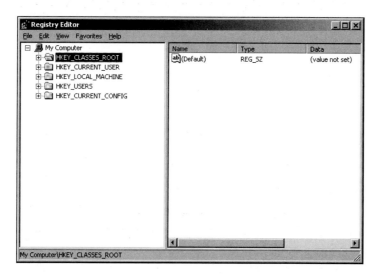

Figure 3-20   Registry Editor

 There are two names for the Registry Editor because in Windows 2000 Server there were two different Registry Editors with different capabilities. At this writing, Windows Server 2003 continues with the same editor names, but both names are for the same program.

Making incorrect changes to the registry can have profound consequences for your operating system—even to the point of possibly disabling your system. Use the following precautions when working with the registry:

- Establish a specific group of administrators who have privileges to open and modify the registry. Take away registry modification privileges from all others by controlling who can use the Registry Editor and .reg files.

- Only make changes to the registry as a last resort, such as those changes recommended in a technical document from Microsoft. It is safer to use tools such as Control Panel options or the Add or Remove Programs tool for changes to information in the registry.

- Regularly back up the registry, such as through the Automated System Recovery set steps discussed in Chapter 2 or through performing a backup via the Backup tool available through the Windows Server 2003 System Tools. Further, always back up the registry prior to reconfiguring it through the Registry Editor.

- Never copy the registry from one Windows-based system over the registry of a different system, regardless of whether or not they use the same operating system or version, because each registry and its contents is unique to the computer and operating system on which it resides. (This does not apply in situations where you create a replica domain controller (DC) by using a tape backup of a DC to restore to a clean computer.)

Registry Contents

The registry is hierarchical in structure (see Figure 3-21) and is made up of keys, subkeys, and entries:

- *Key*—A folder that appears in the left pane of the Registry Editor and can contain subkeys and entries, for example, HKEY_CURRENT_USER

- *Subkey*—A part of the registry that is below a key. A subkey can contain entries or other subkeys.

- *Entry or value*—Appears in the details pane and is the lowest level in the registry. An entry consists of an entry name, its data type, and its value.

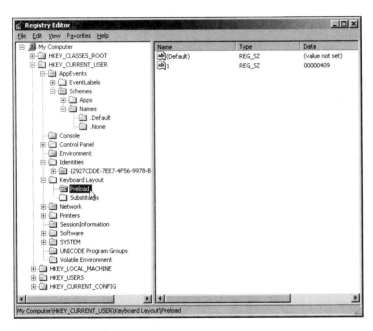

Figure 3-21   Registry's hierarchical structure

A **registry key** is a category or division of information within the registry. A single key may contain one or more lower-level keys called **registry subkeys**, just as a folder may contain several subfolders. A **registry entry** is a data parameter associated with a software or hardware characteristic under a key (or subkey). A registry entry consists of three parts—a name, the data type, and the configuration parameter—for example, ErrorControl:REG_DWORD:0 (ErrorControl is the name, REG_DWORD is the data type, and 0 is the parameter setting). In this registry entry, the option to track errors is turned off if the parameter is 0, and error tracking is turned on if the value is 1. There are three data formats for registry entries: DWORD is hexadecimal, string is text data, and binary is two hexadecimal values.

The Windows Server 2003 registry is made up of five root keys:

- HKEY_LOCAL_MACHINE

- HKEY_CURRENT_USER

- HKEY_USERS

- HKEY_CLASSES_ROOT

- HKEY_CURRENT_CONFIG

A **root key**, also called a **subtree**, is the primary or highest-level category of data contained in the registry. It might be compared to a main folder, such as the \Windows folder, which is at the root level of folders. All root keys start with HKEY to show they are the highest-level key.

HKEY_LOCAL_MACHINE

Under the HKEY_LOCAL_MACHINE root key is information on every hardware component in the server. This includes information about what drivers are loaded and their version levels, what IRQ (interrupt request) lines are used, setup configurations, the BIOS version, and more. Figure 3-22 shows the registry contents, using the Registry Editor to view the HKEY_LOCAL_MACHINE root key information about serial ports.

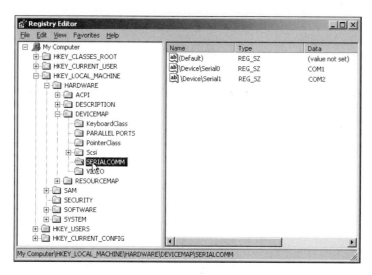

Figure 3-22   The HKEY_LOCAL_MACHINE root key

Under each root key are subkeys, such as the HARDWARE, SAM, SECURITY, SOFTWARE, and SYSTEM subkeys under the root key in Figure 3-22. Each subkey may have subkeys under it, such as the ACPI, DESCRIPTION, DEVICEMAP, and RESOURCEMAP subkeys under the HARDWARE subkey in Figure 3-22.

A few subkeys are stored as a set, called **hives**, because they hold related information. This is true for the SOFTWARE subkey, which holds information about installed software. You can make hardware configuration changes directly from the registry, although this is not recommended (see the following Caution).

 Although it is possible to make hardware configuration changes directly from the registry, this is a dangerous undertaking, because a wrong deletion may mean you cannot reboot your server into Windows Server 2003. It is better to use other options first, such as Control Panel. Make changes in the registry only under the guidance of a Microsoft technical note or a Microsoft support person.

HKEY_CURRENT_USER

The HKEY_CURRENT_USER key contains information about the desktop setup for the account presently logged onto the server console, as opposed to the HKEY_USERS key, which contains profile settings for all users that have logged onto the server. HKEY_CURRENT_USER contains data on color combinations, font sizes and type, the keyboard layout, the taskbar, clock configuration, and nearly any setup action you have made on the desktop. For example, if you want to change the environment parameter governing where temporary files are stored for applications, you could do it from here. The new path is set by clicking the Environment subkey under the HKEY_CURRENT_USER root key and changing the path shown as the value in the right pane. The sounds associated with a given event can be set by clicking the path \HKEY_CURRENT_USER\AppEvents\EventLabels, and then changing the sound value for a particular event, such as the event to close a window, which is a single value in the Close subkey (\HKEY_CURRENT_USER\AppEvents\EventLabels\Close).

Another example is to change a program that runs in association with a particular file extension. For example, click the following path: \HKEY_CURRENT_USER\Software\Microsoft\Windows NT\ CurrentVersion\Extensions. If the Notepad program is associated with files ending in .txt, you can make a change to have WordPad start instead. To do this you would change the value, "txt:REG_SZ:notepad.exe^.txt" to "txt:REG_SZ:write.exe ^.txt," because Write.exe is the file that starts the WordPad application.

HKEY_USERS

The HKEY_USERS root key contains profile information for each user who has logged onto the computer. Each profile is listed under this root key. Within each user profile there is information identical to that viewed within the HKEY_CURRENT_USER root key. The profile used when you are logged on is one of the profiles stored under HKEY_USERS. You can make the same changes just examined, by finding the subkey for your profile and making the changes here instead of under the HKEY_CURRENT_USER root key.

HKEY_CLASSES_ROOT

The HKEY_CLASSES_ROOT key holds data to associate file extensions with programs. This is a more extensive list than the one viewed under HKEY_CURRENT_USER. Associations exist for executable files, text files, graphics files, clipboard files, audio files, and many more. These associations are used as defaults for all users who log onto Windows Server 2003, whereas the associations in HKEY_CURRENT_USER and HKEY_USER are those that have been customized for a given user profile.

HKEY_CURRENT_CONFIG

The last root key, HKEY_CURRENT_CONFIG, has information about the current hardware profile. It holds information about the monitor type, keyboard, mouse, and other hardware characteristics for the current profile. On most servers, there is only one default hardware profile set up. Two or more profiles could be used, but this is more common for a portable computer running Windows XP Professional that is used with and without a docking station. One profile would have the built-in keyboard and monitor used when on the road, and another would have a larger keyboard and monitor used when the computer is docked.

Activity 3-16: Using the Registry Editor

Time Required: Approximately 10 minutes

Objective: Practice using the Registry Editor to view the registry contents.

Description: It is a good idea to have some experience with the Registry Editor before you make changes to the registry, such as changes recommended through a Microsoft TechNet document. In this activity, you use the Registry Editor to view where Control Panel settings are stored.

1. Click **Start**, click **Run**, and type **regedt32** in the Open box. Click **OK**.

2. Double-click **HKEY_CURRENT_USER**, and double-click **Control Panel**.

3. What Control Panel subkeys do you see? Record your observations.

4. Double-click **Accessibility**. What are the subkeys displayed?

5. Click **MouseKeys** to view the values set for that subkey.

6. Click two or three other subkeys to view their values.

7. Click a value, and then click the **Edit** menu to view how to modify a value, delete a value, or add a new one.

Absolutely do not make any changes.

8. Close the Registry Editor.

CHAPTER SUMMARY

- Windows Server 2003 provides a variety of tools that can be used to customize and optimize your server to meet your requirements. Many of these tools also enable you to troubleshoot problems.

- Modern computer hardware and operating systems support Plug and Play for automatic detection of newly installed devices.

- New hardware can be added using the Add Hardware option in Control Panel. Once hardware is installed it can be configured and managed using Device Manager.

- Driver signing enables you to block the installation of drivers and other components that have not been tested and approved by Microsoft.

- Always tune your server for best performance by configuring processor scheduling and memory, virtual memory, and memory used for networking tasks.

- Besides configuring performance options, also plan to configure environment variables, system startup and recovery, power options, and additional protocols.

- Most Windows Server 2003 components are installed using the Network Connections Tool or the Add or Remove Programs tool in Control Panel.

- The registry contains system configuration information. Carefully use the Registry Editor to make changes to the registry, recognizing that the best method for making registry changes is by using the options within Control Panel.

KEY TERMS

driver signing — A digital signature that Microsoft incorporates into driver and system files as a way to verify the files and to ensure that they are not inappropriately overwritten.

hardware profile — A hardware profile is a set of instructions telling the operating system which devices to start or which device settings to use when your computer starts.

hibernate — A mode in which the computer components are shut down, and information in memory is automatically saved to disk before the disk is powered off. The power supply and CPU remain active to startup all components when you press a key or move the mouse.

hive — A set of related registry keys and subkeys stored as a file.

interrupt request (IRQ) line — A hardware line that a computer component, such as a disk drive or serial port, uses to communicate to the processor that it is ready to send or receive information. Intel-based computers have 16 IRQ lines, with 15 of those available for computer components to use.

I/O address — The address in memory through which data is transferred between a computer component and the processor.

paging — Moving blocks of information, called pages, from RAM to virtual memory (the paging file) on disk.

paging file — Disk space, in the form of a file, for use when memory requirements exceed the available RAM.

Plug and Play (PnP) — Ability of added computer hardware, such as an adapter or modem, to identify itself to the computer operating system for installation. PnP also refers to the Intel and Microsoft specifications for automatic device detection and installation. Many operating systems, such as Windows, Macintosh, and UNIX/Linux now support PnP.

registry entry — A data parameter in the registry stored as a value in hexadecimal, binary, or text format.

registry key — A category of information contained in the Windows Server 2003 registry, such as hardware settings or software settings.

registry subkey — A key within a registry key, similar to a subfolder under a folder.

resource — On a network, this refers to an object such as a shared printer or shared directory that can be accessed by users. On workstations as well as servers, a resource is an IRQ line, I/O address, or portion of memory that is allocated to a computer component, such as a disk drive or communications port.

root key — Also called a subtree, the highest category of data contained in the registry. There are five root keys.

Service Advertising Protocol (SAP) — An IPX/SPX-compatible protocol that is used by NetWare clients to identify servers and the network services provided by each server.

system environment variables — Variables defined by the operating system and that apply to any user logged onto the computer.

standby — A mode in which the computer components are shut down and information in memory is not written to disk storage. The power supply and CPU remain active, waiting to start up all components when you press a key or move the mouse.

subtree — Same as root key.

uninterruptible power supply (UPS) — A device built into electrical equipment or a separate device that provides immediate battery power to equipment during a power failure or brownout.

user environment variables — Environment variables that are defined on a per user basis.

virtual memory — Disk storage allocated to link with physical RAM to temporarily hold data when there is not enough free RAM.

REVIEW QUESTIONS

1. Your Windows Server 2003 needs to communicate with a NetWare server that uses IPX routing and applications that use SAP services. What protocol should you configure and how should you configure it?
   a. TCP/IP configured with an external network number
   b. NWLink configured for IP routing
   c. NWLink configured with an internal network number
   d. TCP/IP configured for WINS

2. For which protocol might you have to configure a frame type?
   a. TCP/IP
   b. NWLink
   c. IPv6
   d. AppleTalk

3. One of your critical system files has been overwritten. What utility can you use to have Windows scan and replace protected system files?
   a. System File Checker
   b. Signature Verification
   c. Device Manager
   d. Signature File Analyzer

4. What capability enables automatic detection of new computer hardware when it is attached to a computer?

    a. the Detect Hardware option in Control Panel

    b. Plug and Play

    c. Device Manager

    d. Computer Manager

5. What is the difference between the hibernate and standby modes?

    a. The BIOS setup contents are written to memory in hibernate mode, but not in standby mode.

    b. Standby mode only shuts down the monitor, whereas hibernate shuts down all server components except the NIC.

    c. The page file is moved to memory in standby mode, but not in hibernate mode.

    d. The memory contents are not written to disk in standby mode, but they are in hibernate mode.

6. Once you have created a hardware profile, what tool should you use to disable specific devices?

    a. Add Hardware Wizard

    b. Hardware Manager

    c. Registry Editor

    d. Device Manager

7. The Sigverif tool is used to verify system and critical files to determine if they have a

    _____.

    a. date stamp

    b. manufacturer's ID

    c. signature

    d. parity bit

8. Your server system has 512 MB of RAM. What should the initial amount of virtual memory be set to?

    a. 864 MB

    b. 768 MB

    c. 1024 MB

    d. 512 MB

9. You are concerned about employees installing drivers that are not compatible with Windows Server 2003. Which of the following is the best way to prevent them from installing driver software that may cause damage to the operating system?

    a. Educate users to only install drivers from the hardware manufacturer.

    b. Configure the Add Hardware tool so that it blocks the installation of incompatible software.

    c. Configure driver signing to block the installation of unsigned driver software.

    d. Configure driver signing to prompt users to choose an action.

10. Which of the following are root keys in the Windows Server 2003 registry? (Choose all that apply.)

    a. HKEY_LOCAL_MACHINE

    b. HKEY_CURRENT_USER

    c. HKEY_CLASSES_ROOT

    d. HKEY_USERS

    e. HKEY_COMPUTERS_NET

11. You have set up NWLink so that your Windows 2003 server can communicate with several older NetWare 3.x and 4.x servers in your enterprise. In the process of configuring NWLink, you let it automatically determine the frame type; however, now that it is set up you have problems communicating with some of the NetWare servers. What might you try?

 a. Set up the DLC protocol to communicate with the servers.

 b. Use FAT16 as the file system for the Windows server instead of NTFS.

 c. Find out if the NetWare servers and server applications communicate using more than one frame type.

 d. Make sure that none of the NetWare servers is using a network number that is over four digits.

12. Your organization's Windows 2003 server provides file and print services for users on the network, such as access to folders containing archived and active Word documents and other folders containing spreadsheets. When configuring the properties for File and Printer Sharing for Microsoft Networks, which option should you select?

 a. Minimize memory used

 b. Maximize data throughput for file sharing

 c. Maximize data throughput for network applications

 d. Balance

13. Your server is about two weeks old and has Windows Server 2003 installed. You are now experiencing problems with the floppy disk drive; there are times when it does not seem to communicate with the server. Which tool can help you test the floppy drive?

 a. Control Panel Controllers tool

 b. Network Connections Wizard

 c. Control Panel Add Hardware tool

 d. Hardware Event Detector

14. You have noticed lately that your server is running very slowly, especially when switching between programs. You see that the C: partition is running low on space, limiting the size of your paging file. You have a second partition that has 20 GB of free space. How can you move the paging file from partition C: onto partition D:?

 a. Use the Paging File option in Control Panel and access the Size tab.

 b. Use Device Manager to drag the paging file from partition C: to partition D:.

 c. Reinstall Windows Server 2003 onto partition D:.

 d. Use the Advanced tab of the System option in Control Panel.

15. From where can you set up different hardware profiles?

 a. Control Panel Folder Options selection

 b. Add Hardware Wizard

 c. Control Panel Multimedia option

 d. Control Panel System option

16. You plan to install Internet Information Services (IIS) as a Web Application Server component. Which tool do you use?

 a. Add/Remove Windows Components option in the Add or Remove Programs tool

 b. Change or Remove Programs option in the Network Connections tool

 c. Configure Windows Components option in the Add Hardware Wizard

 d. Change or Remove Programs option in the Folders tool

17. Your college campus has just decided to enable Macintosh computers to access your Windows Server 2003, Standard Edition. How can this be accomplished?

    a. Use the Network Connections tool to install NWLink with the AppleTalk extension.

    b. Use the Network Connections tool to install AppleTalk.

    c. Use the Add/Remove Programs tool to install TCP/IP with the AppleTalk extension.

    d. Windows Server 2003 does not support AppleTalk; thus, you cannot provide this service.

18. Your server did not originally come with a modem, but after you install Windows Server 2003, Standard Edition, you decide to purchase and install a modem. Which of the following tools enable you to install the modem?

    a. Add Hardware Wizard

    b. Add/Remove Programs Wizard

    c. Add New Modem and Fax Wizard

    d. all of the above

    e. none of the above because you must use the Computer Management tool

19. What tool enables you to determine the properties settings and driver associated with a device? (Choose all that apply.)

    a. Device Manager

    b. System Hardware Checker

    c. System File Checker

    d. Driver Setup tool

20. Which of the following are elements of the Windows Server 2003 registry? (Choose all that apply.)

    a. keys

    b. forests

    c. subkeys

    d. entries

    e. subtree

21. From where can you start Device Manager? (Choose all that apply.)

    a. Network Connections option in Control Panel

    b. My Computer

    c. Computer Management tool as part of the Administrative tools

    d. Add or Remove Software option in Control Panel

22. Which of the following is not a Windows Server 2003 component that you can install?

    a. Indexing Service

    b. Remote Installation Services

    c. IBM MVS File Service

    d. Terminal Server

23. ErrorControl:REG_DWORD:0 is an example of:

    a. a Dfs root

    b. a device driver

    c. a registry entry

    d. a startup log script command

24. What is the name of the program used to start the Registry Editor?

    a. Reg16

    b. ER

    c. WordPad

    d. Regedt32

25. Which of the following are types of environment variables?

    a. desktop environment variable

    b. system environment variable

    c. user environment variable

    d. all of the above

    e. only b. and c.

CASE PROJECTS

Case Project Background

Fresh Crops Trucking is a company that ships produce to grocery stores all over the United States. This company has a network that connects users to a mainframe computer and to eight older NetWare 4.x servers configured to use IPX/SPX. The company has an Internet site and already uses TCP/IP for connectivity to the mainframe. All computers have been manually configured with static IP addresses. The company has purchased a new client/server distribution system that runs on two servers configured with Windows Server 2003, Standard Edition. Because they have no administrators on staff who are familiar with Windows Server 2003, they are using Bayside IT Services to install and configure the new servers. You have just installed the servers and now need to configure them.

Case Project 3-1: Configuring to Communicate with NetWare and Troubleshooting a NIC Problem

IPX/SPX is not set up as a protocol in the Windows 2003 servers, and you need to set it up so that both servers can communicate with the NetWare servers, which use the Ethernet II and Ethernet SNAP frame types. Explain how you would set up the Windows 2003 servers to be able to communicate with the NetWare servers.

Further, as you are configuring protocols, you discover that the NIC on one of the servers is not communicating with the network. What steps can you take to troubleshoot the NIC?

Case Project 3-2: Installing a Communications Adapter

Fresh Crops Trucking is planning to connect one of the new Windows 2003 servers to the Internet by installing an Integrated Services Digital Network (ISDN) adapter in an expansion slot. ISDN is a high-speed digital communications service offered by many telecommunication companies and requires a specialized adapter. Explain in general how you would install the adapter in Windows Server 2003, Standard Edition.

Case Project 3-3: Installing the Remote Storage Capability

During the installation of Windows Server 2003, Standard Edition, you omitted installing the Remote Storage capability. Explain in a step-by-step process how you can install this now on both servers.

Case Project 3-4: Optimizing Server Performance

The IT director for Fresh Crops Trucking knows that the mainframe computer and NetWare servers have specialized configuration parameters to optimize performance. She asks you to generally discuss methods for optimizing the Windows Server 2003, Standard Edition, computers.

4

INTRODUCTION TO ACTIVE DIRECTORY AND ACCOUNT MANAGEMENT

After reading this chapter and completing the exercises, you will be able to:

♦ Explain the purpose of Active Directory and its key features

♦ Describe containers in Active Directory

♦ Understand user account management

♦ Explain security group management and implement security groups

♦ Implement user profiles

Good management is essential for all modern networks. Active Directory enables you to bring effective management to a potentially chaotic group of resources, such as user accounts, shared folders, and shared printers. Active Directory accomplishes this by providing a hierarchy of management elements that enable you to organize resources, control who accesses them, and advertise their existence—making the lives of users easier.

In this chapter, you'll begin by learning the basics of Active Directory, including schema, global catalog, and namespace. Additionally, you'll install Active Directory to turn a server into a domain controller. Then you'll go on to learn the basic organizational containers available to organize network resources, such as forests, trees, domains, organizational units, and sites. Further, you'll learn basic guidelines for using the organizational containers in Active Directory. Two of the most important resources that you can manage are accounts and groups. In this chapter, you will learn how to set up and manage both. Finally, you'll learn how to create user profiles for customized account setup features, such as a desktop tailored for your organization.

INTRODUCTION TO ACTIVE DIRECTORY

Active Directory is a **directory service** that houses information about all network resources such as servers, printers, user accounts, groups of user accounts, security policies, and other information. As a directory service, Active Directory is responsible for providing a central listing of resources and ways to quickly find and access specific resources, and for providing a way to manage network resources. In previous versions of Windows NT Server, some of the information now contained in Windows Server 2003 Active Directory, such as information about user accounts, groups, and privileges, is stored in the **Security Account Manager (SAM) database**. The only writeable copy of the SAM is kept on a main server, called the primary domain controller (PDC), and is regularly backed up on other servers called backup domain controllers (BDCs) that contain read-only copies, as Figure 4-1 shows. Every Windows NT Server network can have only one PDC, but many BDCs. If the PDC fails, you manually promote a BDC to become the new PDC.

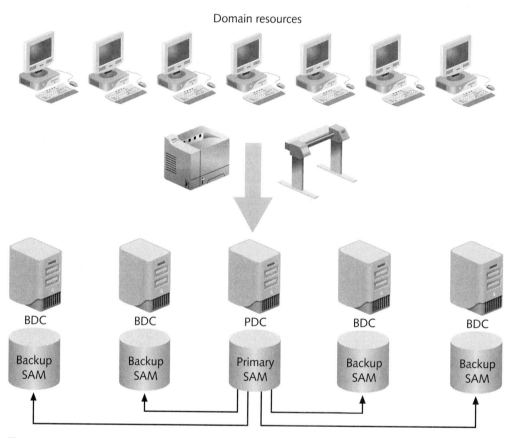

Figure 4-1   Windows NT SAM architecture

Instead of the SAM, Windows 2000 and Server 2003 use Active Directory to manage accounts, groups, and many more services for managing a network. Writeable copies of information in Active Directory are contained in one or more **domain controllers (DCs)**. In Active Directory, a **domain** is a fundamental component or **container** that holds information about all network resources that are grouped within it—servers, printers and other physical resources, users, and user groups. Every resource is called an **object** and is associated with a domain (see Figure 4-2). When you set up a new user account or a network printer, for instance, it becomes an object within a domain.

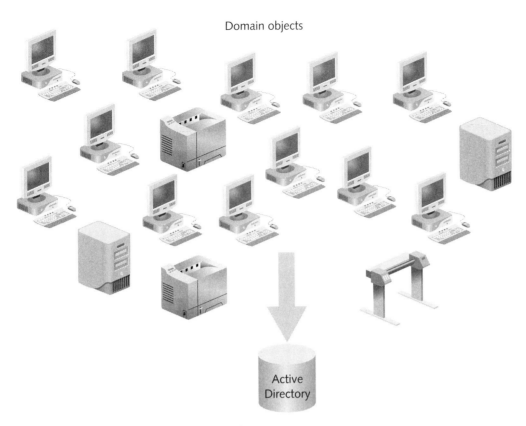

Domain objects

Figure 4-2   Domain objects in Active Directory

In Windows Server 2003, each DC is equal to every other DC in that it contains the full range of information that composes Active Directory. If information on one DC changes, such as the creation of an account, it is replicated to all other DCs in a process called **multimaster replication**. The advantage of this approach is that if one DC fails, Active Directory is fully intact on all other DCs, and there is no visible network interruption.

In Windows Server 2003, you can set replication of Active Directory information to occur at a preset interval instead of as soon as an update occurs. Also, you can determine how much of Active Directory is replicated each time it is copied from one DC to another. In Windows NT 4.0, the process of replicating the PDC to one or more BDCs could create significant network traffic, particularly over a slow wide area network link. This problem has been addressed in Windows Server 2003 in two ways:

- Windows Server 2003 can replicate individual properties instead of entire accounts (as in Windows NT 4.0), which means that a single property can be changed without replicating information for the whole account.

- Windows Server 2003 can replicate Active Directory on the basis of the speed of the network link, such as replicating more frequently over a local area network link than over a wide area network link.

Three general concepts are important as a starting place for understanding Active Directory: schema, global catalog, and namespace. These concepts are described in the next sections.

Activity 4-1: Installing Active Directory

Time Required: Approximately 20 to 30 minutes

Objective: Install Active Directory in Windows Server 2003, Standard Edition.

Description: To make a Windows 2003 server a domain controller, you must install Active Directory. In this activity you learn how to install Active Directory. You will need to log onto Windows Server 2003 as an administrator, and a DNS server should already be set up on your network. Also, before you start, consult with your instructor about what domain name to use.

1. There are two ways to start the Active Directory Installation Wizard. One is to click **Start**, click **Run**, type **dcpromo** on the Open box, and click **OK** (this is the fastest way). An alternative way is to click **Start**, point to **All Programs**, point to **Administrative Tools**, and click the **Configure Your Server Wizard**. Click **Next**, and click **Next** again. (If you see a Configuration Options dialog box, select **Custom configuration**.) In the Server Role box, click **Domain Controller (Active Directory)**, and click **Next**. Click **Next** again.

After Active Directory is installed, you can use dcpromo or the Configure Your Server Wizard to remove Active Directory.

2. Click **Next** when the Active Directory Installation Wizard starts.

3. The Operating System Compatibility dialog box displays a warning that some older versions of Windows will not be able to log on to a domain controller running Windows Server 2003, click **Next**.

4. Click **Domain controller for a new domain**, if this option is not already selected. (Notice that if this were an additional domain controller in an existing domain, you could also set it up through the Active Directory Installation Wizard by using the option Additional domain controller for an existing domain. Click **Next** (see Figure 4-3).

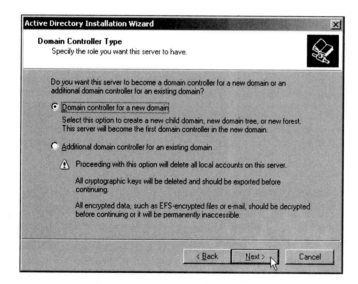

Figure 4-3   Installing a domain controller in a new domain

5. If you see a screen on which to create a new domain tree, click **Create a new domain tree**. Click **Next**.

6. Click **Domain in a new forest**. Click **Next**.

7. Enter the domain name that you selected in consultation with your instructor, or enter your initials plus company.com, such as jpcompany.com. Click **Next**. (At this point the wizard takes a few moments to check that a domain does not already exist and to set up the domain.)

8. Leave the default in the Domain NetBIOS name box (for users of earlier versions of Windows), and click **Next**.

9. Leave C:\WINDOWS\NTDS as the database location and C:\WINDOWS\NTDS as the log location. (Your system may use a different drive location by default, depending on the location of the \WINDOWS folder). Click **Next**.

10. Leave the shared system volume location as the default, such as C:\WINDOWS\SYSVOL. (Again, the exact drive depends on the location of the \WINDOWS folder.) Notice that the

wizard warns that the Sysvol folder must be on a volume formatted with NTFS. Click **Next**. (At this point, if a DNS server is not already installed or available on the network, the wizard provides an option to install it as part of the setup process. If a DNS server is already installed, you will see a DNS Registration Diagnostics dialog box. Verify or supply the requested IP address information about the DNS server and proceed with the installation.)

11. The Permissions dialog box gives you the option to use permissions compatible with pre-Windows 2000 servers, such as Windows NT Server 4.0—or to use permissions compatible only with Windows 2000 or 2003 servers. Click **Permissions compatible only with Windows 2000 or Windows Server 2003 operating systems**, if this option is not already selected. Click **Next**.

12. Enter an Administrator password and confirm it for use in the Directory Services Restore Mode. Click **Next**.

13. Review in the summary scroll box the selections you have made and record them. Is there an option to retrace your steps in case you want to change a parameter? Click **Next** to proceed. (If you do not have permission from your instructor to install Active Directory, click Cancel at this point to exit setup.)

14. Wait a few minutes as the wizard configures Active Directory. Notice the line near the bottom of the dialog box that shows each configuration activity.

15. Click **Finish**.

16. Make sure you have saved any open work, and then click **Restart Now**.

17. If you used the Configure Your Server Wizard in Step 1, click **Finish** after the server reboots and you log onto the Administrator account.

Schema

The Active Directory **schema** defines the objects and the information pertaining to those objects that can be stored in Active Directory. Each kind of object in Active Directory is defined through the schema, which is like a small database of information associated with that object, including the object class and its attributes. Schema information for objects in a domain is replicated on every DC. To help you understand a schema, consider the characteristics associated with a vehicle. First, there are different classes of vehicles, including automobiles, trucks, tractors, and motorcycles. Further, each class has a set of attributes. For automobiles, those attributes include engine, headlights, seats, steering wheel, dashboard, wheels, windshield, CD player, cup holder, and many others. Some of those attributes must be present in every automobile, such as an engine and wheels. Other attributes are optional—whether there is a CD player or cup holder, for instance.

A user account is one class of object in Active Directory that is defined through schema elements unique to that class. The user account class as a whole has the following schema characteristics (see Figure 4-4):

- A unique object name
- A **globally unique identifier (GUID)**, which is a unique number associated with the object name
- Required attributes (those that must be defined with each object)
- Optional attributes (those that are optionally defined)
- A syntax (format) to determine how attributes are defined
- Pointers to parent entities, such as to a parent domain

Examples of required user account attributes that must be defined for each account are:

- Logon name
- User's full name

- Password

- Domain

Optional attributes for a user account include:

- Account description

- Account holder's office number or address

- Account holder's telephone number

- Account holder's e-mail address

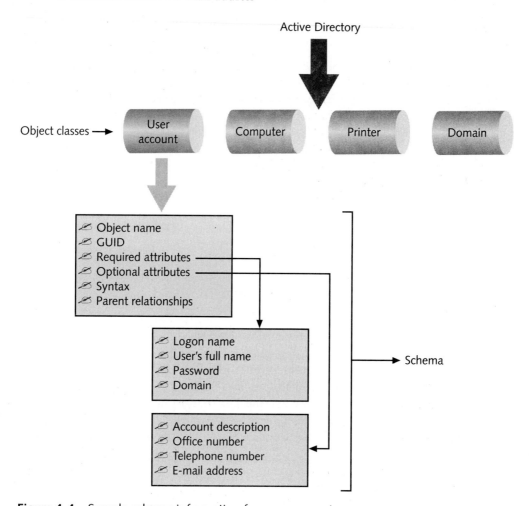

Figure 4-4   Sample schema information for user accounts

Providing an account description or specifying if the account is enabled for remote access over a telephone line are examples of optional attributes that do not have to be completed when you create an account. In some instances, the attributes that are required and those that are optional can be influenced by the security policies that the server administrator sets in Active Directory for a class of objects (see Chapter 10 for more about security policies). This is true, for example, with account passwords because it is possible (but not recommended) for you to have a security policy that does not require account passwords.

Each attribute is automatically given a version number and date when it is created or changed. This information enables Active Directory to know when an attribute value, such as a password, is changed, and update only that value on all DCs. When you install Windows Server 2003 for the first time on a network server, designating it as a domain controller, you also create several object classes automatically. The default object classes include: domain, user account, group, shared drive, shared folder, computer, and printer.

Global Catalog

The **global catalog** stores information about every object within a forest (you learn more about forests later in this chapter). The first DC configured in a forest becomes the global catalog server. The global catalog server stores a full replica of every object within its own domain and a partial replica of each object within every domain in the forest. The partial replica for each object contains those attributes most commonly used to search for objects. The global catalog serves the following purposes:

- Authenticating users when they log on

- Providing lookup and access to all resources in all domains

- Providing replication of key Active Directory elements

- Keeping a copy of the most used attributes for each object for quick access

The global catalog server enables forestwide searches of data. Because it contains attributes pertaining to every object within a forest, users can query this server to locate an object, as opposed to having to perform an extensive search. The global catalog server also can be used for network logons. When a user logs onto the network, the global catalog server is contacted for universal group membership information pertaining to the user's account. In a Windows 2000 domain, if the global catalog was unavailable, the user could only log onto the local computer. In Windows Server 2003, if the global catalog is unavailable for group membership information, the user can log onto the network with cached credentials.

 Cached credentials means that a record is kept in the server cache if a user has successfully logged on previously. Thus, authentication (when the user logs off and then logs on again) can be performed by checking the cached credentials, instead of the global catalog. However, if the user is logging on for the first time and there is no cached credential for that user, then access is only provided to the local computer.

By default the first DC in the forest is automatically designated as the global catalog server. You have the option of configuring another DC to be a global catalog server as well as designating multiple DCs as global catalog servers.

Namespace

Active Directory uses the Domain Name System (DNS), which means there must be a DNS server on the network that Active Directory can access. As you learned in Chapter 1, DNS is a TCP/IP-based name service that converts computer and domain host names to dotted decimal addresses and vice versa, through a process called **name resolution**. A computer running Windows Server 2003 can be set up to act as a DNS server on a network. For example, when a Windows XP Professional client sends a TCP/IP-based request to connect to a specific server on the same network, such as a server named Research, a DNS server on the network can be used to translate Research into its dotted decimal address, 142.78.14.4.

 A DNS server does more than only name resolution; it provides services such as registration of hosts, contains service (SRV) records to identify servers providing particular TCP/IP services, enables transfers of DNS information for redundancy, and provides other services.

A **namespace** is a logical area on a network that contains directory services and named objects, and that has the ability to perform name resolution. Active Directory depends on one or more DNS servers to provide the ability to resolve names in a designated logical DNS namespace. Within Active Directory, there is another namespace which contains named objects, such as accounts and printers, but which Active Directory coordinates with information in the DNS namespace. Both namespaces (DNS and Active Directory) can be on a single computer, such as a Windows 2003 server in a small network, that is set up as a DC and a DNS server. Or, they can be distributed across several servers on a large network, which might have two servers set up as DNS servers and 22 set up as DCs.

Active Directory employs two kinds of namespaces: contiguous and disjointed. A **contiguous namespace** is one in which every child object contains the name of the parent object, such as in the example of the child object *msdn.microsoft.com* and its parent object *microsoft.com*. When the child name does not resemble the name of its parent object, this is called a **disjointed namespace**, such as when the parent for a university is *uni.edu*, and a child is *bio.ethicsresearch.com*.

CONTAINERS IN ACTIVE DIRECTORY

Active Directory has a treelike structure that is similar to the hierarchy of folders and subfolders in a directory structure. For example, in a directory structure information is stored in a root folder, which is at the highest level. The root folder may contain several main folders, 15 or 20, for instance. Under each folder there exist subfolders, and within subfolders there can be more subfolders. Subfolders can have a nearly infinite depth, but typically do not go more than five or ten layers deep. Just as files are the basic elements that are grouped in a hierarchy of folders and subfolders, objects are the basic elements of Active Directory and are grouped in a hierarchy of larger containers. Also, just as the folder structure affects how you can set up security on a server, Active Directory structure affects how you can manage security in an enterprise. The hierarchical elements, or **containers**, of Active Directory include (see Figure 4-5): forests, trees, domains, organizational units, and sites.

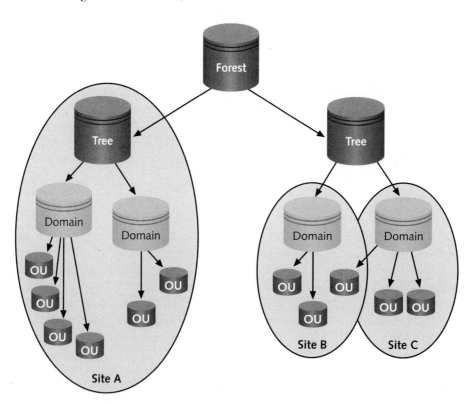

Figure 4-5   Active Directory hierarchical containers

Forest

At the highest level in an Active Directory design is the **forest**. A forest consists of one or more trees that are in a common relationship and that have the following characteristics:

- The trees can use a disjointed namespace.

- All trees use the same schema.

- All trees use the same global catalog.

- Domains enable administration of commonly associated objects, such as accounts and other resources, within a forest.

- Two-way transitive trusts (resources shared equally) are automatically configured between domains within a single forest.

A forest provides a means to relate trees that use a contiguous namespace in domains within each tree but that have disjointed namespaces in relationship to each other. Consider, for example, an international automotive parts company that is really a conglomerate of separate companies, each having a different brand name. The parent company is PartsPlus located in Toronto. PartsPlus manufactures alternators, coils, and other electrical parts at plants in Toronto, Montreal, and Detroit, and has a tree structure for domains that are part of partsplus.com. Another company that they own, Marty and Mike's (2m.com), makes radiators in two South Carolina cities, Florence and Greenville, and radiator fluid in Atlanta. A third member company, Chelos (chelos.com), makes engine parts and starters in Mexico City, Oaxaca, Monterrey, and Puebla, all in Mexico—and also has a manufacturing site in Valencia, Venezuela. In this situation, it makes sense to have a contiguous tree structure for each of the three related companies and to join the trees in a forest of disjointed name spaces, as in Figure 4-6.

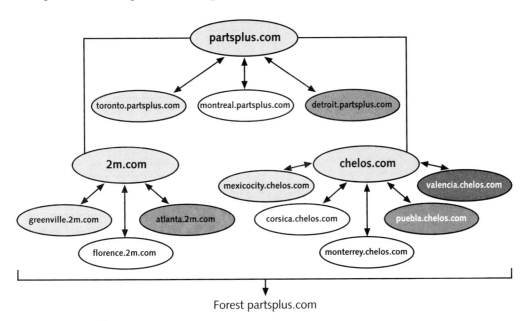

Figure 4-6   A forest

The advantage of joining trees into a forest is that all domains share the same schema and global catalog. A schema is set up in the root domain, which is partsplus.com in our example, and the root domain is home to the master schema server. At least one DC functions as a global catalog server, but in our example, it is likely that you would plan to have a global catalog server located at each geographic location (domain).

 At this writing, Windows Server 2003 Active Directory recognizes two types of forest functional levels. The Windows 2000 forest functional level provides basic forest services compatible with a network that has a combination of Windows NT, Windows 2000, and Windows 2003 servers. The Windows Server 2003 forest functional level is intended for Windows 2003 servers only and enables more functions, such as more options for creating trust relationships between forests. You'll learn more about trust relationships in the next section.

Tree

A **tree** contains one or more domains that are in a common relationship, and has the following characteristics:

- Domains are represented in a contiguous namespace and can be in a hierarchy.

- Two-way trust relationships exist between parent domains and child domains essentially creating a trust path.

- All domains in a single tree use the same schema for all types of common objects.

- All domains use the same global catalog.

The domains in a tree typically have a hierarchical structure, such as a root domain at the top and other domains under the root (similar to a parent-child relationship). Using tracksport.org as an example, tracksport.org might be the root domain and have four domains under the root to form one tree: east.tracksport.org, west.tracksport.org, north.tracksport.org, and south.tracksport.org, as shown in Figure 4-7. These domains use the contiguous namespace format in that the child domains each inherit a portion of their namespace from the parent domain.

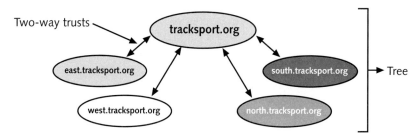

Figure 4-7   Tree with hierarchical domains

The domains within a tree are in what is called a **Kerberos transitive trust relationship**, which consists of **two-way trusts** between parent domains and child domains (see Figure 4-7). A **transitive trust** means that if A and B have a trust and B and C have a trust, A and C automatically have a trust as well. This is similar to the universal or complete trust relationship among domains in Windows NT Server. In a two-way trust, each domain is trusting and trusted. A trusted domain is one that is granted access to resources, whereas a trusting domain is the one granting access. In a two-way trust, members of each domain can have access to the resources of the other.

 Windows Server 2003 also introduces a forest trust. In a forest trust, there is a Kerberos transitive trust relationship between the root domains in Windows Server 2003 forests, resulting in trust relationships between all domains in the forests.

Because of the trust relationship between parent and child domains, any one domain can have access to the resources of all others. The security in the two-way trust relationships is based on Kerberos techniques, using a combination of protocol-based and encryption-based security techniques between clients and servers. A new domain joining a tree has an instant trust relationship with all other member domains through the trust relationship that is established with its parent domain, which makes all objects in the other domains available to the new one.

All domains within a single tree (as well as all trees in a single forest) share the same schema defining all the object types that can be stored within Active Directory. Further, all domains in a tree also share the same global catalog and a portion of their namespace. And, a child domain contains part of the name of the parent domain.

Domain

Microsoft views a **domain** as a partition within an Active Directory forest. A domain is a grouping of objects that typically exists as a primary container within Active Directory. The basic functions of a domain are as follows:

- To provide an Active Directory "partition" in which to house objects, such as accounts and groups, that have a common relationship, particularly in terms of management and security

- To establish a set of information to be replicated from one DC to another
- To expedite management of a set of objects

When you use the server-based networking model described in Chapter 1 to verify users who log on to the network, there is at least one domain. For example, if you are planning Active Directory for a small business of 34 employees who have workstations connected to a network that has one or two Windows 2003 servers, then one domain is sufficient for that business.

The domain functions as a security partition within which to group all of the network resource objects consisting of servers, user accounts, shared printers, and shared folders and files.

In a medium-sized or large business you might use more than one domain—for instance when business units are separated by long distances and you want to limit the amount of DC replication over expensive wide area network links or to manage objects differently between locations, such as through different account or security policies. For example, consider a company that builds tractors in South Carolina and that has a parts manufacturing division in Japan. Each site has a large enterprise network of Windows 2003 servers, and the sites are linked together in a wide area network by an expensive satellite connection. When you calculate the cost of replicating DCs over the satellite link, you cannot justify it in terms of the increased traffic that will delay other vital daily business communications. In this situation, it makes sense to create two separate domains, one for each site, as shown in Figure 4-8.

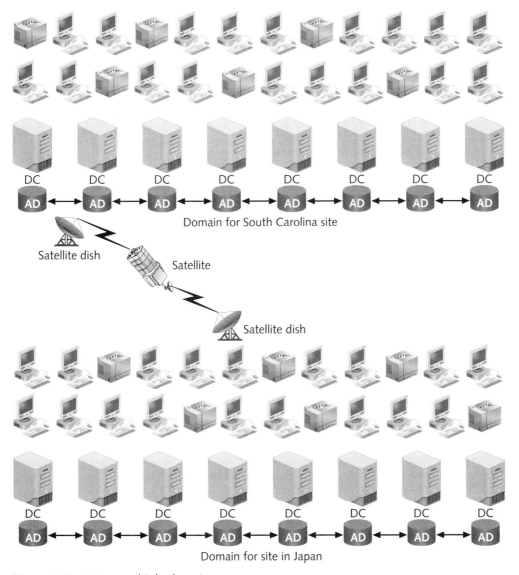

Figure 4-8   Using multiple domains

Activity 4-2: Managing Domains

Time Required: Approximately 10 minutes

Objective: Learn where to manage domains and domain trust relationships.

Description: After Active Directory is installed you may need to customize the properties of a domain or its trust relationships. In this activity, you learn about the tool used to manage domains and trust relationships.

1. Click **Start**, point to **All Programs**, point to **Administrative Tools**, and click **Active Directory Domains and Trusts**.

2. In the left pane, right-click the domain you created in the last project (or an existing domain).

3. Click **Properties**.

4. Click each of the **General**, **Trusts**, and **Managed By** tabs to view their contents. Make notes about their contents.

5. Click **Cancel**.

6. Close the **Active Directory Domains and Trusts** window.

Organizational Unit

An **organizational unit (OU)** offers a way to achieve more flexibility in managing the resources associated with a business unit, department, or division than is possible through domain administration alone. An OU is a grouping of related objects within a domain, similar to the idea of having subfolders within a folder. OUs can be used to reflect the structure of the organization without having to completely restructure the domain(s) when that structure changes.

OUs allow the grouping of objects so that they can be administered using the same group policies, such as security and desktop setup. OUs also make it possible for server administration to be delegated or decentralized. For example, in a software company in which the employees are divided into 15 project teams, the user accounts, shared files, shared printers, and other shared resources of each team can be defined as objects in separate OUs. There would be one domain for the entire company and 15 OUs within that domain, all defined in Active Directory. With this arrangement, file and folder objects can be defined to specific OUs for security, and the management of user accounts, account setup policies, and file and folder permissions (access privileges) can be delegated to each group leader (OU administrator).

OUs can be nested within OUs, as subfolders are nested in subfolders, so that you can create them several layers deep. For example, consider a business that has a Retail Division with its own Accounting Department. Within the Accounting Department there is an Accounts Receivable Group and within that group there is a subgroup of cashiers. You might have one OU under the Retail OU for the Accounting Department, an OU under the Accounting OU for the Accounts Receivable Group, and an OU under Accounts Receivable for the cashiers—creating four layers of OUs. The problem with this approach is that creating OUs many layers deep can get as confusing as creating subfolders several layers deep. It is confusing for the server administrator to track layered OUs, and it is laborious for Active Directory to search through each layer.

When you plan to create OUs, consider following the advice of Microsoft to limit OUs to 10 levels or fewer for easier management. Also, OUs should reflect ways to make resource management easier, and therefore can, but do not have to, reflect the structure of an organization. For example, you might simply use two OUs, one to manage accounts and groups, and one to manage resources, such as published folders and printers.

Activity 4-3: Managing OUs

Time Required: Approximately 10 minutes

Objective: Create an OU and delegate control over it.

Description: One advantage of an OU is that it enables a server administrator to delegate some server management tasks, such as managing user accounts. For example, some organizations prefer to have OUs that reflect the structure of the department. In this way, accounts for a particular department are created within an OU and a department administrator who has authority over an OU can create and manage user accounts for her or his department within the OU. In this activity you learn how to create an OU and delegate authority for account management within that OU.

1. Click **Start**, point to **All Programs**, point to **Administrative Tools**, and click **Active Directory Users and Computers**.

2. Right-click the top domain in the left pane, such as jpcompany.com, point to **New**, and click **Organizational Unit**.

3. Enter **SalesOU** and your initials, such as SalesOUJP. Click **OK**.

4. Double-click the domain in the left pane so that you can see the OU you created listed under the domain.

5. Right-click your OU. What options are available on the shortcut menu?

6. Click **Delegate Control**.

7. Click **Next** when the Delegation of Control Wizard starts.

8. Click **Add**.

9. Click the **Advanced** button.

10. Click **Find Now**.

11. Because you have not yet defined user accounts, click **Administrator** for this activity. Notice that names with a single head icon represent accounts and names with a double head icon represent groups of accounts. Click **OK**.

12. Click **OK** in the Select Users, Computers, or Groups dialog box.

13. Click **Next** in the Delegation of Control Wizard.

14. Click the box for **Create, delete, and manage user accounts**, as shown in Figure 4-9.

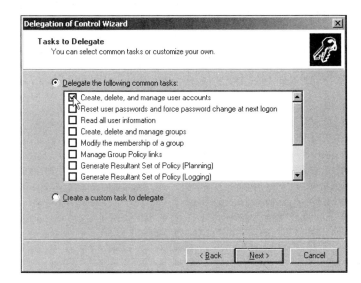

Figure 4-9   Delegating authority over accounts in an OU

15. Click **Next**.

16. Review the tasks that you have completed, and then click **Finish**.

17. Close the **Active Directory Users and Computers** window.

Site

A **site** is a TCP/IP-based concept (container) within Active Directory that is linked to IP subnets and has the following functions:

- Reflects one or more interconnected subnets, usually having good network connectivity
- Reflects the physical aspect of the network
- Is used for DC replication
- Is used to enable a client to access the DC that is physically closest
- Is composed of only two types of objects: servers and configuration objects

Sites are based on connectivity and replication functions. You might think of sites as a way of grouping Active Directory objects by physical location so Active Directory can identify the fastest communications paths between clients and servers and between DCs. The physical representation of the network to Active Directory is accomplished by defining subnets that are interconnected. For this reason, one site may be contained within a single OU or a single domain, or a site may span multiple OUs and domains, depending on how subnets are set up. The most typical boundary for a site consists of the local area network topology and subnet boundaries rather than the OU and domain boundaries.

There are two important reasons to define a site. First, by defining site locations based on IP subnets, you enable a client to access network servers using the most efficient physical route. In the PartsPlus example (discussed under the "Forest" section), it is faster for a client in Toronto to be authenticated by a Toronto global catalog server than for the client to go through Detroit or Mexico City. Second, DC replication is most efficient when Active Directory has information about which DCs are in which locations.

Within a site, each DC replicates forest, tree, domain, and OU naming structures; configuration naming elements, such as computers and printers; and schema information. One advantage of creating a site is that it sets up redundant paths between DCs so that if one path is down, there is a second path that can be used for replication. This redundancy is in a logical ring format, which means that replication goes from DC to DC around a ring until each DC is replicated. If a DC is down along the main route, then Active Directory uses site information to send replication information in the opposite direction around the ring. Whenever a new DC is added or an old one removed, Active Directory reconfigures the ring to make sure there are two replication paths available from each DC. Also, between sites, replication is coordinated through one server at each site that is called a bridgehead server (see Figure 4-10).

Consider a state university's network that might take advantage of sites. The university has three domains, students.uni.edu, faculty.uni.edu, and staffadmin.uni.edu, organized into a single tree. Also, there are three campuses that are in different cities. The domains span each campus location. Therefore, students.uni.edu contains accounts and printers on DCs at all locations, for example. Each domain contains OUs that are appropriate to that domain; for instance, students.uni.edu has an OU for students at each campus for a total of three OUs all at the same level. The campuses are relatively large with 7,000 students, 10,000 students, and 18,000 students, and have networks that are physically divided into subnets. In this situation, you can designate each campus network as a site in Active Directory, which enables it to find the fastest routes for traffic that is on-campus and for traffic that goes between campuses. For example, when a student logs on to students.uni.edu, Active Directory can help that student find the nearest DC and avoid the chance that the logon authentication is performed over a wide area network link at a different campus location. Another advantage is that the DC replication for each domain between sites (over wide area network links) can be set to occur less frequently than replication within a site.

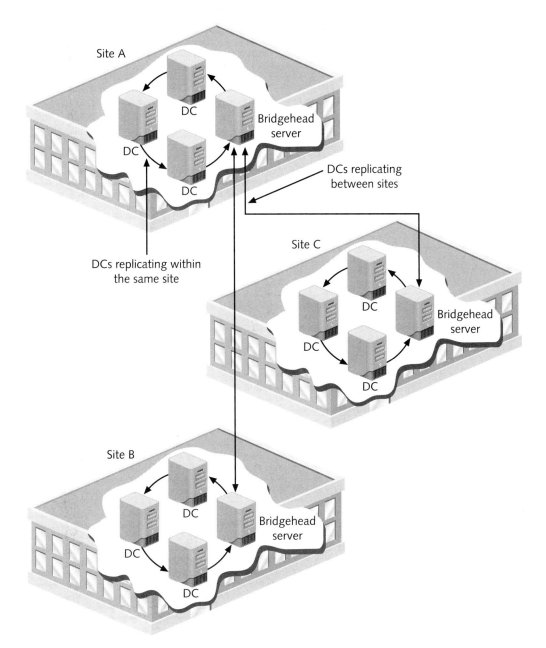

Figure 4-10   DCs replicating within and between sites

Summary of Container Guidelines in Active Directory

Planning the Active Directory structure of forests, trees, domains, and OUs is a potentially complex process. The following guidelines summarize the most important aspects of the Active Directory planning process that you have learned in the previous sections for these containers:

- Above all, keep Active Directory as simple as possible and plan its structure before you implement it.

- Implement the least number of domains possible, with one domain being the ideal and building from there.

- Implement only one domain on most small networks.

- When you are planning for an organization that is likely to reorganize in the future, use OUs to reflect the organization's structure.

- Create only the number of OUs that are absolutely necessary.

- Do not build an Active Directory with more than 10 levels of OUs (and hopefully no more than one or two levels).

- Use domains as partitions in forests to demarcate commonly associated accounts and resources governed by group and security policies.

- Implement multiple trees and forests only as necessary.

- Use sites in situations where there are multiple IP subnets and multiple geographic locations as a means to improve logon and DC replication performance.

USER ACCOUNT MANAGEMENT

Once Active Directory is installed and configured, you enable users to access network servers and resources through user accounts. Several accounts may be set up by default, depending on which Windows components you install, including two primary accounts, Administrator and Guest (Guest is disabled as a security measure).

There are two general environments in which to set up accounts:

- Accounts that are set up through a standalone server that does not have Active Directory installed

- Accounts that are set up in a domain when Active Directory is installed

When accounts are created in the domain through Active Directory, then those accounts can be used to access any domain server or resource.

Creating Accounts

New accounts are created by first installing the MMC Local Users and Groups snap-in for servers that do not use Active Directory. The general steps for creating a local user account on a server that is not part of a domain are as follows:

1. Click **Start**, click **Run**, enter **mmc**, click **OK**, click the **File** menu, click **Add/Remove Snap-in**, click **Add**, double-click **Local Users and Groups**, click **Finish**, click **Close**, and click **OK**.

2. Double-click **Local Users and Groups** in the MMC.

3. Click **Users** and then click the **Action** menu.

4. Click **New User** and complete the information to create the user account.

Symbols that cannot be used in an account name in Windows Server 2003 are: [ ] ; : < > = , + / \ | . Also, each account name must be unique, so that there are no duplicates.

When Active Directory is installed and the server is a domain controller, use the Active Directory Users and Computers tool either from the Administrative Tools menu or as an MMC snap-in. You create each new account by entering account information and password controls.

If you are using Active Directory and are working on a DC, Windows Server 2003 does not allow you to install the Local Users and Groups snap-in; you must use the Active Directory Users and Computers snap-in instead.

Activity 4-4: Creating an Account

Time Required: Approximately 15 minutes

Objective: Learn how to create a user account.

Description: Creating and configuring user accounts is a vital task in server management. In this activity you learn how to set up a new account.

1. Click **Start**, point to **All Programs**, point to **Administrative Tools**, and click **Active Directory Users and Computers**. Or, click **Start**, click **Run**, type **mmc**, and click **OK**. Maximize the console windows, if necessary. Click the **File** menu, and click **Add/Remove Snap-in**. Click **Add** and double-click **Active Directory Users and Computers**. Click **Close** and click **OK**.

2. In the left pane, double-click **Active Directory Users and Computers**, if necessary, to display the elements under it. Double-click the domain name, such as jpcompany.com, to display the folders and OUs under it.

3. Double-click the **Users** folder in the right pane. Are there any accounts already created? What objects are shown along with the accounts?

4. Click the **Action** menu or right-click **Users** in the left pane, point to **New**, and then click **User**.

5. Type your first name in the First name box, type your middle initial (no period) in the Initials box, and type your last name, with the word "test" appended to it, in the Last name box, for example: Peeletest. Enter your initials, with "Test" appended to them, in the User logon name box, for example: JPTest. What options are automatically completed for you? Record your observations. Click **Next** (see Figure 4-11).

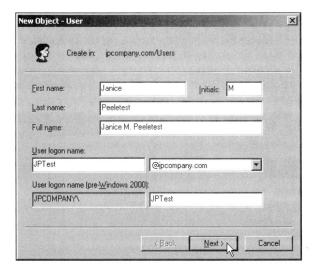

Figure 4-11   Creating a user account

6. Enter a password and enter the password confirmation. (Use a password that meets the security requirements on the server, such as one over a specific number of characters and that uses letters, numbers, and symbols inside the password.) Click the box to select **User must change password at next logon**, if necessary. This option forces users to enter a new password the first time they logon, so that the account creator will not know their password. The User cannot change password option means that only the account administrator can change the user's password. Password never expires is used in situations in which an account must always be accessed, such as when a program accesses an account to run a special process. The Account is disabled option provides a way to prevent access to an account without deleting it. Click **Next**.

7. Verify the information you have entered, and click **Finish**.

8. To continue configuring the account, in the right pane, right-click the account you just created, such as Janice M. Peeletest, and click **Properties**.

9. Notice the tabs that are displayed for the account properties and record them.

10. Click the **General** tab, if it is not already displayed, and enter a description of the account, such as Test account.

11. Click the **Account** tab. What information is already completed on this tab?

12. Click the tabs you have not yet viewed to find out what information can be configured through each one. Which tab enables you to record information about the user's e-mail address?

13. Click **OK**.

14. Leave the Active Directory Users and Computers window open for the next activity.

The following is a brief summary of the account properties that can be set.

- *General tab*—Enables you to enter or modify personal information about the account holder that includes the first name, last name, and name as it is displayed in the console, description of the user or account, office location, telephone number, e-mail address, and home page. There are also optional buttons to enter additional telephone numbers and Web page addresses for the account holder.

- *Address tab*—Used to provide information about the account holder's street address, post office box, city, state or province, postal code, and country or region

- *Account tab*—Provides information about the logon name, domain name, and account options, such as requiring the user to change her or his password at next logon, and account expiration date, if one applies. There is also a Logon Hours button on this tab that enables you to set up an account so that the user only logs onto the domain at designated times, such as during backups and at times designated for system work on the server. Also, the Log On To button enables you to limit from which computer a user can log on to the server or domain.

- *Profile tab*—Enables you to associate a particular profile with a user or set of users, such as a common desktop (profiles are discussed later in this chapter). This tab also is used to associate a logon script and a home folder (directory) with an account. A logon script is a file of commands that are executed at logon, and a home folder is a folder that is the user's main folder, such as a folder on a particular server.

 You can use the %username% variable to automatically create a user's home folder with her or his logon name. For example, to automatically create a home folder for the user RKurkowski, simply enter the universal naming convention name and the variable (*servername**sharename*\\%username%).

- *Telephones tab*—Enables you to associate specific types of telephone contact numbers for an account holder, which include one or more numbers for home, pager, mobile, fax, and IP

- *Organization tab*—Provides a place to enter the account holder's title, department, company name, and the name of the person who manages the account holder

- *Member Of tab*—Used to add the account to an existing group of users that have the same security and access requirements (you'll learn more about groups later in this chapter). The tab also is used to remove the account from a group.

- *Dial-in tab*—Permits you to control remote access from dial-in modems or from virtual private networks (VPNs)

- *Environment tab*—Enables you to configure the startup environment for clients that access one or more servers using terminal services (for running programs on the server)

- *Sessions tab*—Used to configure session parameters for a client using terminal services, such as a session time limit, a limit on how long a session can be idle, what to do when a connection is broken, and how to reconnect

4

- *Remote control tab*—Enables you to set up remote control parameters for a client that uses terminal services. The remote control capability enables you to view and manipulate the client session while it is active in order to troubleshoot problems.
- *Terminal Services Profile tab*—Used to set up a user profile for a client that uses terminal services
- *COM+ tab*—Used to specify the COM+ partition set of which the user is a member

Disabling, Enabling, and Renaming Accounts

When a user takes a leave of absence, you have the option to disable his or her account. Your organization may also disable someone's account when that person leaves, and then later rename and enable the account for that person's replacement (this is easier than deleting the account and creating a new one).

Activity 4-5: Disabling, Renaming, and Enabling an Account

Time Required: Approximately 5 minutes

Objective: Practice disabling, renaming, and then enabling an account.

Description: In this activity, you learn how to disable an account, rename the account, and then enable that account.

1. Access the Active Directory Users and Computers window, or if it is closed, click **Start**, point to **All Programs**, point to **Administrative Tools**, and click **Active Directory Users and Computers**.

2. Browse to find the account, such as the one you created in Activity 4-4 under the Users folder within the domain that you created.

3. Right-click the account, and click **Disable Account** on the shortcut menu as shown in Figure 4-12.

Figure 4-12 Disabling an account

4. Click **OK** when you see the informational dialog box that verifies you have disabled the account. The account icon has an "X" in a red circle to show that it is disabled. No one can use the account until you enable it.

5. To rename the account, right-click it, and click **Rename** (see Figure 4-12). Enter a new name, such as Martin Sanchez, and then press **Enter**.

6. When you see the Rename User dialog box, change the First name and the Last name boxes to reflect the new name. Change the User logon name, such as to MSTest. Click **OK**.

7. Make sure the account is now listed as Martin Sanchez in the Users folder.

8. Right-click the account you renamed, and click **Enable Account**. Click **OK**. What happens to the display of the account in the Users folder?

9. Leave the Active Directory Users and Computers window open for the next activity.

Moving an Account

When an employee moves from one department to another, for example from the Payroll Department to the budget office, you may need to move their account from one container to another—between OUs, for example.

Activity 4-6: Moving an Account

Time Required: Approximately 5 minutes

Objective: Practice moving an account.

Description: If your organization uses OUs to reflect different departments, then you may need to move accounts between OUs as people are transferred to different departments. In this activity, you move the account you renamed in Activity 4-5 to the OU that you created in Activity 4-3.

1. Access the Active Directory Users and Computers window, or if it is closed, click **Start**, point to **All Programs**, point to **Administrative Tools**, and click **Active Directory Users and Computers**.

2. Right-click the account you renamed.

3. Click **Move** (see Figure 4-12).

4. Find the OU that you created in Activity 4-3, such as SalesOUJP, and click it. Click **OK** (see Figure 4-13).

Figure 4-13   Moving an account

5. In the tree of the left pane, double-click the OU to which you moved the account. Is the account displayed in the right pane?

6. Leave the Active Directory Users and Computers window open for the next activity.

Resetting a Password

Sometimes users change their passwords or go several weeks without logging on—and forget their passwords. You do not have the option to look up a password, but you can reset it for the user. For organizations that have accounts that manage sensitive information, particularly financial information, it is advisable to have specific guidelines that govern the circumstances under which an account password is reset. For example, an organization might require that the account holder physically visit his or her account manager, rather than to place a telephone call because there is no way to verify the authenticity of the request by telephone.

 Accounts that handle financial information are typically audited by independent financial auditors. These auditors may require that you keep records of each time a password is reset, so that they can examine them along with other financial information.

Activity 4-7: Changing an Account's Password

Time Required: Approximately 5 minutes

Objective: Practice changing an account's password.

Description: One of the most common account management tasks is resetting passwords. In this activity you learn how to reset the password for a user.

1. Access the Active Directory Users and Computers window, or if it is closed, click **Start**, point to **All Programs**, point to **Administrative Tools**, and click **Active Directory Users and Computers**.

2. Open the OU folder that contains the account, such as SalesOUJP, if necessary.

3. Right-click the account for which you want to reset the password, such as Martin Sanchez.

4. Click **Reset Password** (see Figure 4-12).

5. Enter the new password, and then confirm it. (Use a password that meets the security requirements on the server, such as one over seven characters in length and that uses letters, numbers, and symbols inside the password.)

6. Click the **User must change password at next logon** box (see Figure 4-14). Checking this box enables you to force the user to change the password you set, so that you will not know the new password, which is a best practice endorsed by Microsoft and often a requirement of financial auditors who scrutinize networks that handle financial information.

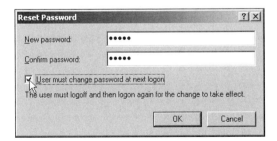

Figure 4-14   Resetting a password

7. Click **OK** in the Reset Password dialog box. Click **OK** in the information box.

8. Continue to leave the Active Directory Users and Computers window open for the next activity.

Deleting an Account

Plan to practice good account management by deleting accounts that are no longer in use. If you don't, the number of dormant accounts may grow into a confused tangle of accounts, and you expose your company to security risks. When you delete an account, its globally unique identifier (GUID) is also deleted and is not reused even if you create another account using the same name.

Activity 4-8: Deleting an Account

Time Required: Approximately 5 minutes

Objective: Practice deleting an account.

Description: In this project, you delete the account that you renamed in Activity 4-5.

1. Access the Active Directory Users and Computers window (if it is closed, click **Start**, point to **All Programs**, point to **Administrative Tools**, and click **Active Directory Users and Computers**).

2. If necessary, open the OU folder that contains the account you want to delete, such as SalesOUJP.

3. Right-click the account you want to delete, such as Martin Sanchez, and click **Delete** (see Figure 4-12).

4. Click **Yes** to verify that you want to delete this account.

5. Close the **Active Directory Users and Computers** window (also, if you have been using the Active Directory Users and Computers snap-in, click **No** when asked to save the console settings).

SECURITY GROUP MANAGEMENT

One of the best ways to manage accounts is by grouping together accounts that have similar characteristics, such as those that are in a single department, in a specific project group, or that access the same folders and printers. The group management concept saves time by eliminating repetitive steps in managing user and resource access. Windows 2000 and Server 2003 expand on the concept of groups from the one used in Windows NT Server. In Windows NT Server, there are two types of groups: local groups that are used to manage resources on a single workstation or on domain controllers in one domain, and global groups that are used to manage resources across multiple domains. With the introduction of Active Directory, Windows 2000 and Server 2003 expand the use of groups through the concept of **scope of influence** (or **scope**), which is the reach of a group for gaining access to resources in Active Directory. When Active Directory is not implemented, the scope of a group is limited to the standalone server, and only local groups are created. In contrast, the implementation of Active Directory increases the scope from a local server or domain to all domains in a forest. The types of groups and their associated scopes are as follows:

- *Local*—Used on standalone servers that are not part of a domain. The scope of this type of group does not go beyond the local server on which it is defined.

- *Domain local*—Used when there is a single domain or used to manage resources in a particular domain so that global and universal groups can access those resources

- *Global*—Used to manage group accounts from the same domain so that those accounts can access resources in the same domain and in other domains

- *Universal*—Used to provide access to resources in any domain within a forest

All of these groups can be used for security or distribution groups. **Security groups** are used to enable access to resources on a standalone server or in Active Directory. **Distribution groups** are used for e-mail or telephone lists, to provide quick, mass distribution of information. In this section, the focus is on security groups.

Implementing Local Groups

A **local security group** is used to manage resources on a standalone computer that is not part of a domain and on member servers in a domain (non-DCs). For example, you might use a local group in a small office situation in which there are only a few users, such as 5, 15, or 30. Consider an office of mineral resource consultants in which there are 18 user accounts on the server. Four of these accounts are used by the founding partners of the consulting firm, who manage employee hiring, payroll, schedules, and general accounting. Seven accounts are for consultants who specialize in coal-bed methane extraction, and the seven remaining accounts belong to consultants who work with oil extraction. In this situation, the company may decide not to install Active Directory, and divide these accounts into three local groups. One group would be called Managers and consist of the four founding partners. Another group would be called CBM for the coal-bed methane consultants, and the third group would be called Oil and used for the oil consultants. Each group would be given different security access based on the resources at the server, which would include access to folders and to printers.

 You create local groups by using the Local Users and Groups MMC snap-in.

Implementing Domain Local Groups

A **domain local security group** is used when Active Directory is deployed. This type of group is typically used to manage resources in a domain and to give global groups from the same and other domains access to those resources. As shown in Table 4-1, a domain local group can contain user accounts, global groups, and universal groups.

Table 4-1   Membership capabilities of a domain local group

Active Directory Objects That can be Members of a Domain Local Group	Active Directory Objects That a Domain Local Group can Join as a Member
User accounts in the same domain	Access control (security) lists for objects in the same domain, such as permissions to access a folder, shared folder, or printer
Domain local groups in the same domain	Domain local groups in the same domain
Global groups in any domain in a tree or forest (as long as there are transitive or two-way trust relationships maintained)	
Universal groups in any domain in a tree or forest (as long as there are transitive or two-way trust relationships maintained)	

The scope of a domain local group is the domain in which the group exists, but you can convert a domain local group to a universal group as long as the domain local group does not contain any other domain local groups. Also, to convert any group, the domain must be in the Windows Server 2003 mode, and not the Windows 2000 mixed or native modes. Windows 2000 mixed mode means there are a combination of Windows NT 4.0, Windows 2000, and Windows 2003 servers. In Windows 2000 native mode there are only Windows 2000 and Windows 2003 servers. Windows Server 2003 mode means there are only Windows 2003 servers in a domain.

 Depending on how you install Windows Server 2003, the default mode is either Windows 2000 mixed mode (if you specified there are Windows NT servers on the network), or Windows 2000 native mode. To check the mode (domain functional level) or to change it, click Start, point to All Programs, point to Administrative Tools, and click Active Directory Domains and Trusts. Next, right-click the domain, and click Raise Domain Functional Level to view the Raise Domain Functional Level dialog box as shown in Figure 4-15.

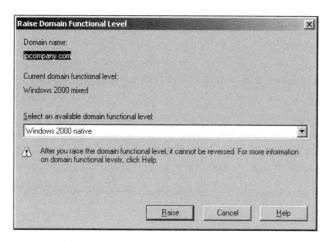

Figure 4-15   Viewing the domain functional level

Although a domain local group can contain any combination of accounts, global, and universal groups, the typical purpose of a domain local group is to provide access to resources, which means that you grant access to servers, folders, shared folders, and printers to a domain local group. Under most circumstances you should plan to put domain local groups in access control lists only, and the members of domain local groups should be mainly global groups. An **access control list (ACL)** is a list of security descriptors (privileges) that have been set up for a particular object, such as a shared folder or shared printer. You'll learn more about how ACLs are configured as you learn about permissions in Chapter 5. Generally, a domain local group does not contain accounts, because account management is more efficient when you handle it through global groups. Examples of using domain local groups with global groups are presented in the next section.

Implementing Global Groups

A **global security group** is intended to contain user accounts from a single domain and can also be set up as a member of a domain local group in the same or another domain. This capability gives global groups a broader scope than domain local groups, because their members can access resources in other domains. A global group can contain user accounts and other global groups from the domain in which it was created.

Nesting global groups to reflect the structure of OUs means that global groups can be layered. For example, your organization might consist of an OU for management, an OU under the management OU for the Finance Department, and an OU under the Finance Department for the budget office—resulting in three levels of OUs. Also, you might have a global group composed of the accounts of vice presidents in the management OU, a global group of accounts for supervisors in the Finance Department OU, and a global group of all members of the budget office in the budget OU. The global group membership can be set up to reflect the structure of OUs, as shown in Figure 4-16.

4

*Managers global group (top-level global group)
   Amber Richards
   Joe Scarpelli
   Kathy Brown
   Sam Rameriz
   **Finance global group (second-level global group)
      Martin LeDuc
      Sarah Humphrey
      Heather Shultz
      Sam Weisenberg
      Jason Lew
      ***Budget global group (third-level global group)
         Michele Gomez
         Kristin Beck
         Chris Doyle

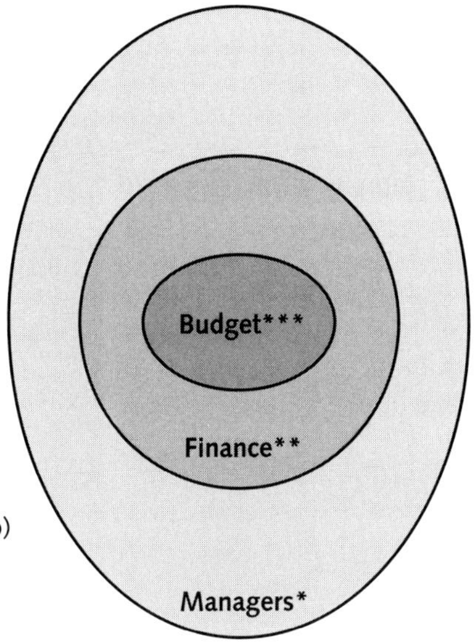

Figure 4-16   Nested global groups

 Plan nesting of global groups carefully. You can convert a global group to a universal group at a later time, but only if it is not a member of another global group. Also, global groups can only be nested in Windows 2000 native or Windows Server 2003 mode domains.

A global group can be converted to a universal group as long as it is not nested in another global group or in a universal group. In the example shown in Figure 4-16, the Finance and Budget global groups cannot be converted to universal groups because they already are members of the Managers and Finance groups, respectively.

A typical use for a global group is to build it with accounts that need access to resources in the same or in another domain and then to make the global group in one domain a member of a domain local group in the same or another domain. This model enables you to manage user accounts and their access to resources through one or more global groups, while reducing the complexity of managing accounts.

For example, consider a college that has a domain for students, a domain for faculty and staff, and a domain for research organizations that are associated with the college. The college's executive council, consisting of the college president and vice presidents, needs access to resources in all three domains. One way to enable the executive council to have access is to create a domain local group called LocalExec in each domain that provides the appropriate access to folders, files, and other resources. Next, create a GlobalExec global group in the faculty and staff domain that has the president's and vice presidents' user accounts as members (see Figure 4-17). These steps enable you to manage security for all of their accounts at one time from one global group. If the president or a vice president leaves to take another job, you simply delete (or disable) that person's account from the global group and later add an account (or rename and enable the old account) for her or his replacement. You also can manage access to resources in each domain using one step, by giving the domain local group access, resulting in much less management work. If a new printer is added to a domain, for example, you can give the domain local group full privileges to the printer.

When the Active Directory structure becomes complex enough in a large organization so that many domains, trees, and forests are in use, global groups are used as members of universal groups to manage accounts, as described in the next section, "Implementing Universal Groups."

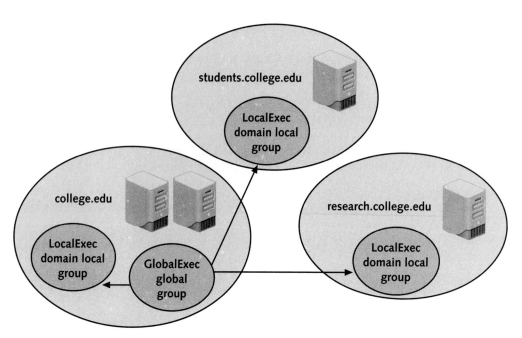

Figure 4-17   Managing security through domain local and global groups

Activity 4-9: Creating Domain Local and Global Security Groups

Time Required: Approximately 15 minutes

Objective: Create a domain local and a global security group and make the global group a member of the domain local group.

Description: In this project, assume that you have been asked to set up groups to manage access for the managers in an Active Directory that has four domains. You begin the setup by creating a domain local group that will be used to manage resources and a global group of accounts. Next, you add the global group to the domain local group. To complete the assignment, you first need an environment in which Active Directory is installed and two accounts that are already set up by your instructor (or that you create in advance).

1. Install and use the Active Directory Users and Computers snap-in in the MMC, or click **Start**, point to **All Programs**, point to **Administrative Tools**, and click **Active Directory Users and Computers**.

2. Double-click **Active Directory Users and Computers**, and the domain, such as jpcompany.com, if the contents of these are not displayed in the tree.

3. Double-click **Users** in the tree.

4. Click the **Action** menu, point to **New**, and click **Group**. What defaults are already selected in the New Object – Group dialog box? Record your observations.

5. In the Group name box, enter **DomainMgrs** plus your initials, for example DomainMgrsJP. What is the pre-Windows 2000 group name?

6. Click **Domain local** under Group scope, and click **Security** (if it is not already selected) under Group type.

7. Click **OK** and then look for the group you just created in the right pane within the Users folder.

8. Click the **Create a new group in the current container** icon (with two heads) on the button bar.

9. In the Group name box, type **GlobalMgrs** plus your initials, for example, GlobalMgrsJP.

10. Click **Global** under Group scope, and click **Security** under Group type, if they are not already selected.

11. Click **OK** and then look for the group you just created in the right pane.

12. Double-click the global group you created.

13. Click the **Members** tab. Are there any members already associated with the group?

14. Click the **Add** button.

15. Click the **Advanced** button.

16. Click **Find Now**.

17. Press the **Ctrl** key, and click each of the two users provided by your instructor. Click **OK** (see Figure 4-18).

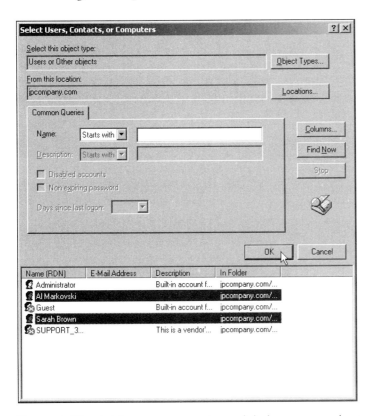

Figure 4-18 Adding user accounts as global group members

18. Make sure that the users you selected are shown in the Select Users, Contacts, or Computers dialog box. Click **OK**.

19. Again, be sure that both accounts are shown in the Members box on the Members tab. Click **OK**.

20. Double-click the domain local group, such as DomainMgrsJP, and then click the **Members** tab. What members are shown?

21. Click **Add**, and then click **Advanced**.

22. Click **Find Now**.

23. Locate the global group you created, such as GlobalMgrsJP. Click that global group, and click **OK**.

24. Verify that the global group is displayed in the Select Users, Contacts, Computers, or Groups dialog box, and then click **OK**.

25. Make sure the global group is listed under Members on the Members tab. Click **OK**.

26. Close the **Active Directory Users and Computers** tool.

Implementing Universal Groups

In an Active Directory context in which there are multiple hierarchies of domains, trees, and forests, **universal security groups** provide a means to span domains and trees. Universal group membership can include user accounts from any domain, global groups from any domain, and other universal groups from any domain.

Universal groups are offered to provide an easy means to access any resource in a tree or among trees in a forest. If you carefully plan the use of universal groups, then you can manage security for single accounts with a minimum of effort. That planning is done in relation to the scope of access that is needed for a group of accounts. Here are some guidelines to help simplify how you can use groups:

- Use global groups to hold accounts as members—and keep the nesting of global groups to a minimum (or do not use nesting), to avoid confusion. Give accounts access to resources by making the global groups to which they belong members of domain local groups or universal groups or both.

- Use domain local groups to provide access to resources in a specific domain. Avoid placing accounts in domain local groups—but do make domain local groups members of access control lists for specific resources in the domain, such as shared folders and printers.

- Use universal groups to provide extensive access to resources, particularly when Active Directory contains trees and forests, or to simplify access when there are multiple domains. Make universal groups members of access control lists for objects in any domain, tree, or forest. Manage user account access by placing accounts in global groups and joining global groups to domain local or universal groups, depending on which is most appropriate to the scope required for access.

 As of this writing, if you attempt to create a new universal group, but find that the option button in the Create New Object – (Group) dialog box is deactivated, this means that the domain is set up in Windows 2000 mixed or native mode and you must convert the domain to Windows Server 2003 mode.

In the example of setting up access for the executive council in a college that has three domains, an alternative is to create one universal group that has access to all resources in the three domains—create one global group containing the president and vice presidents, and make that global group a member of the universal group. In this model there are only two groups to manage, as shown in Figure 4-19.

Properties of Groups

All of the groups that you can create in Windows Server 2003 have a set of properties that can be configured. As you probably noticed in Activity 4-9, you can configure the properties of a specific group by double-clicking that group in the Local Users and Groups tool for a standalone (nondomain) or member server; or in the Active Directory Users and Computers tool for DC servers in a domain. The properties are configured using the following tabs:

- *General*—Used to enter a description of the group, change the scope and type of group, and provide e-mail addresses for a distribution group

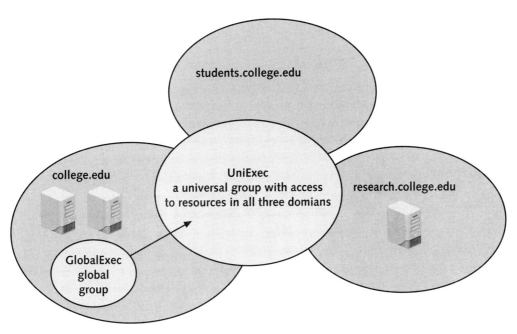

Figure 4-19   Managing security through universal and global groups

- *Members*—Used to add members to a group, such as adding user accounts to a global group; it also enables members to be removed

- *Member Of*—Used to make the group a member of another group, or to remove the group's membership

- *Managed By*—Used to establish an account or group that manages the group, if the manager is other than the server administrator; also, the location, telephone number, and fax number of the manager can be provided

IMPLEMENTING USER PROFILES

Client access to Windows Server 2003 can be customized through user profiles. A **local user profile** is automatically created at the local computer when you log on with an account for the first time, and the profile can be modified to consist of desktop settings that are customized for one or more clients who log on locally.

User profiles provide the following advantages:

- Multiple users can use the same computer and maintain their own customized settings. When users log on they receive their own personalized settings that were saved when they last logged off.

- Profiles can be stored on a network server so they are available to users regardless of the computer they log on.

- Profiles can be made mandatory so users have the same settings each time they log on. When a user logs on, he or she can modify the settings but the changes are never saved when the user logs off.

 Profiles are used in Microsoft operating systems to provide a consistent working environment for one or more users. A local user profile is a particular desktop setup that always starts in the same way and is stored on the local computer. A **roaming profile** is a desktop setup that starts in the same way from any computer used to access an account, including remote connections from home or on the road. In a network environment where users are moving between computers, a roaming profile is ideal so the users' settings are available from any computer.

For example, if there are two server administrators and two backup operators who primarily run backups, you might create one profile for the administrators and a different one for the backup operators. That can be useful if each type of account needs to have certain program icons, startup programs, or some other prearranged desktop settings. Also, a user profile can be set up on a server so it is downloaded to the client workstation each time a specific account is logged on. This is a roaming profile, which enables a user to start off with the same desktop setup, no matter which computer she or he uses. In some circumstances, you need to set up profiles so that certain users cannot change their profiles. This is done by creating a **mandatory user profile** in which the user does not have permission to update the folder containing her or his profile. A mandatory user profile overrides the user's locally stored profile if it has been changed from the version stored on the server. This means that when a user logs on she or he can make changes to the profile and customize it, but when the user logs off the changes are not saved. To make a server profile (either local or roaming) mandatory, rename the user's Ntuser.dat file in the user's profile folder as Ntuser.man. The user's profile folder is found in \Documents and Settings*username*.

An easy way to set up a profile is to first set up a generic account on the server or use the Guest account as a model with the desired desktop configuration, including desktop icons, shortcut folders, and programs in the Startup folder to start when the client workstation starts. Then copy the Ntuser.dat file to the \Documents and Settings\All Users (or Default User, depending on your setup) folder. This step makes that profile the default for new users. You can also create a profile to use as a roaming profile for specific users. To create a roaming profile, set up a generic account and customize the desktop. For example, you might create an account called BUDGET for users in the budget office and customize the desktop, start menu, and network and printer connections. After you create that account, set up those users to access that profile by opening the Profile tab in each user's account properties and entering the path to that profile as shown in Figure 4-20. You can also use the System icon (Advanced tab) in Control Panel to copy profiles from one location to another.

Activity 4-10: Creating a Default User Profile

Time Required: Approximately 20 to 30 minutes

Objective: Create a default profile for newly created accounts.

Description: In this activity, you configure a default user profile for new accounts created in Windows Server 2003. (Before starting, either you or your instructor need to set up an account that has access to log on locally to the computer. One way to do this is to create an account and then make it a member of the Server Operators group in the Users folder. Another option is to enable the Guest account and log onto it from a client computer, such as Windows XP Professional, but make sure that another profile is not associated with the Guest account.)

1. If you use the Guest account, you may need to activate that account before you start. Log onto an account that has Administrator privileges. Click **Start**, point to **All Programs**, point to **Administrative Tools**, and click **Active Directory Users and Computers**. Open the **Users** folder in the tree. Right-click **Guest**, and click **Enable Account**. Click **OK**. Next, make sure that the Guest account has a password and that you know it. Right-click **Guest**, and click **Reset Password**. Enter a password and confirm it. Click **OK**. Click **OK** again. Close the Active Directory Users and Computers window.

2. Click **Start** and click **Log Off**. Alternatively, you can press **Ctrl+Alt+Del**, and click **Log Off**. Click **Log Off** again.

3. Press **Ctrl+Alt+Del** and log on to the account created for this activity or to the **Guest** account. (If this is the first time the account has been used, you may be prompted to change the password.)

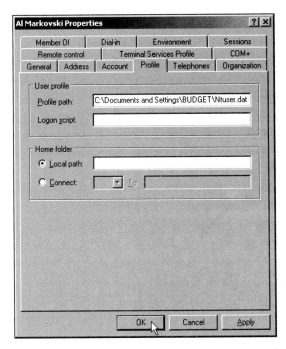

Figure 4-20   Setting a roaming profile in an account's properties

4. Click **Start**, point to **Control Panel**, click **Display**, and click the **Desktop** tab. (Or, if you are logging on from Windows XP Professional using the new XP desktop theme, click **Start**, click **Control Panel**, click **Appearance and Themes**, and click **Change the desktop background**.)

5. Under Background, click the **Ascent** option. Click **Apply**. Click the **Screen Saver** tab. Set the Wait time to **7** minutes and make sure that the **On resume, password protect** box is checked. (Password protect is a good way to provide security for workstation clients when the user is away from his or her desk, because after the screen saver starts in seven minutes, the user must enter his or her password to resume.)

6. Click **OK** in the Display Properties dialog box (and close the Appearance and Themes dialog box, if you are using Windows XP Professional with the new XP desktop theme).

7. Log off the account by clicking **Start**, clicking **Log Off**, and clicking **Log Off** again.

8. Log onto your Windows Server 2003 account with Administrator privileges (if you logged off).

9. Click **Start**, point to **Control Panel**, and click **System**. Click the **Advanced** tab, and click the **Settings** button in the User Profiles section.

10. Click the account you accessed in Step 3, such as JPCOMPANY\Guest.

11. Click the **Copy To** button.

12. Click the Browse button, locate and then click the Default User subfolder in the Documents and Settings folder, for example, C:\Documents and Settings\Default User. Click **OK** in the Browse for Folder dialog box.

13. Click **OK** in the Copy To dialog box, and click **Yes** to confirm the copy (replace the current settings).

14. Click **OK** in the User Profiles dialog box, and click **OK** in the System Properties dialog box.

15. If you used the Guest account in this activity, disable the account.

CHAPTER SUMMARY

- Active Directory is a directory service that is like the central nervous system of a network because it is used to provide ways to manage resources including user accounts, groups of user accounts, security policies, and other information.

- The most basic component of Active Directory is an object. Each object is defined through an information set called a schema.

- The global catalog stores information about every object, replicates key Active Directory elements, and is used to authenticate user accounts when they log on.

- A namespace consists of using the Domain Name System for resolving computer and domain names to IP addresses and vice versa. Named objects in Active Directory also exist in a namespace. Active Directory requires a Domain Name System server to help with the management of network resources.

- Active Directory is a hierarchy of logical containers: forests, trees, domains, and organizational units. Forests are the highest-level containers and organizational units are the lowest level. Another important container is the site, which is created out of IP subnets.

- When you design the Active Directory structure, follow some basic rules so that your design meets the needs of your organization. Perhaps the most basic of these rules is to keep your design as simple as possible.

- User accounts are vital to a network, because they enable individual users to access specific resources, such as folders and files. There are many, many properties that can be associated with accounts for customization. Besides customizing account properties, other ways to manage accounts include disabling, enabling, renaming, moving, and deleting them. Further, resetting account passwords is one of the most common account management tasks.

- On a standalone or member server, you can create local groups to help manage user accounts. When Active Directory is installed, you can use domain local, global, and universal groups for managing accounts.

- User profiles are tools for customizing accounts, such as customizing desktop and other user features.

KEY TERMS

access control list (ACL) — A list of all security descriptors that have been set up for a particular object, such as for a shared folder or a shared printer.

container — An Active Directory object that houses other objects, such as a tree that houses domains or a domain that houses organizational units.

contiguous namespace — A namespace in which every child object has a portion of its name derived from its parent object.

directory service — A large container (database) of network data and resources, such as computers, printers, user accounts, and user groups that enables management and fast access to those resources.

disjointed namespace — A namespace in which the child object name does not resemble the name of its parent object.

distribution group — A list of users that enables one e-mail message to be sent to all users on the list. A distribution group is not used for security and thus cannot appear in an ACL.

domain — A grouping of resource objects, such as servers and user accounts, that is one element of Active Directory in Windows Server 2003. A domain usually is a higher-level representation of how a business, government, or school is organized, for example reflecting a geographical location or major division of that organization.

domain controller (DC) — A Windows 2003 server that contains a full copy of the Active Directory information. You can add a new object to Active Directory via a domain controller, such as a new user account. Also, a Windows 2003 server configured as a domain controller replicates any changes made to its copy of Active Directory to every other domain controller in the same domain.

domain local security group — A group that is used to manage resources—shared folders and printers, for example—in its home domain, and that is primarily used to give global groups access to those resources.

forest — A grouping of trees that each have contiguous namespaces within their own domain structure, but that have disjointed namespaces between trees. The trees and their domains use the same schema and global catalog.

global catalog — A grand repository for all objects and the most frequently used attributes for each object in all domains. Each forest has a single global catalog that can be replicated onto multiple servers.

global security group — A group that typically contains user accounts from its home domain, and that is a member of domain local groups in the same or other domains, so as to give that global group's member accounts access to the resources defined to the domain local groups.

globally unique identifier (GUID) — A unique number, up to 16 characters long, that is associated with an Active Directory object.

Kerberos transitive trust relationship — A set of two-way trusts between two or more domains (or forests in a forest trust) in which Kerberos security is used.

local security group — A group of user accounts that is used to manage resources on a standalone computer.

local user profile — A desktop setup that is associated with one or more accounts to determine what startup programs are used, additional desktop icons, and other customizations. A user profile is local to the computer in which it is stored.

mandatory user profile — A user profile set up by the server administrator that is loaded from the server to the client each time the user logs on; changes that the user makes to the profile are not saved.

multimaster replication — In Windows Server 2003, there can be multiple servers, called domain controllers (DC)s, that store Active Directory information and replicate it to each other. Because each DC acts as a master, replication does not stop when one is down, and updates to Active Directory continue, as when creating a new account.

name resolution — A process used to translate a computer's logical or host name into a network address, such as to a dotted decimal address associated with a computer—and vice versa.

namespace — A logical area on a network that contains directory services and named objects, and that has the ability to perform name resolution.

object — A network resource, such as a server or a user account, with distinct attributes or properties, that is defined in a domain, and exists in Active Directory.

organizational unit (OU) — A grouping of objects within a domain that provides a means to establish specific policies for governing those objects and that enables object management to be delegated.

roaming profile — Desktop settings that are associated with an account so that the same settings are employed no matter which computer is used to access the account (the profile is downloaded to the client from a server).

schema — Elements used in the definition of each object contained in Active Directory, including the object class and its attributes.

scope of influence (scope) — The reach of a type of group such as access to resources in a single domain or access to all resources in all domains in a forest (see domain local, global, and universal security groups). (Another meaning for the term "scope" is the beginning through ending IP addresses defined in a DHCP server for use by DHCP clients; see Chapter 8).

Security Account Manager (SAM) database — A database of information about user accounts, groups, and privileges stored in a Windows NT domain.

security group — Used to assign a group of users permission to access network resources.

site — An option in Active Directory to interconnect IP subnets so that the server can determine the fastest route to connect clients for authentication and to connect DCs for replication of Active Directory. Site information also enables Active Directory to create redundant routes for DC replication.

transitive trust — A trust relationship between two or more domains in a tree in which each domain has access to objects in the others.

tree — Related domains that use a contiguous namespace, share the same schema, and have two-way transitive trust relationships.

two-way trust — A domain relationship in which both domains are trusted and trusting, enabling one to have access to objects in the other.

universal security group — A group that is used to provide access to resources in any domain within a forest. A common implementation is to make global groups that contain accounts members of a universal group that has access to resources.

REVIEW QUESTIONS

1. Your organization has a root domain called consult.com and other child domains called web.cs.com and products.conslt.com. This is an example of a _____.

   a. disjointed namespace

   b. contiguous namespace

   c. commercial namespace

   d. nonreciprocal namespace

2. Which of the following are schema characteristics you would find in the user account class? (Circle all that apply.)

   a. required attributes

   b. optional attributes

   c. pointers to parent entities

   d. tree priority

3. Your Active Directory planning committee is currently working on a plan for OUs in your company, which makes auto parts. One of the committee members wants to create a top-level OU called parts and then to create under it OUs for each of the 500 parts manufactured by the company. Which of the following matches your response?

   a. You recommend creating an additional set of OUs so that there is one for each employee.

   b. You endorse the plan.

   c. You recommend instead that the company create five OUs in a horizontal structure, so that there is one OU for each of the five major departments in the company.

   d. You recommend creating trees for each of the 500 parts, because trees can have their own schemas.

4. The first domain controller created in a tree that will have 10 domain controllers automatically becomes _____.

   a. the main domain controller (MDC)

   b. a global catalog server

   c. the master accounts controller

   d. the domain registrar

5. Your organization's network extends to several locations in three states. Also, these networks are divided into multiple IP subnets. What Active Directory containers should you configure on the basis of the IP subnets to enable faster access to the network and its resources by users?

   a. OUs

   b. forests

   c. trees

   d. sites

6. You want to create a mandatory user profile for a group of tellers in a bank. To do this, you create a file for these users called _____.

   a. Userman.txt

   b. Profile.txt

   c. Ntuser.man

   d. Netuser.dat

7. Which of the following is true about all trees in a forest? (Choose all that apply.)

   a. All trees use the same schema.

   b. All trees must have no more than two domains.

   c. All trees use the same global catalog.

   d. All trees must have OUs.

8. A group of 25 physicians is implementing a new network that uses two Windows 2003 servers and that will have Internet access. Besides the physicians, there is a bookkeeper, a business manager, five billing clerks, 28 nurses, and five nurse practitioners. Each will have a connection to the network. How many domains are needed when Active Directory is configured?

   a. 1

   b. 2, one for access within the building, and one for physicians who remotely dial in from home

   c. 3, one for the physicians, one for the nurse practitioners and nurses, and one for the remaining staff

   d. 4, one for the physicians, one for the nurse practitioners, one for the nurses, and one for the remaining staff

9. You have a network of Windows 2003 servers and you've decided to create a universal security group called AdminSecure for the server administrators. However, when you try to create the group, the option for Universal is deactivated. What is the problem?

   a. Windows Server 2003 does not support universal security groups.

   b. You must convert the domain to Windows Server 2003 mode.

   c. You must convert the domain to Windows 2000 mixed mode.

   d. You must create the AdminSecure local computer group and then create the universal group.

10. You can use the _____ tool to delegate management of an OU.

   a. Computer Management

   b. Schema Editor

   c. Local Users and Computers

   d. Active Directory Users and Computers

11. The accounting manager in your company is concerned about using Windows Server 2003 because he has heard that user accounts can only be created on one server, and that there is no automatic backup of the account information, even though your network has 24 servers. What is your response?

   a. This is a problem with Windows Server 2003, but it is best addressed by taking daily backups.

   b. This is not a problem because Windows Server 2003 uses backup domain controllers to save the account information.

   c. This problem was addressed long ago through automatic floppy disk transaction update files.

   d. This is not a problem because Windows Server 2003 uses multimaster replication.

12. Which of the following are important elements of namespace logic? (Choose all that apply.)

    a. deployment of multiple OUs

    b. one DHCP server

    c. Active Directory as a container for named objects

    d. one or more DNS servers

13. In a schema, objects have _____.

    a. attributes

    b. valences

    c. forests

    d. trees

14. You are the server administrator in the IT Department of a community college. The head of the Psychology Department has just resigned and his user account has access to many databases and spreadsheets related to the department's budget. What is the easiest way to create an account for his replacement, who will be selected in two weeks?

    a. Set the current department head's account to expire in two weeks.

    b. Delete the department head's account immediately and then create a new account with the same privileges after the new department head is selected.

    c. Disable the current department head's account, and when the new department head takes over, rename the account and then enable it.

    d. Move the current department head's account to the Temp subfolder in the \Windows folder and then move it back when the new head is selected.

15. One way to enable users to have their individual desktop configurations follow them when they log onto computers at different locations is to _____.

    a. create traveling accounts for those users

    b. create roaming profiles for those users

    c. use the Desktop Configuration tool to create remote user account desktops

    d. limit user access to the network to only one computer per user

16. You have an Active Directory structure that contains four domains. How might you plan to use groups in this situation?

    a. Use global groups to provide access to resources and domain local groups to contain user account members.

    b. Use only local groups to manage all access because you do not have enough domains to merit using universal groups.

    c. Use domain local and universal groups to manage resources and global groups to contain user account members.

    d. Use only universal groups because they are the best management technique when you have more than two domains.

17. When a DNS server converts a computer name to a dotted decimal address, this is called _____.

    a. name recognition

    b. name resolution

    c. piping

    d. pinging

18. The default accounts in Windows Server 2003 are located in the _____.

    a. Builtin folder

    b. Domain Controllers OU

    c. NETUsers OU

    d. Users folder

19. You need to configure accounts so they cannot log onto the network on Friday nights between 8:00 p.m. and midnight. How can you do this? (Choose all that apply.)

    a. Use the Computer Management tool to configure shared access.

    b. Use the Logon Hours button on the Account tab for the properties of each account.

    c. Configure the General tab for the properties of the default user account template.

    d. Use the Profiles button on the Advanced tab in the System option of Control Panel.

20. Which of the following is (are) properties of groups? (Choose all that apply.)

    a. Member Of

    b. Members

    c. General

    d. Managed By

CASE PROJECTS

Case Project Background

Moose Jaw Outfitters is a mail-order company that sells outdoor clothing in Canada and the United States. Although they are known as a mail-order company, Moose Jaw Outfitters does most of its business via telephone and an Internet Web site. Actual orders sent through the mail represent their third largest source of sales. The company also has two large outlet stores, one in Winnipeg, Canada, and another in St. Cloud, Minnesota, which represent their fourth largest source of income.

The Winnipeg store is the location of the main headquarters for Moose Jaw Outfitters, where the company employs customer service representatives to take telephone orders, maintains a Web site for Internet orders, processes mail orders, keeps its main inventory of products, and handles their general business and accounting functions. There are clothing factories in both Winnipeg and St. Cloud. The St. Cloud location also employs customer service representatives for telephone orders. The company has hired you through Bayside IT Services to help their IT Department implement new servers. Most of the IT Department members are located in Winnipeg, but the St. Cloud site also has some IT staff. Both sites have computer resources that are networked via local area networks linked together through a wide area network. The company wants to implement Active Directory for their networks in Winnipeg and St. Cloud. The Winnipeg location has a medium-sized network of 170 users, and five subnets using TCP/IP. That location also has Internet connectivity and maintains a Web server. Both sites have Customer Service, Business, Inventory, and IT Department members. The Winnipeg location houses most of the management team, but St. Cloud, which has two subnets, has a vice president in charge of that location, an operations manager, and supervisors for the Customer Service, Business, Inventory, and IT groups at that location. Winnipeg also has a Marketing Department.

Case Project 4-1: A Presentation for the IT Department

The IT Department is very inexperienced with Active Directory. Create a brief presentation for them about Active Directory, including its purpose, Active Directory elements, how it is backed up, and the information contained in Active Directory.

Case Project 4-2: Implementing an Active Directory Structure

After the presentation, the IT Department asks for your preliminary evaluation of how Active Directory might be implemented. On the basis of what you already know about this company, explain how you would use the following Active Directory elements and why: OUs, domains, trees, forests, and sites.

Case Project 4-3: Setting Up Accounts

Moose Jaw Outfitters has decided to have the managers or supervisor's of each department create and manage the accounts for the employees they supervise. Prepare a set of general instructions showing how to set up a user account.

Case Project 4-4: Creating Roaming Profiles

Each department has decided to create roaming profiles for its account users. Discuss the general steps for two possible methods they can use to create roaming profiles. Which method do you recommend?

5

CONFIGURING, MANAGING, AND TROUBLESHOOTING RESOURCE ACCESS

After reading this chapter and completing the exercises, you will be able to:

- ♦ Manage object security for files and folders
- ♦ Configure shared folders and share permissions
- ♦ Publish a shared folder in Active Directory
- ♦ Configure Web sharing
- ♦ Troubleshoot a security conflict
- ♦ Implement the Distributed File System
- ♦ Configure disk quotas

Users benefit from access to Windows Server 2003 through using vital resources, such as documents, spreadsheets, databases, and software. Windows Server 2003 offers many ways to make resources available to users, including ways to secure resources so that only the designated users can access them. Some information stored on servers is confidential and must be protected. Other information is targeted to reach as many users as possible, such as on a Web site.

In this chapter, you will learn how to manage network resource objects, such as folders and files. You'll learn how to set up attributes and permissions for these objects, as well as how to set up auditing and troubleshoot access problems. You will learn how to create and manage a shared folder, how to publish a shared folder in Active Directory, and how to configure Web sharing. To ensure broad and fail-safe access to shared information, you'll learn how to set up and manage the Microsoft Distributed File System. Finally, you will learn how to set up disk quotas, so that your server does not run out of disk space for the resources that are managed and shared.

MANAGING OBJECTS AND OBJECT SECURITY

In Chapter 4, you learned how to create and manage groups. The purpose in creating groups is to help you to manage objects on a local server and in Active Directory. The objects you manage through groups include disk volumes, folders, files, printers, software, program processes, and network services. Each of these objects has an access control list (ACL) to which you can add a group, such as a domain local group, so that an object can be managed as a shared resource. Access to objects is controlled through common security techniques. The object security techniques that you learn in the next sections include the following object access controls for folders and files:

- Attributes
- Permissions
- Auditing
- Ownership

Configuring Folder and File Attributes

Use of **attributes** is retained in the File Allocation Table (FAT) file system and the NT File System (NTFS) in Windows Server 2003 as a carryover from earlier DOS-based systems. Also, the attributes provide a partial migration path to convert files and directories from a Novell NetWare file server. DOS and NetWare systems use file attributes as a form of security and file management. Attributes are stored as header information with each folder and file, along with other characteristics including volume label, designation as a subfolder, date of creation, and time of creation.

FAT File System

The folder and file attributes available in a FAT-formatted Windows Server 2003 disk are read-only, hidden, and archive. They are accessed from the General tab when you right-click a folder or file and click Properties, such as from My Computer or Windows Explorer. If you check read-only for a folder, the folder is read-only, but not the files in the folder. This means the folder cannot be deleted or renamed from the command prompt. Also, the folder cannot be deleted or renamed by a user other than one belonging to the Administrators group. If a server administrator attempts to delete or rename the folder, a warning message states the folder is read-only and asks whether to proceed. Most Windows Server 2003 server administrators leave the read-only box blank and set the equivalent protection in permissions instead, because the read-only permissions apply to the folder and can be inherited by its files.

 Folders can be marked as hidden to prevent users from viewing their contents, which is a carryover from MS-DOS operating systems. The hidden attribute can be defeated by any Windows 98, Windows NT, Windows 2000, Windows XP, or Windows 2003 client if the user selects the view hidden files and folders option from the View or Tools menus (depending on the version of Windows) in Windows Explorer or My Computer.

The archive attribute is checked to indicate the folder or file needs to be backed up because the folder or file is new or changed. Most network administrators ignore the folder archive attribute, but instead rely on it for files. Files, but not folders, are automatically flagged to archive when they are changed. File server backup systems can be set to detect files with the archive attribute to ensure those files are backed up. The backup system ensures each file is saved following the same folder or subfolder scheme as on the server.

NT File System

An NTFS volume also has the read-only, hidden, and archive attributes; plus it has the index, compress, and encrypt attributes. The read-only and Hidden attributes are on the General tab in an NTFS folder's or file's properties dialog box and the other attributes, called extended attributes, are accessed by clicking the General tab's Advanced button (see Figure 5-1). When you make a change to one of the attributes in the Advanced

Attributes dialog box in a folder's properties, you have the option to apply that change to only the folder and the files in that folder or to apply the change to the folder, its files, and all subfolders and files within the folder (make sure you click the OK button when you return to the General tab).

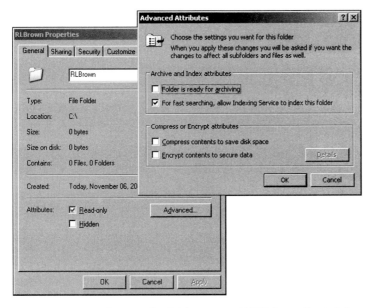

Figure 5-1   Attributes of a folder on an NTFS formatted disk

Index Attribute   The NTFS index attribute is used to index the folder and file contents so that text, creation date, and other properties can be quickly searched in Windows Server 2003 using the Search button in My Computer or Windows Explorer.

 The index attribute relies on two preceding steps in order to work. The first step is that the Indexing Service must already be installed as a Windows Server 2003 component (see Chapter 3). Also, the service should be set to start automatically after it is installed by clicking Start, pointing to All Programs, pointing to Administrative Tools, clicking Computer Management, double-clicking Services and Applications in the left pane (if necessary), clicking Services in the left pane, double-clicking Indexing Service in the right pane, and setting the Startup type box to Automatic.

A folder and its contents can be stored on the disk in compressed format, which is an option that enables you to reduce the amount of disk space used for files, particularly in situations in which disk space is limited or for directories that are accessed infrequently, such as those used to store accounting data from a previous fiscal year. Compression saves space, but it takes longer to access information because each file must be decompressed before it is read.

 If you are concerned about security and want to use the encrypt attribute, do not compress files because compressed files cannot be encrypted.

Encrypt Attribute   The NTFS encrypt attribute protects folders and files so that only the user who encrypts the folder or file is able to read it. As a server administrator, you might use this option to protect certain system files or new software files that you are not yet ready to release for general use. An encrypted folder or file uses the Microsoft **Encrypting File System (EFS)**, which sets up a unique, private encryption key that is associated with the user account that encrypted the folder or file. The file is protected from network intruders and in situations in which a server or hard drive is stolen. When you move an encrypted file to another folder, that file remains encrypted, even if you also rename it. You can decrypt a folder or file by using Windows Explorer or My Computer to remove the encrypt attribute and then apply the change. Folders and files can also be encrypted or decrypted by using the cipher command at the command prompt (type cipher /? to view the command's switch options).

Activity 5-1: Encrypting the Contents of a Folder

Time Required: Approximately 15 minutes

Objective: Encrypt the files in a folder.

Description: There have been cases in the news about theft in organizations in which a computer's drive has been stolen because of its valuable contents, such as business secrets or information crucial to national security. One way to provide security in these situations is to use the Encrypting File System to protect files. In this activity, you practice encrypting the contents of a folder.

1. Use My Computer or Windows Explorer to create a new folder. For example, click **Start**, click **My Computer**, double-click a local drive (NTFS formatted), such as **Local Disk C:**, click **File**, point to **New**, click **Folder**, and enter a folder name that is a combination of your last name and initials, such as RLBrown, and press **Enter**. Find a file to copy into the folder, such as a text or another file already in the root of drive C. To copy the file, right-click it, drag it to the folder you created, and click **Copy Here**.

2. Right-click your new folder, such as **RLBrown**, and click **Properties**. Make sure that the **General** tab is displayed, and if it is not, then click it.

3. What attributes are already checked? Record your observations.

4. Click the **Advanced** button. Record which attributes are already checked in the Advanced Attributes dialog box.

5. Check **Encrypt contents to secure data**, and then click **OK**.

6. Click **Apply**.

7. Be certain that **Apply changes to this folder, subfolders and files** is selected, and click **OK**.

8. Make a note of how you would verify that the file you copied into the folder is now encrypted. How would you decrypt the entire folder contents?

9. Decrypt the folder so that you can use it for another activity.

10. Close the folder's **Properties** dialog box.

11. Close My Computer or Windows Explorer.

Configuring Folder and File Permissions

Permissions control access to an object, such as a folder or file. For example, when you configure a folder so that a domain local group has access to only read the contents of that folder, you are configuring permissions. At the same time you are configuring that folder's access control list (ACL) of security descriptors.

Use the Add and Remove buttons on the folder properties Security tab (see Figure 5-2) to change which groups and users have permissions to a folder. To add a group, for example, click Add, click the Advanced button, click Find Now, scroll to the group you want to add, double-click that group, click OK, and then select the permissions. Also, for groups and users that are already set up with permissions, you can modify the permissions by clicking the group and checking or removing checks in the Allow and Deny columns as shown in Figure 5-2.

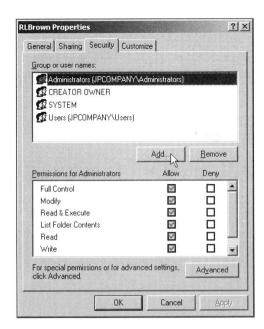

Figure 5-2   Folder properties Security tab

Table 5-1 lists the folder and file permissions supported by NTFS.

Table 5-1   NTFS folder and file permissions

Permission	Description	Applies to
Full Control	Can read, add, delete, execute, and modify files plus change permissions and attributes, and take ownership	Folders and files
Modify	Can read, add, delete, execute, and modify files; cannot delete subfolders and their file contents, change permissions, or take ownership	Folders and file
Read & Execute	Implies the capabilities of both List Folder Contents and Read (traverse folders, view file contents, view attributes and permissions, and execute files)	Folders and files
List Folder Contents	Can list (traverse) files in the folder or switch to a subfolder, view folder attributes and permissions, and execute files, but cannot view file contents	Folders only
Read	Can view file contents, view folder attributes and permissions, but cannot traverse folders or execute files	Folders and files
Write	Can create files, write data to files, append data to files, create folders, delete files (but not subfolders and their files), and modify folder and file attributes	Folders and files

If none of the Allow or Deny boxes are checked, then the associated group or user has no access to the folder. Also, when a new folder or file is created, it typically inherits permissions from the parent folder or from the root. Finally, if the Deny box is checked, this overrides any other access. For instance, if an account in a group has Allow checked for a specific permission, but the group to which the account belongs has Deny checked—Deny prevails, even for the account with Allow checked.

Activity 5-2: Configuring Folder Permissions

Time Required: Approximately 10 minutes

Objective: Configure permissions on a folder so that users can modify the contents.

Description: In some organizations, there is a group of server operators who perform the day-to-day management of servers for an organization. Assume that you need to create a Utilities folder for the server operators so that they can place new utilities in the folder, plus list the folder's contents and execute utilities out of that folder.

1. Use My Computer or Windows Explorer to create a folder called Utilities plus your initials, such as UtilitiesJP.

2. Right-click the new folder, click **Properties,** and then click the **Security** tab.

3. What users and groups already have permissions to access the folder? Click each group and user to determine what permissions they have, and record your results. Notice that some boxes are checked and deactivated.

4. Click the **Add** button.

5. Click the **Advanced** button. Click **Find Now.** Double-click **Server Operators** in the list at the bottom of the box. Click **OK.**

6. Click **Server Operators** to highlight this group. What permissions do they have by default?

7. Click the **Allow** box for **Modify.**

8. Click **OK** in the folder's Properties dialog box.

9. Close My Computer or Windows Explorer.

As you noticed in Activity 5-2, some of the Allow boxes for permissions are checked and deactivated. These are **inherited permissions**, which means that the same permissions on a parent object, such as the root folder in this case, apply to the child objects such as files and subfolders within the parent folder. If you want to change inherited permissions that cause Allow or Deny boxes to be deactivated (and checked), you can do this by removing the inherited permissions.

Activity 5-3: Removing Inherited Permissions

Time Required: Approximately 5 minutes

Objective: Remove inherited permissions on a folder.

Description: Often you want to remove inherited permissions for specific situations. In this activity, you reconfigure the inherited permissions so that you can remove the Users group from those who can access the Utilities folder.

1. Using Windows Explorer or My Computer, find the Utilities folder that you created in the last activity. Right-click the folder, and click **Properties.**

2. Click the **Security** tab.

3. Click the **Advanced** button.

4. Remove the check mark from the box for **Allow inheritable permissions from the parent to propagate to this object and all child objects. Include these with entries explicitly defined here.**

5. Notice that there are three options from which to select, as shown in Figure 5-3. One is to copy back the inherited permissions (if you have removed them already), one is to remove the inherited permissions, and one is to cancel this operation. Click **Remove.**

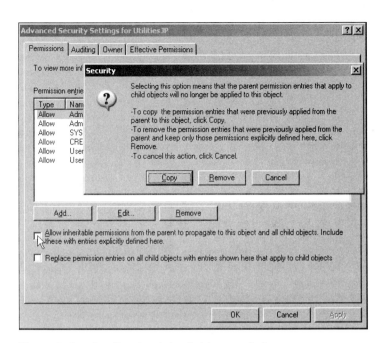

Figure 5-3   Configuring inheritable permissions

6. Click **OK**.

7. Compare the groups that now remain to those you recorded in Step 3 of Activity 5-2. Notice that the User group is no longer on the list for access.

8. Click **OK** in the folder's Properties dialog box.

9. Close My Computer or Windows Explorer.

If you need to customize permissions, you have the option to set up special permissions for a particular group or user. Figure 5-4 illustrates the special permissions that you can set up and Table 5-2 explains each of the special permissions.

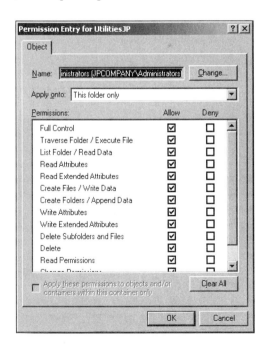

Figure 5-4   Special permissions

Table 5-2   NTFS folder and file special permissions

Permission	Description	Applies to
Full Control	Can read, add, delete, execute, and modify files, plus change permissions and attributes, and take ownership	Folders and files
Traverse Folder / Execute File	Can list the contents of a folder and execute program files in that folder; keep in mind that all users are automatically granted this permission via the Everyone and Users groups, unless it is removed or denied by you	Folders and files
List Folder / Read Data	Can list the contents of folders and subfolders and read the contents of files	Folders and files
Read Attributes	Can view folder and file attributes (read-only and hidden)	Folders and files
Read Extended Attributes	Enables the viewing of extended attributes (index, compress, encrypt)	Folders and files
Create Files / Write Data	Can add new files to a folder and modify, append to, or write over file contents	Folders and files
Create Folders / Append Data	Can add new folders and add new data at the end of files, but otherwise cannot delete, write over, or modify data	Folders and files
Write Attributes	Can add or remove the read-only and hidden attributes	Folders and files
Write Extended Attributes	Can add or remove the archive, index, compress, and encrypt attributes	Folders and files
Delete Subfolders and Files	Can delete subfolders and files (the following Delete permission is not required)	Folders and files
Delete	Can delete the specific subfolder or file to which this permission is attached	Folders and files
Read Permissions	Can view the permissions (ACL information) associated with a folder or file (but does not imply you can change them)	Folders and files
Change Permissions	Can change the permissions associated with a folder or file	Folders and files
Take Ownership	Can take ownership of the folder or file (Read Permissions and Change Permissions automatically accompany this permission)	Folders and files

Activity 5-4: Configuring Special Permissions

Time Required: Approximately 15 minutes

Objective: Configure special permissions for a folder to give a group extra access.

Description: Sometimes the regular NTFS permissions do not quite enable you to create exactly the type of access you want on a folder. In this activity, you set up special permissions for the Server Operators group on the Utilities folder you created and configured earlier.

1. Using Windows Explorer or My Computer, find the Utilities folder that you created in Activity 5-2. Right-click the folder, and click **Properties**.

2. Click the **Security** tab.

3. Click the **Advanced** button.

4. Click **Server Operators** in the Permissions entries box, and click the **Edit** button.

5. Notice that the Server Operators group does not have permissions to delete subfolders and files. You want them to have these permissions so that they can remove old utilities and keep the Utilities folder contents up to date. Click the **Allow** box for **Delete Subfolders and Files**.

6. Click **OK** in the Permissions Entry dialog box.

7. Click **OK** in the Advanced Security Setting for Utilities dialog box.

8. Click **OK** in the Properties dialog box.

9. Close My Computer or Windows Explorer.

Microsoft provides guidelines for setting permissions as follows:

- Protect the \Windows folder that contains operating system files on Windows 2003 servers and its subfolders from general users through allowing limited access, such as Read & Execute and List Folder Contents or by just using the special permission to Traverse Folder / Execute File, but give the Administrators group Full Control access.

- Protect server utility folders, such as for backup software and network management, with access permissions only for the Administrators, Server Operators, and Backup Operators groups.

- Protect software application folders with Read & Execute and Write to enable users to run applications and write temporary files.

- Create publicly used folders to have Modify access, so users have broad access except to take ownership, set permissions, and delete subfolders and files.

- Provide users Full Control of their own home folders.

- Remove general access groups, such as Everyone and Users from confidential folders, as in those used for personal mail, for sensitive files, or for software development projects.

Always err on the side of too much security. It is easier, in terms of human relations, to give users more permissions later than it is to take away permissions.

Configuring Folder and File Auditing

Accessing folders and files can be tracked by setting up **auditing,** which in Windows Server 2003 enables you to track activity on a folder or file, such as read or write activity. Some organizations choose to implement auditing on folders and files that involve financially sensitive information, such as those involving accounting and payroll. Other organizations monitor access to research or special marketing project information stored in folders and files. Windows Server 2003 NTFS folders and files enable you to audit a combination of any or all of the activities listed as special permissions in Table 5-2. When you set up auditing, the options for each type of access are to track successful and failed attempts. For example, consider a situation in which your organization's financial auditors specify that all accounting files in the Accounting folder must create an "audit trail" for each time a person who has access changes the contents of a file in the folder. Further, the financial auditors may want to verify that only groups that have access to write to files are those in the Accounting and Administrator groups. You would set up auditing by configuring the folder's security to audit each successful type of write event, such as Create Files / Write Data and Create Folders / Append Data. For extra information, you might track permission, attribute, and ownership changes by monitoring successful attempts to Write Attributes, Write Extended Attributes, Change Permissions, and Take Ownership. Audited events are recorded in the Windows 2003 security log that is accessed from Event Viewer (see Chapter 12).

Activity 5-5: Auditing a Folder

Time Required: Approximately 10 minutes

Objective: Configure auditing on a folder to monitor how it is accessed and who is making changes to the folder.

Description: In a meeting with the server operators in your organization, several of the operators mention that someone has been putting programs in the Utilities folder other than those the group has agreed to have in that folder, including games. One way to track the culprit and to determine if there is a problem with the way you have configured permissions for that folder is to set up auditing, which you do in this activity.

1. Find the Utilities folder you created by using Windows Explorer or My Computer. Right-click the folder, and click **Properties**.

2. Click the **Security** tab.

3. Click the **Advanced** button.

4. Click the **Auditing** tab.

5. Click **Add**, click **Advanced**, click **Find Now**, double-click the **Server Operators** group, and click **OK**.

6. Click the Successful boxes for **Create Files / Write Data**, **Create Folders / Append Data**, **Delete Subfolders and Files**, and **Delete**, as shown in Figure 5-5. This enables you to monitor the server operators who are creating new information in the folder and who might be deleting information after they create it. Click **OK**. How would you configure auditing instead to track everyone who might be creating new information or deleting information in the folder?

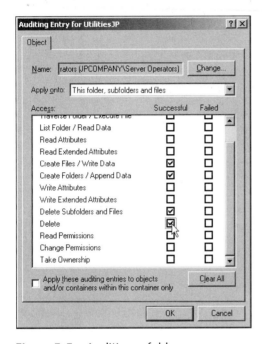

Figure 5-5   Auditing a folder

7. Notice that there is now an entry for Server Operators in the Auditing entries box.

8. Click **OK**, and click **OK** again.

9. Close My Computer or Windows Explorer.

Troubleshooting Auditing

To fully configure auditing for an object—an account or folder, for example—you need to set up an auditing policy. If the policy is not set up, you may see an error message when you configure auditing in the object's properties, such as when you configure auditing for a folder. For a standalone server, you configure the audit policy for the local computer, and for DCs in an Active Directory domain, you configure the domain security policy. You need to log on using an account that has Administrator privileges.

Activity 5-6: Configuring an Auditing Policy

Time Required: Approximately 10 minutes

Objective: Configure an auditing policy in the default security policies for a domain.

Description: After you configure auditing in the Utility folder's properties, you also need to configure an auditing policy, which you accomplish in this activity.

1. Click **Start**, point to **All Programs**, point to **Administrative Tools**, and click **Domain Security Policy**.

2. Double-click **Local Policies** in the tree, if necessary to display the elements under it. Click **Audit Policy** in the tree (see Figure 5-6). What options are available in the right pane?

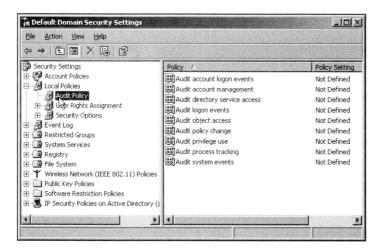

Figure 5-6   Accessing the Audit Policy

3. In the right pane, double-click **Audit object access**.

4. Click **Define these policy settings**.

5. Click the boxes for **Success** and **Failure** (see Figure 5-7).

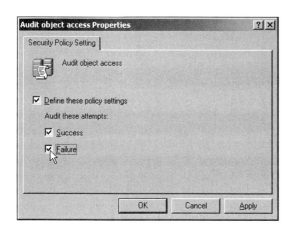

Figure 5-7   Configuring Audit Policy

6. Click **OK**.

7. Close the **Default Domain Security Settings** window.

Configuring Folder and File Ownership

With permissions and auditing set up, you may want to verify the **ownership** of a folder. Folders are first owned by the account that creates them, such as the Administrator account. Folder owners have the ability to change permissions for the folders they create. Also, ownership can be transferred only by having the Take Ownership special permission or Full Control Permission (which includes Take Ownership). These permissions enable a user to take control of a folder or file and become its owner. Taking ownership is the only way to shift control from one account to another. The Administrators group always has the ability to take control of any folder, regardless of the permissions, particularly because there are instances in which the server administrator needs to take ownership of a folder, such as when someone leaves an organization. The general steps you use to take ownership of a folder, using your account with Administrator privileges, are as follows:

1. Right-click the folder for which you want to take ownership, and click **Properties**.

2. Click the **Security** tab.

3. Click the **Advanced** button.

4. Click the **Owner** tab.

5. In the Name box, click the **Administrators group**, as shown in Figure 5-8.

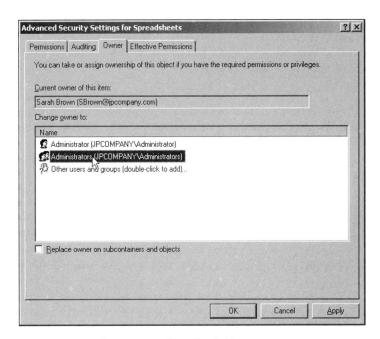

Figure 5-8   Taking ownership of a folder

6. Click **OK**.

7. Click **OK** in the folder's Properties dialog box.

CONFIGURING SHARED FOLDERS AND SHARED FOLDER PERMISSIONS

Along with establishing folder permissions, auditing, and ownership, a folder can be set up as a shared folder for users to access over the network. To share a server folder, access the Sharing tab in the folder properties dialog box (right-click the folder and click Sharing and Security). As Figure 5-9 shows, the Sharing tab has two main options: to share or to not share the folder. To share a folder so network users can access or map it, click the Share this folder option button. The Maximum allowed option button enables as many accesses as there are Windows Server 2003 client access licenses. The other option, Allow this number of users, enables you to specify a limit to the number of simultaneous users. This is one way to ensure the licensing restrictions for software are followed.

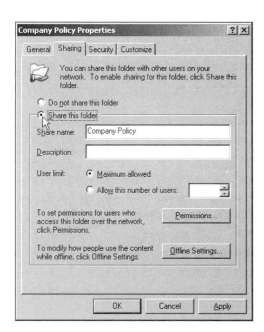

Figure 5-9   Folder Sharing tab options

For example, consider that you have an accounting software package in a folder and have only two licenses. In this case, you would set the Allow this number of users parameter to 2 so the license requirement is honored.

You can set permissions for the share from this tab by clicking the Permissions button. **Share permissions** for an object can differ from basic access permissions set through the Security tab, and the permissions are cumulative, with the exception of permissions that are denied. There are three share permissions that are associated with a folder (see Figure 5-10):

- *Full Control*—Provides full access to the folder including the ability to take control or change share permissions

- *Change*—Enables users to read, add, modify, execute, and delete files

- *Read*—Permits groups or users to read and execute files

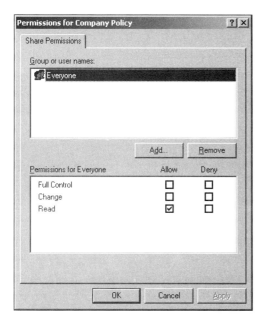

Figure 5-10   Share permissions

Before setting the share permissions, first make sure you have selected the appropriate groups and users, such as by specifying the Everyone or Users groups for a publicly accessed folder. Use the Add button in the Permissions dialog box to set up additional groups and the Remove button to delete a group's access to a shared folder. For example, you can remove a group by highlighting it in the list box in the Group or user names dialog box and clicking Remove. To set the share permissions, highlight a group, and click the appropriate Allow and Deny boxes for the permissions.

The Offline Settings button in Figure 5-9 enables you to set up a folder so that it can be accessed by a client even when the client computer is not connected to the network, such as when the network connection is lost or when a user disconnects a laptop computer to take home. "Offline" in this situation means that the folder is cached on the client computer's hard drive for continued access after losing the network connection and that the folder location remains unchanged in Windows Explorer and My Computer. When the network connection is resumed, any offline files that have been modified can be synchronized with the network versions of the files. If two or more users attempt to synchronize a file, they have the option of choosing whose version to use or of saving both versions. A folder can be cached in three ways:

- *Only the files and programs that users specify will be available offline*—Files and programs are cached only per the user's request per each document (the default option).

- *All files and programs that users open from the share will be automatically available offline*—Files and programs are cached without user intervention, which means that all files in the folder which are opened by the client or which are executed by the client are cached automatically.

- *Files or programs from the share will not be available offline*—Files and programs are not cached on the computer's hard drive.

When you share a folder, there is an option to hide that shared folder so that it does not appear on a browser list, as in My Network Places in Windows 2000 or XP clients, or in Network Neighborhood in Windows 98 or Windows NT clients. To hide a share, place the dollar sign ($) just after its name. For instance, if the Share name text box contains the share name Budget, you can hide the share by entering Budget$. (This is an actual example of what one university does to discourage general scanning of a folder containing budget worksheets. However, departmental accounting technicians who know of the folder's existence can map it to help with budget planning.)

 When you right-click on a folder to view its properties, the sharing option on the shortcut menu may be missing or you may not see the Sharing tab. You can troubleshoot this problem by making sure that the Server Service is started, and even if it is, you can restart it in case the service is hung (make sure no users are on if you restart it). To start or restart the Server Service, click Start, point to All Programs, point to Administrative Tools, and click Computer Management. Double-click Services under the Services and Applications container, scroll to find the Server Service, and check for "Started" in the status column. Right-click the service; if it is stopped, click Start, and if it is already started, click Restart.

Activity 5-7: Sharing a folder

Time Required: Approximately 15 minutes

Objective: Configure a shared folder, share permissions, and offline access.

Description: As a server administrator, one of the most important tasks you perform is to enable folder sharing. In this activity, you configure the folder you created in Activity 5-1 for sharing.

1. Use My Computer or Windows Explorer to find the folder you created in Activity 5-1, such as RLBrown.

2. Right-click the folder, and click **Sharing and Security**.

3. Click **Share this folder**. What name automatically appears in the Share name box?

4. In the Share name box, enter **Data Files**.

5. Click the **Allow this number of users** option button, and enter **15** in the box, to limit simultaneous access to 15 users.

6. Click the **Permissions** button.

7. Click **Add**, click **Advanced**, and click **Find Now**.

8. Locate the Domain Managers group that you created in Chapter 4, such as DomainMgrsJP, and double-click it (remember that you create access to resources, such as shared folders by using domain local groups).

9. Click **OK**.

10. In the Permissions for (folder) dialog box, click **Everyone**, and click the **Remove** button to remove the Everyone group from having access to this shared folder (see Figure 5-11).

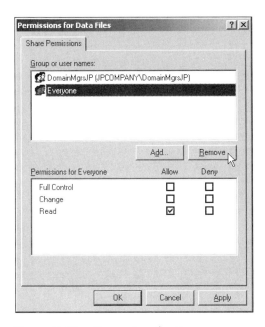

Figure 5-11   Removing the Everyone group from access

11. Make sure that the Domain Managers group, such as DomainMgrsJP, is highlighted, and that there is a check mark in the **Allow** box for **Read**.

12. Click the **Allow** box for **Change** so that members of the Domain Managers group can add or delete files to this folder.

13. Click **OK**.

14. Click the **Offline Settings** button.

15. Click **All files and programs that users open from the share will be automatically available offline**. What does selecting this option accomplish? Click **OK**.

16. Click **OK** in the folder's Properties dialog box.

17. Close My Computer or Windows Explorer.

Activity 5-8: Accessing a Shared Folder

Time Required: Approximately 10 minutes

Objective: Access the shared folder you configured.

Description: In this activity, you practice connecting to the server and accessing the shared folder that you configured in Activity 5-7. This enables you to make sure that it is properly set up and can be accessed over the network.

1. Click **Start** and click **My Computer**.

2. Click the down arrow in the Address box, and click **My Network Places**.

3. Double-click **Entire Network**.

4. Double-click **Microsoft Windows Network**.

5. Double-click your domain name, such as jpcompany.

6. Double-click the name of your server.

7. Double-click the **Data Files** shared folder. You should see a warning box that access is denied, as in Figure 5-12. Why do you see this warning? Make a note of the location of the Data Files Folder for use in Activity 5-9.

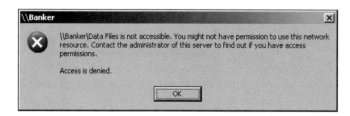

Figure 5-12   Access denied warning

8. Click **OK**.

9. Minimize the server's window (leaving it open in the background).

10. Click **Start** and click **My Computer**. Locate the folder you configured in Activity 5-7, such as RLBrown, right-click it and click **Sharing and Security**. (Remember that the name of the folder in My Computer is RLBrown, for example, but the name for display as a shared folder over the network is Data Files.)

11. Click the **Permissions** button. Click **Add**, click **Advanced**, click **Find Now**, and double-click the **Administrators** group. Click **OK**. Notice that this group has Allow checked for Read by default.

12. Click **OK,** and click **OK** again.

13. Maximize the server window that you minimized in Step 9.

14. Double-click **Data Files**. You now have access to this shared folder.

15. Close all open windows.

PUBLISHING A SHARED FOLDER IN ACTIVE DIRECTORY

One reason for having Active Directory is to enable certain objects to be "published" so that users can find and access those objects quickly. **Publishing** an object means that it is made available for users to access when they view Active Directory contents and that the information associated with the object can be replicated. For example, a shared folder or a shared printer can be published in Active Directory for clients to access. Publishing an object also makes it easier to find when a user searches for that object, such as by using My Network Places in Windows 2000 or Windows XP (see Figure 5-13). Once an object is published, information associated with that object is duplicated in copies of Active Directory that are kept when there are multiple domain controllers on a network. This enables a published object to be accessed even when one domain controller is down.

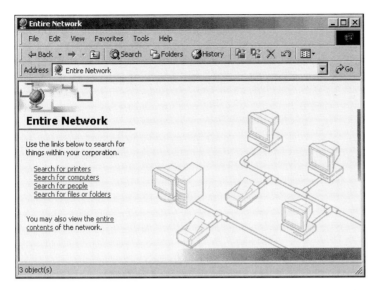

Figure 5-13   Searching by using My Network Places in Windows 2000

Active Directory search capabilities are automatically built into all Windows 2000 Professional and Windows XP Professional clients. Earlier Windows-based operating systems such as Windows 95 and Windows 98 are able to search Active Directory when the **Directory Service Client (DSClient)** software is installed on those systems. The Directory Service Client software is available from Microsoft as the program, Dsclient.exe.

The Directory Service Client software installs Active Directory search features at the client, such as the ability to search for a printer even if the client does not know the specific name of the printer. To search Active Directory for a printer using Windows 98 for example, click Start, point to Find, and click Printers (Printers is a new option added by the Directory Service Client).

When you publish an object, you can publish it to be shared for domainwide access or to be shared and managed through an organizational unit (OU). A shared folder, for example, might be used only by a department in a company. If you publish the shared folder in that department's OU, then the accounts (users) that manage that OU can also manage the shared folder and how it is accessed.

Activity 5-9: Publishing a Shared Folder

Time Required: Approximately 5 minutes

Objective: Publish a shared folder in Active Directory.

Description: In this activity you learn how to use the Active Directory Users and Computers tool to publish the shared folder you configured in Activity 5-7.

1. Click **Start**, point to **All Programs**, point to **Administrative Tools**, and click **Active Directory Users and Computers**.

2. Double-click the **Users** folder in the tree (or you could double-click an OU at this point to control administration of the published folder from an OU by delegating authority over the OU).

3. Right-click the **Users** folder, and point to **New**. What are two objects that you can publish using this menu?

4. Click **Shared Folder**.

5. Enter the name for the published shared folder, such as Data Files. Enter the network path to the share, such as *servername*\Data Files. Click **OK**. Notice that the shared folder is now one of the objects listed in the right pane within the Users (or OU) folder.

6. Close the **Active Directory Users and Computers** window.

CONFIGURING WEB SHARING

Some folders and files stored in Windows Server 2003 may be intended for HTML or FTP access through a Web server. When you install the Internet Information Services (IIS) on a Windows 2003 server, a new Web Sharing tab becomes available from a folder's properties dialog box (see Figure 5-14). This tab enables you to configure the folder for access and application permissions when it is made available on the Web.

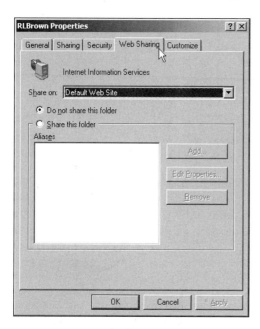

Figure 5-14   Web Sharing tab

    IIS is a Windows component that is part of the Application Server component that can be installed by using the Control Panel Add or Remove Programs option (refer to Chapters 3 and 8).

Tables 5-3 and 5-4 describe the access and application permissions that you can select.

Table 5-3   Web sharing access permissions

Access Permission	Description
Read	Enables clients to read and display the contents of folders and files via the Internet or an intranet
Write	Enables clients to modify the contents of folders and files; includes the ability to upload files through FTP
Script source access	Enables clients to view the contents of scripts containing commands to execute Web functions
Directory browsing	Enables clients to browse the folder and subfolders; this is helpful, for instance, with FTP access

Table 5-4   Web sharing application permissions

Application Permission	Description
None	No access to execute a script or application
Scripts	Enables the client to run scripts to perform Web-based functions
Execute (includes scripts)	Enables clients to execute programs and scripts via the Internet or an intranet or virtual private network (VPN) connection

Activity 5-10: Configuring Web Sharing

Time Required: Approximately 10 minutes

Objective: Configure a folder for Web sharing.

Description: On a Web server, you might have a folder that is shared over the network for programmers and that is also made available through the Internet. In this activity, you practice configuring the folder you created in Activity 5-1 (and set up for sharing in Activity 5-7) so that it is also configured for Web sharing. IIS must already be installed on the server.

1. Use My Computer or Windows Explorer to find the folder that you created in Activity 5-1, such as RLBrown.

2. Right-click the folder, click **Properties**, and click the **Web Sharing** tab.

3. Use the Share on box to specify Default Web Site (which is the default selection) on which the folder will be shared.

4. Click **Share this folder**.

5. Specify an alias for the folder, which enables clients to view it by a name other than the actual folder's name, such as Data Files.

6. Under Access permissions, click **Read**, if it is not already selected.

7. Under Application permissions, click **Execute (includes scripts)** as shown in Figure 5-15.

8. Click **OK**, and click **OK** again to save your changes.

9. Close My Computer or Windows Explorer.

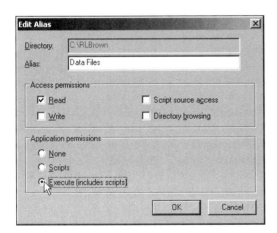

Figure 5-15   Configuring Web sharing permissions

TROUBLESHOOTING A SECURITY CONFLICT

Sometimes you set up access for a user, but find that the user does not actually have the type of access you set up. Consider the example of Cleo Jackson, an English professor who maintains a shared subfolder called Assignments for his students from the account CJackson. Assignments is a subfolder under the parent folder English, which contains folders used by all English professors. CJackson needs to update files, copy in new files, and delete files. As Administrator, you have granted CJackson Modify access permissions to Assignments. However, you omitted the step of reviewing the groups to which CJackson belongs, such as the Paper group, which consists of Cleo Jackson and the student newspaper staff. The Paper group has been denied all access to the English folder and all of its subfolders. When Cleo Jackson attempts to copy a file to the Assignments folder, he receives an access denied message.

To troubleshoot the problem, you should review the folder permissions and share permissions for the CJackson account and for all of the groups to which CJackson belongs. In this case, because the Paper group is denied access, CJackson is also denied. The easiest solution is to remove CJackson from the Paper group and perhaps create a group of English professors, such as EngProfs, who all have access to the same resources as the Paper group.

Windows 2000 Server and Windows Server 2003 make determining a user's or group's effective permissions much simpler than previous versions of Windows. In these server operating systems, the properties of a folder or file include an Effective Permissions tab. To access this tab, right-click a folder or file, click Properties, click the Security tab, click the Advanced button, and click the Effective Permissions tab. Using the Effective Permissions tab, you can view the effective permissions assigned to a user or group. The calculation takes into account group membership as well as permission inheritance. After the calculation is complete, a user's or group's effective permissions are indicated with a check mark beside them.

When you troubleshoot permissions, also take into account what happens when a folder or files in a folder are copied or moved. When a file is copied, the original file remains intact and a copy is made in another folder. Moving a file causes it to be deleted from the original location and placed in a different folder on the same or on a different volume. Copying and moving works the same for a folder, but the entire folder contents (files and subfolders) are copied or moved. When a file or folder is created, copied, or moved, the file and folder permissions can be affected in the following ways (depending on how inheritance is set up in the target location):

- A newly created file inherits the permissions already set up in a folder.

- A file that is copied from one folder to another on the same volume inherits the permissions of the folder to which it is copied.

- A file or folder that is moved from one folder to another on the same volume takes with it the permissions it had in the original folder. For example, if the original folder had Read permissions for the Users domain local group and the folder to which it is transplanted has Modify permissions for Users, that file (or folder) will still only have Read permissions.

- A file or folder that is moved or copied to a folder on a different volume inherits the permissions of the folder to which it is moved or copied.

- A file or folder that is moved or copied from an NTFS volume to a folder in a FAT volume is not protected by NTFS permissions, but it does inherit share permissions if they are assigned to the FAT folder.

- A file or folder that is moved or copied from a FAT volume to a folder in an NTFS volume inherits the permissions already assigned in the NTFS folder.

Activity 5-11: Troubleshooting Permissions

Time Required: Approximately 10 minutes

Objective: View the effective permissions on a folder.

Description: The Effective Permissions tab in a folder's properties is an excellent place to start when you are troubleshooting a security conflict, such as when you think someone should be able to access a folder, but the system prevents them from accessing it. In this activity, you practice using the Effective Permissions tab.

1. Find the folder that you created in Activity 5-1, such as RLBrown, via My Computer or Windows Explorer.

2. Right-click the folder, and click **Properties**.

3. Click the **Security** tab.

4. Click the **Advanced** button.

5. Click the **Effective Permissions** tab.

6. Click the **Select** button, click **Advanced**, click **Find Now**, and double-click **Administrators**. Click **OK**.

7. Scroll through the Effective permissions box (see Figure 5-16)

8. Click **Cancel,** and click **Cancel** again.

9. Close My Computer or Windows Explorer.

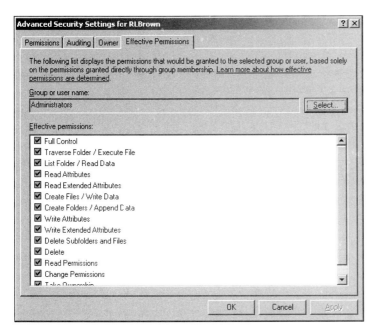

Figure 5-16   Examining effective permissions as a troubleshooting aid

IMPLEMENTING THE DISTRIBUTED FILE SYSTEM

The **Distributed File System (DFS)** enables you to simplify access to the shared folders on a network by setting up folders to appear that they are accessed from only one place. If the network, for example, has eight Windows 2003 servers that make a variety of shared folders available to network users, DFS can be set up so that users do not have to know what server offers which shared folder. All of the folders can be set up to appear as though they are on one server and under one broad folder structure. DFS also makes managing folder access easier for server administrators. DFS is configured using the Distributed File System tool in the Administrative Tools menu (click Start, point to All Programs, and point to Administrative Tools) or the Distributed File System MMC snap-in.

If DFS is used in a domain, then shared folder contents can be replicated to one or more DCs or member servers, which means that if the original server goes offline, its shared folders are still available to users through the replica servers. Also, from the server administrator's perspective, he or she can update software in a shared folder without having to make the folder temporarily inaccessible during the update. DFS offers the following advantages:

- Shared folders can be set up so that they appear in one hierarchy of folders, enabling users to save time when searching for information.

- NTFS access permissions fully apply to DFS on NTFS-formatted volumes.

- Fault tolerance is an option by replicating shared folders on multiple servers resulting in uninterrupted access for users.

- Access to shared folders can be distributed across many servers, resulting in the ability to perform **load balancing**, so that one server does not experience more of a load than others.

- Access is improved to resources for Web-based Internet and intranet sites.
- Vital shared folders on multiple computers can be backed up from one set of master folders.

Besides enabling users to be more productive, server administrators are also immediately more productive because DFS reduces the number of calls to server administrators asking where to find a particular resource. Another advantage of DFS in a domain is that folders can be replicated automatically or manually through Microsoft File Replication Service. When you set up DFS so that shared folders are replicated on two or more servers (called targets), the Microsoft File Replication Service performs the copying to the target servers. Each time the contents of a DFS folder are changed, the Microsoft File Replication Service goes into action. Shared folders in DFS are copied to each designated target computer, which yields two significant advantages:

- Important information is not lost when a disk drive on one server fails.
- Users always have access to shared folders even in the event of a disk failure.

 In a Windows 2000 mixed-mode domain that has a combination of Windows 2003 and Windows NT 4.0 servers, DFS can be fully implemented on the Windows NT 4.0 servers as long as Service Pack 3 or above is installed.

DFS Models

There are two models for implementing DFS: standalone and domain based. The standalone DFS model offers more limited capabilities than the domain-based model. In the **standalone DFS model** there is no Active Directory implementation to help manage the shared folders, and this model provides only a single or flat level share, which means that the main DFS shared folder does not contain a hierarchy of other shared folders. Also, the standalone model does not have DFS folders that are linked to other computers through a DFS container that has a main root and a deep, multilevel hierarchical structure.

The **domain-based DFS model** has more features than the standalone approach. Most importantly, the domain-based model takes full advantage of Active Directory and is available only to servers and workstations that are members of a domain. The domain-based model enables a deep root-based hierarchical arrangement of shared folders that is published in Active Directory. DFS shared folders in the domain-based model are replicated for fault tolerance and load balancing, whereas the standalone DFS model does not implement these features.

DFS Topology

The hierarchical structure of DFS in the domain-based model is called the **DFS topology**. There are three elements to the DFS topology:

- The DFS root
- The DFS links
- Replica sets (targets)

A **DFS root** is a main container in Active Directory that holds links to shared folders that can be accessed from the root. The server that maintains the DFS root is called the host server. When a network client views the shared folders in the DFS root, all of the folders appear as though they are in one main folder on the same computer, which is the Windows 2003 server containing the DFS root—even though the folders may actually reside on many different computers in the domain.

A **DFS link** is a designated access path between the DFS root and shared folders that are defined to the root. For example, a DFS root might be set up to contain all shared research folders for a plant biology research group that has folders on four different servers. Those folders can be shared via links drawn from them to the DFS root so that all of the folders appear as though they are available from one place through the published information in Active Directory. DFS links can also be made to another DFS root on a different computer or to an entire shared volume on a server.

A **replica set** is a set of shared folders that is replicated or copied to one or more servers in a domain. In the plant biology example, the replica set would consist of all shared folders under the DFS root that are designated to be replicated to other network servers. Part of this process means that links are established to each server that participates in the replication. Another part of the process is to set up synchronization so that replication takes place among all servers at a specified interval, such as every 15 minutes.

Configuring the Standalone DFS Model

A standalone DFS installation is configured on a local server by using the Distributed File System management tool. The installation steps for a standalone DFS installation are as follows:

1. Click **Start**, point to **All Programs**, point to **Administrative Tools**, and click **Distributed File System**. (Alternatively, to create a customized MMC window, click **Start,** click **Run**, enter **mmc** in the Open box, click **OK,** click the **File** menu, click **Add/Remove Snap-in**, click the **Add** button, double-click **Distributed File System**, click **Close**, and click **OK**.)

2. Make sure that **Distributed File System** is highlighted. Click the **Action** menu, and click **New Root** to start the Welcome to the New Root Wizard.

3. Click **Next**.

4. Click **Standalone root**, and click **Next** (see Figure 5-17).

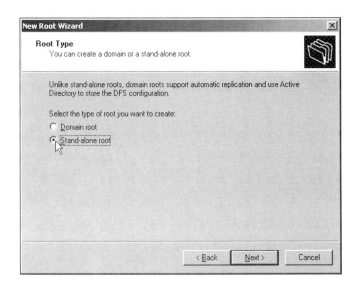

Figure 5-17   Specifying the standalone DFS model

5. Enter the name of the server that will host the DFS root. Click **Next**.

6. Enter a unique name for the root, and click **Next**.

7. Browse to find the folder to share. Click **OK** after you find it, and then click **Next**.

8. Review the information that has been entered, and click **Finish**; or click **Back** to go back and change information that is already entered.

After the standalone DFS shared root folder is created, it is displayed in the Distributed File System console window. If you are using the MMC, make sure that you save the changes and provide a name for the console so that you can easily view the DFS shared folder the next time that you open the console.

Configuring the Domain-based DFS Model

Installing a domain-based DFS root is similar to installing a standalone DFS root, but there are some differences, such as specifying the domain in which the root resides. Follow the steps in Activity 5-12 to practice a DFS installation.

Activity 5-12: A Domain-based DFS Installation

Time Required: Approximately 10 minutes

Objective: Install DFS for a domain.

Description: In this activity, you use a domain-based model to implement DFS for the folder, such as RLBrown, that you shared in Activity 5-7.

1. Click **Start**, point to **All Programs**, point to **Administrative Tools**, and click **Distributed File System**.

2. Click **Action** and then click **New Root**.

3. Click **Next** after the Welcome to the New Root Wizard starts.

4. Click **Domain root**, if it is not already selected. Click **Next**.

5. Use the default domain name, such as jpcompany.com (see Figure 5-18). Click **Next**.

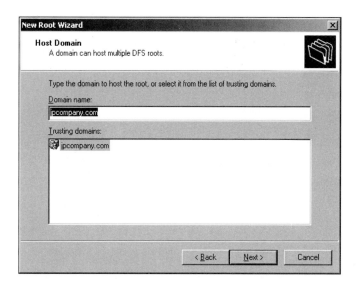

Figure 5-18   Entering the domain name

6. Enter the server name or use the Browse button to find the server, and then click **Next**. The server name is identified with the domain in which it resides.

7. Enter a unique name for the root, such as Research Data Files, and click **Next**.

8. **Browse** to find the folder to share, such as the folder you created in Activity 5-1. Click **OK** after you find it, and then click **Next**.

9. Review the information that has been entered, and click **Finish**.

10. Close the **Distributed File System** window.

Managing a Domain-based DFS Root System

After the DFS root system is set up, there are several tasks involved in managing the root which can include:

- Publishing a DFS root
- Deleting a DFS root

- Adding and removing a DFS link
- Adding root and link replica sets
- Troubleshooting a root or link

Each of these tasks is described in the following sections.

Publishing a DFS Root

DFS shared folders can be published in Active Directory for easier management and to facilitate user access. When you use DFS and Active Directory is available, plan to publish at the root level.

Activity 5-13: Publishing a DFS Root

Time Required: Approximately 10 minutes

Objective: Publish the root folder of a DFS installation.

Description: In this activity, you learn how to publish a DFS root. A DFS root folder should already be installed before you start.

1. Click **Start**, point to **All Programs**, point to **Administrative Tools**, and click **Distributed File System**.
2. Right-click the DFS root just under Distributed File System in the tree in the left pane.
3. Click **Properties**.
4. Click the **Publish** tab.
5. Click the box, **Publish this root in Active Directory**.
6. Enter a description of the DFS root.
7. Enter the user account that owns the DFS root. What other information can you configure?
8. Click **OK**.
9. Close the **Distributed File System** window.

Deleting a DFS Root

After a DFS root is created, it is possible to delete it, as may occur when, for example, you want to configure it differently. The general steps to delete a DFS root are as follows:

1. Provide users with a warning that the root will be deleted to make sure that no one is accessing the root prior to when you delete it.
2. Open the **Distributed File System management tool** via the MMC or from the Administrative Tools menu.
3. Right-click the root that you want to delete under Distributed File System in the tree.
4. Click **Delete Root**.
5. Click **Yes**.

Adding and Removing a DFS Link

A link to a DFS root can be established to a shared folder on the same computer as the root or to another computer that is a member of the domain. For example, there might be three servers that contain spreadsheets that should be placed under the DFS root for easy access. To set up a link, follow these general steps:

1. Open the **Distributed File System** management tool and right-click the root under the tree in the left pane.
2. Click **New Link**.

3. Enter a name that users will see for the link. Use the Browse button to find the computer and shared folder that you want to link to the DFS root. Provide a comment to describe the link.

4. Establish the cache timeout (described in the following paragraph) in seconds for the link.

5. Click **OK.**

When you create a link, the first link automatically becomes the **master folder** for replication, which is the folder that contains the master copy replicated to the other links. Also, the security, such as access permissions and auditing, that is already set up for the shared folder that becomes a link to a DFS root is retained after the link is established. The **DFS cache timeout** is the amount of time that a shared folder is retained in the client operating system's cache for fast access. 1800 seconds is the default implementation for the timeout value. The cache timeout can be adjusted after a DFS link is created by right-clicking the link, clicking Properties, and resetting the cache timeout in the General tab.

A link is removed from the DFS root by using the following steps:

1. Right-click the link in the left pane.

2. Click **Delete Link**.

3. Click **Yes**.

Adding DFS Root and Link Replicas

An entire DFS root or specific DFS links in a root can be replicated on servers other than the one that contains the master folder. The replication capability is what enables you to provide fault tolerance and to create load balancing. On a network in which there are multiple servers, replication can prove to be a vital service to provide uninterrupted access for users, in case the computer with the master folder is inaccessible. Load balancing also is vital as a way to provide users with faster service and better network performance because it enables users to access the nearest server containing the DFS shared folders.

You can replicate the root and all of its links to shared folders to one or more computers other than the one that houses the original DFS root and links. Each computer that contains a replica of the original root and links cannot already have any DFS roots, because you can only create one root per computer. To create a replica of an entire root, first determine which domain controllers or member servers do not already contain a DFS root. Next, right-click the DFS root that you want to replicate using the Distributed File System management tool. Click New Root Target, and use the New Root Wizard to provide the name of the server on which to place the replica, the path for the replica, and whether to manually or automatically synchronize the information between the master and the replica.

The replication is handled by the Windows 2003 File Replication Service. If automatic synchronization is used, then the default synchronization interval is every 15 minutes. When manual synchronization is used instead of automatic synchronization, new links must be manually built in each root replica by an Administrator. Normally, you set this up to use automatic synchronization, but manual synchronization is an alternative if you do not want to fully replicate all links, for example. If you attempt to create a DFS root replica on a server that already has a root, the New Root Wizard provides a message that one already exists on that computer. Depending on the domain and server DFS architecture and planning, it may be desirable to replicate designated DFS links. For example, you might set up link replication as a way to load balance access to specific folders on a busy network. Consider a business campus on which the accounting office is located several buildings away from the budget office. A DFS link to shared accounting files might be replicated on servers that are located near the Accounting Department, while a link to shared budget files is replicated on a server located near the budget office. To set up replication of a designated link, use these general steps:

1. Right-click the DFS link in the Distributed File System tool, and click **New Target**.

2. Enter the computer name and shared folder on the computer to use for the replica; or use the Browse button to locate the computer and shared folder in the domain. The computer name

and shared folder are specified in UNC format. Check the box for **Add this target to the replication set**, if it is not checked by default.

3. Click **OK**.

4. Click **Yes** to set the replication policy, and complete the setup steps through the Configure Replication Wizard.

Checking the Status of a Root or Link for Troubleshooting Connectivity

The most common problem associated with DFS shared folders is that one or more DFS links are inaccessible because a particular server is disconnected from the network or has failed. You can quickly check the status of a DFS root, DFS link, or replica by right-clicking it in the Root Target column of the Distributed File System management tool, and then clicking Check Status. A DFS root, link, or replica that is working and fully connected has a green check mark in a white circle through its folder icon. One that is disconnected will have a white "x" in a red circle through its folder icon.

CONFIGURING DISK QUOTAS

One reason why setting up shared folders and DFS shared folders using NTFS-formatted volumes (instead of FAT) works well is that NTFS offers the ability to establish **disk quotas**. Using disk quotas has the following advantages:

- Prevents users from filling the disk capacity

- Encourages users to help manage disk space by deleting old files when they receive a warning that their quota limit is approaching

- Tracks disk capacity needs on a per user basis for future planning

- Provides server administrators with information about when users are nearing or have reached their quota limits

Disk quotas can be set on any local or shared volume. By simply enabling the disk quota feature on a volume, you can determine how much disk capacity is occupied by each user without specifically setting quotas on those users. Another option is to set default quotas for all users, particularly on volumes that house user home folders. For example, many organizations establish a default quota of 50 to 100 MB per user on home folder volumes. The default quota prevents a few users from occupying disk space needed by all users. Disk quotas also can be established on a per user basis or special exceptions can be made for users who need additional space, such as a newspaper publishing group on a college campus that requires a large amount of space for text and graphics files.

The general parameters that can be configured for disk quota management include:

- *Enable quota management*—Starts tracking disk quotas and sets up quota management

- *Deny disk space to users exceeding quota limit*—Prevents users from writing new information to disk after they have exceeded their quotas

- *Do not limit disk usage*—Tracks disk usage without establishing quotas on users, such as to gather statistics for disk capacity planning

- *Limit disk space to*—Sets the default amount of disk space that users can use

- *Set warning level to*—Sets the default amount of disk space that users can occupy before triggering a warning message to users that they are reaching their quota

- *Log event when a user exceeds their quota limit*—Causes an event to be entered in the system log to notify the Administrator that the user has reached his or her quota

- *Log event when the user exceeds their warning level*—Causes an event to be entered in the system log to notify the Administrator that the user is approaching his or her quota

Activity 5-14: Configuring Disk Quotas

Time Required: Approximately 10 minutes

Objective: Enable disk quotas and then set a disk quota for a specific group of users.

Description: In this activity you begin by enabling default disk quotas on the C: volume of a server for all users. Next, you set a special disk quota exception for a user account. The volume you use should be formatted for NTFS.

1. Open **My Computer** or **Windows Explorer**.
2. Right-click **Local Disk (C:)** (or click whichever drive is a local disk formatted for NTFS), and click **Properties**.
3. Click the **Quota** tab.
4. Click the box to **Enable quota management**.
5. Click the box for **Deny disk space to users exceeding quota limit**.
6. Click the option button to **Limit disk space to**, and enter the limitation value, such as 100 MB.
7. Enter a value in the **Set warning level to** boxes, such as 90 MB.
8. Place a check in front of **Log event when a user exceeds their quota limit**.
9. Place a check in front of **Log event when a user exceeds their warning level** (see Figure 5-19).

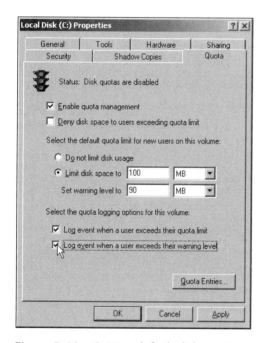

Figure 5-19   Setting default disk quotas

10. Disk quotas for specific user accounts that are exceptions to the default quotas are set by clicking the Quota Entries button. Click **Quota Entries**.
11. Click the **Quota** menu, and click **New Quota Entry**.
12. Click the **Advanced** button, click **Find Now**, and double-click an account in the list that you or your instructor have created previously. Click **OK**.
13. Click **Limit disk space to**, and enter **200 MB**.
14. Click **Set warning level to**, and enter **180 MB**.
15. Click **OK**.

16. Close the **Quota Entries for Local Disk (C:)** window. (Note that the drive on your system may not be C:.)

17. Click **OK**. Click **OK** again.

18. Close the My Computer or Windows Explorer Window.

CHAPTER SUMMARY

❑ Windows Server 2003 objects are managed through tools that include folder and file attributes, permissions, auditing, and ownership.

❑ Attributes enable you to manage folder and file properties such as read-only, archiving, compression, and encryption. Permissions are set to control who has access to a folder or file and auditing is used to monitor who has been accessing a folder or file. Ownership is used to grant full control over a folder or file.

❑ Folders can be shared over a network and their security is configured through share permissions. After a folder has been shared, it can be published in Active Directory for better management.

❑ Folders and files intended for access through the Web can be specially configured for Web sharing properties.

❑ Sometimes when you configure the security for a folder or file, specific people who are supposed to have access do not. Use security troubleshooting techniques and Windows Server 2003 troubleshooting tools to diagnose a security conflict.

❑ The Distributed File System (DFS) enables you to set up shared folders so they are easier for users to access and can be replicated for backup and load distribution.

❑ Use disk quotas to manage the resources that are put on a server disk volume so you do not prematurely or unexpectedly run out of disk space.

KEY TERMS

attribute — A characteristic associated with a folder or file used to help manage access and backups.

auditing — In Windows Server 2003, a security capability that tracks activity on an object, such as reading, writing, creating, or deleting a file in a folder.

DFS cache timeout — The amount of time that a DFS shared folder is retained in the client operating system's cache for fast access.

DFS link — A path that is established between a shared folder in a domain and a DFS root.

DFS root — The main Active Directory container that holds DFS links to shared folders in a domain.

DFS topology — Applies to a domain-based DFS model and encompasses the DFS root, DFS links to the root, and servers on which the DFS structure is replicated.

Directory Service Client (DSClient) — Microsoft software for pre-Windows 2000 clients that connect to Windows 2000 Server and Windows Server 2003 and enables those clients to view information published in Active Directory.

disk quota — Allocating a specific amount of disk space to a user or application with the ability to ensure that the user or application cannot use more disk space than is specified in the allocation.

Distributed File System (DFS) — A system that enables folders shared from multiple computers to appear as though they exist in one centralized hierarchy of folders instead of on many different computers.

domain-based DFS model — A DFS model that uses Active Directory and is available only to servers and workstations that are members of a particular domain. The domain-based model enables a deep root-based hierarchical arrangement of shared folders that is published in Active Directory. DFS shared folders in the domain-based model can be replicated for fault tolerance and load balancing.

Encrypting File System (EFS) — Set by an attribute of NTFS, this file system enables a user to encrypt the contents of a folder or a file so that it can only be accessed via private key code by the user who encrypted it. EFS adheres to the Data Encryption Standard's expanded version for data protection.

5

inherited permissions — Permissions of a parent object that also apply to child objects of the parent, such as to subfolders within a folder.

load balancing — On a single server, distributing resources across multiple server disk drives and paths for better server response; on multiple network servers, distributing resources across two or more servers for better server and network performance.

master folder — The main folder that provides master files and folders for a DFS root or link when replication is enabled.

ownership — Having the privilege to change permissions and to fully manipulate an object. The account that creates an object, such as a folder or printer, initially has ownership.

permissions — In Windows Server 2003, privileges to access and manipulate resource objects, such as folders and printers, or a privilege to read a file or to create a new file.

publish — Making an object, such as a printer or shared folder, available for users to access when they view Active Directory contents and so that the data associated with the object can be replicated.

replica set — A grouping of shared folders in a DFS root that are replicated or copied to all servers that participate in DFS replication. When changes are made to DFS shared folders, all of the participating servers are automatically or manually synchronized so that they have the same copy.

share permissions — Permissions that apply to a particular object that is shared over a network, such as a shared folder or printer.

standalone DFS model — A DFS model in which there is no Active Directory implementation to help manage the shared folders. This model provides only a single or flat level share.

REVIEW QUESTIONS

1. Which of the following is not a Web sharing application permission?

   a. None

   b. Full Control

   c. Scripts

   d. Execute

2. You have set up a special Planning folder for the Promotions Planning Task Force composed of members of the Marketing Department at your corporation. The folder is set up to give the Promo domain local group Full Control access permissions and Full Control share permissions. Also, you have a global group, called GlobalPromo, that contains only the members of the task force and is a member of the Promo group. However, after you set up the folder, no one in the GlobalPromo group can access it. Which of the following might explain why?

   a. You set up the Promo group to have access to the Planning folder, but did not allow or deny any permissions.

   b. You failed to set up automatic document caching for the Planning folder for the GlobalPromo group.

   c. You earlier made the GlobalMkt group a member of the Promo group, but also denied all permission access for GlobalMkt to the Planning folder when you set up the folder.

   d. all of the above

   e. only a and b

   f. only a and c

3. Which of the following are DFS models that you can set up in Windows Server 2003 Server? (Choose all that apply.)

   a. transitive

   b. two-way access

   c. domain-based

   d. standalone

5

4. On the Windows NT servers originally on your network, one problem was that users put so much material in folders that you often ran out of disk space and had to buy larger disks. Now that you've converted to Windows Server 2003, what is the best way to control this situation, but to still enable users to access files on servers?

a. Change the permissions of user folders only to allow for Read.

b. Use dynamic disks instead of basic disks.

c. Enable disk quotas and set quota defaults.

d. Publish user folders.

5. Your organization uses shared folders for office associates to access Word documents that are shared and often revised by different offices. Some of these documents are revised and needed on a moment's notice. Which of the following is a good strategy for sharing these documents?

a. Configure them to be available in DFS and use replication.

b. Place them all on one server and connect that server to a UPS.

c. Frequently back up these files to CD-RWs and distribute copies to each department on a weekly basis.

d. Give each department Full Control access to the shared folders for maximum flexibility.

6. One of the server operators in your organization seems to have problems accessing folders containing programs he needs to run. What tool might help diagnose the problem most immediately?

a. Active Directory Domains and Trusts

b. Computer Management

c. Add or Remove Programs in Control Panel

d. Effective Permissions in a folder's properties

7. Your college's president has several sensitive budget spreadsheets located in the Budgets subfolder under her home folder on a Windows 2003 server, and she wants to make sure that only she can read them. How can she set up security to be sure that only she can access and read those files?

a. Use the Encrypting File System to protect the files in her Budgets subfolder.

b. Set up the Users and Everyone groups to be denied access to the Budgets subfolder by using the All Permissions attribute.

c. Set up the president's account password so it must be changed every week.

d. Hide the Budgets subfolder using the hidden attribute.

8. Normally, the servers in the machine room of your organization are connected to a large UPS. However, that UPS has failed and your organization has decided to purchase a new large UPS system that is also connected to a backup diesel generator system. How can you help assure that the president's office will have access to a specific folder of documents also used by the board of trustees, during the two weeks when there will be no UPS backup?

a. Place the server containing the files in the president's office.

b. Use file compression, which offers the best protection against corruption for folders and files on computers that are subject to unexpected shut downs.

c. Use the automatic Print Backup feature of Windows Server 2003, that creates hardcopies of designated files each evening.

d. Use the Offline Settings feature of NTFS for this folder.

9. When you attempt to set up auditing on a folder, you discover that no auditing is actually taking place. What might be the cause of the problem?

   a. You have not enabled auditing an object as a Group Policy.

   b. The auditing service is not set to start automatically.

   c. You do not have Active Directory installed with an OU for auditing.

   d. You are trying to set up auditing on a folder that is formatted for NTFS instead of FAT.

10. Which of the following are examples of extended attributes in NTFS? (Choose all that apply.)

    a. read-only

    b. encrypt

    c. indexing

    d. show

11. As Administrator, you have set up a shared folder for the manager of the Inventory Department and you ask him to take ownership and set up the permissions he wants. Later, you receive a telephone call from him about a problem with a file in that folder. You log onto your account, which is a member of Domain Admins group, and find that you cannot access the shared folder. Why not (after all, you created it)?

    a. Even Administrators cannot access files owned by another user.

    b. The problem with the file has spread to the entire folder and the folder must be restored.

    c. The manager of the Inventory Department did not set up permissions access for the Builtin Administrators group or for the Domain Admins group.

    d. You must have ownership to access a folder through the Domain Admins group.

12. You are consulting for a doctor's office consisting of 18 networked workstations and one Windows 2003 server that is used to share folders. The office has a demo of a new medical database, but the licensing requires that not more than two people access it at the same time. How can you accommodate this requirement most easily?

    a. Set up the database in a hidden folder, because the access limit on a hidden folder is 2.

    b. Set up the database in a shared folder and set the user limit to 2.

    c. Set up the database in a shared folder, but change the permissions daily to a different combination of two people.

    d. Set up user rights to the server so that no more than 2 people can access the server at once.

13. Which of the following is (are) part of the DFS topology when DFS is set up in a domain? (Choose all that apply.)

    a. roots

    b. replica sets

    c. links

    d. bus connections

14. What tool can you use to publish a shared folder?

    a. Active Directory Publish

    b. Active Directory Users and Computers

    c. Services

    d. Control Panel Publish

15. How can you delete a DFS link?

   a. Right-click the link in the Distributed File System management tool, and click Delete Link.

   b. Deactivate the DFS link, and then purge it.

   c. Delete the link's root in the Distributed File System management tool, and then purge the link.

   d. To ensure security, you cannot delete a link after it is created.

16. The director of finance has called you into a planning meeting because your school has just determined that an accountant who quit four months ago embezzled $50,000 from the school. Besides setting permissions, the director wants to know other ways to help prevent this type of situation. What do you recommend?

   a. Deny access to log on locally to Windows 2003 servers.

   b. Establish an alert to the Administrators group whenever any folders and files are accessed.

   c. Set up auditing on specific folders and files and regularly review the audit events.

   d. Regularly remove the archive attribute on specific folders so you can track how often they are accessed.

17. Which of the following are permissions that can be set up on NTFS folders? (Choose all that apply.)

   a. Modify

   b. Read & Execute

   c. List Folder Contents

   d. Write

18. You are setting up permissions on a development folder for a group of programmers, each of whom sometimes individually accesses the server console to move programs into production or to diagnose the problems with specific programs. The typical permissions do not quite satisfy how you want to set up security. What can you do?

   a. Transfer ownership of the folder to the programmers.

   b. Configure customized attributes.

   c. Configure special permissions.

   d. Use the permissions extension feature to program new permissions.

19. You need to set up Web sharing on a folder in Windows Server 2003, but there is no Web sharing tab. What might be the problem?

   a. You are using Windows Server 2003, Standard Edition, which does not support Web sharing.

   b. You need to change the NTFS permissions on that folder to Full Control so that Web sharing is enabled.

   c. You first need to publish the folder in Active Directory.

   d. You need to install IIS on the server.

20. Your boss is a busy person and wants you to give him ownership of several folders so that he does not have to spend time on the task. As Administrator, how do you accomplish transferring ownership?

   a. Simply give him Take Ownership permission, and he has ownership.

   b. Give him Full Control permissions and then transfer ownership to him.

   c. You can give him Take Ownership permission, but he must take ownership himself.

   d. Add him to the Domain Administrators group, and he automatically has ownership.

CASE PROJECTS

Case Project Background

Precision Digital is a company that makes compact discs for digital use, such as CD-ROMs, CD-Rs, and CD-RWs. They design, manufacture, sell, and research discs entirely for computer-related digital applications. Precision Digital has employees located in four buildings and there is a Windows Server 2003, Standard Edition server, in each building. All servers are in one domain. One building houses the administrative and business offices, one is used for research teams, and the other two are used to manufacture discs. Precision Digital's server administrator has just resigned and they are in the process of hiring a new one. In the interim, they have hired you through Bayside IT Services to help work on several special projects.

Case Project 5-1: Setting Up Shared Folders

Two of the members of the business management staff need training in how to set up shared folders with access permissions and share permission security. Develop a set of instructions they can follow showing how to configure shared folders, folder permissions, and share permissions.

Case Project 5-2: Setting Up Web Sharing

The Marketing Department has a Web site from which to advertise products and take orders. Two of the marketing staff need training in how to manage Web sharing from a folder. They ask you for an explanation. Create a document they can use that illustrates the tasks involved in managing Web sharing from a folder.

Case Project 5-3: Using DFS for Folder Sharing

Each server contains from 10 to 20 shared folders that are accessed by various users throughout the company. The problem is that users are still very confused about which folders are on which servers. As a result, they waste a lot of time trying to find the information that they need. Precision Digital asks you to help them develop a way to make the folders easier to find and access. Explain to Precision Digital's administrative team how DFS works and how it can be of value in their situation. Design a very general DFS folder structure that they might implement.

Case Project 5-4: Setting Up DFS

After making your presentation about DFS, the human resources director at Precision Digital calls to let you know that they have hired a new server administrator, but the new administrator has only worked with other server operating systems and not with Windows Server 2003. Prepare a document for the new administrator that explains how to set up a DFS root and links in a domain.

CHAPTER

6

CONFIGURING WINDOWS SERVER 2003 PRINTING

After reading this chapter and completing the exercises, you will be able to:

♦ Explain basic printing concepts, how network printing works, and how Internet printing works

♦ Install local and shared printers

♦ Configure Windows Server 2003 printing properties

♦ Configure nonlocal or Internet printing

♦ Manage print jobs

♦ Troubleshoot common printing problems

Network printing is one of the most used resources on any network, because the word processing, database, computer graphics, and other work performed by users often end with a printed document as the final product. Printed materials are used for important meetings, presentations, information analysis, and in a huge realm of other activities. Because printing is so important, it is also a major source of frustration to users when it does not work well. Fortunately, Windows Server 2003 has simplified printing and made it more reliable.

In this chapter, you'll learn the basics of how Windows Server 2003 printing works on a local computer, a network, and the Internet. Next, you'll learn how to install printers for local use and for sharing on a network. After installing a printer, you will learn to configure, monitor, and control how the printer is accessed. Also, you'll learn how to configure Internet printing and how to manage network printers from a server. After a printer is installed and configured, you will learn to monitor and manage print jobs. You'll also learn to solve problems when printing does not go as planned, such as when printing fails on a server and you need to restart the process that controls printing.

AN OVERVIEW OF WINDOWS SERVER 2003 PRINTING

The network printing process on Windows Server 2003 LANs begins when a client decides to print a file, either on a printer locally connected to the client's computer (a **local print device**), on a shared network printer (a **network print device**), or through Internet printing (also a network print device). A shared network printer can be connected to a workstation sharing a printer, a printer attached to a server, or a printer attached to a print server device. The workstation or application that initially generates the print job is the network **print client**, and the computer or print server device offering the printer share is the network **print server**.

A shared network printer device is an object, like a folder, that is made available to network users for print services. When the printout goes to a printer share, it is temporarily spooled in specially designated disk storage and held until it is sent to be printed. **Spooling** frees the server CPU to handle other processing requests in addition to print requests.

When its turn comes, the print file is sent to the printer along with formatting instructions. A **printer driver** that holds configuration information for the given printer provides the formatting instructions. The formatting and configuration information includes instructions to reset the printer before starting, information about printing fonts, and special printer control codes.

The printer driver resides on the computer offering the printer services (for local and network print jobs) and also can reside on the workstation client sending the print job. For example, when you send a print job to be printed on a Windows Server 2003 print share, your printout is formatted using the printer driver at your workstation and then further interpreted by print services software on the print server. The printer driver is either contained on the Windows Server 2003 CD-ROM or obtained from the printer manufacturer.

How Network Printing Works

In technical terms, both the network print client and the network print server run specific processes to finally deliver a print job to a printer. The following steps outline the printing process:

1. The first stage in the process is when the software application at the client generates a print file.

2. As it creates the print file, the application communicates with the Windows **graphics device interface (GDI)**. The GDI integrates information about the print file—such as word-processing codes for fonts, colors, and embedded graphics objects—with information obtained from the printer driver installed at the client for the target printer, in a process that Microsoft calls rendering.

3. When the GDI is finished, the print file is formatted with control codes to implement the special graphics, font, and color characteristics of the file. At the same time, the software application places the print file in the client's spooler by writing the file, called the **spool file**, to a subfolder used for spooling. In the Windows 95, 98, NT, 2000, XP, and 2003 operating systems, a **spooler** is a group of DLLs, information files, and programs that processes print jobs for printing.

Large print files cannot be processed if there is inadequate disk space on which to store spooled files. Make sure clients and the server have sufficient disk space to handle the largest print requests, particularly for huge graphics and color files that are targeted for a color printer or plotter.

4. The remote print provider at the client makes a remote procedure call to the network print server to which the print file is targeted, such as a Windows 2003 server. If the print server is responding and ready to accept the print file, the remote printer transmits that file from the client's spooler folder to the Server Service on Windows Server 2003.

5. The network print server uses four processes to receive and process a print file: router, print provider, print processor, and print monitor. The router, print provider, and print processor all are pieces of the network print server's spooler.

6. Once it is contacted by the remote print provider on the print client, the Server Service calls its router, the Print Spooler Service. The router directs the print file to the print provider, which stores it in a spool file until it can be sent to the printer.

7. While the file is spooled, the print provider works with the print processor to ensure that the file is formatted to use the right data type, such as TEXT or RAW.

8. When the spool file is fully formatted for transmission to the printer, the print monitor pulls it from the spooler's disk storage and sends it to the printer.

Activity 6-1: Print Spooler Service

Time Required: Approximately 5 minutes

Objective: Learn about the Print Spooler Service and services upon which it depends.

Description: The Print Spooler Service works in conjunction with the Remote Procedure Call service to help make Windows Server 2003 printing possible. In this activity, you use the Computer Management tool to view the Print Spooler service as well as services upon which it depends.

1. Click **Start**, right-click **My Computer**, and click **Manage**.

2. Click **Services** in the tree under Services and Applications.

3. Scroll the right pane to find the Print Spooler service. Click **Print Spooler**, if necessary. Notice the description of the Print Spooler Service as shown in Figure 6-1.

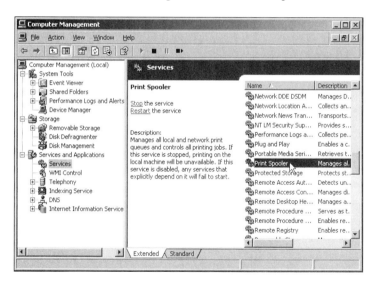

Figure 6-1   Viewing the description of the Print Spooler Service

4. Double-click **Print Spooler** to view its properties.

5. Click the **Dependencies** tab. What service(s) depend on the Print Spooler Service? On what service(s) does the Print Spooler depend?

6. Click **Cancel**.

7. Close the **Computer Management** window.

How Internet Printing Works

When a print job is processed over the Internet or an intranet, the Internet Information Services (IIS) must be installed and running in Windows Server 2003, and the client must connect to the Windows Server 2003 IIS using a Web browser, such as Internet Explorer. The print process on the client is nearly the same as for network printing, with a couple of exceptions. One exception is that it is the browser that sends the print file to the GDI instead of a software application such as Word. Another exception is that the remote print provider at the client makes a remote procedure call to the IIS on the Windows Server 2003. The remote procedure call is made through the TCP/IP-based Hypertext Transfer Protocol (HTTP) protocol, which transports another protocol, called the **Internet Printing Protocol (IPP)**. The IPP encapsulates both the remote procedure call and print process information and is transported in HTTP just as a human passenger is transported inside a bus along a highway. IIS sends the IPP encapsulated information to its HTTP print server. The HTTP print server works with the regular Windows Server 2003 spooler services—the print provider, print processor, and print monitor processes—to prepare the print file for transmission to the target printer.

INSTALLING LOCAL AND SHARED PRINTERS

On a Microsoft network, any server or workstation running Windows Server 2003, Windows XP, Windows 2000, or Windows NT, 98, or 95 can host a shared printer for others to use through network connectivity. In Windows Server 2003, you configure a printer that is attached to the server computer as a local printer and then enable it as a shared printer. When you share a printer, the Windows 2003 server becomes a print server. Figure 6-2 is a simplified representation of how shared printers are connected to a network, including printers connected to servers, workstations, and print server devices.

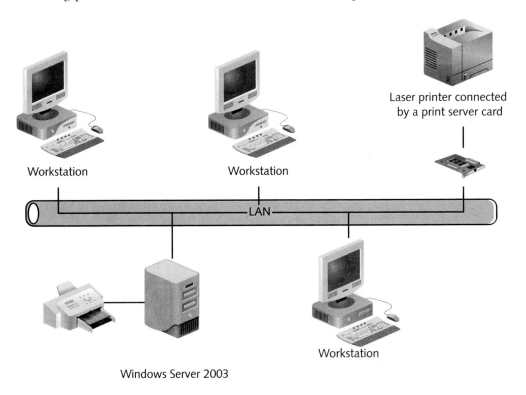

Figure 6-2   Shared network printers

If you are setting up a computer as a print server make sure it has sufficient RAM to process the documents and sufficient disk space to store the spooled documents.

The steps to installing a printer in Windows Server 2003 depend on the type of printer you are adding. If you are installing a printer that is compatible with Plug and Play, Windows Server 2003 automatically detects and installs the new hardware. If the printer is not automatically detected, you can use the Add Printer Wizard to install it. Printers that are added using the Add Printer Wizard are by default shared and published within Active Directory. Printers installed using Plug-and-Play technology are not automatically shared and must be configured for sharing after installation.

Activity 6-2: Installing a Printer

6

Time Required: Approximately 15 minutes

Objective: Install a printer using the Add Printer Wizard.

Description: In this activity, you install a printer using the Add Printer Wizard. For this activity it is not required to have a printer attached to the computer, because you practice a manual configuration without automatic detection.

1. Click **Start**, point to **Control Panel**, point to **Printers and Faxes**, and click **Add Printer**.

2. Click **Next** after the Add Printer Wizard starts.

3. Notice the options to install a local or a network printer (see Figure 6-3). A local printer is one that is physically attached to the computer and a network printer is one that is connected to a different computer or to a dedicated print server device and that is shared over the network. For this activity, click **Local printer attached to this computer**, if necessary. Notice that you can have the Add Printer Wizard automatically detect the printer or you can manually configure. For this activity you will configure it manually to learn all of the steps; therefore, remove the check mark from **Automatically detect and install my Plug and Play printer**. Click **Next**.

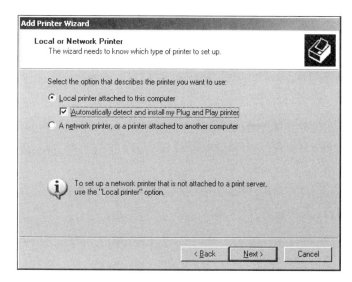

Figure 6-3 Setting up a local printer

4. Click the **down** arrow for Use the following port. What options are available?

5. Leave LPT1: (Recommended Printer Port) as the default selection, and click **Next**.

6. If you have a printer connected, select the printer manufacturer and model. If no printer is connected, select **HP** under Manufacturer, and select **HP Color LaserJet**. (Notice that you can use the Windows Update button to obtain newer printer driver files or you can use the Have Disk button to obtain printer drivers from the manufacturer's disk.)

7. Click **Next**.

8. If the printer has been installed previously and then deleted, you'll see a Use Existing Driver screen. If you see this screen, select **Keep existing driver (recommended)** and click **Next**.

9. For the name, type **HP Color LaserJet** plus your initials, such as HP Color LaserJetJP. If you see the option, **Do you want to use this printer as the default printer?** select **Yes**. Click **Next**.

10. On the Printer Sharing dialog box, leave the Share name option button selected (the default). Enter a share name including the word **Room** and your initials, such as HP Color LaserJet RoomJP (see Figure 6-4). This is the name that users on the network will see. Click **Next**.

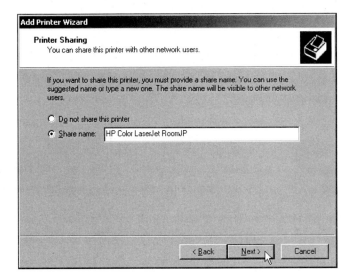

Figure 6-4   Sharing a printer

Use the following guidelines when choosing a share name:
- Compose names that are easily understood and spelled by those who will use the printer.
- Include a room number, floor, or workstation name to help identify where the printer is located.
- Include descriptive information about the printer, such as the type, manufacturer, or model.

11. Click **Yes**, if a warning box appears warning that your share name may not be accessible from MS-DOS clients.

12. In the Location box, enter **Color printer in *your initials* room**. In the Comment text box enter **Color printer shared for all students to use**. Click **Next**.

13. If you have a printer physically connected to the computer, select **Yes** to print a test page. If not, click **No**. Click **Next**.

14. Review your configuration, and click **Finish**.

15. Wait a moment for the installation to complete.

16. If you clicked **Yes** in Step 13, you see a box asking if the test page printed. Click **OK**, but notice that if you have trouble, there is the option to click Troubleshoot to get help.

CONFIGURING WINDOWS SERVER 2003 PRINTING

The setup information that you specify while stepping through the Add Printer Wizard can be modified and further tuned by accessing the Properties dialog box for a printer. Printer properties are available by pointing to Control Panel, pointing to Printers and Faxes, right-clicking the printer you want to modify, and clicking Properties. You can manage the following functions associated with a printer from the tabs in the Properties dialog box:

- General printer information
- Printer sharing
- Printer port setup
- Printer scheduling and advanced options
- Security
- Device settings

 Note These are the main printer properties available after a printer is installed. Other properties and tabs may be available, depending on the printer and its driver, such as a Color Management tab for printers that support color printing.

General Printer Specifications

The title bar and top portion of the General tab in a printer's properties show the name of the printer (see Figure 6-5). The Location and Comment boxes are used to store special notes about the printer that can help distinguish it from other printers, particularly for the sake of users if the printer is shared on the network. Below the Comment box is the printer model name, and under that is an area that describes features of the printer, such as its speed and resolution. The Printing Preferences button is used to specify additional information about printing, such as whether to use portrait or landscape printing as the default and the default paper source, if the printer supports special trays and sheet or envelope feeders. Also, the Print Test Page button enables you to print a test page as a way to verify that the printer is working.

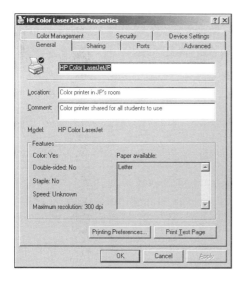

Figure 6-5   Printer Properties General tab

Activity 6-3: Viewing Printing Preferences

Time Required: Approximately 5 minutes

Objective: Verify the default setup for printing preferences on a printer.

Description: After you install a printer, it is a good idea to verify the printing preferences to make certain they match the intended use of the printer. In this activity you view the printing preferences for the printer you installed in Activity 6-2.

1. Click **Start**, point to **Control Panel**, point to **Printers and Faxes**, and right-click the printer you installed in Activity 6-2, such as HP Color LaserJetJP. Click **Properties**.

2. Make sure the General tab is displayed. Click the **Printing Preferences** button near the bottom of the dialog box. What tabs are shown? What are the options on the tabs that can be configured?

3. Click **Cancel**. Close the Properties dialog box.

Sharing Printers

The Sharing tab is used to enable or disable a printer for sharing, as well as to specify the name of the share (see Figure 6-6). The choices are (1) to turn off sharing, select Do not share this printer, and (2) to turn on sharing, select Share this printer. If you enable sharing, provide a name for the shared printer and check the List in the directory check box to publish the printer through Active Directory. When you publish a printer, Windows XP and Windows 2000 clients as well as other client operating systems that have the Directory Service Client software installed can easily find it using the Search function.

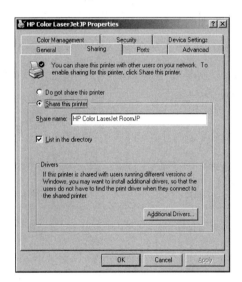

Figure 6-6   Configuring printer sharing

Another way to publish a printer in Active Directory is to open the Active Directory Users and Computers tool, right-click the domain (or an OU in the domain), point to New, click Printer, and enter the UNC (Universal Naming Convention) path to the shared printer.

The Additional Drivers button on a printer's properties Sharing tab is used to add new types of clients, if there are clients who will access the shared printer from computers running other Windows operating systems. For example, if there are Windows 98 clients and Windows NT 4.0 clients, click the Additional Drivers button and check the boxes for these operating systems. When you check these boxes, the appropriate printer drivers are installed so users can automatically download them when they connect to the print server for the first time.

The first time clients connect to the printer they must download and install the appropriate driver. Windows NT 4.0, Windows 2000, and Windows XP clients check the printer driver each time they connect to the printer. If the driver on any of these clients is not current, the driver is automatically updated. Clients running Windows 95 or Windows 98 do not automatically update the driver. If the driver for these clients is updated, the new driver must be manually installed.

Activity 6-4: Configuring the Domain's Group Policy to Enable Publishing a Printer

Time Required: Approximately 10 minutes

Objective: Learn how to enable printer publishing in the domain's Group Policy.

Description: Publishing a printer for domainwide access must be enabled in a domain's Group Policy within Active Directory. In this activity, you make certain that the domain's Group Policy for publishing printers is enabled.

1. Click **Start** and click **Run**.
2. Enter **mmc** in the Open box and click **OK**.
3. Maximize the console windows.
4. Click the **File** menu and click **Add/Remove Snap-in**.
5. Click the **Add** button and then double-click **Group Policy Object Editor**.
6. Click the **Browse** button and double-click **Default Domain Policy**.
7. Click **Finish**.
8. Click **Close** and click **OK**.
9. Double-click the following, if necessary, to open these folders in the tree, **Console Root**, **Default Domain Policy**, **Computer Configuration**, **Administrative Templates**, and **Printers**.
10. Double-click **Allow printers to be published**. How is this policy currently configured?
11. Click the option button for **Enabled**, if it is not already selected. Click **OK**.
12. In addition to enabling printer publishing, you may want to enable the ability for browse master servers to include published printers when users browse for network printers while installing them through their operating system's version of the Add Printer Wizard. To enable printer browsing, double-click **Printer browsing**, select **Enabled**, and click **OK**.
13. Close the **Console1** window.
14. Click **No** so that you don't save the console settings.

Port Specifications

The Ports tab has options to specify which server port, such as LPT1, is used for the printer, and options to set up bidirectional printing and printer pooling (see Figure 6-7). **Bidirectional printing** is used with printers that have bidirectional capability. A bidirectional printer can engage in two-way communications with the print server and with software applications. This allows the printer driver to determine how much memory is installed in the printer, or if it is equipped with PostScript print capability. The printer also may be equipped with the ability to communicate that it is out of paper in a particular drawer or that it has a paper jam.

Before you connect a printer, consult the manual to determine whether the printer is bidirectional. If so, the printer requires a special bidirectional cable labeled as an IEEE 1284 cable, and the printer port may need to be designated as bidirectional in the computer's BIOS setup program. Check both of these contingencies if you have a bidirectional printer; by default, the bidirectional box is deactivated on the Ports tab.

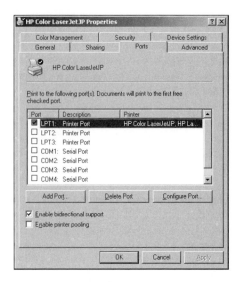

Figure 6-7 Configuring printer ports

Printer pooling involves configuring two or more identical printers connected to one print server. For example, you might connect three identical laser printers (except for port access) to one parallel port and two serial ports on a Windows 2003 server. On the Ports tab, check the Enable printer pooling box, and then check all of the ports to which printers are attached, such as LPT1, COM2, and COM3.

All of the printers in a pool must be identical so that they use the same printer driver and handle print files in the same way. The advantage of having a printer pool is that the Windows Server 2003 print monitor can send print files to any of the three printers (or however many you set up). If two of the printers are busy, it can send an incoming file to the third printer. Printer pooling can significantly increase the print volume in a busy office, without the need to configure network printing for different kinds of printers.

 It is wise to locate pooled printers close to each other, because users are not able to tell to which pooled printer a print job may be sent.

The Add Port button enables you to add a new port, such as a new print monitor or a fax port. Click this button if you need to configure print monitors for specialized printing needs. The default options are (see Figure 6-8):

- *Local Port*—The Local Port print monitor handles print jobs sent to a local physical port on the server, such as an LPT or COM port. It also sends print jobs to a file, if you specify FILE as the port. When a print job is sent to FILE, there is a prompt to supply a filename.

- *LPR Port*—The Line Printer Remote (LPR) print monitor is employed for transmitting files by means of the Microsoft TCP/IP Printing service for printers connected to a UNIX, DEC VAX, or IBM mainframe computer or from these computers as clients to printers attached to Windows 2003 servers. To use this, you first need to install the TCP/IP protocol in Windows Server 2003 and Print Services for UNIX (part of the Other Network File and Print Services that is a Windows component installed through Add or Remove Programs in Control Panel). Also, to use LPR, there must be a Line Printer Daemon (LPD) server. The LPD server can be a UNIX computer, an MVS (IBM mainframe) computer with TCP/IP, a computer running Windows 2000 or 2003, or a print server device such as a Hewlett-Packard JetDirect card in a Hewlett-Packard printer. If you create an LPR port on the server, you need to provide the IP address of the LPD server.

- *Standard TCP/IP Port*—This print monitor is used for TCP/IP-based printers that are connected to the network through print server cards or print servers.

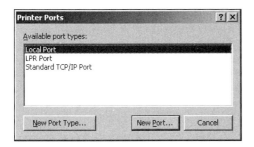

Figure 6-8 Port options

The Delete Port button is used to remove a port option from the list of ports. The Configure Port button is used to tune the configuration parameters that are appropriate to the type of port. On an LPT port, click the Configure Port button to check the port timeout setting. This setting is the amount of time the server continues to try sending a print file to a printer while the printer is not responding. The default setting is normally 90 seconds. Consider increasing the setting to 120 seconds or more if you are installing a printer to handle large print files, such as files for combined graphics and color printing. On a COM port, the Configure Port button is used to set the serial port speed in bits per second, the data bits, parity, stop bits, and flow control.

Activity 6-5: Configuring Printer Pooling

Time Required: Approximately 10 minutes

Objective: Learn how to configure printer pooling.

Description: Printer pooling can enable users in a busy office to be more productive by not making them wait on printouts. In this activity, you practice configuring printer pooling (you do not need an additional printer for this activity, but you would, of course in an actual office situation).

1. Click **Start**, point to **Control Panel**, point to **Printers and Faxes**, and right-click the printer you installed in Activity 6-2, such as HP Color LaserJetJP. Click **Properties**.

2. Click the **Ports** tab.

3. Click **Enable printer pooling**.

4. Click **COM3** or another port that is not in use.

5. Click **Apply**. How has that port's printer assignment changed? Record your observations. How could you print a test page?

6. Leave the Properties dialog box open for the next activity.

Activity 6-6: Transferring Print Jobs

Time Required: Approximately 15 minutes

Objective: Learn how to transfer print jobs from a malfunctioning printer.

Description: Assume that you have a small network in which there is a printer connected to the server, the printer has failed, but there is an identical printer shared by a workstation on the network that is working. You practice configuring the print monitor associated with the Local Port option and at the same time learn how to transfer print jobs to the other printer. You need a printer set up in Windows Server 2003; and obtain from your instructor the name of a workstation (or server) that has a shared printer.

1. Make sure the Ports tab is still displayed from Activity 6-5.

2. Click the **Add Port** button. What port types are available? Record your observations.

3. Click **Local Port** and click the **New Port** button (do not click the New Port Type button). Enter the UNC name of the workstation and printer provided by your instructor, such as \\Lab1\HPLaser and click **OK**. (Note that if your server has two printers connected you can also enter the server name and the name of the other printer.)

4. Click **Close**. Is the new port added to the list of ports? What is the Port name and description?

5. Click **Close**.

Printer Scheduling and Advanced Options

The Advanced tab allows you to have the printer available at all times or to limit the time to a range of hours (see Figure 6-9). To have the printer available at all times, click Always available; to limit printer use to only certain times, click Available from and enter the range of times when the printer can be used, such as from 8:00 a.m. to 10:00 p.m.

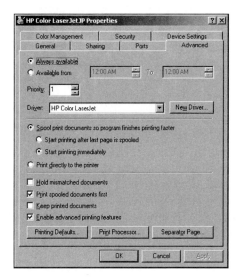

Figure 6-9   Advanced printer properties

You can set the priority higher to give a particular printer or printer pool priority over other printers attached to the server, which applies only if there are two or more printer icons set up in the Printers folder. The priority can be set from 1 to 99. For example, if the server is managing several printer shares, one may be set for higher priority because it prints payroll checks or is used by the company president.

Printer scheduling can be useful when there is one printer and two printer objects (shares) for that printer. One object can be set up for immediate printing, and the other can be used for long print jobs that are not immediately needed. The object for the longer jobs that can wait might be set up so those print jobs are scheduled to print between 6:00 p.m. and midnight. Another way to handle the longer jobs is to pause that printer object and resume printing when the printer has a light load, such as at noon or during slow times of the day.

The Advanced tab provides the option to use spooled printing or to bypass the spooler and send print files directly to the printer. It works best to spool print jobs so they are printed on a first-come, first-served basis and to enable background printing so the CPU can work on other tasks. Printing directly to the printer is not recommended, unless there is an emergency need to focus all resources on a specific print-out. Print spooling also helps ensure that jobs are printed together, so a long Word document is not interrupted by a one-page print job. Without spooling, such an interruption can happen if the one-page job is ready to print at the time the Word job is pausing to read the disk. The spool option is selected by default, with the instruction to start printing before all the pages are spooled. This is an appropriate option in a small office in which most print files are not resource-intensive and there is infrequent contention for printers, reducing the odds of intermixing printouts.

 If there is a problem with pages intermixing from printouts, as in a busy office, for example, click the option to Start printing after last page is spooled.

The Hold mismatched documents option causes the system to compare the setup of the printer to the setup in the document. For example, if the printer is set up in a print share as a Hewlett-Packard 5Si and the document is formatted for a plotter, the print job is placed on hold. The job does not print until the document is released by the user, a member of the Print Operators or Server Operators group, or an Administrator.

 The Hold mismatched documents option is a good way to save paper in a heterogeneous situation, such as a student lab, where users have very different formatted print jobs. One mismatch situation can use hundreds of pages printing one character per page.

The Print spooled documents first option enables jobs that have completed spooling to be printed, no matter what their priority. Where there is high-volume printing, this speeds the process by reducing the wait for long print jobs to spool. The Keep printed documents option retains documents in the spooler after they have printed, which enables the network administrator to re-create a printout damaged by a printer jam or other problem. For example, if a large number of paychecks are printing and a printer problem strikes in the middle of the printout, this critical option makes it possible to reprint the damaged checks. However, this option should be accompanied by a maintenance schedule to delete documents no longer needed. The Enable advanced printing features option permits you to make use of special features associated with a particular printer, such as the ability to print booklets or to vary the order in which pages are printed—back to front, for example.

The Printing Defaults button enables you to specify default settings for print jobs, unless they are over-ridden by control codes in the print file. These can include the print layout, page print order (front to back), and paper source, depending on the printer.

Use the Print Processor button to specify one of the print processors and data types, for example, when using the WinPrint print processor (the default) and the EMF data type for Windows-based clients. The **data type** is the way in which information is formatted in a print file; and the data types include:

- *RAW*—A print file formatted as the **RAW** data type is often used for files sent from MS-DOS, Windows 3.x, and UNIX clients. It is also the default setting for a PostScript printer. A RAW print file is intended to be printed by the print server with no additional formatting.

- *RAW (FF appended)*—In this data type, the FF is a form-feed code placed at the end of the print file. Some non-Windows and old 16-bit Windows software do not place a form feed at the end of a print file. The form feed is used to make sure the last page of the file is printed.

- *RAW (FF auto)*—In this data type, the print processor checks the print file for a form feed as the last character set before appending a form feed at the end. If there already is one, it does not add anything to the file.

- *NT EMF (different versions)*—Windows 95, 98, Me, NT, 2000, XP, and 2003 clients use the **enhanced metafile (EMF)** data type. This is the data type that is created when a print file is prepared by the GDI at the client. EMF print files offer a distinct advantage in Windows operating system environments because they are very portable from computer to computer.

- *TEXT*—The **TEXT** data type is used for printing text files formatted according to the ANSI standard that uses values between 0 and 255 to represent characters, numbers, and symbols. You use the TEXT data type for printing many types of MS-DOS print files, such as text files printed from older word processors or MS-DOS text editors.

The Separator Page button is used to place a blank page at the beginning of each printed document. This helps designate the end of one printout and the beginning of another, so that printouts do not get mixed together, or so that someone does not take the wrong printout in a medium-sized or large office setting in which many people share the same printer. Another advantage of using a separator page is that it sends control codes to the printer to make sure that the special formatting set for the last printout is reset prior to the next one. In small offices, a separator page may not be needed, because print formatting may not vary, and users can quickly identify their own printouts. Windows Server 2003 has four separator page files from which to choose, located in the \Windows\System32 folder:

- *Sysprint.sep*—Used with PostScript-only printers and prints a separator page at the beginning of each document

- *Sysprtj.sep*—Used in the same way as Sysprint.sep, but for documents printed in the Japanese language

- *Pcl.sep*—Used to print a Printer Control Language (PCL) separator page on a printer that handles PCL and PostScript

- *Pscript.sep*—Used to print a PostScript separator page on a printer that handles PCL and PostScript

A **PostScript** printer is one that has special firmware or cartridges to print using a page-description language (PDL). Most non-PostScript laser printers use a version of the **Printer Control Language (PCL)**, which was developed by Hewlett-Packard.

Consider the cost of paper before you set up separator pages. If you set up a separator page for each document, and each user also specifies a banner page from the client, the resulting paper costs quickly mount. For example, depending on the setup, there can be one or more extra pages printed per document, turning a one-page original document into two, three, or more printed pages. Many offices sharing a printer simply decide to forgo separator and banner pages, because each person knows what he or she printed anyway.

Activity 6-7: Changing Data Types

Time Required: Approximately 10 minutes

Objective: Learn how to change the data type when printing problems occur.

Description: In this activity, you practice changing the data type to accommodate UNIX and mainframe clients that print to a printer connected to Windows Server 2003. Assume you have been experiencing garbled printouts using the TEXT setup and a problem with getting the first page to print. To solve the problem, you change the data type to RAW with FF appended.

1. Click **Start**, point to **Control Panel**, point to **Printers and Faxes**, and right-click the printer you installed in Activity 6-2, such as HP Color LaserJetJP. Click **Properties**.

2. Click the **Advanced** tab, and click the **Print Processor** button. What print processors and data types are listed? Record your results.

3. Click **WinPrint** (if it is not already selected), and click **RAW [FF appended]**.

4. Click **OK**. What are some other parameters that you can set on the Advanced tab? Record several of these.

5. Click **Apply** and close the Properties dialog box.

Configuring Security

As an object, a shared printer can be set up to use security features such as share permissions, auditing, and ownership. To configure security for a printer, you must have Manage Printers permissions for that printer. Use the Security tab to set up printer share permissions (see Figure 6-10).

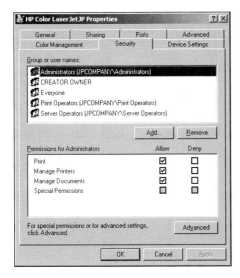

Figure 6-10   Configuring security

Once a printer is shared, the default permissions are as follows:

- *Administrators, Server Operators, Print Operators*—Print, Manage Printers, and Manage Documents
- *Everyone group*—Print
- *Creator Owner*—Manage Documents

Click an existing group to modify its permissions, and use the Add button to add new groups or the Remove button to delete a group from accessing the printer. Table 6-1 lists the printer share permissions that can be set.

Table 6-1   Printer share permissions

Share Permission	Access Capability
Print	Users can connect to the shared printer, send print jobs, and manage their own print requests (such as to pause, restart, resume, or cancel a print job)
Manage Documents	Users can connect to the shared printer, send print jobs, and manage any print job sent (including jobs sent by other users)
Manage Printers	Users have complete access to a printer share, including the ability to change permissions, turn off sharing, configure printer properties, and delete the share
Special Permissions	Similar to configuring special permissions for a folder, special permissions can be set up for a printer from the Advanced tab

By clicking the Advanced button on the Security tab you can:

- Set up special printer permissions for a specific group or user (click the Permissions tab, click the group or user, and click Edit)
- Add or remove a group or user for security access or denial (click the Permissions tab)
- Set up printer auditing (click the Auditing tab)

- Take ownership of a printer (click the Owner tab)
- View the effective permissions for a user or group (click the Effective Permissions tab)

Special permissions enable you to fine-tune shared printer permissions, as when configuring a group that has Manage Printers permissions to be able to perform all functions except taking ownership.

Any user account or group can be set up for auditing by clicking the Auditing tab and the Add button. Before you set up printer auditing, make sure that there is a Group Policy or default domain security policy that enables object auditing on the basis of successful and failed activity attempts. For a shared printer you can track successful or failed attempts to:

- Print jobs
- Manage printers
- Manage documents
- Read printer share permissions
- Change printer share permissions
- Take ownership of the printer

Activity 6-8: Configuring Printer Security

Time Required: Approximately 10 minutes

Objective: Learn how to set up security on a shared printer.

Description: Configuring security is very important on a shared printer. You want to control who has access and assure the productivity of the printer's users. In this activity, you remove the Everyone group from access to a printer, and provide access to the domain local group that you created in Chapter 4. You also set up auditing of failed printing attempts for the domain local group you created.

1. Click **Start**, point to **Control Panel**, point to **Printers and Faxes**, and right-click the printer you installed in Activity 6-2, such as HP Color LaserJetJP. Click **Properties**.

2. Click the **Security** tab. What security is set up already? Record your observations.

3. Click the **Everyone** group, and click **Remove**. Is the Name box updated to reflect the change?

4. Click the **Add** button, click the **Advanced** button, click **Find Now**, double-click the domain local group you created in Chapter 4, such as DomainMgrsJP, and click **OK**. What permissions are given to this group by default?

5. Make sure that **Print** is checked for **Allow**.

6. Click the **Advanced** button.

7. Click the **Auditing** tab.

8. Click **Add**, click the **Advanced** button, click **Find Now**, double-click the domain local group you created in Chapter 4, such as DomainMgrsJP, and click **OK**.

9. Make sure **This printer and documents** is selected.

10. Click the **Failed** box for Print (notice that Read Permissions is also checked automatically), and click **OK** (see Figure 6-11). What information now appears in the Auditing entries box?

11. Click **OK**. If there is a message that auditing is not turned on as a Group Policy, how would you turn it on?

12. Click **OK**.

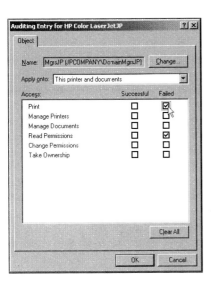

Figure 6-11   Configuring shared printer auditing

6

Configuring Device Settings

The Device Settings tab enables you to specify printer settings that are specific to the printer you have installed, such as printer trays, memory, paper size, fonts, and installable options (see Figure 6-12). For example, in many cases, if you have a multiple-tray printer you can leave the paper tray assignment on Auto Select (not shown in Figure 6-12, but available on some printers) and let the software application at the client specify the printer tray. Or, if your organization uses special forms such as paychecks, you can specify use of a designated paper tray when checks are printing.

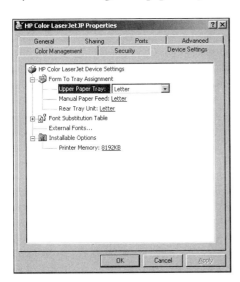

Figure 6-12   Configuring printer device settings

The printer memory is usually automatically detected in bidirectional printers, but if it is not, you can specify the amount of memory in the Printer Memory option under Installable Options. In the client operating systems, such as Windows 2000 Professional, Windows XP Professional, or Windows 98, the workstation printer setup also can have information about how much memory is installed in a shared printer.

Make sure the memory reported in the device settings matches the memory installed in the printer, because this enables the print server to offload more work to the printer, improving the speed at which print jobs are completed, as well as server performance. Most other settings are better left to the software at the client end to handle. For example, a client printing in Microsoft Word can specify font and paper tray instructions inside the document and by using the Printer Setup.

CONFIGURING A NONLOCAL PRINTER OR AN INTERNET PRINTER

There are times when you want to enable a Windows 2003 server to connect to a printer that is not directly connected to one of its ports, for example a printer shared from a workstation, another server, the Internet or an intranet, or one that is connected to the network through a print server card or device. You can connect to a network printer by using the Add Printer Wizard and following these general steps:

1. Click **Start**, point to **Control Panel**, point **to Printers and Faxes**, and click **Add Printer**.

2. Click **Next**.

3. Select **A network printer, or a printer attached to another computer** (see Figure 6-3), and click **Next**.

4. The Specify a Printer window opens (see Figure 6-13), with options to: (1) Find a printer in the directory (for Active Directory installations), (2) Connect to this printer (or to browse for the printer, select this option and click Next), or (3) Connect to a printer on the Internet or on a home or office network. Click the appropriate option, and click **Next**. If you specify Find a printer in the Directory, the Find Printers dialog box opens from which you can enter the printer's name or use the Browse button to locate the printer. If you choose Connect to this printer, you simply enter the UNC of the printer as illustrated under the Name box. If you want to Connect to a printer on the Internet or on a home or office network, then you need to provide the URL.

5. Follow the instructions to complete the installation, which in most cases involves clicking **Yes** to print a test page, then clicking **Next**, and clicking **Finish**.

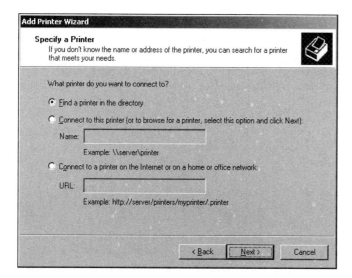

Figure 6-13   Specifying printer options

When the remote printer is installed on a domain controller, you can change the properties of the shared printer you just installed, even though you are not logged on to its host computer. This means you can manage any remote shared network printer, even though it is not connected to a port on the server. For example, open Control Panel's Printers and Faxes option and right-click the remote printer you installed. Click the Properties selection and make any changes you desire. This capability is very useful when you manage a large network with network printers located in distant buildings. If you need to change the print processor used by a shared printer that is a block away, you can do so without leaving your office.

MANAGING PRINT JOBS

In the time after a print job is sent and before it is fully transmitted to the printer, there are several options for managing that job. Users with Print permissions can print and manage their own jobs. Also members of the Printer Operators, Server Operators, and Administrators groups can manage the jobs of others through the Manage Documents and Manage Printers permissions. To manage printed documents, access Control Panel's Printers and Faxes option, and click the appropriate printer. The following options are available to users with Print permissions:

- Send print jobs to the printer
- Pause, resume, and restart their own print jobs
- Cancel their own print jobs

Print Operators, Server Operators, and other groups having Manage Documents permissions can:

- Send print jobs to the printer
- Pause, resume, and restart any user's print jobs
- Cancel any user's print jobs

Administrators, Print Operators, Server Operators, and any other groups having Manage Printers permissions can do all of the same things as those with Manage Documents permissions, but they also can change the properties of the printer, for example, start and stop sharing, configure printer properties, take ownership, change permissions, and set the default printer for the Windows 2003 server.

Controlling the Status of Printing

In Windows Server 2003, printer control and setup information for a particular printer is associated with that printer's selection in Control Panel's Printers and Faxes option. For example, if you have two printers installed, HPLaser_Rm20 and InkJet_Rm8, there is a set of properties and printer control information for each printer. If you want to pause a print job on the HPLaser_Rm20 printer, click Start, point to Control Panel, point to Printers and Faxes, and click HPLaser_Rm20. If you want to delete a print job on the InkJet_Rm8 printer, find that printer within Printers and Faxes, and click it.

Sometimes you need to pause a printer to fix a problem, for example, to reattach a loose cable or to power the printer off and on to reset it. You can pause printing to that printer by clicking it in Printers and Faxes, clicking the Printer menu, and clicking the Pause Printing option so there is a check mark beside it (see Figure 6-14). Remember that you need to uncheck Pause Printing before print jobs can continue printing. The Pause Printing capability is particularly important if a user sends an improperly formatted document to the printer, for example a PostScript-formatted document to a non-PostScript printer. If you do not have Hold mismatched documents enabled, the printer may print tens or hundreds of pages with a single control code on each page. By pausing printing, you have time to identify and delete the document before too much paper is used.

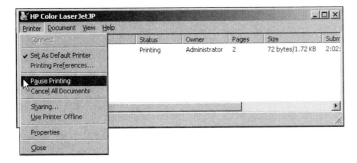

Figure 6-14   Pausing printing

Controlling Specific Print Jobs

You can pause, resume, restart, or view the properties of one or more documents in the print queue of a printer. A **print queue** is like a stack of print jobs, with the first job submitted at the top of the stack and the last job submitted at the bottom, and all of the jobs waiting to be sent from the spooler to the printer.

In Windows Server 2003, to pause a print job, click Start, point to Control Panel, point to Printers and Faxes, and click the appropriate printer. The resulting window shows a list of jobs to be printed, the status of each job, the owner, the number of pages to be printed, the size of the print file, and when the print job was submitted. Click the document you want to pause, click the Document menu, and then click Pause. That print job stops printing until you highlight the document and click Resume or Restart on the Document menu. Resume starts printing at the point in the document where the printing was paused. Restart prints from the beginning of the document. You also can use the Document menu to cancel a print job. First click the job in the status window, click the Document menu, and click Cancel.

Jobs print in the order they are received, unless the administrator changes their priority. Jobs come in with a priority of 1, but can be assigned a priority as high as 99. For example, if you work for a university, the president may need to quickly print a last-minute report before going to a meeting with the trustees. You can give the president a 99 priority by clicking her print job in the window listing the print jobs. Next click the Document menu, click Properties, and access the General tab. The Priority box is in the middle of the General tab. Move the slider from Lowest (1) to Highest (99), depending on your requirements and click OK (see Figure 6-15).

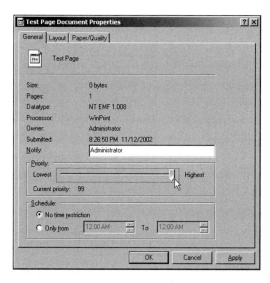

Figure 6-15 Changing the print priority

You also can use the General tab to set a time for selected jobs to print on a printer. For example, if the server is very busy during the day, you can ease the load by setting jobs to print at a certain time of day, such as from noon to 1 p.m. The General tab also provides basic information about the file such as the size, the owner, the data type used, the print processor used, and when the job was submitted.

Activity 6-9: Pausing a Printer and Canceling a Document

Time Required: Approximately 5 minutes

Objective: Learn how to pause a printer and then cancel a document.

Description: Assume that your office has a printer that is printing sheet after sheet of garbled text and you need to pause printing to that printer until you can cancel the print job. This activity enables you to do just that.

1. Click **Start**, point to **Control Panel**, point to **Printers and Faxes**, and click the printer you installed in Activity 6-2, such as HP Color LaserJetJP.

2. Click the **Printer** menu, and click **Pause Printing**. Has the title bar of the printer window changed, and if so how?

3. Create a document using a word processor or using Notepad that contains only one or two words, such as **Test**. Send the document to the printer that you have paused.

4. When the document appears in the printer window, click it.

5. Click the **Document** menu. What options are available to you to control a print job? Click the **Properties** option. How would you reset the priority of this print job from the General tab? Click the **Cancel** button to close the Properties dialog box.

6. Right-click the document that you sent to the printer, and click **Cancel**. Click **Yes** to confirm that you want to delete the selected print job.

7. Click the **Printer** menu, and click **Pause Printing** to remove the check. Has the title bar of the printer window changed?

8. Close the **printer** window.

TROUBLESHOOTING COMMON PRINTING PROBLEMS

One common printing problem occurs when the Windows Server 2003 Print Spooler Service experiences a temporary difficulty, gets out of synchronization, or hangs. Because the spooler contains several complex pieces, it is a possible source of printer problems. The result is that print jobs are not processed until the problem is solved. If a print job is not going through, and you determine that one or more printers are not paused, and that the cable connection is good, then stop and restart the Print Spooler Service by using the following general steps:

1. Click **Start**, point to **All Programs**, point to **Administrative Tools**, and click **Computer Management**.

2. Click **Services** in the tree under Services and Applications.

3. Scroll to Print Spooler.

4. Check the status column to determine if the Print Spooler service is started, and make sure that it is set to start automatically. If it is not started, if it is not set to start automatically, or if you need to stop and restart the spooler, double-click **Print Spooler**. To start the service, click **Start**. If you need to set it to start automatically, set this option in the Startup type box; to stop and restart the service, click **Stop**, and then click **Start**. Make sure that the service status is Started and that the startup type is Automatic. Click **OK**.

5. Close the **Computer Management** window.

 Warn users before you stop and restart the Print Spooler Service, because queued print jobs will be deleted.

Because the Print Spooler Service is dependent on the Remote Procedure Call (RPC) Service, check to make sure that the Remote Procedure Call Service is also started and set to start automatically. Further, make sure that the Server Service is working and that the TCP/IP Print Server Service is working, if you have spooler problems.

There are several other common problems that can occur that are summarized in Table 6-2.

Table 6-2 Troubleshooting printing problems

Network Printing Problem	Solutions
Only one character prints per page	1. If only one workstation experiences this problem, reinstall the printer driver on that workstation using the Add Printer Wizard. 2. If all workstations are experiencing the problem, reinstall the printer and printer driver at the computer or print server offering the printer share (using the Add Printer Wizard). 3. Check the print monitor and data type setup.
Some users get a no-access message when trying to access the printer share	Check the share permissions. Make certain the clients belong to a group for which at least Print permission has been granted and that none of the groups to which these users belong are denied Print permissions.
Printer control codes are on the printout	1. If only one workstation experiences the problem, reinstall the printer driver on that workstation using the Add Printer Wizard. Also, make sure the software generating the printout is installed correctly. 2. If all workstations are experiencing the problem, reinstall the printer and printer driver at the computer or print server offering the printer share (using the Add Printer Wizard). 3. Make sure the share is set up for all operating systems that access it, that the correct print monitor is installed, and that the right data type is used.
A print job shows it is printing, the printer looks fine, but nothing is printing	1. Click the printer in Control Panel's Printers and Faxes option. Check for a problem with the print job at the top of the queue. If it shows the job is printing but nothing is happening, delete the print job because it may be hung (and resubmit the print job). 2. Also, try stopping and restarting the Print Spooler Service (warn users first).
Some clients find that the ending pages are not printed for large print jobs	Check the disk space on the server or workstation in which the job is spooled. It may not have enough space to fully spool all jobs.
On some long print jobs, pages from other print jobs are found in the printout	Set the printer's properties so that the printer starts printing only after all pages are spooled. To do that, right-click the printer in Control Panel's Printers and Faxes option, click Properties on the shortcut menu, click the Advanced tab, click the Spool print documents so program finishes printing faster option button, click the Start printing after last page is spooled option button, and click OK.
Extra separator pages are printed or print jobs seem to get stuck in the printer for all users	Check the print processor in use by accessing the printer's Properties dialog box, click the Advanced tab, click the Print Processor button, and check the print processor in use. Also check the data type. If the problem continues, try a different data type.
Some clients occasionally send a document that prints garbage on hundreds of pages before anyone notices and can stop the printing	Have the spooler automatically hold printer jobs that contain the wrong printer setup information. To do that, access the printer's Properties dialog box, click the Advanced tab, click the check box to Hold mismatched documents, and click OK on the Properties dialog box.

CHAPTER SUMMARY

- A Windows 2003 server can be configured to provide local or network printing.
- Network printing works through the use of the HTTP protocol and the Internet Printing Protocol.
- Local and shared printers are installed by using the Add Printer Wizard from Control Panel's Printers and Faxes option.
- The properties associated with a printer enable you to configure general printer information, printer sharing, printer port setup, printer scheduling, advanced printer options, printer security, and device settings, such as paper trays.
- Use the Add Printer Wizard to install a nonlocal printer or an Internet printer. When these are configured from a Windows 2003 server, it is possible to manage their properties configurations from the server.

❑ Managing a printer entails actions such as pausing and resuming printing and setting the default printer. Specific print jobs can be canceled, paused, started, and resumed. Also, each print job has associated properties, such as the priority setting for the print job.

❑ There are many ways to troubleshoot printing problems, such as restarting the Print Spooler Service.

KEY TERMS

bidirectional printing — Ability of a printer connected to a computer's parallel port to conduct two-way communications between the printer and the computer, such as to provide out of paper information; also bidirectional printing supports Plug and Play and enables an operating system to query a printer about its capabilities.

data type — The way in which information is formatted in a print file.

enhanced metafile (EMF) — A data type for printing used by Windows 95, 98, Me, NT, 2000, XP, and 2003 operating systems. EMF print files offer a distinct advantage in Windows operating system environments because they are very portable from computer to computer.

graphics device interface (GDI) — An interface on a Windows network print client that works with a local software application, such as Microsoft Word, and a local printer driver to format a file to be sent to a local printer or a network print server.

Internet Printing Protocol (IPP) — A protocol that is encapsulated in HTTP and that is used to print files over the Internet.

local print device — A printer, such as a laser printer, physically attached to a port on the local computer.

network print device — A printing device, such as a laser printer, connected to a print server through a network.

PostScript printer — A printer that has special firmware or cartridges to print using a page-description language (PDL).

print client — Client computer or application that generates a print job.

print queue — A stack or lineup of print jobs, with the first job submitted at the top of the stack and the last job submitted at the bottom, and all of the jobs waiting to be sent from the spooler to the printer.

print server — Network computer or server device that connects printers to the network for sharing and that receives and processes print requests from print clients.

Printer Control Language (PCL) — A printer language used by non-PostScript Hewlett-Packard and compatible laser printers.

printer driver — Contains the device-specific information that Windows Server 2003 requires to control a particular print device, implementing customized printer control codes, font, and style information so that documents are converted into a printer-specific language.

printer pooling — Linking two or more identical printers with one printer setup or printer share.

RAW — A data type often used for printing MS-DOS, Windows 3.x, and UNIX print files.

spool file — A print file written to disk until it can be transmitted to a printer.

spooler — In the Windows 95, 98, Me, NT, 2000, XP, and 2003 environment, a group of DLLs, information files, and programs that process print jobs for printing.

spooling — A process working in the background to enable several print files to go to a single printer. Each file is placed in temporary storage until its turn comes to be printed.

TEXT — A data type used for printing text files formatted using the ANSI standard that employs values between 0 and 255 to represent characters, numbers, and symbols.

REVIEW QUESTIONS

1. An office of software programmers has called you because they have one printer that everyone uses to print programs on which they are working. Some of the programs generate pages of output causing long backups in the print queue. A manager has offered to give this office a new printer that is identical to the one they have already. Which of the following would work best in setting up this new printer?

   a. Make the new printer the default printer and give it the highest priority, so that the old printer does not wear out faster.

   b. Adjust the timing to be equal for the print queues associated with both printers.

   c. Configure both printers as pooled, so there is the least impact on the office users.

   d. Use an alternate printer driver for the new printer, so that the network does not confuse it with the original printer.

2. The Research Department in your company wants to be able to work with database files on a Windows 2003 server and then have print jobs from that database be transferred to a printer connected to a UNIX computer located in their office. How would you set up the printer properties on the Windows 2003 server for printouts transferred to the UNIX printer? (Choose all that apply.)

   a. Configure an LPR Port in the printer properties.

   b. Configure a Conversion File Port in the printer properties.

   c. Configure the printer properties so that there is a UNIX tray in the device settings.

   d. Install Print Services for UNIX on the Windows 2003 server.

   e. Windows Server 2003 no longer supports UNIX printing.

3. Your company's president is going out of town shortly and her administrative assistant needs to print several documents as soon as possible. The problem is that the printer used by the administrative assistant is shared by several people and there are already 28 documents in the print queue. What can you do to help?

   a. Cancel the print jobs that are ahead of the administrative assistant's, but reschedule them to print later.

   b. Pause and restart the printer to clear the queue, and then submit the administrative assistant's print jobs.

   c. Stop and restart the print queue, and then submit the administrative assistant's print jobs.

   d. Have the administrative assistant submit the print jobs and then give each one a priority of 99.

4. As the printer administrator for your company, you need to establish a backup person who not only can manage all print jobs to all printers, but also can change sharing properties and permissions for printers. What shared printer permissions should you give to your backup person? (Choose all that apply.)

   a. Manage Printers

   b. Full Control

   c. Documents Control

   d. Print

   e. Manage Documents

5. The power supply in one of your shared printers has burned out. You plan to purchase an identical printer, but not for two weeks. Which of the following enables you to prevent users from trying to use that printer?

   a. Disable the printer sharing.

   b. Change permissions so that no one but you can access the printer.

   c. Set up auditing on the Everyone group using the failure option.

d. all of the above

e. only a and b

f. only b and c

6. Someone in your office often sends documents formatted for PostScript to the office's PCL printer, causing it to print page after page of garbage and thus waste paper. How can you best solve this problem?

a. Configure the printer's properties to hold mismatched documents.

b. Use Postscript spooling for the PCL printer.

c. Configure the printer to use a separator page to give you time to cancel these printer jobs.

d. Determine who is sending the documents and take away his or her permissions to use the printer.

7. Most of the users of a shared printer you are configuring on a Windows 2003 server have Windows 2000 Professional workstations. What data type should you configure for these users?

a. RAW

b. RAW (FF appended)

c. NT EMF

d. TEXT

8. Your office can only afford one printer. The problem is that some people occupy the printer by sending 100-page print jobs that do not need to print immediately. What solution can you use to solve this problem?

a. Frequently monitor the print queue and pause the long print jobs until near the end of the workday.

b. Develop a voluntary system so that users with jobs over 50 pages print only during the lunch hour or after 5 p.m.

c. Change permissions for users who send long print jobs from Print to Limited Print, and then set the limited print jobs to 25 pages or less.

d. Set up two printer objects for one printer, but implement one object for long print jobs and schedule it to print after the workday or overnight.

9. Your boss has purchased a new bidirectional printer to attach to one of the Windows 2003 servers used by your company. Which of the following should you do to set up the printer? (Choose all that apply.)

a. Configure the Advanced settings in the printer's properties to enable flash printing.

b. Check to make sure you attach the printer using an IEEE 1284 cable.

c. Check the BIOS setup in the computer to make sure that bidirectional is enabled for the port to which the printer is attached.

d. Enable bidirectional support in the Ports settings in the printer's properties.

10. Your printer has extra memory, but it does not seem to process print jobs any faster than printers with less memory. What should you check?

a. Make sure that the printer's properties are configured to Print directly to the printer.

b. Disable printer scheduling in the printer's properties.

c. Check the Device Settings tab in the printer's properties to make sure the amount of memory recorded there matches the amount in the printer.

d. Configure the Advanced tab in the printer's properties for automated sharing, which enables the print processor to fully use the memory in the printer.

11. You are in a meeting to troubleshoot a problem with printing checks for your organization, which has 500 employees. Last night, the printer jammed when checks were printing and the payroll office spent hours resetting the payroll program to only print certain checks that were damaged. How can you prevent such drastic time loss next time, so the payroll office can go home earlier?

    a. Set the printer to print from Tray 2, because Tray 1 is more likely to cause jams.

    b. Configure that printer to Enable advanced printing features, and then have it pause two seconds between each check to give the printer more time to reset.

    c. Schedule paychecks to print at night so there is more time to deal with this problem.

    d. Just before printing the paychecks, configure that printer to Keep printed documents.

12. Which of the following protocols is (are) important for Internet printing through a Windows 2003 server? (Choose all that apply.)

    a. IPP

    b. NetBEUI

    c. IPX

    d. NWLink

13. Your printer uses the Printer Control Language and you have been asked to set up a separator page in the printer's properties. Which of the following should you use for the separator page?

    a. Sysprint.sep

    b. Sysprtj.sep

    c. Pcl.sep

    d. Post.sep

14. A user is calling you to report that he sent a print job to the printer at least four hours ago and it still has not printed. How can you verify the exact time when the job was submitted to help in your analysis of the problem?

    a. Check the properties of the printer.

    b. Check the properties of the print job.

    c. Check the printer's Advanced tab.

    d. That information is not available.

15. _____ a printer so that it can be managed and accessed as a resource through Active Directory.

    a. Bond

    b. Transfer ownership of

    c. Publish

    d. Set special permissions on

16. You have set up a shared printer on a Windows 2003 server, but Marsha Valdez gets an access denied message when she attempts to use the printer. Marsha belongs to two global groups, Managers and Sales, which are members of the domain local groups Managers and Marketing, respectively. Which of the following might be a problem?

    a. You have granted Print permissions to the global groups, but not to the domain local groups.

    b. The Managers domain local group is denied Print permissions.

    c. You have granted Print permissions to the domain local groups, but not to the global groups.

    d. The Sales global group must also be a member of the Print Operators group.

17. Is there a tool in Windows Server 2003 that enables you to troubleshoot a problem like the one in Question 16?

    a. Yes, diagnose the problem using the audit capability of a printer's properties.

    b. Yes, diagnose the problem by determining the effective permissions for a printer.

    c. Yes, use the Printer Permissions Troubleshooting Wizard for that printer.

    d. No, there is no specialized tool to help you diagnose permissions conflicts for shared printers.

18. Which document printing option commences a print job from where it left off?

    a. renew

    b. reset

    c. restart

    d. resume

19. The Sales Department for your company has one network printer attached to its Windows 2003 server and currently the printer is unable to process print requests, even though nothing appears to be wrong with the printer. Which of the following should you try? (Choose all that apply.)

    a. Make sure that there is sufficient disk space to handle large spool files.

    b. Reinstall the printer driver in case it is corrupted.

    c. Stop and restart the Print Spooler service.

    d. Delete the print job at the top of the print queue.

20. The Payroll Department has one network printer, called PAY, that is used only to print checks. The printer is always loaded with checks, but kept in a locked room. What other steps would you take to secure this printer?

    a. Set the permissions so that only the Payroll Department can access the printer.

    b. Audit the Everyone group for successful printing to that printer.

    c. Have the Payroll Department take ownership of the printer.

    d. all of the above

    e. only a and b

    f. only a and c

21. The clients of a Windows 2003 server shared printer are running Windows XP Professional and Windows 98. The Windows XP Professional clients are using the shared printer successfully, but not the Windows 98 clients. Which of the following might be the solution?

    a. Install the Directory Service Client on the Windows 98 computers.

    b. Configure additional drivers for Windows 98 in the printer's properties.

    c. Set the printer's Device Settings to enable Windows 95/98

    d. Enable use of short MS-DOS printer names in the printer's properties.

22. You want to configure Windows Server 2003 to use a printer that is connected through the Internet. How is this possible?

    a. Use the Add Printer Wizard, and select to install a network printer.

    b. Use the Add Printer Wizard, and select to install a local printer.

    c. Set up the printer first, and then configure the Ports tab for Local Port, providing the IP address of the Internet printer.

    d. Use the Tools menu in Internet Explorer.

23. Which printer properties tab enables you to configure the times during which a printer is available for use?

    a. General

    b. Ports

    c. Security

    d. Advanced

24. In Windows Server 2003 printing, the _____ integrates information about the print file with information obtained from the printer driver installed at the client.

    a. spool monitor

    b. graphics device interface

    c. TCP/IP protocol

    d. scheduler

25. Which of the following can a user perform who has Print permissions for a shared printer? (Choose all that apply.)

    a. Send print jobs to that printer.

    b. Cancel their own print jobs.

    c. Cancel the print jobs of others.

    d. Pause the printer.

CASE PROJECTS

Case Project Background

Modern Cuisine Utensils manufactures cooking utensils, such as iron and porcelain pans and pots, as well as stoneware. The company's manufacturing building has three servers, one that is used for manufacturing, one that tracks inventory, and one that handles product distribution. Because each server is in a central location for its associated function, the company has purchased two identical printers to connect to each server for a total of six printers. Modern Cuisine Utensils contracts out many IT functions and has hired Bayside IT Services to advise them on the setup of the printers.

Case Project 6-1: Installing the Printers

The manufacturing building has two people who are assigned to manage the printers for the entire building. Modern Cuisine Utensils asks you to explain how to install the printers that are attached to the servers. Develop a general instruction set to which they can refer when setting up a printer. As you develop your instructions, keep in mind that the workstations accessing the printers are running either Windows 2000 Professional or Windows 98. The network is TCP/IP based.

Case Project 6-2: Configuring Permissions

Explain what permissions should be granted to the two people who will be setting up and managing the printers and explain how to set up the permissions.

Case Project 6-3: Additional Configuration Questions

The two printer coordinators have some extra questions about the following:

- Is there a way to set up large print jobs so that they only print after 7 p.m. when most employees have gone home?

- How can a printer be stopped from printing while it is being maintained?

- Is there a way to retain print files so that they can be reprinted? And if so, how are they deleted when no longer needed?

Prepare a document to answer their questions.

6

Case Project 6-4: A Printing Problem

Printouts on the printers connected to the manufacturing server often have pages from other printouts mixed in. How can you solve this problem?

CONFIGURING AND MANAGING DATA STORAGE

After reading this chapter and completing the exercises, you will be able to:

♦ Understand the Windows Server 2003 storage options, including basic and dynamic disks

♦ Perform disk management and troubleshooting on partitions, volumes, and mounted drives

♦ Configure and manage RAID volumes for fault tolerance

♦ Perform disk backups

♦ Restore data to a disk

When Intel-based servers first appeared on the scene, disk storage options were limited because disk sizes were relatively small at 20 to 40 MB. At 20 GB and beyond, disk storage has come a long way and is arguably one of the most important server elements that you can configure and maintain. Server activities are typically related to providing files, databases, and applications to clients—and all of these require disk storage.

In this chapter, you'll learn the fundamentals of Windows Server 2003 disk storage. You will learn both disk types (basic and dynamic) supported by Windows Server 2003, including how to configure and manage each one. You'll also discover the different RAID options available to provide fault tolerance and how these options are used in Windows Server 2003. Further, you will learn how to protect your valuable data and operating system files by performing backups and restores.

WINDOWS SERVER 2003 STORAGE OPTIONS

Windows Server 2003 supports two data storage types: basic disks and dynamic disks. A **basic disk** is one that uses traditional disk management techniques and contains primary partitions, extended partitions, and logical drives. A **dynamic disk** is one that does not use traditional partitioning. Dynamic disk architecture provides new flexibility so there is virtually no restriction to the number of volumes that can be on one disk. Both types of data storage are discussed in the next sections.

Basic Disks

Because a basic disk uses traditional disk management techniques, it is partitioned and formatted and can be set up to employ disk sets. **Partitioning** is a process that blocks a group of tracks and sectors to be used by a particular file system, such as FAT or NTFS. **Formatting** is a process that creates a table containing file and folder information for a specific file system in a partition. Formatting also creates a root directory (folder) and a volume label.

Basic disks recognize primary and extended partitions, which are discussed in the next section. Basic disks also can be configured for any of three RAID levels: disk striping (RAID level 0), disk mirroring (RAID level 1), and disk striping with parity (RAID level 5). **RAID** stands for **redundant array of inexpensive** (or **independent**) **disks**—a set of standards for lengthening disk life and preventing data loss. Disk **striping** is the ability to spread data over multiple disks or volumes. For example, part of a large file may be written to one disk and part to another. The goal is to spread disk activity equally across all disks, preventing wear from being focused on a single disk in a set. **Disk mirroring** is the practice of creating a mirror image of all data on an original disk, so that the data is fully copied or mirrored to a backup disk. The sole purpose of the backup disk is to go into live production, but only if the original disk fails.

Any disks that are added to a computer running Windows Server 2003 are automatically configured as basic disks. Also, if you upgrade any of the Windows NT Server 4.0, 3.51, or 3.5 operating systems to Windows Server 2003, all disks are initialized as basic disks. Further, if you upgrade a Windows 2000 server that has basic disks, the resulting Windows 2003 server will have basic disks.

Primary and Extended Partitions

A partition may be set up as primary or extended. A basic disk must contain at least one **primary partition** and can contain up to a maximum of four per disk. A primary partition is one from which you can boot an operating system, such as Windows Server 2003, Standard Edition. Or a primary partition may simply hold files in a different file system format. When you boot from a primary partition, it contains the operating system startup files in a location at the beginning of the partition. For example, the startup files for Windows 98 include Io.sys and Msdos.sys. For Windows Server 2003, the startup files include Boot.ini, Ntldr (treated as a .sys file), and Ntdetect.com, for example. At least one primary partition must be marked as active and only one primary partition can be active at a given time. The **active partition** is the partition where your computer looks for the hardware-specific files to start the operating system (system partition).

An **extended partition** is created from space that is not yet partitioned. The purpose of an extended partition is to enable you to exceed the four-partition limit of a basic disk. There can be only one extended partition on a single basic disk. An extended partition is not actually formatted and assigned a drive letter. Once an extended partition is created, it is further divided up into logical drives. The logical drives are then formatted and assigned drive letters.

A computer with multiple partitions boots from the partition that is designated as the active partition, which must also be the system partition containing the startup files. To determine which partition is designated as active, look for the "(System)" designation in the Disk Management tool pane that gives information about the disk's size and file system.

Two other references to partitioning used by Microsoft are important to understand. The **system partition** is the partition that contains the hardware specific files, such as Boot.ini, Ntldr, and Ntdetect.com, needed to load the operating system. The **boot partition** is the partition that contains the operating system files located in the \Windows folder. The system partition has to be on a primary partition, while the boot partition can be installed on a primary or extended partition.

Activity 7-1: Viewing the Active Partition

Time Required: Approximately 5 minutes

Objective: Verify which partition is marked as active.

Description: In this activity, you use the Computer Management window to access the Disk Management tool and verify which is the active partition, along with other information about the disks on your system. Also, you learn how to mark a partition as active.

1. Click **Start**, right-click **My Computer**, and click **Manage**.

2. Double-click **Storage** under the tree, if the tools under it are not displayed. What tools are available?

3. Click **Disk Management** in the tree. Notice the active partition, as illustrated in Figure 7-1. Also, in Figure 7-1, the disks are configured as basic disks. What type(s) of disks are on the computer you are using for this activity? Which disk on your computer is designated as the system disk? What file systems are used on your computer?

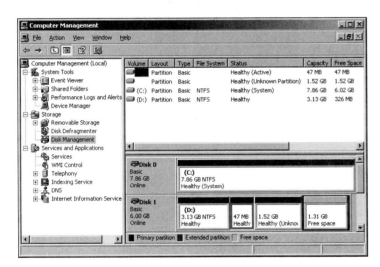

Figure 7-1   Verifying the Active partition

4. In the lower-right area of the window, find a partition that is not labeled as the system partition, and right-click it (do not click in the area that says Disk 0 or Disk 1, but do click in the area labeled as (D:), for example).

5. Notice the Mark Partition as Active option on the shortcut menu (see Figure 7-2). This is the option you would click to mark a partition as active. (Do not mark the partition active in this practice session, unless your instructor gives you permission.)

6. Close the **Computer Management** window.

Figure 7-2   Shortcut menu

Activity 7-2: Customize the MMC to Access Disk Management Tools

Time Required: Approximately 10 minutes

Objective: Create a customized console from which to perform disk management and disk defragmentation.

Description: Some server managers prefer to customize an MMC window from which to access disk management tools. In this activity you customize an MMC window to contain the Disk Management tool and the Disk Defragmenter.

1. Click **Start** and click **Run**. Enter **mmc** in the Open box, and click **OK**.

2. Maximize the Console windows, if necessary. Click the **File** menu, and click **Add/Remove Snap-in**.

3. Click the **Add** button, and double-click **Disk Management**.

4. Use the default selection, **This computer**, and click **Finish**.

5. Double-click **Disk Defragmenter**. If you wanted to manage removable storage from the same customized console, what additional snap-in might you add?

6. Click **Close** and then click **OK**. Your customized console window should look similar to Figure 7-3.

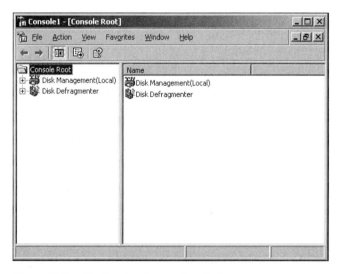

Figure 7-3   Customized console window

7. Notice the title bar of the window reads Console1 – [Console Root].

8. Click the **File** menu, and click **Save As**. Enter Disk Tools plus your initials, such as **Disk ToolsJP.msc** as the name for this Console setup, and click **Save**. What is on the title bar now?

9. Close the console window.

10. Click **Start**, point to **All Programs**, point to **Administrative Tools**, and notice that your customized console is listed, such as Disk ToolsJP.msc.

Volume and Stripe Sets

Under Windows NT 4.0 you can create multidisk volumes also known as volume sets and stripe sets. A **volume set** consists of two or more partitions that are combined to look like one volume with a single drive letter. A **stripe set** is two or more disks that are combined like a volume set, but that are striped for RAID level 0 or RAID level 5 (RAID is discussed later in this chapter). Windows Server 2003 (and Windows 2000 Server) provides backward compatibility with basic disk volume and stripe sets that have previously been created through Windows NT. If you have any of these multidisk volumes on a computer running Windows NT 4.0, you can still use them after you upgrade to Windows Server 2003, but you cannot create new volume or stripe sets should the disks fail. For this reason, after a Windows NT server is upgraded to Windows Server 2003, you should plan to convert basic disks to dynamic disks in order to implement any new multidisk volumes.

Dynamic Disks

A dynamic disk does not use traditional partitioning, which makes it possible to set up a large number of volumes on one disk and provides the ability to extend volumes onto additional physical disks. There is an upward limit of 32 disks that can be incorporated into one spanned volume. Besides volume extensions and spanned volumes, dynamic disks support RAID levels 0, 1, and 5. Dynamic disks can be formatted for FAT16, FAT32, or NTFS and are used when you do not implement a dual-boot system. Also, dynamic disks can be reactivated, should they go offline because they have been powered down or disconnected.

Plan to convert basic disks to dynamic disks after you install Windows Server 2003, so that you can take advantage of the richer set of options associated with dynamic disks. There are five types of dynamic disk configurations: simple volumes, spanned volumes, mirrored volumes, striped volumes, and RAID-5 volumes. The functional concepts of these disk configurations are similar to those used for Windows NT 4.0-compatible basic disks, but the Windows Server 2003 dynamic disks have better disk management options and do not use partitioning. For example, the dynamic disk equivalent of a basic disk volume set is called "spanned volumes," and the equivalent of a basic disk stripe set is called "striped volumes."

On dynamic disks, instead of using the basic disk terminology of boot partition and system partition, the volume that contains the \Windows folder of system files is called the boot volume, and the volume that contains the files used to boot the computer is called the system volume.

In the next sections, you'll learn more about simple, spanned, and striped volumes. Later, in the "Introduction to Fault Tolerance" section, you'll learn about dynamic disk mirrored volumes and RAID-5 volumes, plus additional information about using striped volumes.

 Dynamic disks are recognized by both the Windows 2000 and Windows Server 2003 operating systems. Earlier operating systems such as Windows Me, Windows 98, Windows 95, and MS-DOS do not support dynamic disks. Keep this in mind if you are planning a dual-boot configuration consisting of Windows Server 2003 and Windows Me, for example. Any operating systems that do not support dynamic disks cannot access dynamic volumes on the local computer.

Simple Volume

A **simple volume** is a portion of a disk or an entire disk that is set up as a dynamic disk. If you do not allocate all of a disk as a simple volume, you have the option to later take all or a portion of the unallocated space and add it to an existing simple volume, which is called extending the volume. A simple volume can be extended onto multiple sections of the same disk (up to 32 sections). A simple volume does not provide fault tolerance, because it cannot be set up for any RAID level (see the "Introduction to Fault Tolerance" section later in the chapter).

Spanned Volume

A **spanned volume** contains two to 32 dynamic disks that are treated as one volume. For example, you might create a spanned volume if you have four separate small hard disks, 2 GB, 2 GB, 3 GB, and 4 GB as shown in Figure 7-4. Another reason to use a spanned volume is if you have several small free portions of disk space scattered throughout the server's disk drives. You might have 600 MB of free space on one drive, 150 MB on another, and 70 MB on a third. All of these free areas can be combined into a single 820 MB spanned volume with its own drive letter, with the advantage that you reduce the number of drive letters needed to make use of the space.

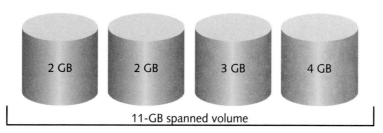

Figure 7-4 Creating one spanned volume from four disks

As you add new disks, the spanned volume can be extended to include each disk. Volumes formatted for NTFS can be extended, but those formatted for FAT16 and FAT32 cannot. The advantage of creating spanned volumes is the ability to more easily manage several small disk drives or to maximize the use of scattered pockets of disk space across several disks.

 The disadvantage of using a spanned volume is that if one disk fails, the entire volume is inaccessible. Also, if a portion of a spanned volume is deleted, the entire disk set is deleted. For these reasons, avoid placing mission-critical data and applications on a spanned volume.

Striped Volume

Striped volumes are often referred to as RAID level 0. The main purpose for striping disks in a volume is to extend the life of hard disk drives by spreading data equally over two or more drives. Spreading the data divides the drive load so that one drive is not working more than any other. Another advantage of striping is that it increases disk performance. Contention among disks is equalized and data is accessed faster for both reading and writing than when it is on a single drive, because Windows Server 2003 can write to all drives at the same time.

In Windows Server 2003, striping requires at least two disks and can be performed over as many as 32. All of the striped disks taken together is called a striped volume. Equal portions of data are written in 64 KB blocks in rows or stripes on each disk. For example, consider that you have set up striping across five hard disks and are working with a 720 KB data file. The first 64 KB portion of the file is written to disk 1, the next 64 KB portion is written to disk 2, the third portion is written to disk 3, and so on. After 320 KB are spread in the first data row across disks 1 through 5, the next 320 KB are written in 64 KB blocks in the second row across the disks. Finally, there will be 64 KB in the third row on disk 1 and 16 KB in the third row on disk 2 (see Figure 7-5).

Because of its high performance, striping is useful for volumes that store large databases or for data replication from one volume to another. Striping is not a benefit when most of the data files on a server are very small, such as under 64 KB.

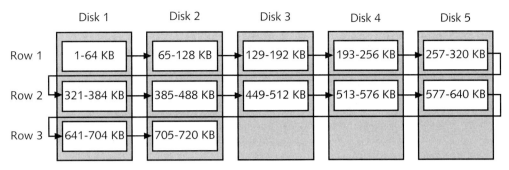

Figure 7-5   Disks in a striped volume

Data can be lost when one or more disks in the striped volume fail, because the system has no automated way to rebuild data. If you use striping to increase disk performance for a critical database, consider frequently backing up that database on tape (backups are discussed later in this chapter).

 You also can create mirrored volumes and RAID-5 volumes on a dynamic disk for fault tolerance. Fault tolerant volumes will be covered later in this chapter.

DISK MANAGEMENT

Disk Management tasks can be performed using the Disk Management tool. This tool provides a central location for viewing disk information and performing tasks such as creating and deleting partitions and volumes. The following sections will introduce you to the different tasks you can perform using the Disk Management tool: creating partitions, creating volumes, and converting to dynamic disks. Also in the next sections, you'll learn how to manage and troubleshoot disks using the Disk Defragmenter, Check Disk, and chkdsk tools.

Creating Partitions

Basic disks are divided into primary and extended partitions. When you partition a disk, leave 1 MB or more of the disk space free. This is the amount of workspace that Windows Server 2003 needs to convert a basic disk to a dynamic disk, in case you want to upgrade later.

Partitions operate as separate storage units on a hard disk. This allows you to better organize your data and make better use of your hard disk space. For example, you can create one partition on which to install the operating system and another partition for user data.

 In terms of configuring your server, it is always a good idea to keep the operating system on a partition separate from user data. This way if you need to reinstall the operating system, all your data still remains intact (unless you format the partition the data is stored on during the reinstall).

 ## Activity 7-3: Creating a New Partition

Time Required: Approximately 10 to 30 minutes

Objective: Create a new partition from unpartitioned disk space.

Description: This activity enables you to create a new partition. You will need access to a server that has some amount of unpartitioned disk space or free space on an extended partition. If a server is not available with unpartitioned space, remember the location of this activity so you can refer to these steps before partitioning disk space in a live work situation.

1. Open the customized MMC you created in Activity 7-2, by clicking **Start**, pointing to **All Programs**, pointing to **Administrative Tools**, and clicking **Disk ToolsJP.msc**. Maximize the console windows, and also click **Disk Management(Local)** in the Console Root tree, if necessary.

2. If you have unallocated disk space, right-click that space, and click **New Partition**. If, instead you see free space in an extended partition, right-click the free space, and click **New Logical Drive**.

3. Click **Next** at the **New Partition Wizard**.

4. Choose the type of partition you want to create. If you are partitioning unallocated space, click **Primary partition** or **Extended partition** (ask your instructor if you have questions about which to create). If you are partitioning free space on an extended partition, click **Logical drive** (see Figure 7-6). Click **Next**. (Note that if you create an extended partition you will not see Steps 6 and 7.)

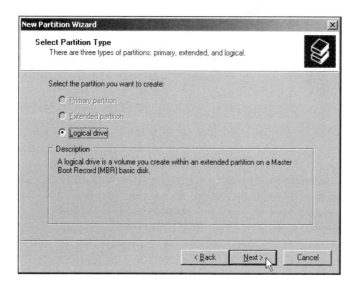

Figure 7-6   Partitioning a logical drive

5. Specify the size of the partition (or use the default), and click **Next**.

6. What options do you see next? Make sure the option to **Assign the following drive letter** is selected, and choose a drive letter to assign, such as the one offered by default. Click **Next**.

7. What file systems can you select to format the partition? Also, what options appear under the volume label box? For this activity, use the default selections, making sure that NTFS is selected as the file system. Click **Next**.

8. Click **Finish** in the summary window.

9. Leave the Disk Management tool open for the next activity.

You can delete a partition using the Disk Management tool, as well. To delete a partition, right-click the partition you want to delete. The partition will have a dark gray border and shading to indicate that you have selected it. Click Delete Partition on the shortcut menu. The Disk Management Snap-in gives you a warning that data will be lost. Click Yes to continue the delete process.

When you step through the New Partition Wizard, you have the option of not formatting the partition. If you do not format a partition when it is created, it still needs to be formatted for a particular file system before it can be used. As you already learned, Windows Server 2003 supports the FAT16, FAT32, and NTFS file systems. Once a partition is formatted, it is called a **volume** and can be assigned a drive letter. Assigning a drive letter makes it easier to refer to the volume, for example, assigning it drive letter C:. You can also provide a customized volume label to reflect what is contained in the volume.

To format a partition that is not already formatted, open the Disk Management tool, right-click the partition to be formatted, and click Format. You can specify a volume label, the file system to use, and the allocation unit size. Also, you can select to use the quick format option and to enable file and folder compression.

If you are formatting a volume on a dynamic disk through the Disk Management tool, you only have the option of formatting with NTFS.

Converting a Partitioned Basic Disk to a Dynamic Disk

Converting a partitioned basic disk to a dynamic disk is accomplished from the Disk Management tool. When you convert from a basic to dynamic disk, the process does not damage data in any way, but you must be certain there is 1 MB or more of free space on the basic disk before you convert it.

7

Activity 7-4: Converting a Basic Disk

Time Required: Approximately 10 minutes

Objective: Convert a partitioned basic disk to a dynamic disk.

Description: In this activity you convert a basic disk, such as the one you partitioned in Activity 7-3, to a dynamic disk. Before you start, make sure you have permission from your instructor to convert the disk. If you do not have permission to convert the disk, click Cancel at Step 5.

1. Open the **Disk Management** tool if it is closed.

2. Right-click the disk you want to convert, such as the disk you partitioned in Activity 7-3.

Make sure that you right-click the disk, for example Disk 0, and not the volume, for example (C:), or else the upgrade option will not be displayed.

3. Click **Convert to Dynamic Disk** as shown in Figure 7-7.

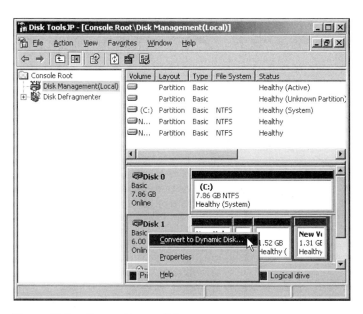

Figure 7-7   Converting a disk

4. Make sure that the correct disk is selected, such as Disk 0 or Disk 1 (check all that apply) in the Convert to Dynamic Disk dialog box. Click **OK**.

5. Verify the disk or disks to convert in the Disks to Convert dialog box, and click **Convert**. Or, if you do not have permission to convert the disk, click **Cancel**.

6. Click **Yes** in the Disk Management information box.

7. Click **Yes** to acknowledge that the file systems on the disk will be dismounted. What happens to the color bar in the lower-right portion of the Disk Management window? To complete the conversion, click the **Action** menu and click **Rescan Disks**. Or, if you see a confirmation box to complete the process, click **OK** to reboot the computer. If you reboot, reopen the Disk Management tool.

8. Notice under the Layout column that Simple now appears.

9. Leave the Disk Management tool open for the next activity.

There are circumstances when you may need to change a dynamic disk back to a basic disk, such as when you want to implement a dual-boot setup, or when you want to remove Windows Server 2003 from the computer so that a different operating system—such as Windows XP—can be loaded. Before reverting back to a basic disk, the disk must be empty; therefore, the data on the disk must be backed up or moved to another disk. A dynamic disk can be converted back to a basic disk by using the following general steps:

1. Back up all data on the dynamic disk volume before you start.

2. Delete the dynamic disk volume, using the Disk Management tool, by right-clicking the volume, such as **(D:)**, and clicking **Delete Volume**.

3. Right click the **dynamic disk**, and choose **Convert to Basic Disk**.

4. Use the Disk Management tool to partition and format the disk.

Creating Volumes

If you have converted your basic disk to dynamic, you will be creating volumes, as opposed to partitions, using the Disk Management tool. The type of volumes you can create include: simple, spanned, and striped volumes (you also learn how to create dynamic disk mirrored and RAID-5 volumes in the "Introduction to Fault Tolerance" section of this chapter).

Activity 7-5: Creating a Simple Volume

Time Required: Approximately 10 to 15 minutes

Objective: Create a simple volume on a dynamic disk.

Description: After you create a dynamic disk, if you have unallocated disk space on the disk, you may want to turn it into a simple volume, which you learn in this activity. You need a dynamic disk with unallocated disk space. (Note that if you do not have unallocated space after you complete Activity 7-4, try clicking a volume on the dynamic disk and deleting it.)

1. Open the **Disk Management** tool, if necessary.

2. Find the unallocated disk space, and right-click it.

3. Click **New Volume** as shown in Figure 7-8.

4. Click **Next** in the Welcome to the New Volume Wizard window.

5. What volume options do you see? Select **Simple**, and click **Next**.

6. If the disk you want to work on is not already in the Selected box, choose that disk under the Available box, click **Add**, and enter the size of the volume. Click **Next**.

7. Assign a drive letter to the new volume. What other options do you see? Click **Next**.

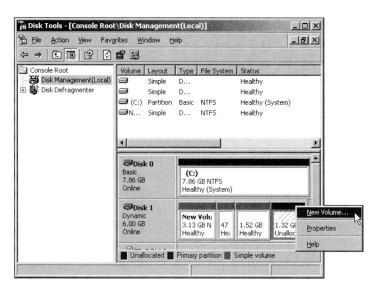

Figure 7-8   Selecting New Volume

8. Leave the default option to format the volume using **NTFS**. What other file systems could you use? Click **Next**.

9. Click **Finish** (or click Cancel if you do not want to create the simple volume at this time).

10. Leave the Disk Tools window (the Disk ToolsJP.msc that you created earlier) open for the next activity.

Mounting a Drive

Windows Server 2003 enables you to mount a drive as an alternative to giving it a drive letter. A **mounted drive** is one that appears as a folder and that is accessed through a path like any other folder. You can mount a basic or dynamic disk drive, a CD-ROM, or a Zip drive. Only an empty folder on a volume formatted for NTFS can be used for mounting a drive. Once a drive is mounted, other drives can be added to the same folder to appear as one drive. There are several reasons for using mounted drives. The most apparent reason is that Windows operating systems are limited to 26 drive letters and mounting drives enables you to reduce the number of drive letters in use, because they are not associated with letters. Another reason for creating a mounted drive is for user home directories that are stored on the server. A **home directory** or **home folder** is a server folder that is associated with a user's account and that is a designated workspace for the user to store files. (Microsoft sometimes uses the term "home directory" instead of "home folder" for consistency with earlier versions of Windows NT and with Novell NetWare terminology.) As server administrator, you might allocate one drive for all user home directories and mount that drive in a folder called Users. The path to the drive might be C:\Home or C:\Users. In another situation, you might have a database that you want to manage as a mounted drive so that it is easier for users to access. Also, by mounting the drive, you can set up special backups for that database by simply backing up its folder.

Activity 7-6: Configuring a Mounted Drive

Time Required: Approximately 10 to 15 minutes

Objective: Learn how to set up a mounted drive.

Description: This activity enables you to create a mounted volume. In the first series of steps you create a folder on an NTFS formatted volume or disk that will hold the mounted drive. After those steps, you mount the drive into the folder. You need an available disk drive to mount into the folder (or stop at Step 9).

1. Open **Windows Explorer** or **My Computer**, and click a main volume that is formatted for NTFS, such as drive C:.

2. Click the **File** menu, point to **New**, and click **Folder**. Enter your initials appended to Mount for the folder name, such as JPMount. Press **Enter**.

3. Access the **Disk Management** tool.

4. Right-click the disk drive, such as D:, you want to mount into the folder, and click **Change Drive Letter and Paths**.

5. Click the existing drive letter for the drive, such as D:, in the Name box, and click the **Add** button.

6. Click **Mount in the following empty NTFS folder**, if necessary.

7. Click the **Browse** button, and locate the folder you created, then click that folder, such as JPMount.

8. Click **OK** in the Browse for Drive Path dialog box.

9. Click **OK** in the Add Drive Letter or Path dialog box (or click Cancel if you do not want to complete mounting the drive).

10. Go back to Windows Explorer or My Computer and find the mounted volume you created. What icon is used to represent it?

11. Right-click the mounted volume to examine its properties. Record your observations about the mounted volume's icon and properties.

12. Close the mounted volume's properties dialog box, and close Windows Explorer or My Computer. Leave open the Disk Tools window (Disk ToolsJP.msc).

Managing Disks

Once you have your physical disks partitioned and formatted, they are ready to be used as storage mediums. In order to ensure system performance, the disks must still be maintained. Windows Server 2003 includes several tools, such as Disk Defragmenter, Check Disk, and chkdsk, that can be used to diagnose disk problems and maintain disk performance.

Using Disk Defragmenter

When you save a file to a disk, Windows Server 2003 saves the file to the first area of available space. The file may not be saved to a contiguous area of free space, and therefore the disk gradually becomes **fragmented**, particularly as more and more files are created and deleted. When your computer attempts to access the file, it may have to be read from different areas on a disk, slowing access time and creating disk wear. The process of **defragmenting** locates fragmented folders and files and moves them to a location on the physical disk so they are in contiguous order.

 On a busy server, drives should be defragmented every week to two weeks. On less busy servers, defragment the drives at least once a month.

Activity 7-7: Using the Disk Defragmenter

Time Required: Depends on the size of your disk (10 to more than 40 minutes)

Objective: Practice using the disk defragmenter.

Description: This activity enables you to use the Windows Server 2003 Disk Defragmenter.

1. Open the Disk Tools console you created earlier, such as **Disk ToolsJP.msc**, if it is not already open.

2. Click **Disk Defragmenter** in the left pane.

3. To determine if a disk or volume needs to be defragmented, click it in the upper-right pane, and click the **Analyze** button as shown in Figure 7-9.

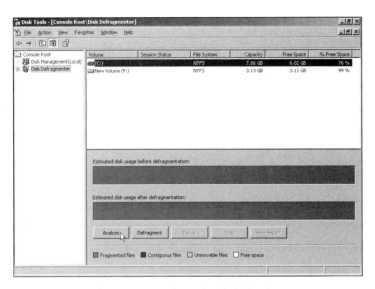

Figure 7-9   Selecting to analyze the disk for fragmentation

4. After the analysis is done, click the **View Report** button. Notice that at the top of the Analysis Report box there is a recommendation about whether or not you need to defragment the disk (see Figure 7-10). What does your report say?

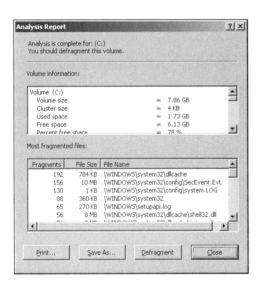

Figure 7-10   Analysis Report box

5. Click the **Defragment** button whether or not defragmentation is recommended, so that you can view the process.

6. Click **View Report**. Were there any files that could not be defragmented?

7. Click **Close**.

8. Close your customized **Disk Tools** console window. Click **Yes** to save the console settings.

Using Check Disk

The Check Disk tool allows you to scan your disk for bad sectors and file system errors. This is a tool that is meant for use when there are no users that need to access the files on the disk you want to check, because the disk is made unavailable during the scan for problems. The Check Disk tool is started from the Properties dialog box for a disk.

When you start the Check Disk tool, there are two options:

- *Automatically fix file system errors*—Select this option to have Windows repair any errors in the file system that it finds during the disk-checking process. In order to use this option, all programs must be closed.

- *Scan for and attempt recovery of bad sectors*—Select this option to have the system find and fix bad sectors and file errors, recovering any information that it can read. Choosing this option also includes the file system fixes that are performed by the Automatically fix file system errors option.

Activity 7-8: Using Check Disk

Time Required: Depends on the size of the disk and number of files (10 to more than 40 minutes)

Objective: Learn how to use Check Disk.

Description: In this activity you practice using Check Disk to scan your disk. If you are using a multiple disk system, ask your instructor which disk to scan. Also, if you have a large disk with many files, you may want to stop at Step 6.

1. Click **Start** and click **My Computer**.
2. Right-click the disk you want to scan, such as **Local Disk (C:)**.
3. Click **Properties**.
4. Click the **Tools** tab. What are the tools you can use on this tab?
5. Click **Check Now**.
6. Click the box, Scan for and attempt recovery of bad sectors, as shown in Figure 7-11.

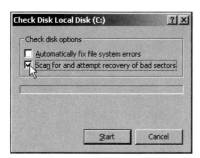

Figure 7-11   Selecting a Check Disk option

7. Click **Start**.
8. After the scan is completed, click **OK**.
9. Close the disk's **Properties** dialog box.
10. Close the **My Computer** window.

Using chkdsk

You can also check your disk for errors by running the chkdsk command, by clicking the Start button, clicking Run, entering chkdsk, and clicking OK (or use this command from the command line). Chkdsk also starts automatically when you boot Windows Server 2003 and the boot process detects a corrupt file allocation table or corrupted files.   The chkdsk utility is much more robust in Windows Server 2003, Windows 2000, and Windows NT than it is in most other versions of Windows. In Windows Server 2003, it can be used to check FAT16, FAT32, NTFS, or a combination of these (on a dual-boot computer). When the file system is FAT16 or FAT32, the utility checks the file allocation table, folders, files, disk sectors, and disk allocation units. In NTFS, it checks files, folders, indexes, security descriptors, user files, and disk allocation units. Table 7-1 summarizes the different switches that can be used with the chkdsk command.

Allow plenty of time for chkdsk to run on large disk systems, such as a system having over 10 GB. If you have multiple disks, you may want to stagger running chkdsk, on different disks for each week. Also, the presence of some bad sectors is normal. Many disks have a few bad sectors that are marked by the manufacturer during the low-level format and on which data cannot be written.

When chkdsk finds lost allocation units or chains, it prompts you with the Yes or No question: Convert lost chains to files? Answer Yes to the question so that you can save the lost information to files. The files that chkdsk creates for each lost chain are labeled Filexxx.chk and can be edited with a text editor to determine their contents.

Table 7-1   Chkdsk switch and parameter options

Switch/Parameter	Purpose
[volume] (such as C:)	Specifies that chkdsk only check the designated volume
[filename] (such as *.dll)	Enables a check of the specified file or files only
/c	For NTFS only, chkdsk uses an abbreviated check of the folder structure
/f	Instructs chkdsk to fix errors that it finds
/i	For NTFS only, chkdsk uses an abbreviated check of indexes
/L:size	For NTFS only, enables you to specify the size of the log file created by the disk check
/r	Searches for bad sectors, fixes problems, and recovers information (when not possible, use the Recover command on separate files)
/v	For FAT16/FAT32, shows the entire path name of files; for NTFS, it shows cleanup messages associated with errors
/x	Dismounts or locks a volume before starting

Activity 7-9: Using chkdsk

Time Required: Approximately 5 to 15 minutes

Objective: Learn how to use chkdsk from the command line.

Description: You run the chkdsk command-line utility to examine a disk for errors.

1. Click **Start**, point to **All Programs**, point to **Accessories**, and click **Command Prompt**.

2. Type **chkdsk** and press **Enter** (see Figure 7-12). What happens when you run chkdsk without the /f option?

```
Command Prompt                                              _|□|x|
WARNING! F parameter not specified.
Running CHKDSK in read-only mode.

CHKDSK is verifying files (stage 1 of 3)...
File verification completed.
CHKDSK is verifying indexes (stage 2 of 3)...
Index verification completed.
CHKDSK is verifying security descriptors (stage 3 of 3)...
Security descriptor verification completed.
CHKDSK is verifying Usn Journal...
Usn Journal verification completed.

  8241313 KB total disk space.
  1731304 KB in 11541 files.
     3448 KB in 1093 indexes.
        0 KB in bad sectors.
    75593 KB in use by the system.
    43264 KB occupied by the log file.
  6430968 KB available on disk.

     4096 bytes in each allocation unit.
  2060328 total allocation units on disk.
  1607742 allocation units available on disk.

C:\Documents and Settings\Administrator>
```

Figure 7-12   Chkdsk results

3. Close the **Command Prompt** window.

INTRODUCTION TO FAULT TOLERANCE

Fault tolerance is the ability of a system to gracefully recover from hardware or software failure. Servers often store critical data that must have high availability. Windows Server 2003 provides a level of fault tolerance through software RAID. RAID is not meant as a replacement for performing regular backups of data, but it increases the availability of disk storage. For example, if a hard disk fails and you have not implemented fault tolerance, any data stored on that disk is lost and unavailable until the drive is replaced and data is restored from backup. With fault tolerance, data is written to more than one drive; in the event one drive fails, data can still be accessed from one of the remaining drives.

RAID Volumes

Because hard disk drives are prone to failure, one of the best data security measures is to plan for disk redundancy in servers and host computers. This is accomplished in two ways: by performing regular backups and by installing RAID drives.

RAID is a set of standards for lengthening disk life, preventing data loss, and enabling relatively uninterrupted access to data. There are six basic levels of RAID (other RAID levels exist beyond the basic levels), beginning with the use of disk striping.

The six basic RAID levels are as follows:

- *RAID level 0*—Striping with no other redundancy features is RAID level 0. Striping is used to extend disk life and to improve performance. Data access on striped volumes is fast because of the way the data is divided into blocks that are quickly accessed through multiple disk reads and data paths. A significant disadvantage to using level 0 striping is that if one disk fails, you can expect a large data loss on all volumes. Windows Server 2003 supports RAID level 0, using two to 32 disks in a set. In Windows Server 2003, this is called striped volumes, previously referred to as striped sets in Windows NT 4.0.

- *RAID level 1*—This level employs simple disk mirroring and provides a means to duplicate the operating system files in the event of a disk failure. Disk mirroring is a method of fault tolerance that prevents data loss by duplicating data from a main disk to a backup disk (see Figure 7-13). **Disk duplexing** is the same as disk mirroring, with the exception that it places the backup disk on a different controller or adapter than is used by the main disk (see Figure 7-14). Windows Server 2003 supports level 1, but includes disk duplexing as well as mirroring through the fault-tolerance driver Ftdisk.sys. If there are three or more volumes to be mirrored or duplexed, this solution is more expensive than the other RAID levels. When you plan for disk mirroring, remember that write access is slower than read access, because information must be written twice, once on the primary disk and once on the secondary disk. Some server administrators consider disk mirroring and disk duplexing to offer one of the best guarantees of data recovery when there is a disk failure.

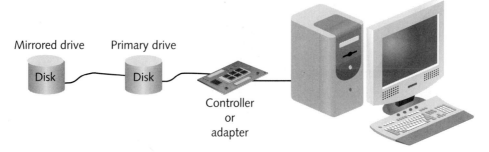

Figure 7-13   Disk mirroring

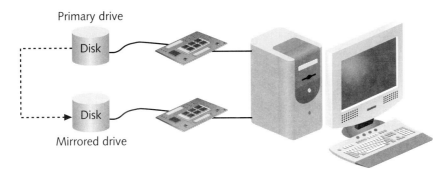

Primary drive

Disk

Disk

Mirrored drive

Figure 7-14   Disk duplexing

- *RAID level 2*—This uses an array of disks whereby the data is striped across all disks in the array. Also, in this method all disks store error-correction information that enables the array to reconstruct data from a failed disk. The advantages of level 2 are that disk wear is reduced and data can be reconstructed if a disk fails.

- *RAID level 3*—Like level 2, RAID level 3 uses disk striping and stores error-correcting information, but the information is only written to one disk in the array. If that disk fails, the array cannot rebuild its contents.

- *RAID level 4*—This level stripes data and stores error-correcting information on all drives, in a manner similar to level 2. An added feature is its ability to perform checksum verification. The checksum is a sum of bits in a file. When a file is recreated after a disk failure, the checksum previously stored for that file is checked against the actual file after it is reconstructed. If the two do not match, the file may be corrupted. Windows Server 2003 does not support RAID levels 2 through 4.

- *RAID level 5*—Level 5 combines the best features of RAID, including striping, error correction, and checksum verification. Windows Server 2003 supports level 5, calling it "stripe set with parity on basic disks" or a RAID-5 volume (for dynamic disks), depending on the disk architecture. Whereas level 4 stores checksum data on only one disk, level 5 spreads both error-correction and checksum data over all of the disks, so there is no single point of failure. This level uses more memory than other RAID levels, with at least 16 MB recommended as additional memory for system functions. In addition, level 5 requires at least three disks in the RAID array. Recovery from a failed disk provides roughly the same guarantee as with disk mirroring, but takes longer with level 5. RAID level 5 can recover from a single disk failure. However, if more than one drive in the array fails, all data is lost and must be restored from backup.

Windows Server 2003 supports RAID levels 0, 1, and 5 for disk fault tolerance (each of these levels is discussed further in the sections that follow), with levels 1 and 5 recommended. RAID level 0 is not recommended in many situations because it does not really provide fault tolerance, except to help extend the life of disks while providing relatively fast access. All three RAID levels support disks formatted with FAT or NTFS. When you decide upon using RAID level 1 or RAID level 5, consider the following:

- The boot and system files can be placed on RAID level 1, but not on RAID level 5. Thus, if you use RAID level 5, these files must be on a separate disk or a separate RAID level 1 disk set.

- RAID level 1 uses two hard disks, and RAID level 5 uses from three to 32.

- RAID level 1 is more expensive to implement than RAID level 5, when you consider the cost per megabyte of storage. Keep in mind that in RAID level 1, half of your total disk space is used for redundancy, whereas that value is one-third or less for RAID level 5. The amount of RAID level 5 used for parity is 1/n where n is the number of disk drives in the array.

- RAID level 5 requires more memory than RAID level 1.

- Reading from disk is faster in RAID level 1 and RAID level 5 than is write access, with read access for RAID level 1 identical to that of a disk that does not have RAID.

- Because RAID level 5 involves more disks and because the read/write heads can acquire data simultaneously across striped volumes, it has much faster read access than RAID level 1.

Using a Striped Volume (RAID Level 0)

As you learned earlier in this chapter, the reasons for using a RAID level 0 or a striped volume in Windows Server 2003 are to:

- Reduce the wear on multiple disk drives by equally spreading the load

- Increase disk performance compared to other methods for configuring dynamic disk volumes

Although striped volumes do not provide fault tolerance, other than to extend the life of the disks, there are situations in which they might be used. Consider, for example, an organization that maintains a "data warehouse" in which vital data is stored and updated on a mainframe; and a copy is downloaded at regular intervals to a server housing the data warehouse. The purpose of the data on the server is to create reports and to provide fast lookup of certain kinds of data, without slowing down the mainframe. In this instance, the goal is to provide the fastest possible access to the data and not fault tolerance, because the original data and primary data services are on the mainframe. For this application, you might create a striped volume on the server used for the data warehouse, because it yields the fastest data access.

To create a striped volume, right-click the unallocated space for the volume, click New Volume, click Next after the New Volume Wizard starts, click the option button for Striped, and complete the remaining steps in the New Volume Wizard.

Using a Mirrored Volume (RAID Level 1)

Disk mirroring involves creating a shadow copy of data on a backup disk and is known as RAID level 1. Only dynamic disks can be set up as a **mirrored volume** in Windows Server 2003. It is one of the most guaranteed forms of disk fault tolerance because the data on a failed drive is still available on the mirrored drive (with a short down time to make the mirrored drive accessible). Also, disk read performance is the same as reading data from any single disk drive. The disadvantage of mirroring is that the time to create or update information is doubled because it is written twice, once on the main disk and once on the shadow disk. However, writing to disk in mirroring is normally faster than writing to disk when you use RAID level 5. A mirrored volume cannot be striped and requires two dynamic disks.

A mirrored volume is particularly well suited for situations in which data is mission critical and must not be lost under any circumstances, as with customer files at a bank. A mirrored volume is also valuable for situations in which a computer system must not be down for long, such as for medical applications or in 24-hour manufacturing. The somewhat slower update time is offset by the assurance that data cannot be lost through disk failure, and that the system will quickly be functioning again after a disk failure. However, if fast disk updating is the most important criterion for disk storage, such as when copying files or taking orders over a telephone, then a striped volume may be a better choice than a mirrored volume.

 The Windows Server 2003 system and boot volumes can be in a mirrored volume, but they cannot be in a striped or RAID-5 volume.

A mirrored volume is created through the Disk Management tool. To create the volume, right-click the unallocated space on one disk, click New Volume, click Next, and choose the Mirrored option in the New Volume Wizard.

Using a RAID-5 Volume

Fault tolerance is better for a RAID-5 volume than for a simple striped volume. A **RAID-5 volume** requires a minimum of three disk drives. Parity information is distributed on each disk so that if one disk fails, the information on that disk can be reconstructed. The parity used by Microsoft is Boolean (true/false, one/zero) logic, with information about the data contained in each row of 64 KB data blocks on the striped disks. Using the example of storing a 720 KB file across five disks, one 64 KB parity block is written on each disk. The first parity block is always written in row 1 of disk 1, the second is in row 2 of disk 2, and so on, as illustrated in Figure 7-15 (compare this figure to Figure 7-5 for a striped volume).

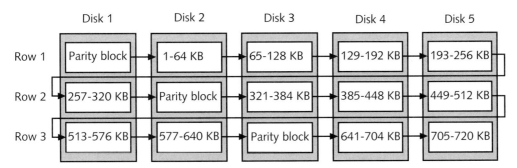

Figure 7-15   Disks in a RAID-5 volume

When you set up a RAID-5 volume, the performance is not as fast as with a striped volume, because it takes longer to write the data and calculate the parity block for each row. However, reading from the disk is as fast as a striped volume. A RAID-5 volume is a viable choice for fault tolerance with mission-critical data and applications when full mirroring is not feasible due to the expense. Also, disk arrays are compatible with RAID level 5. A RAID-5 volume is particularly useful in a client/server system that uses a separate database for queries and creating reports, because disk read performance is fast for obtaining data. In applications such as a customer service database that is constantly updated with new orders, disk read performance is slower than with striping without parity.

 If you create a RAID-5 volume, consider adding 16 MB or more of RAM, because a RAID-5 volume uses more memory than mirroring or simple striping. Also, a RAID-5 volume takes up additional disk space for the parity information.

The amount of storage space used is based on the formula $1/n$ where n is the number of physical disks in the volume. For example, if there are four disks, the amount of space taken for parity information is 1/4 of the total space of all disk drives in the volume. This means you get more usable disk storage if there are more disks in the volume. A set of eight 2 MB disks yields more usable storage than a set of four 4 MB disks using RAID level 5.

Use the Disk Management tool to create a RAID-5 volume. To start, right-click the unallocated or free space on a disk that is to be part of the volume, click New Volume, click Next, and select the RAID-5 volume option in the New Volume Wizard.

Software RAID versus Hardware RAID

Actually, two approaches to RAID can be implemented on a server: software RAID and hardware RAID. Software RAID implements fault tolerance through the server's operating system, such as using RAID levels 0, 1, or 5 through the Windows Server 2003 Disk Management tool. Hardware RAID is implemented through the server hardware and is independent of the operating system. Many manufacturers implement hardware RAID on the adapter, such as a SCSI adapter, to which the disk drives are connected. The RAID logic is contained in a chip on the adapter. Also, there often is a battery connected to the chip that ensures that the chip never loses power and has fault tolerance to retain the

RAID setup even when there is a power outage. Hardware RAID is more expensive than software RAID, but offers many advantages over software RAID:

- Faster read and write response

- The ability to place boot and system files on different RAID levels, such as RAID levels 1 and 5

- The ability to "hot-swap" a failed disk with one that works or is new, thus replacing the disk without shutting down the server (this option can vary by manufacturer)

- More setup options to retrieve damaged data and to combine different RAID levels within one array of disks, such as mirroring two disks using RAID level 1 and setting up five disks for RAID level 5 in a seven disk array (the RAID options depend on what the manufacturer offers)

Disk Backup

RAID is one of the ways that you can provide fault tolerance for your server's hard disks. Most software implementations of RAID can only recover from single disk failure so it is still no substitute for performing regular, scheduled backups. One of the best ways to make sure you do not lose valuable information on a hard disk is to fully back up information on a regular basis, using backup media, such as tapes or CD-Rs. These backups can be performed from the server or from a workstation on the network.

There are several advantages to performing backups from a tape drive installed on the server:

- Tapes can hold more data than most other backup media, including CD-Rs or CD-RWs.

- There is no extra load on the network from traffic caused by transferring files from the server to a tape drive on a workstation.

- Equipping each server with its own tape drive gives you a way to perform backups on a multiple-server network even if one of the tape drives fails on a server. Backups can be performed from the tape drive on one of the other servers.

- Backing up from a tape drive on a server provides more assurance that the registry is backed up, since access to the registry is limited to backups performed at the server. The registry contains vital information about a server's setup.

The advantages of performing a network backup are that backup jobs can be stored on a single backup media and one administrator can be responsible for backing up multiple servers. The main disadvantages are the increase in network traffic and the registry cannot be backed up from across the network.

Backup Options

There are five different types of backups that can be performed using the Windows Server 2003 Backup utility:

- Normal

- Incremental

- Differential

- Copy

- Daily

A **normal backup** is a backup of an entire system, including all system files, programs, and data files. A normal backup is a backup of all files that you have selected, usually an entire partition or volume. The normal backup changes each file's archive attribute to show that it has been backed up. As you will recall from Chapter 5, each FAT16, FAT32, and NTFS folder or file has an archive attribute that can be set to show whether that folder or file has been backed up since the last change to it. A normal backup is usually performed the first time you back up a server, and afterwards once a night, once a week, or at a regular interval, depending on the number of files on your server and your organization's particular needs.

An **incremental backup** only backs up files that are new or that have been updated. The Windows Server 2003 incremental option backs up only files that have the archive attribute marked. When it backs up a file, the incremental backup removes the archive attribute to show that the file has been backed up.

A **differential backup** is the same as an incremental backup, but it does not remove the archive attribute. Incremental or differential backups are often mixed with full backups. The advantage of the differential backup is the restore process is quicker because only the most recent normal backup and the most recent differential backup are required to restore data. That saves time over incremental restores, which require a full backup and all the incremental backups dating back to the last normal backup.

Another Windows Server 2003 option is the **copy backup**, which backs up only the files or folders selected. The archive attribute, showing that a file is new or updated, is left unchanged. For example, if the archive attribute is present on a file, the copy backup does not remove it. Copy backups are used in exceptional cases where a backup is performed on certain files, but the regular backup routines are unaffected because the copy backup does not alter the archive attribute.

The **daily backup** option backs up only files that have been changed or updated on the day the backup is performed. It leaves the archive attribute unchanged, so regular backups are not affected. A daily backup is valuable, for example, when there is a failing hard disk and little time to save the day's work to that point. It enables the administrator to save only that day's work, instead of all changed files, which may span more than a day.

Activity 7-10: Backing Up a Server

Time Required: Approximately 10 to 30 minutes

Objective: Practice taking a normal backup.

Description: In this activity, you practice backing up a disk drive, without configuring the backup through a wizard (so you'll learn more about the backup process). You need a computer running Windows Server 2003, Standard Edition, that is set up with a tape drive, and you need a tape. (If your system does not have a tape drive, you can still practice by simply backing up a folder to a CD-R/CD-RW, Zip disk, or to another disk drive on the computer).

1. Insert a tape into the tape drive of the computer (or if you are using a CD-R, CD-RW, or Zip disk, insert it).

2. Click **Start**, point to **All Programs**, point to **Accessories**, point to **System Tools**, and click **Backup**. (Alternatively, you can open My Computer or Windows Explorer, right-click a drive, click **Properties**, click the **Tools** tab, and click the **Backup Now** button.) If at any point after you insert the tape or CD-R/CD-RW, or Zip disk you see a Recognizable Media Found message box, click **Allow Backup Utility to use all the recognized media**, and click **OK**.

3. Click **Advanced Mode** when you see the Welcome to the Backup or Restore Wizard.

4. Click the **Backup** tab.

5. Check the box of a drive on the computer, such as drive **C:** or **D:** (you may need to consult with your instructor about which drive to back up). Double-click that drive and notice which folders are checked for the backup. How would you back up only a portion of a drive, such as one or two folders–as when you are backing up specific information to a CD-R, CD-RW, or to a shared folder? Record your observations.

When you are selecting the drives (or folders) you want to back up, notice there is a check box for System State. This enables you to back up critical system files. You'll learn more about this option in Chapter 12.

6. In the Backup destination box, select the backup media, which reflects the type of media available on your computer such as a **Travan** or **8mm DAT** tape drive, or **File**. (Note that if you are using a CD-R/CD-RW, Zip disk, or are backing up to a file, select the **File** option instead of a tape drive—but also make sure you have only selected one or two folders to back up.)

7. Click the **Start Backup** button.

8. Enter a description and label for the backup, such as **Drive C: backup created 12/19/05 at 10:00 PM** and **Tape 1 of 1 created 12/19/05**. If you are using a new tape or an old one that you can write over, click **Replace the data on the media with this backup**. If instead you want to retain data already on the tape, click **Append this backup to the media**.

9. Click the **Advanced** button (see Figure 7-16).

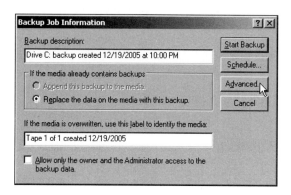

Figure 7-16   Backup Job Information dialog box

10. Click **If possible, compress the backup data to save space**.

11. Click the Backup Type list box, and view the options. Record the options you see, and note which dialog box enables you to access them. Select **Normal** as the option for this backup. What other options are available in the Advanced Backup Options dialog box?

12. Click **OK**.

13. Click the **Start Backup** button (or you can click **Cancel** if you do not have a tape or other media for practice). After you click the Start Backup button, you may see a dialog box with a warning that "There is no 'unused' media available," which means that the tape (or other media) has been used previously. Click **Yes** if you see this warning.

14. Click **Close** when the backup is complete, and then close the Backup utility.

15. Close any open windows.

Scheduling Backups

Windows Server 2003 includes a scheduling capability so that you can have the server automatically start backups after regular work hours or at a specific time of day. For example, you may schedule full backups to start at 7:00 p.m. after everyone has left work. An accounting office in an organization may perform a daily closing routine in which they stop processing by 4:20 p.m. and start backing up accounting files at 4:30 p.m.

The following general steps illustrate how to create and schedule a backup:

1. Insert a tape into the tape drive of the computer (or if you are using a CD-R, CD-RW, or Zip disk, insert it).

2. Click **Start**, point to **All Programs**, point to **Accessories**, point to **System Tools**, and click **Backup**.

3. Click **Advanced Mode** when you see the Welcome to the Backup or Restore Wizard.

4. Click the **Backup** tab.

5. Select the drives and folders that you want to back up. Also, select the backup destination.

6. Click **Start Backup**.

7. Provide the backup job information, such as the backup description, how to write on the media, and a label for the backup.

8. Click the **Schedule** button, and click **Yes**.

9. Provide a filename in which to store the selection parameters for the backup job, and click **Save**.

10. Provide a password for the account from which the job will run, and confirm the password. Click **OK**.

11. On the Schedule tab, enter the job name.

12. Click the **Properties** button to specify the scheduling information, such as how often to run the backup, the start time, and the day or days of the week on which to run it. Figure 7-17 shows the display after you select **Weekly** in the Schedule Task box.

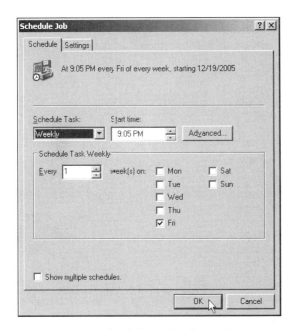

Figure 7-17   Scheduling a backup job

13. Click **OK** to close the Schedule Job dialog box.

14. Click **OK** in the Scheduled Job Options dialog box.

15. Leave the Backup utility open.

RESTORING BACKED UP FILES

Use the Backup utility to perform a restore from removable media. The Restore Wizard in the Backup utility takes you through a restore step by step, or you can perform a restore without the Restore Wizard's help by using the Restore tab in the Backup utility. For example, if you use the Restore tab, follow these steps after inserting the medium from which you will perform the restore:

1. Click **Start**, point to **All Programs**, point to **Accessories**, point to **System Tools**, and click **Backup**.

2. Click **Advanced Mode** when you see the Welcome to the Backup or Restore Wizard.

3. Click the **Restore and Manage Media** tab.

4. In the left pane, double-click the medium from which to perform the restore, such as **File** (for a Zip drive, for example) or **Travan** (for a tape drive). In the right pane (or on the left pane under the medium) find the label of the backup that you want to restore, and double-click it.

5. Double-click down through the levels of the drives, folders, and subfolders to find what you want to restore. Place a check mark in front of the drives, folders, and files that you want to restore.

6. In the Restore files to box, select a location where you want the files and folders restored. The options are to restore to the original location, to restore to an alternate location, or to restore to a single folder. The first two options retain the original folder structure as reflected on the backup medium. In the third option, restore to a single folder, the original folder structure is not retained, which means that the target folder will contain only files after the restore.

7. Click the **Start Restore** button.

8. Click **Advanced** on the Confirm Restore dialog box, if you want to modify any of the restore options—for example, if you want to restore security information. Click **OK** if you decide to modify the advanced options.

9. Click **OK** to start the restore. Prior to starting, you may be prompted to supply the location, if you are restoring from a file.

10. Click **Close** and close the Backup tool.

Chapter Summary

- Windows Server 2003 supports two different disk configurations: basic and dynamic. Basic disks are backward-compatible to earlier operating systems, such as Windows NT Server, and provide rudimentary disk handling. Dynamic disks can be configured for more comprehensive disk management involving simple, spanned, striped, mirrored, and RAID-5 volumes.

- The Disk Management tool provides you with a graphical view of your disk configuration. Using this through the Computer Management tool or as an MMC snap-in, you can perform most disk management tasks.

- Use the Disk Management tool to create basic disk partitions or dynamic disk volumes.

- Mounting a drive enables you to save drive letter assignments and to access a drive through a folder, such as a shared folder.

- Plan to regularly defragment disks using the Disk Defragmenter tool.

- Use the Check Disk and chkdsk tools to find and repair disk problems.

- RAID provides fault tolerance for your server's hard disks. Windows Server 2003 supports RAID level 0, 1, and 5. RAID level 0, also known as striping, provides no actual fault tolerance other than to help extend the life of the disks.

- With disk mirroring or disk duplexing (RAID level 1), the same data is written to a partition on each of the two disks included in the mirror. With RAID level 5, data is written across a minimum of three disks in 64 KB chunks. Parity information is added to achieve fault tolerance.

- Use the Windows Server 2003 Backup utility to regularly back up your important data and system files. This utility works with all kinds of removable media, such as tapes, CD-Rs, CD-RWs, and Zip disks.

- The restore capability in the Backup utility enables you to restore an entire server, one disk drive, specific folders on a disk drive, or only specific files.

KEY TERMS

active partition — The partition from which a computer boots.

basic disk — In Windows Server 2003, a partitioned disk that can have up to four partitions and that uses logical drive designations. This type of disk is compatible with MS-DOS, Windows 3.x, Windows 95, Windows 98, Windows NT, Windows 2000, Windows XP, and Windows Server 2003.

boot partition — Holds the Windows Server 2003 \Windows folder containing the system files.

copy backup — Backs up only files or folders that are manually selected for the backup, and the archive attribute is not changed or reset to show the files or folders have been backed up.

daily backup — Backs up only files that have been changed or updated on the day the backup is performed.

defragmenting — A software process that rearranges data to fill in the empty spaces that develop on disks and makes data easier to obtain.

differential backup — A backup of new or changed files; the archive attribute is not reset after the file is backed up.

disk duplexing — A method of fault tolerance similar to disk mirroring in that it prevents data loss by duplicating data from a main disk to a backup disk; disk duplexing places the backup disk on a different controller or adapter than is used by the main disk.

disk mirroring — A method of fault tolerance that prevents data loss by duplicating data from a main disk to a backup disk. Some operating systems also refer to this as disk shadowing.

dynamic disk — In Windows Server 2003, a disk that does not use traditional partitioning, which means that there is no restriction to the number of volumes that can be set up on one disk or to the ability to extend volumes onto additional physical disks. Dynamic disks are only compatible with Windows Server 2003 and Windows 2000 Server platforms.

extended partition — A partition that is created from unpartitioned free disk space and is linked to a primary partition in order to increase the available disk space.

fault tolerance — Techniques that employ hardware and software to provide assurance against equipment failures, computer service interruptions, and data loss.

formatting — A process that prepares a hard disk partition for a specific file system.

fragmented — A normal and gradual process in which files become spread throughout a disk, and empty pockets of space develop between files.

home directory or **folder** — A server folder that is associated with a user's account and that is a designated workspace for the user to store files.

incremental backup — A backup of new or changed files. The archive attribute is removed once the file is backed up.

mirrored volume — Two dynamic disks that are set up for RAID level 1 so that data on one disk is stored on a redundant disk.

mounted drive — A physical disk, CD-ROM, or Zip drive that appears as a folder and that is accessed through a path like any other folder.

normal backup — A backup of an entire system, including all system files, programs, and data files.

partitioning — Blocking a group of tracks and sectors to be used by a particular file system, such as FAT or NTFS.

primary partition — Partition or portion of a hard disk that is bootable.

RAID-5 volume — Three or more dynamic disks that use RAID level 5 fault tolerance through disk striping and creating parity blocks for data recovery.

redundant array of inexpensive (or independent) disks (RAID) — A set of standards designed to extend the life of hard disk drives and to prevent data loss from a hard disk failure.

simple volume — A portion of a disk or an entire disk that is set up as a dynamic disk.

spanned volume — Two or more Windows Server 2003 dynamic disks that are combined to appear as one disk.

stripe set — Two or more basic disks set up so that files are spread in blocks across the disks.

striped volume — Two or more dynamic disks that use striping so that files are spread in blocks across the disks.

striping — A data storage method that breaks up data files across all volumes of a disk set to minimize wear on a single volume.

system partition — Partition that contains boot files, such as Boot.ini and Ntldr in Windows Server 2003.

volume — A basic disk partition that has been formatted for a particular file system, a primary partition, a volume set, an extended volume, a stripe set, a stripe set with parity, or a mirror set. Or a dynamic disk that is set up as a simple volume, spanned volume, striped volume, RAID-5 volume, or mirrored volume.

volume set — Two or more formatted basic disk partitions (volumes) that are combined to look like one volume with a single drive letter.

REVIEW QUESTIONS

1. You have two 5 GB hard drives. You need 2.2 GB of space to store data. Which of the following RAID implementations should you use to provide fault tolerance for your operating system files?

   a. RAID level 0

   b. disk mirroring

   c. RAID level 5

   d. volume spanning

2. If you have four disks in a RAID level 5 implementation, how much space is available for actual data storage?

   a. 90%

   b. 75%

   c. 65%

   d. 50%

3. Your company is planning to purchase a server and it wants to provide at least two options for backup media used with the Windows Server 2003 Backup utility. Which of the following options are supported by the utility? (Choose all that apply.)

   a. tapes

   b. CD-Rs

   c. CD-RWs

   d. Zip disks

4. You perform a normal backup on Monday. Tuesday through Friday you perform incremental backups. Late Thursday night after the backups, the server's disk subsystem fails and you need to restore your data. Which tapes will you need to restore from?

   a. Thursday only

   b. Monday and Thursday

   c. Monday through Thursday

   d. Monday only

5. You have just upgraded your Windows NT 4.0 server to Windows Server 2003. You open the Disk Management tool and attempt to create a new mirrored volume to provide fault tolerance for your operating system files but are unsuccessful. What is causing the problem?

   a. The partitions are not formatted with NTFS.

   b. The disks need to be converted to basic disks.

   c. Windows Server 2003 does not support software RAID.

   d. The disks need to be converted to dynamic disks.

6. You are consulting for a small organization that has used their server for over two years without maintaining it, other than to replace a defective monitor. They are complaining that the server performance has gotten slower over the past several months. What would you do first to improve performance?

   a. Defragment the disks.

   b. Add much more RAM.

   c. Increase the initial page file size by at least 1 GB.

   d. Purchase faster disks.

7. Which of the following provide fault tolerance?

   a. volume sets

   b. mirrored volumes

   c. striped volumes

   d. striped volumes with parity

   e. spanned volumes

8. On an NTFS volume, you want to perform a fast check of indexes. To do this, use _____ in the Command Prompt window.

   a. dskchk /index

   b. chkindex

   c. chkdsk /i

   d. fdisk /ab /i

9. In order to boot from a basic disk, which of the following must be true? (Choose all that apply.)

   a. It is a spanned volume.

   b. It is a primary partition.

   c. It is an active partition.

   d. It has a default disk quota of over 1 GB.

10. You are setting up an experimental server that has three disk drives. You are not concerned about fault tolerance, but you are interested in configuring dynamic disks to have relatively fast read/write performance, and you want to extend the life of each disk. Which of the following would you use?

   a. a striped volume

   b. disk duplexing

   c. a simple volume

   d. a spanned volume

11. The dynamic disk that contains the \Windows folder is called the _____.

   a. system partition

   b. system disk

   c. operating volume

   d. boot volume

12. On the old server in your department, it was necessary for the server administrator to come back after 10 p.m. each night to back up the server. Now that you have a new Windows 2003 server, is this still necessary?

   a. No, because if you configure for dynamic disks the department cannot lose vital information, even if two or more disks fail.

   b. No, because you can use RAID level 0 to assure fault tolerance.

   c. No, because you can schedule backups to automatically start after 10 p.m.

   d. Yes, because the Windows Server 2003 Backup utility requires a server operator to perform a tape verification check.

13. How much free space is needed on a basic disk to convert it to a dynamic disk?

    a. 1 MB

    b. 5 MB

    c. 10 MB

    d. none of the above

14. Which of the following is (are) true about basic and dynamic disks in Windows Server 2003? (Choose all that apply.)

    a. Dynamic disks can be partitioned, but basic disks cannot.

    b. At least three basic disks are required to configure disk mirroring after the server is installed.

    c. Basic disks are formatted, but dynamic disks are not.

    d. Dynamic disks can be configured to use RAID levels 0, 1, or 5.

15. You have recently deleted a large number of files off of your server's hard disk. As users continue to add new files, you notice it is taking longer to gain access to them. What can you do to improve access time?

    a. Use the Disk Defragmenter tool to defragment the hard disk.

    b. Use the Check Disk tool to scan the hard disk for bad sectors.

    c. Format the hard disk and restore data from backup.

    d. Upgrade the disk from basic to dynamic.

16. Which tool can you use to determine which partition is designated as the system partition?

    a. Disk Management

    b. Removable Storage

    c. System Tools

    d. Backup

17. Which of the following can be performed by the Check Disk utility? (Choose all that apply.)

    a. Mount a dismounted disk.

    b. Fix bad sectors.

    c. Fix file system errors.

    d. Find files that are no longer used.

18. Which of the following backup options are you most likely to use when you want to back up all files on a server?

    a. copy

    b. incremental

    c. differential

    d. normal

    e. daily

19. You want to set up a mounted volume on your Windows 2003 server. As you go through the steps to mount the volume in the Disk Management Snap-in, you find there is no option to mount the volume. What is the problem?

    a. You did not first set up the target folder as a shared resource.

    b. The target folder is not compressed.

    c. The disk containing the target folder for the mounted volume is formatted for FAT32 and not for NTFS.

    d. Only a CD-ROM can be mounted, and you are trying to mount a dynamic disk.

20. You are setting up a server for an accounting firm. They want fast access to data, but are not concerned with the write speed. They would also like to implement fault tolerance for the data. What type of volume would you configure on the server?

    a. a spanned volume

    b. a striped volume

    c. a RAID-5 volume

    d. a simple volume

21. You have the following disks: 2 GB, 5 GB, 5 GB, 10 GB, and 16 GB. If you create a spanned volume, how much usable disk space will you have?

    a. 28.5 GB

    b. 38 GB

    c. 34.2 GB

    d. 31 GB

22. On your server there are four basic disks set up to look like one disk with a single drive letter. This is called _____.

    a. disk quadraplexing

    b. disk matching

    c. a volume set

    d. a basic mounted group

23. An extended partition in Windows Server 2003 would be on a _____.

    a. basic disk

    b. dynamic disk

    c. striped volume

    d. mirrored volume

24. You have set up a spanned volume, and one disk has failed. What are your alternatives?

    a. Use the Disk Management Snap-in to start the parity repair tool.

    b. There is no problem because the other disks will take over.

    c. Use the Disk Management Snap-in to make the remaining disks simple volumes, and then recover the data.

    d. Replace the disk, repair the spanned volume, and perform a full restore.

25. When you perform a restore, which of the following options are available to you? (Choose all that apply.)

    a. Restore to a single folder.

    b. Restore to a tape.

    c. Restore to the original location.

    d. Restore to an alternate location.

CASE PROJECTS

Case Project Background

Country Fresh Breads is a large bakery in Los Angeles that supplies baked goods to grocery and convenience stores. Their information technology group is implementing a new server with Windows Server 2003. It will be used to track sales and distribution data. Sales are handled over the telephone by customer representatives, who take weekly orders from grocery stores for bakery items to be delivered. Currently,

Country Fresh Breads is using an aging UNIX server for the sales and distribution functions. The Country Fresh Breads customer representatives look up information when each store calls, and then place the store's order via the computer. The disk response time on the UNIX server is relatively slow, and they are hoping to have faster look-up response on the new Windows 2003 server. The new server has a disk array containing eight 20 GB disks. Four of the disks are on one SCSI adapter, and four are on another SCSI adapter. The information technology group is contacting you through your firm, Bayside IT Services, to help in setting up the server. Their current need is to have you assist with the disk storage and in setting up backups.

Case Project 7-1: Planning Disk Storage

To begin, the information technology group asks for the following recommendations about planning the disk storage:

1. What type of disk storage do you recommend that Country Fresh Breads use on this sever: basic or dynamic disks?

2. What fault tolerance do you recommend that they use, if any?

Create a planning document for the information technology group that discusses your recommendations, including the reasons behind your recommendations. If your document recommends fault tolerance, discuss in general terms how to set it up.

Case Project 7-2: Configuring Home Folders

Country Fresh Breads wants to use one disk on this server for users' home folders. Modify the planning document that you created in Case Project 7-1 so that it has a section explaining how you would implement the disk for this purpose. Outline the steps to follow in setting it up.

Case Project 7-3: Devising Backup Plans

Country Fresh Breads is very concerned about formulating a backup plan. Create a separate backup planning document that explains how you would set up backup systems for the following purposes:

1. Daily backups of the server

2. Weekly backups of sales information contained in the five folders to import into the accounting system on another server

3. Yearly archiving of all sales data

Case Project 7-4: Repairing Disk Errors

After you have copied data to the new server and taken one backup, there seem to be some disk errors reported in the server's logs. You are working with a member of the information technology group, Mahalia Yablonsky, who has been assigned to work with you to resolve this type of problem. Create an explanation for Mahalia that includes one or more tools Country Fresh Breads can use to examine the disks and try to repair any problems. Also, explain how to use the tool(s) you suggest.

8

MANAGING WINDOWS SERVER 2003 NETWORK SERVICES

After reading this chapter and completing the exercises, you will be able to:

♦ Implement Microsoft DHCP

♦ Implement Microsoft DNS

♦ Implement Microsoft WINS

♦ Install and configure Internet Information Services

♦ Configure a Telnet server

Network services include those used to manage a network, enable users to access Web resources, and provide all types of network connectivity. Windows Server 2003 offers a wide range of network services including DHCP, DNS, WINS, IIS, and Telnet. DHCP, DNS, and WINS servers provide vital behind-the-scenes functions on networks by automatically leasing IP addresses and by translating computer names to IP addresses. IIS enables an organization to operate a Web server for e-mail communications, purchasing goods and services, disseminating information, advancing scientific research, and a wide range of other uses. Telnet enables clients with or without Windows operating systems to access a server over a network or through the Internet.

In this chapter you will learn how to install and configure DHCP, DNS, and WINS servers. Next, you'll discover how to install and manage IIS, including Microsoft Windows Media Services. Finally, you will configure Windows Server 2003 as a Telnet server.

IMPLEMENTING MICROSOFT DHCP

The Dynamic Host Configuration Protocol (DHCP) is a protocol in the TCP/IP suite that is used along with DHCP Services to detect the presence of a new network client and assign an IP address to that client. When you set up a Windows 95, 98, Me, NT, 2000, or XP client to automatically obtain an IP address, the client contacts a DHCP server to obtain that address. The DHCP server has an assigned range of IP addresses from which it can draw to give to new clients. Each address is assigned for a specific period of time, such as eight hours, two weeks, a month, a year, or even permanently. A range of contiguous addresses is called the **scope**. A single Microsoft DHCP server can support the following:

- Dynamic configuration of DNS server forward and reverse lookup zone records

- Up to 1,000 different scopes (not the theoretical upward limit, but a Microsoft recommendation)

- Up to 10,000 DHCP clients (also not the theoretical upward limit, but a Microsoft recommendation)

A Windows server can be configured as a DHCP server using Microsoft DHCP Services. When you set up a Microsoft DHCP server, you have the option to set it up to automatically register forward and reverse lookup zone records with a Microsoft DNS server (you'll learn about these later in this chapter). The DHCP server automatically updates the DNS server at the time it assigns an IP address. Using dynamic DNS updates can significantly save time in creating DNS lookup zone records.

Multiple scopes are supported in a single Microsoft DHCP server, because it is often necessary to assign different address ranges, such as one range that is 129.70.10.1 to 129.70.10.122 and another that is 129.71.20.10 to 129.71.20.182. As this example illustrates, you can assign address ranges to reflect the network subnet structure or other network divisions (see Figure 8-1).

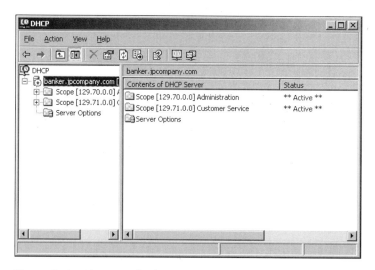

Figure 8-1   Using multiple scopes

 If your network has Internet connectivity, make sure you obtain IP address ranges from your Internet service provider so that you use addresses specifically assigned to your organization and recognized as valid by the Internet community.

Activity 8-1: Installing DHCP

Time Required: Approximately 15 minutes

Objective: Learn how to install DHCP.

Description: DCHP is installed using the Control Panel Add or Remove Programs tool as a networking service in the Windows components. To install DHCP, you need access to an account that has Administrator privileges (for this and all activities in this chapter) and keep the Windows Server 2003, Standard Edition, CD-ROM handy.

1. Click **Start**, point to **Control Panel**, and click **Add or Remove Programs**.

2. Click **Add/Remove Windows Components**.

3. Double-click **Networking Services**.

4. Click the box for **Dynamic Host Configuration Protocol (DHCP)** as shown in Figure 8-2.

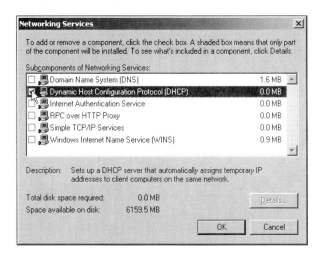

Figure 8-2 Selecting to install DHCP

5. Click **OK**.

6. Click **Next**. (If requested, insert the Windows Server 2003, Standard Edition, CD-ROM, and click **OK**. Also, exit out of the CD-ROM's auto run program, if it starts.) Windows Server 2003 takes a few minutes to install the files. (Also, if your server already has a dynamically configured IP address, an information box enables you to change to a static IP address. Click **OK** and provide a static address, if necessary.)

7. Click **Finish**.

8. Close the **Add or Remove Programs** window.

Configuring a DHCP Server

After DHCP is installed, it is necessary to configure the DHCP server. First, set up one or more scopes of contiguous address ranges and activate each scope.

Secondly, authorize the DHCP server. The process of authorizing the server is a security precaution to make sure IP addresses are only assigned by DHCP servers that are managed by network and server administrators. The security is needed because it is critical for IP address leasing to be carefully managed, ensuring that only valid IP addresses are used and no duplicate IP addresses can be leased. DHCP servers that are not authorized are prevented from running on a network.

Third, a step that is not required, but that saves time in managing DNS, is to configure the DHCP server and its clients to automatically update DNS records.

 Only domain controllers and member servers can be authorized as DHCP servers when Active Directory is in use on the network. If Active Directory is not implemented, a standalone server can be authorized.

Activity 8-2: Configuring DHCP Scopes

Time Required: Approximately 15 minutes

Objective: Learn how to configure a DHCP scope.

Description: In this activity, you practice configuring a scope on a DHCP server. Before you start, obtain the address or computer name of a DNS server from your instructor and ask for a range of addresses for the scope, plus an address to exclude from the scope. You will also need to know the subnet mask.

1. Click **Start**, point to **All Programs**, and point to **Administrative Tools**. Notice the DHCP option. It may be a different color (such as yellow) than the other options on the menu, indicating that it needs to be configured.

2. Click **DHCP**. (Note that instead of following Steps 1 and 2, you can use the MMC DHCP Snap-in).

3. Double-click **DHCP** in the tree, if the DHCP server name is not already displayed. Click the DHCP server. Notice the information provided in the right pane about configuring a scope.

4. Right-click the DHCP server, such as **banker.jpcompany.com [129.70.10.1]**, and click **New Scope** (see Figure 8-3).

Figure 8-3 Configuring a new scope

5. Click **Next** after the New Scope Wizard starts.

6. Enter a name for the scope so it is easy for you to identify as you maintain it, such as **Tellers** and enter a description for the scope, such as **Tellers area subnet**. Click **Next**.

7. Enter the start and end IP addresses, such as **129.70.19.51** and **129.70.19.99**. To go from field to field, press the **period (.)** key. Further, enter the subnet mask, if the desired value is different from the default 255.255.0.0. If you change the subnet mask, such as to **255.255.255.0**, click inside the Length box to automatically reset the subnet mask length (see Figure 8-4). Click **Next**.

8. Enter an address, such as **129.70.19.70**, in the Start IP address box, and click **Add**. What happens after you click Add? Do you need to enter an ending address? Record your observations. Click **Next**.

9. What is the default lease time? For what types of situations would this default be appropriate? Record your answers. Change the default lease time to **4** days. Click **Next**.

10. Click **Yes, I want to configure these options now**, if necessary, and click **Next**.

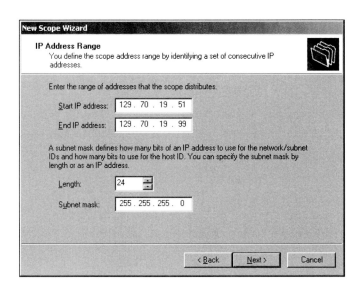

Figure 8-4 Configuring the scope

11. The next dialog box offers the ability to enter an IP address for a router or default gateway. You configure this information if access to the addresses in this scope is through a router or gateway. Click **Next**.

12. Enter the parent domain in which DNS name resolution will occur, such as **jpcompany.com**. Enter the name of the DNS server obtained from your instructor, and click **Resolve**, or enter the DNS server's IP address. Click **Add**. How would you enter more than one DNS server? Click **Next**.

13. In the next dialog box, you can enter the names and IP addresses of WINS servers. These are used on networks with NetBIOS naming to map names to IP addresses. Click **Next**.

14. Click **Yes, I want to activate this scope now**, if necessary, and then click **Next** (or click **Cancel**, if you do not have permission from your instructor to finish creating the scope).

15. Click **Finish**. What now appears in the right pane of the DHCP window?

16. Next, you need to authorize the DHCP server. Right click the server as you did in Step 4, and click **Authorize.**

17. Close the **DHCP** window.

 Set the duration of a lease on the basis of the type of connection. For desktop computers that are connected on a more permanent basis, set leases to expire after a longer period such as from three days to a couple weeks. Particularly use a longer lease period on medium and large networks in which you have a large number of IP addresses that can be used. For laptop and portable computers that are less permanent on the network, set leases to expire after the duration of the communication session, such as 8 to 24 hours.

When it is installed, a DHCP server is automatically configured to register IP addresses at the DNS servers, but you must also provide the DNS servers' IP addresses when you configure each scope. Also, you can manually configure automatic DNS registration through a DHCP server, as you learn in the next activity.

Activity 8-3: Configuring Automatic DNS Registration

Time Required: Approximately 5 minutes

Objective: Verify that a DHCP server is configured to automatically register IP addresses with a DNS server.

Description: In this activity, you verify two things: that the DHCP server you have configured is set up to automatically register with a DNS server the IP addresses that it leases, and that the DHCP server is configured for the types of clients on your network.

1. Click **Start**, point to **All Programs**, point to **Administrative Tools**, and click **DHCP**.

2. Right-click the server in the DHCP management tool, and then click **Properties**.

3. Click the **DNS** tab (see Figure 8-5), and make sure that the box for **Enable DNS dynamic updates according to the settings below** is checked. Clients running Windows 2000, Windows XP, or Windows Server 2003 operating systems can request to update a DNS server. If you have only these clients, click the box for **Dynamically update DNS A and PTR records only if requested by the DHCP clients**. If there are other operating systems connecting to the network, such as Windows 98 or Windows NT, which do not request to update a DNS server, click instead **Always dynamically update DNS A and PTR records**—which means that the DHCP server takes the responsibility to update the DNS server's records every time a client obtains the IP address. Also, make sure that **Discard A and PTR records when lease is denied** is checked, so that the DHCP server alerts the DNS server to delete a record each time a lease is up. If some clients are running Windows 95, 98, and NT, also check **Dynamically update DNS A and PTR records for DHCP clients that do not request updates (for example, clients running Windows NT 4.0)**.

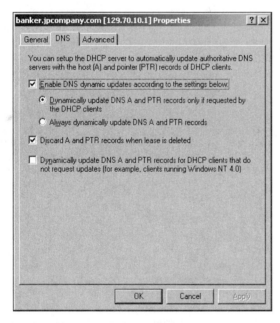

Figure 8-5   Configuring automatic updates for DNS servers

4. Click **OK**.

5. Close the **DHCP** window.

Troubleshooting DHCP

When you set up a DHCP server, it is possible for problems to occur. Some possible problems include that the server is stopped or not working, that it is creating extra network traffic, that it is not automatically registering with DNS servers, and others. Table 8-1 presents several typical problems and their resolution.

Table 8-1   Troubleshooting a DHCP server

Problem	Solution
The DHCP server does not start	1. Use the Computer Management tool to make sure that the DHCP Client and DHCP Server services are started and set to start automatically. If the DHCP Server Service does not start, make sure that the Remote Procedure Call (RPC) and the Security Accounts Manager Services are already started, because the DHCP Server Service depends on both. 2. Make sure that the DHCP server is authorized. 3. Use the Event Viewer to check the System log (see Chapter 12).
The DHCP server creates extra or excessive network traffic (as determined by using the System Monitor as discussed in Chapter 11)	Increase the lease period in each scope, so there is less traffic caused by allocating new leases when the old ones expire.
The DNS lookup zone records are not automatically updated	1. Make sure that DNS servers and IP addresses are set up in each DHCP scope. 2. Make sure that the DHCP server's properties are set up to automatically update the DNS server. Also, have the DHCP server do the updating instead of clients, when there are pre-Windows 2000 clients. Lastly, enable DNS updating for clients that do not dynamically support it.
One of the leased IP addresses is conflicting with a permanent IP address leased to a computer, such as a server	Exclude that IP address from the scope.
Your network has a large number of portable and laptop computers and is in short supply of IP addresses	Reduce the lease duration so that leases expire sooner and can be reassigned.
The system log is reporting Jet database error messages	The DHCP database is corrupted. Have users log off from the network and disable the server's connection (use the Control Panel's Network Connections tool). Use the DHCP management tool to reconcile the scopes (right-click the server and click Reconcile All Scopes). Another option is to open the Command Prompt window and use the Jetpack.exe program to repair the database. A third option is to use the Nesh.exe command to dump the database and then reinitialize it.
The DHCP server is not responding	Use the control panel's Network Connections tool to make sure that the server is connected to the network.

IMPLEMENTING MICROSOFT DNS

One of the requirements for using Active Directory on a Windows Server 2003 network is to have the DNS available to it. When you set up a Windows Server 2003 network, if there are no DNS servers that have been implemented, plan to use Windows Server 2003 DNS, because it is most compatible with Active Directory. Non-Microsoft DNS servers can be used, but then it is necessary to make sure they are compatible with Active Directory. Also, non-Microsoft versions of DNS do not offer the DNS replication advantages (you learn about these shortly) through Active Directory.

DNS servers provide the DNS namespace for an enterprise (see Chapter 4), including providing a way to resolve computer names to IP addresses and IP addresses to computer names, as well as many other services. In the following sections, you'll learn how to install DNS, how to set up zones and services in DNS, and you'll learn about DNS replication.

 Microsoft recommends that DNS servers have a static IP address (one that is manually configured and not automatically leased by DHCP). Also, before installing DNS on a server when Active Directory is in use on a network, make sure that the server is a DC or promote it to be a DC if it is not. Use the Dcpromo tool or the Configure Your Server Wizard (see Chapter 4), if you need to promote a member server to a DC.

Installing DNS Services

The installation steps for DNS are similar to those for DHCP, because both are installed as Windows components. Also, if you want to use Active Directory on a network, plan to install DNS before you install Active Directory—or you can install DNS at the same time you are installing Active Directory (see Chapter 4).

Activity 8-4: Installing DNS

Time Required: Approximately 10 minutes

Objective: Learn how to install DNS separately from the Active Directory installation.

Description: In this activity, you use the Add or Remove Programs tool to install DNS.

1. Click **Start**, point to **Control Panel**, and click **Add or Remove Programs**.

2. Click **Add/Remove Windows Components**.

3. Double-click **Networking Services**.

4. Click **Domain Name System (DNS)** and make sure that you do not remove check marks for any other services, such as DHCP.

5. Click **OK** (see Figure 8-6).

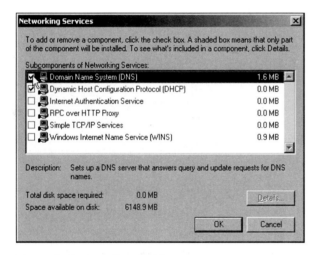

Figure 8-6   Installing DNS

6. Click **Next**. (If requested, insert the Windows Server 2003, Standard Edition, CD-ROM, and click **OK**. Also, exit out of the auto run program, if it starts.)

7. Click **Finish**.

8. Close the **Add or Remove Programs** window.

DNS Zones

DNS name resolution is enabled through the use of tables of information that link computer names and IP addresses. The tables are associated with partitions in a DNS server that are called **zones** and that contain resource records. Each zone houses tables, called the zone file or zone database, of different types of resource records, such as records that link a computer name to an IP address.

The zone that links computer names to IP addresses is called the **forward lookup zone**, which holds host name records, which are called address records. Each IP-based server and client should have a host record so that it can be found through DNS. For example, if the DNS server name is Banker, with the IP address 129.70.10.1, then the forward lookup zone maps Banker to 129.70.10.1. In IP version 4, a host record is called a **host address (A) resource record**. IP version 6 (IPv6), the newer version of IP that is used primarily on education and experimental networks, consists of a 128-bit address (instead of the 32-bit address used with IPv4). An IPv6 record is called an **IPv6 host address (AAAA) resource record**. Microsoft, along with other major network software and hardware vendors, has made a commitment to implement IPv6. When you install DNS on a domain controller (DC) in a domain, a forward lookup zone is automatically created for the domain with the DNS server's address record already entered. You must enter the records of other hosts or configure DHCP to automatically update the DNS forward lookup zone each time it leases an IP address.

Depending on the domain structure and Internet connectivity, a DNS server can have several forward lookup zones, but there should be at least one for the parent domain, such as jpcompany.com. Another zone, called the **reverse lookup zone**, holds the **pointer (PTR) resource** record, which contains the links from IP addresses to host names. The reverse lookup zone is not used as commonly as the forward lookup zone, but can be important to create for those instances when a network communication requires associating an IP address to a computer name, such as for monitoring a network using IP address information. Because it is used less commonly, the reverse lookup zone is not automatically configured when DNS is installed. However, if you anticipate that there will be users with off-site access to your network, such as over the Internet, plan to implement information in a reverse lookup zone. Table 8-2 summarizes the commonly used resource records in DNS.

8

Table 8-2   DNS resource records

Resource Record	Description
Host (A)	Links a computer or network host name to its IP address
Canonical name (CNAME)	Links an alias to a computer name
Load sharing	Used to spread the load of DNS lookup requests among multiple DNS servers as a way to provide faster resolution for clients and better network response
Mail exchanger (MX)	Provides the IP addresses for SMTP servers that can accept e-mail for users in a domain
Name server (NS)	Provides information in response to queries about secondary DNS servers for an authoritative server (described later in this section) and information about off-site primary servers that are not authoritative for the domain
Pointer record (PTR)	Associates an IP address to a computer or network host name
Service (SRV) Locator	Associates a particular TCP/IP service to a server along with the domain of the server and its protocol
Start of authority (SOA)	Is the first record in a zone and also indicates if this server is authoritative for the current zone
Windows Internet Naming Service (WINS)	Used to forward a lookup request for a NetBIOS name to a WINS server when the host name cannot be found in DNS
Windows Internet Naming Service Reverse (WINS-R)	Used to forward a reverse lookup (IP address to computer name) request to a WINS server

Activity 8-5: Creating a Reverse Lookup Zone

Time Required: Approximately 10 minutes

Objective: Learn how to create a reverse lookup zone.

Description: If you plan to use a reverse lookup zone, create it before DNS forward lookup zone records are created. The reason for this is that when a DNS forward lookup zone record is created, either manually or through dynamic updating, an associated reverse lookup zone PTR record can be created automatically.

1. Click **Start**, point to **All Programs**, point to **Administrative Tools**, and click **DNS**. Double-click the server in the tree, if necessary to display the items under it. Click **Reverse Lookup Zones** to highlight it.

2. Right-click the **Reverse Lookup Zones** folder in the tree under the DNS server, and click **New Zone** (see Figure 8-7).

Figure 8-7   Creating a reverse lookup zone

3. Click **Next** after the New Zone Wizard starts.

4. Notice the zone options that are available, and then click **Primary zone**, if necessary. Also, click the box for **Store the zone in Active Directory (available only if DNS server is a domain controller)**, if necessary. This last option enables the DNS server contents to be replicated to other DNS servers on the network (you'll learn more about this later in the chapter).

5. Click **Next**.

6. In the Active Directory Zone Replication Scope window, you can select how the DNS server is replicated through Active Directory. Make sure that **To all domain controllers in the Active Directory domain** *domainname* is selected, and then click **Next**.

7. Enter the network ID of the reverse lookup zone (which is the first two or three octets that identify the network, depending on the subnet mask that you use). This information is used to build the "in-addr.arpa" reverse lookup zone name. For example, if your zone network address is 129.70 then the in-addr.arpa reverse lookup zone is named 70.129.IN-ADDR.ARPA. The wizard automatically builds the in-addr.arpa name format when you enter the network address (see Figure 8-8). Click **Next**.

8. Configure the security of updates made through DHCP by making sure that **Allow only secure dynamic updates** is selected. Click **Next**.

9. Review the information you have entered, and click **Finish**. You should see the new reverse lookup zone displayed in the right pane.

10. Leave the DNS tool open for the next activity.

If you are using subnets, you can create a folder for each one under the parent reverse lookup zone by double-clicking Reverse Lookup Zones in the tree to show the new zone, right clicking the new zone, such as 129.70.*x.x* Subnet, clicking New Domain, and entering the subnet value, such as 10 (for subnet 129.77.10). Click OK, and repeat this step for each subnet.

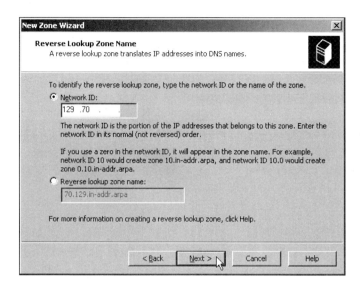

Figure 8-8   Configuring the in-addr.arpa reverse lookup zone name

Activity 8-6: Manually Creating DNS Host Address A Resource Records

Time Required: Approximately 10 minutes

Objective: Create a host address A resource record.

Description: In this activity you learn how to configure a host address A resource record in a forward lookup zone.

1. Open the **DNS** tool, if it is not still open.

2. Double-click **Forward Lookup Zones**, and double-click the domain name (see Figure 8-9).

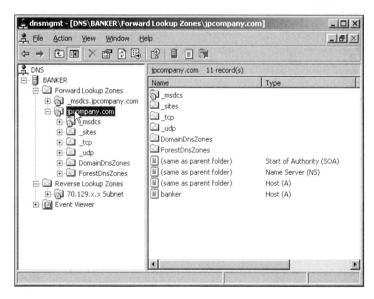

Figure 8-9   Opening the DNS tree

3. Click the **Action** menu. What are the options in this menu?

4. Click **New Host (A)**.

5. Enter the name of the host computer, such as **Teller1**, and its IP address, such as **129.70.10.50** in the New Host dialog box.

6. Check the box to **Create associated pointer (PTR) record** (note that the reverse lookup zone must be created first, as in Activity 8-5).

7. Check the box to **Allow any authenticated user to update DNS records with the same owner name** (for computers running Windows 2000, XP, and Server 2003 that can update in coordination with DHCP; this option also ensures security, because it associates an ACL with the record).

8. Click **Add Host** (see Figure 8-10). Click **OK**.

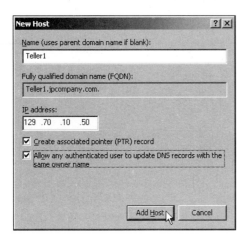

Figure 8-10   Configuring a new host record

9. Click **Done**.

10. Leave the DNS tool open for the next activity.

Using the DNS Dynamic Update Protocol

Microsoft DNS is also called **Dynamic DNS (DDNS)**, which is a modern form of DNS that enables client computers and DHCP servers to automatically register IP addresses. The **DNS dynamic update protocol** enables information in a DNS server to be automatically updated in coordination with DHCP. Using the DNS dynamic update protocol can save network administrators a great deal of time, because they no longer have to manually register each new workstation or to register a workstation each time its IP lease is up and a new IP address is issued. After you configure DNS, always make sure that it is configured to use the DNS dynamic update protocol.

Activity 8-7: Verifying the DNS Dynamic Update Configuration

Time Required: Approximately 5 minutes

Objective: Verify that DNS is configured to be dynamically updated using the DNS dynamic update protocol.

Description: In this activity you make certain that dynamic DNS updating is properly configured. This step is important in two respects. One is to ensure that the workload for the DNS server administrator is reduced and the other ensures that security is set on dynamic updating.

1. Open the **DNS** tool, if it is not still open.

2. In the left pane under Forward Lookup Zones, right-click the domain, and click **Properties**.

3. Make sure that the **General** tab is displayed. In the Data is stored in Active Directory section of the dialog box, check the setting for Dynamic updates? The best practice, as shown in Figure 8-11, is for this parameter to be configured as Secure only, so that an ACL is associated with a host record (only an authorized client can perform an update). Click the down arrow in the list box to view the other options and record what they are.

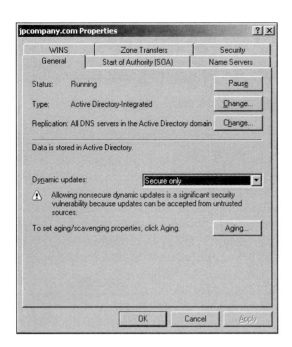

Figure 8-11   Dynamic updates configuration

    4. Click **OK**.

    5. Close the **DNS management tool**.

Keep in mind that the DHCP server must also be configured to perform automatic DNS registration, as you learned in Activity 8-3.

DNS Replication

DNS servers on a network fall into two broad categories: primary and secondary. A **primary DNS server** is the DNS server that is the main administrative server for a zone and thus is also the *authoritative* server for that zone. For example, when you first create a forward lookup zone on a DNS server for the york.com domain, you create an SOA resource record identifying that DNS server as authoritative for the domain. This means that all changes to the zone, the creation of address A resource records, new SRV resource records, and so on, must be made on that DNS server.

You have the option to create one or more backup DNS servers, called **secondary DNS servers** for a primary DNS server. A secondary DNS server contains a copy of the primary DNS server's zone database, but is not used for administration (it is not authoritative). It obtains that copy through a zone transfer over the network. There are three vital services performed by secondary DNS servers. One is to make sure that there is a copy of the primary DNS server's data, in case the primary server fails. Another function is to enable DNS load balancing (via the load sharing resource records) among a primary DNS server and its secondary servers. Load balancing means that if the primary DNS server is busy performing a name resolution, a different request for a name resolution that is received at the same time can be fielded by a secondary DNS server for faster response to users. A third advantage to using secondary DNS servers is that they can be spread to different parts of a network, such as to different sites (this applies to geographic locations and to Active Directory sites), so that you can reduce the congestion in one part of the network.

One DNS server can be authoritative for multiple domains because it can have multiple zones. Also, because one server can have multiple zones, a single DNS server can be a secondary server for more than one primary server. Plus, one DNS server can be a primary server for one zone and a secondary server for another zone.

If you use Active Directory and have two or more DCs, plan to set up Microsoft DNS services on at least two of the DCs, because the multimaster replication model (see Chapter 4) enables you to replicate DNS information on each DC. The advantage of replicating DNS information is that if one DC that hosts DNS services fails, another DC is available to provide uninterrupted DNS services for the network. This is especially critical on a network that provides Internet access and Web-based SMTP e-mail services. Whenever you create a zone, as you practiced in Activity 8-5, select the option to Store the zone in Active Directory (available only if a DNS server is a domain controller), which enables you to take advantage of multimaster replication.

Troubleshooting DNS

If DNS is installed, but is not resolving names or does not seem to be working, check to make sure that the DNS Server and DNS Client services are both started and set to start automatically on the DNS server. To check these services, click Start, point to All Programs, point to Administrative Tools, and click Computer Management. Double-click Services and Applications, if necessary, and click Services. Scroll to view the DNS Client and DNS Server services and then check the status and startup type information for both. If you need to start one or both services, double-click the service and click the Start button. Also, make sure that the Startup type box is set to Automatic.

IMPLEMENTING MICROSOFT WINS

Windows Internet Naming Service (WINS) is used to register NetBIOS computer names and map them to IP addresses for any systems that use NetBIOS name resolution (often it is pre-Windows 2000 servers and pre-Windows 2000 clients that particularly use NetBIOS names). WINS automatically registers network clients that use NetBIOS, and builds a database that other network clients can query in order to locate a computer. For example, if there is a Windows 98 network computer called Eggplant that offers a shared folder for other network clients, those other clients can query WINS to find Eggplant.

The steps for installing WINS are similar to those for installing DHCP and DNS, because all three are installed from the Control Panel's Add or Remove Programs option.

Activity 8-8: Installing WINS

Time Required: Approximately 10 minutes

Objective: Learn how to install WINS.

Description: In this activity, you use the Add or Remove Programs tool to install WINS.

1. Click **Start**, point to **Control Panel**, and click **Add or Remove Programs**.

2. Click **Add/Remove Windows Components**.

3. Double-click **Networking Services**.

4. Click the box for **Windows Internet Name Service (WINS)**. Leave all other boxes that are already checked as is. Click **OK**.

5. Click **Next**. Windows Server 2003 takes a few minutes to install the files. (If your server already has a dynamically configured IP address, an information box enables you to change to a static IP address. Click **OK** and provide a static address, if necessary.) Further, if requested, insert the Windows Server 2003, Standard Edition, CD-ROM, click **OK**, and exit out of the auto run program, if it starts.

6. Click **Finish**.

7. Close the **Add or Remove Programs** window.

Typically, you will use the default configuration for WINS after it is installed. If you need to manage WINS, you can access the WINS management tool as an MMC snap-in or from the Administrative Tools menu. For example, you can use this tool to import a special database of computers to register or to set up replication with other WINS servers in a domain.

If the WINS server experiences problems, you can troubleshoot by making sure WINS is started, or by stopping and restarting it to reinitialize the service. To do this, open the WINS tool from the Administrative Tools menu or as an MMC snap-in. Double-click the WINS server in the tree to display the elements under it, then right-click the WINS server in the tree and point to All Tasks. If WINS is stopped, click Start; or if WINS is started, click the Restart option to stop and restart it.

IMPLEMENTING MICROSOFT INTERNET INFORMATION SERVICES

Microsoft **Internet Information Services (IIS)** is a component included on the Windows Server 2003, Standard Edition, CD-ROM that enables you to offer a complete Web site from a Windows server. Your Web site might fulfill any number of functions. On a college campus you might use it to enable applicants to apply for admission, or to allow currently enrolled students to view their progress toward completing degree requirements. Many companies use their Web sites for multiple purposes such as to announce new products, provide product support, take product orders, and advertise job openings. Another use is to provide training to company employees on using software such as an inventory or order entry system.

IIS benchmarks prove these services are fast and the software design enables the use of extensions to link other software applications to an IIS server, such as a distributed client/server system that implements Web-based features. One reason why IIS services are fast and can be integrated with other programs is the built-in **Internet Server Application Programming Interface (ISAPI)**. ISAPI is a group of DLL (dynamic-link library) files that are applications and filters. The applications files enable developers to link customized programs into IIS and to speed program execution. IIS filters are used to automatically trigger programs, such as a Microsoft Access database lookup or a security program to authorize a user to access specific Web functions. The IIS component contains the World Wide Web services which are vital for a Web site. The Web, of course, is a series of servers with software such as Microsoft IIS that make HTML and other Web documents available for workstations. Another service that can be employed through IIS is the **File Transfer Protocol (FTP)** service. FTP is a TCP/IP-based application protocol that handles file transfers over a network. Also, there are additional services that you can install to make an IIS server function as an e-mail server using the **Simple Mail Transfer Protocol (SMTP)** and as a **Network News Transfer Protocol (NNTP)** server. An SMTP server acts as an Internet gateway and in partnership with e-mail services, such as Microsoft Exchange, accepts incoming e-mail from the Internet and forwards it to the recipient. It also forwards outgoing e-mail from a network's e-mail service to the Internet. NNTP is used over TCP/IP-based networks by NNTP servers to transfer news and informational messages organized and stored in newsgroups for clients to access.

There are several reasons why Windows Server 2003 makes a good candidate as a Web server. One reason is that Windows Server 2003's privileged-mode architecture (see Chapter 1) and fault-tolerance capabilities make it a reliable server platform. Another reason is that Windows Server 2003 is compatible with small databases, such as Microsoft Access, and large databases, such as SQL Server and Oracle. Also, users can log directly into a database through the IIS **Open Database Connectivity (ODBC)** drivers. ODBC is a set of database access rules used by Microsoft in its ODBC application programming interface (API) for accessing databases and providing a standard doorway to database data. This makes IIS very compatible with Web-based client/server applications. IIS also is compatible with Microsoft Point-to-Point Encryption (MPPE) security, IP Security (IPSec), and the Secure Sockets Layer (SSL) encryption technique. SSL is a dual-key encryption standard for communication between a server and a client and is also used by Internet Explorer. IIS enables security control on the basis of username and password, IP address, and folder and file access controls.

Table 8-3 shows the main components that can be used with IIS.

8

Table 8-3   IIS components

IIS Component Option	Purpose
Background Intelligent Transfer Service (BITS) Server Extensions	Used to enhance control and speed for IIS-based data transfers
Common files	Files needed for general IIS functions that must be installed, but should not be installed without installing other services
File Transfer Protocol (FTP) Service	Used to set up FTP Server Services for Internet, intranet, and virtual private network (VPN) file transfers between the Windows 2003 server and a client
FrontPage 2002 Server Extensions	Used to work with Microsoft FrontPage and Visual InterDev for creating and publishing Web materials developed through those tools (both tools are purchased separately)
Internet Printing	Used for printing to shared printers and for managing IIS printing
Internet Services Manager	Installs an MMC snap-in that is used to manage an IIS server
NNTP service	Enables an IIS server to function as a Network News Transfer Protocol server to provide news groups and news messages to client subscribers
SMTP service	Enables an IIS server to function as a Simple Mail Transfer Protocol server to distribute SMTP-formatted e-mail messages on a network or through the Internet
World Wide Web server	Enables the IIS server to function as a Web server on the Internet, via an intranet, or through a VPN

Installing a Web Server

There are several requirements for installing and using IIS on the Internet:

- Windows Server 2003 installed on the computer selected to host IIS
- TCP/IP installed on the IIS host
- Access to an Internet service provider (ISP). (Ask the ISP for your IP address, subnet mask, and default gateway IP address.)
- Sufficient disk space for IIS and for Web site files (the required space depends on the number of Web files that you publish)
- Disk storage formatted for NTFS (IIS can run on FAT, but NTFS has better performance and security)
- A method for resolving IP addresses to computer or domain names, such as DNS and WINS

You can install IIS when you install Windows Server 2003. If you do not install IIS during the Windows Server 2003 installation, you can install it later by using the Control Panel Add or Remove Programs icon, as in the next activity.

Activity 8-9: Installing IIS

Time Required: Approximately 15 minutes

Objective: Learn how to install IIS.

Description: This activity enables you to install IIS. (IIS may already be installed, but you can follow these steps anyway.)

1. Click **Start**, point to **Control Panel**, and click **Add or Remove Programs**.
2. Click **Add/Remove Windows Components**.
3. Double-click **Application Server**.

4. Click the box for **Internet Information Services (IIS)**. Notice the amount of disk space required, which is relatively substantial compared to other services you have installed. Double-click **Internet Information Services (IIS)** to view the IIS subcomponents that are selected by default. How could you select to install FTP services? Click **OK**.

5. Click **OK**.

6. Click **Next**. (If requested, insert the Windows Server 2003, Standard Edition, CD-ROM, and click **OK**. Exit out of the CD-ROM's auto run program, if it starts.)

7. Click **Finish**.

8. Close the **Add or Remove Programs** window.

Creating a Virtual Directory

A **virtual directory** is really a physical folder or a redirection to a **Uniform Resource Locator (URL)** that points to a folder, so that it can be accessed over the Internet, an intranet, or VPN. This means that the folder can reside on the same computer that hosts IIS or it can be on another computer. The reason for creating a virtual directory is to provide a shortcut path to specific IIS server content. For example, one reason for creating a virtual directory is to provide an easy way for multiple users to publish on the Web site, by modifying and uploading files to the virtual directory. A URL is a special addressing format used to find, for example, particular Web locations or FTP sites. When you set up a virtual directory, you give it an alias, which is a name to identify it to a Web browser. The URL format for accessing a file in a virtual directory entails providing the server name, the virtual directory alias, and the file name, such as \\Banker\Webpub\Mypage.html. In this example, Banker is the server name, Webpub is the alias of the virtual directory, and Mypage.html is the file.

When you create a virtual directory, you can choose the security options you want to apply, as shown in Table 8-4.

Table 8-4   Virtual directory security options

Security Option	Purpose
Directory browsing (or Browse when you configure it)	Enables users to browse the contents of the virtual directory
Execute	Enables users to execute programs and scripts
Read	Enables users to open files in the virtual directory
Run scripts	Enables users to run command scripts
Write	Enables users to add new files to the virtual directory and to modify the contents of existing files

After a virtual directory is created, you can modify its properties in the Internet Information Services tool, by clicking Default Web Site in the tree under the server, right-clicking the virtual directory's alias, such as WebdocsJP, and then clicking Properties (see Figure 8-12). Table 8-5 presents a general description of the properties that can be configured for a virtual directory.

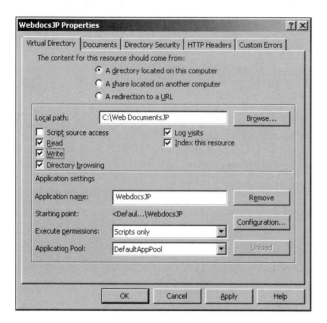

Figure 8-12   A virtual directory's properties

Table 8-5   Virtual directory properties tabs

Properties Tab	Purpose
Custom Errors	Used to set up error messages that are displayed in a client's browser when specific errors occur
Directory Security	Used to fine-tune security including whether or not to allow anonymous access, to set IP address restrictions and restrictions on domain names that can access the site, and to require secure communications through certificates
Documents	Used to define a default Web page and to specify a footer for Web documents
HTTP Headers	Used to set an expiration date on the directory contents, to set properties of headers that are returned to the client's browser, to set content ratings (such as for content limited to adults), and to specify Multipurpose Internet Mail Extensions (MIME)
Virtual Directory	Used to specify general properties that include the computer on which the physical folder is located, the local path, security, and application settings

The physical folder properties, including permissions, share permissions, and Web sharing permissions can also be modified by right-clicking the folder on drive C: in Windows Explorer or My Computer when you are directly logged on to the server.

Activity 8-10: Creating a Virtual Directory

Time Required: Approximately 10 minutes

Objective: Set up a virtual directory.

Description: In this activity, you set up a virtual directory from which to publish documents for the IIS Web server that you installed in Activity 8-9. Before you start, create a folder on drive C: called Web Documents with your initials at the end of the folder name, such as Web DocumentsJP

1. Click **Start**, point to **All Programs**, point to **Administrative Tools**, and click **Internet Information Services (IIS) Manager**.

2. In the tree, double-click the name of the server, if necessary, on which you installed IIS.

3. Double-click the **Web Sites** folder.

4. Right-click **Default Web Site** in the right pane, point to **New**, and click **Virtual Directory** as shown in Figure 8-13.

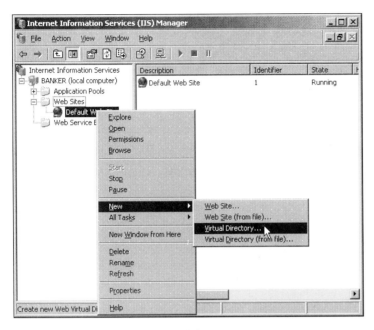

Figure 8-13   Creating a virtual directory

5. Click **Next** after the Virtual Directory Creation Wizard starts.

6. Enter an alias for the virtual directory, which users will employ to access it, such as Webdocs plus your initials at the end, such as WebdocsJP. Click **Next**.

7. Enter the path to the physical folder you created before starting this assignment, such as C:\Web DocumentsJP (or use the Browse button to find it). Click **Next**.

8. What security options are available for you to set? What options would you need to set to enable users to copy HTML documents to the virtual directory? Similarly, how would you provide users access to only read, browse, and view the source code for scripts? Record your observations. Click the options for **Read**, **Run** scripts (such as ASP), and **Browse**, so that there is a check mark in each of these boxes. Click **Next** after you have configured the security options.

9. Click **Finish**.

10. How would you use the Internet Information Services tool to view the properties of the new virtual directory? Leave the Internet Information Services tool open for the next project.

Managing and Configuring an IIS Web Server

After it is installed, you can manage a Web server using the Internet Information Services tool, described in the previous section. The Internet Information Services tool enables you to manage the following types of IIS components:

- Application pools
- Web sites
- Web service extensions
- SMTP virtual server (if you have installed the SMTP Service)
- NNTP virtual server (if you have installed the NNTP Service)

You can also manage an FTP site from the Internet Information Services tool, if you have previously installed the File Transfer Protocol (FTP) Service when you installed IIS (see Activity 8-9).

Application pools enables you to group similar Web applications into pools or groups for management, such as for common settings. Web sites is a folder used to manage multiple Web sites from one administrative Web server, and one Default Web site is automatically set up within the Web sites folder. Web service extensions are for compatibility with Microsoft FrontPage for Web design use, plus they enable the use of other extensions such as for Active Server pages and Internet printing. The SMTP and NNTP virtual server components are used to manage Internet e-mail and newsgroup services on an IIS server. To manage and configure any of these components, open the Internet Information Services tool, and double-click the IIS server in the tree under Internet Information Services. Next, click or double-click the component under the tree, such as Web Sites.

To configure an IIS Web server, open the Internet Information Services tool, and double-click Web Sites in the tree. Start by configuring the Default Web Site by right-clicking it, and clicking Properties. Configure the properties on the tabs as shown in Figure 8-14. There are many parameters that you can configure for a Web site, but the best advice is to start by configuring the basic properties, such as configuring performance to match the number of users, and configuring security. Table 8-6 summarizes the configuration options associated with each tab for a Web site's properties.

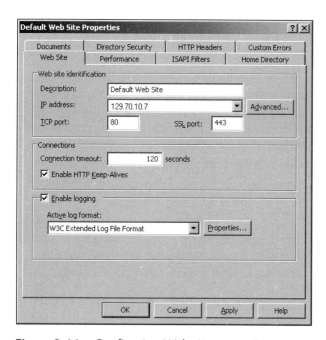

Figure 8-14   Configuring Web site properties

Table 8-6   Web site properties tabs

Properties Tab	Purpose
Custom Errors	Used to set up error messages that are displayed in a client's browser when specific errors occur while accessing the Web server
Directory Security	Used to set up security for a Web site that includes whether or not to allow anonymous access, authentication methods, IP address and domain restrictions, and use of certificate security
Documents	Defines a default Web page for the Web site and enables you to specify a footer for Web documents

Table 8-6   Web site properties tabs (continued)

Properties Tab	Purpose
Home Directory	Specifies the location of the main folder in which Web programs and processes are stored, which is usually \\server\inetpub\wwwroot; enables you to set security on that folder
HTTP Headers	Used to set an expiration date on the directory contents, to set properties of headers that are returned to the client's browser, to set content ratings (such as for content limited to adults), and to specify Multipurpose Internet Mail Extensions (MIME)
ISAPI Filters	Used to set up Internet Server Application Programming Interface (ISAPI) filters, which are used to provide special instructions on how to handle specific HTTP requests
Performance	Used to optimize performance on the basis of bandwidth allocated for the Web site and the number of connections
Web Site	Used to configure Web site identification, connection timeout, and activity logging

Activity 8-11: Configuring a Web Site

8

Time Required: Approximately 15 minutes

Objective: Learn how to configure a Web site.

Description: In this activity, you practice configuring the connection timeout, number of connections, and anonymous user authentication for the Default Web site. You also learn where to set restrictions on who can access a Web server.

1. Open the **Internet Information Services** tool, if necessary.

2. Double-click the **Web Sites** folder, if necessary, to view the Default Web Site.

3. Right-click **Default Web Site** in the left pane, and click **Properties**.

4. On the Web Site tab, verify the IP address (click the down arrow to view the selections).

5. Set the Connection timeout box to **240** seconds.

6. Click the **Performance** tab. What is the default setting for Web site connections?

7. Click the option button for **Connections limited to**, and set the number of connections to **500**.

8. Click the **Directory Security** tab. What options are on this tab?

9. Click the top **Edit** button for the Authentication and access control section to see the dialog box shown in Figure 8-15. Notice that anonymous access is enabled by default (access in which the user does not have to provide identification). Also, notice the types of Authenticated access:

   - *Integrated Windows authentication*—Employs the user's currently logged on credentials which are passed to the Web server from the user's Web browser.

   - *Digest authentication for Windows domain servers*—Used to transmit a hashed security communication and not a password between the Web server and the client. A hashed value is created by using a mathematical formula to create a random value.

   - *Basic authentication (password is sent in clear text)*—Used for clients that do not send an encrypted password.

   - *.NET Passport authentication*—Hands over authentication to .NET Passport, an authentication service provided by Microsoft.

10. Make sure that **Integrated Windows authentication** is selected (the default), and click **OK**.

11. In the IP address and domain name restrictions section, click the **Edit** button.

12. Click the **Add** button. What are the three ways in which you can deny access to this Web server? Select each option to view the information you would enter to deny access (click **OK** if you see a warning box). Click **Cancel**.

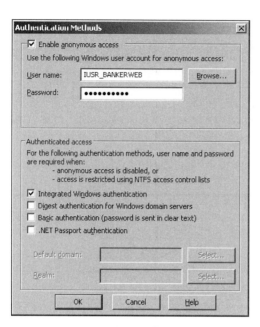

Figure 8-15   Configuring the Authentication Methods

13. Click **Cancel** in the IP Address and Domain Name Restrictions dialog box.

14. Click **OK** in the Default Web Site Properties dialog box.

15. Close the **Internet Information Services** window.

Troubleshooting a Web Server

Occasionally a Web server can experience problems, such as users not being able to connect to the server or the server not enabling e-mail to be sent. Table 8-7 illustrates possible problems and their solutions.

Table 8-7   Troubleshooting IIS

Problem	Solution
The Web server is not responding	1. Use the Control Panel's Network Connections tool to make sure that the server's connection to the network or Internet is enabled. 2. Right-click the Web server in the Internet Information Services Manager tool, point to All Tasks, and click Restart IIS to restart the IIS service. 3. Use the Computer Management tool to make sure that the Server service is started and set to start automatically.
No one can access the Web server, but the server is booted and its network and Internet connections are enabled	1. Make sure that the DNS server(s) is (are) connected and working on the network. 2. Use a Web browser from different computers and locations to test the connection and determine if the problem is due to a network segment location, the Internet connection, or a specific client that cannot access the server.
Clients can connect to the Web server, but cannot access its contents	1. Make sure that the authentication and encryption set at the server matches the authentication and encryption properties that the client computers can support. 2. Check the Web sharing permissions on Web folders to make sure that they enable the appropriate client access, such as permission to read files and run scripts (try using the Effective Permissions tool for help). 3. Make sure that no NTFS permissions on Web folders are set to Deny. 4. Make sure that the \Inetpub\wwwroot folder is intact and contains all of the necessary HTML files (open the Internet Information Services tool, right-click Default Web Site, and click Open).

Table 8-7   Troubleshooting IIS (continued)

Problem	Solution
E-mail is not going through an SMTP server	Use the Computer Management tool to make sure that the Simple Mail Transfer Protocol service is started and set to start automatically.
Newsgroups are not supported on an NNTP server	Make sure there are virtual directories set up for newsgroups and that the permissions are appropriately set for users to access, such as permissions to browse and read.
Users cannot publish using FrontPage	1. Make sure that the FrontPage Server Extensions are installed and up to date. 2. Encourage users to upgrade to the most recent versions of FrontPage for best compatibility. 3. Check the authoring permissions.

Installing Windows Media Services

When multimedia applications are played in **streaming** mode, the audio and video begin playing as soon as received, without waiting for the entire file to be received at the client. A Windows 2003 Web Server can be set up to provide streaming media services by installing the Windows Media Services component. The Windows Media Services component is separate from the Internet Information Services component and can be installed after you install IIS. Windows Media Services enable you to serve voice and video multimedia applications from a Web server, such as an audio/video lesson demonstrating a hazardous chemistry experiment that is too dangerous for students to try in a lab on their own.

When you install Windows Media Services, also plan to install the Administrator for the Web for management. After Windows Media Services is installed, open the Windows Media Services tool by clicking Start, pointing to All Programs, pointing to Administrative Tools, and clicking Windows Media Services. Use the options in the right pane to get started and learn about streaming media, or click the server name in the tree and click the Getting Started tab.

Activity 8-12: Installing Windows Media Services

Time Required: Approximately 10 minutes

Objective: Learn how to install Windows Media Services.

Description: In this activity you install Windows Media Services, including components for Web-based activities.

1. Click **Start**, point to **Control Panel**, and click **Add or Remove Programs**.

2. Click **Add/Remove Windows Components**.

3. Double-click **Windows Media Services**. What subcomponents can you select to install?

4. Check all of the subcomponents. If you see warning boxes that IIS must first be installed, click **OK** in those boxes.

5. Click **OK** in the Windows Media Services dialog box.

6. Click **Next**. (If requested, insert the Windows Server 2003, Standard Edition, CD-ROM, and click **OK**. Exit out of the CD-ROM's auto run program, if it starts.)

7. Click **Finish**.

8. Close the Add or Remove Programs window.

CONFIGURING A TELNET SERVER

Another way for clients to access resources on a Windows 2003 server is to use Telnet. Telnet is particularly useful for non-Windows clients such as UNIX clients and others that support Telnet. **Telnet** is a member of the TCP/IP application suite that enables a client to act as a terminal to access a server. Telnet is a technology that is almost as old as TCP/IP and is a TCP/IP application used to set up one computer as a network host and other computers as clients. Instead of running Windows-based terminal services, the client runs TCP/IP-based Telnet and accesses the Windows 2003 server, which is set up as a Telnet server. The access is accomplished in a character-based mode and requires two elements:

- Telnet Server running on Windows Server 2003

- Microsoft Telnet Client or some other version of Telnet on the client computer

The server and client must be configured for TCP/IP prior to running either Telnet Server or the client software. When a user Telnets to a server, he or she must have a user account and supply the account name and password. Telnet can use NTLM authentication (NT LAN Manager) to protect access to the server, but you must first turn on NTLM from the client (by entering the NTLM command in Telnet, if the client supports NTLM). Once connected, the user can execute programs and processes on the server for which that user has permissions. Telnet Server supports up to 63 clients.

The Windows Server 2003 Telnet Server Service is started on one of two ways, through the Computer Management tool or through the Command Prompt window.

Activity 8-13: Starting Telnet Server Using the Computer Management Tool

Time Required: Approximately 5 minutes

Objective: Start the Telnet server via the Computer Management tool.

Description: In this activity you install and start the Telnet Server Service and configure it by using the Computer Management tool.

1. Click **Start**, right-click **My Computer**, and click **Manage**.

2. Click **Services** in the tree under Services and Applications.

3. Scroll the right pane to find **Telnet**, right-click the service, and click **Properties**.

4. In the Startup type box, select **Automatic**.

5. Click the **Apply** button.

6. Click the **Start** button as shown in Figure 8-16.

7. Click **OK**.

8. Close the **Computer Management** tool.

Activity 8-14: Starting Telnet Server from the Command Prompt Window

Time Required: Approximately 5 minutes

Objective: Start the Telnet server using the Command Prompt window.

Description: In this activity you start the Telnet Server Service using the alternative method, which is from the Command Prompt window.

1. Click **Start**, point to **All Programs**, point to **Accessories**, and click **Command Prompt**.

2. Because you started the Telnet server in Activity 8-13, you'll first need to stop it. At the prompt, type **net stop tlntsvr** and press **Enter**.

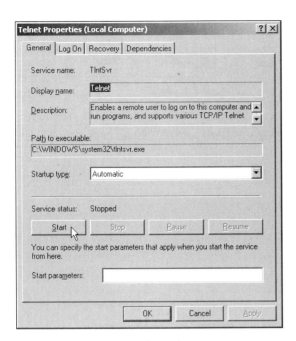

Figure 8-16   Starting the Telnet service

3. At the prompt, type **net start tlntsvr**, and press **Enter**. You should see a message that says:

```
The Telnet service is starting.
The Telnet service was started successfully.
```

4. Close the **Command Prompt** window.

The client computer must have Telnet installed, such as Windows Telnet Client. The Windows Telnet Client is started from the Command Prompt window. To find out about Telnet commands, enter *telnet /?* in the Command Prompt window, or to connect to a server, enter Telnet and the name of the host computer, such as *telnet Server1*. To disconnect from a server, enter *exit*. When a user starts Telnet and connects to the server, he or she views a command prompt window that is very similar to the same window on the client, but that window is actually on the server. On other systems, such as UNIX or Linux systems not operating from an X Window GUI desktop, Telnet may simply consist of command-line operations without a GUI-based command window.

Out of the box, Windows Server 2003 is licensed to use only two simultaneous Telnet connections. More licenses are available when you purchase the add-on pack for Microsoft Windows Services for UNIX.

There are several different versions of Telnet client software, such as SDI's TN3270 Plus, Ericom's PowerTerm, Distinct's IntelliTerm, and Windows Telnet Client. Make sure that users who telnet into a Telnet server have set a password on the client side, or else intruders can telnet into their computers.

CHAPTER SUMMARY

- DHCP is a work-saving protocol because it enables IP addresses to be leased dynamically. Use the Control Panel's Add or Remove Programs tool to install DHCP.

- Configuring DHCP involves configuring scopes that are ranges of IP addresses from which addresses are leased to clients.

- Plan to configure DHCP to dynamically update DNS.

❏ DNS is installed using the Control Panel's Add or Remove Programs tool.

❏ Part of configuring DNS involves configuring forward and reverse lookup zones.

❏ Configure Dynamic DNS to enable automated IP address registration in coordination with a DHCP server.

❏ Plan to set up two or more DNS servers on most networks and to integrate DNS with Active Directory for DNS replication and load balancing.

❏ If your network uses NetBIOS naming, install WINS.

❏ To implement a Web server, install Internet Information Services.

❏ Create IIS virtual directories to enable multiple users to publish on a Web site.

❏ Plan to configure each Web site to control client timeout, server bandwidth, number of connections, and authentication.

❏ By installing Window Media Services, you enable a Windows 2003 server, including one configured with IIS, to provide streaming multimedia.

❏ If you have users, such as UNIX computers, that need to connect using Telnet, configure Windows Server 2003 as a Telnet server.

KEY TERMS

DNS dynamic update protocol — A protocol that enables information in a DNS server to be automatically updated in coordination with DHCP.

Dynamic DNS (DDNS) — A form of DNS that enables client computers to update DNS registration information so that this does not have to be done manually. DDNS is often used with DHCP servers to automatically register IP addresses on a DNS server.

File Transfer Protocol (FTP) — Available through the TCP/IP protocol suite, FTP enables files to be transferred across a network or the Internet between computers or servers.

forward lookup zone — A DNS zone or table that maps computer names to IP addresses.

host address (A) resource record — A record in a DNS forward lookup zone that consists of a computer or domain name correlated to an IPv4 (or 32-bit) address.

Internet Information Services (IIS) — A Microsoft Windows Server 2003 component that provides Internet Web, FTP, mail, newsgroup, and other services, and that is particularly offered to set up a Web server.

Internet Server Application Programming Interface (ISAPI) — A group of dynamic-link library (DLL) files that consist of applications and filters to enable user customized programs to interface with IIS and to trigger particular programs, such as a specialized security check or a database lookup.

IPv6 host address (AAAA) resource record — A record in a DNS forward lookup zone that consists of a computer or domain name mapped to an IPv6 (or 128-bit) address.

Network News Transfer Protocol (NNTP) — Used over TCP/IP-based networks by NNTP servers to transfer news and informational messages organized and stored in newsgroups.

Open Database Connectivity (ODBC) — A set of database access rules used by Microsoft in its ODBC application programming interface for accessing databases and providing a standard doorway to database data.

pointer (PTR) resource record — A record in a DNS reverse lookup zone that consists of an IP (version 4 or 6) address correlated to a computer or domain name.

primary DNS server — A DNS server that is used as the main server from which zones are administered, as when updating records in a forward lookup zone for a domain. A primary DNS server is also called the authoritative server for that zone.

reverse lookup zone — A DNS server zone or table that maps IP addresses to computer or domain names.

scope — A range of IP addresses that a DHCP server can lease to clients.

secondary DNS server — A DNS server that is a backup to a primary DNS server and therefore is not authoritative.

Simple Mail Transfer Protocol (SMTP) —An e-mail protocol used by systems having TCP/IP network communications.

streaming — Playing a multimedia audio, video, or combined file received over a network before the entire file is received at the client.

Telnet — A TCP/IP-based application that provides terminal emulation services for access to a server, such as Windows Server 2003.

Uniform Resource Locator (URL) — An addressing format used to find an Internet Web site or page.

virtual directory — A URL formatted address that provides an Internet location (virtual location) for an actual physical folder on a Web server that is used to publish Web documents.

zone — A partition or subtree in a DNS server that contains specific kinds of records in a lookup table, such as a forward lookup zone that contains records in a table for looking up computer and domain names in order to find their associated IP addresses.

REVIEW QUESTIONS

1. Your company has set up a Web server to publish special promotions that have expiration dates. The marketing group is asking you if IIS has features to help with expiring promotional Web files after a certain number of days. How might this be possible?

   a. Configure the Operators default Web site properties to issue an alert to Web operators when files need to be deleted.

   b. Set up multiple Web publishing folders containing information that expires at the same time. Manually delete a folder on its expiration date.

   c. Create a Web-based spreadsheet showing when promotions expire and what files need to be deleted. Delete the files on the basis of checking the spreadsheet each morning.

   d. Configure the HTTP Headers default Web site properties to expire documents.

2. Your users are calling to complain that e-mail is not going through an IIS server. How might you troubleshoot this problem?

   a. Check the permissions on FTP folders for those users.

   b. Make sure the Simple Mail Transfer Protocol service is started.

   c. Make sure that the FTP Mail Publishing service is started.

   d. Make sure that the Telnet service is set up in IIS

3. You have set up a Web server and now your users are asking for a better way to publish their Web pages than to hand carry them to your office for you to install on the server. Which of the following can you set up to make you and the users more productive?

   a. Create one or more virtual directories.

   b. Install Web services on all of their client computers and make pointers from the Web server to the clients.

   c. Configure Dfs for Web-only publishing.

   d. There is no more efficient way for users to publish Web pages.

4. You are in a planning meeting to set up a new network that will have Internet access, one Windows 2003 Web server, and four Windows 2003 servers for general file and printing access. Many of the clients are still using Windows 98 and NetBIOS applications. The organization for which you are planning has decided to implement Active Directory. Which of the following should they include in their planning? (Choose all that apply.)

   a. Make at least two of the Windows 2003 servers domain controllers (DCs).

   b. Make at least two of the Windows 2003 servers DNS servers.

   c. Make at least one of the Windows 2003 servers a WINS server.

   d. Install IIS on the Web server.

5. You are planning to implement a Web server that will also handle Internet newsgroups. Which of the following services specifically enables you to support newsgroups?

   a. SMTP

   b. NNTP

   c. FTP

   d. PPTP

6. You have configured DHCP to automatically update DNS servers, but the problem is that old leases are sometimes not removed or updated in the DNS servers. This is causing some mismatched IP resolutions. What can you do to solve the problem?

   a. This problem is most common on large networks and you must disable automatic updating.

   b. This problem is caused by using TCP with IP on the network, and you must convert DNS servers to instead use UDP with IP.

   c. You need to configure DHCP to discard lookup records when their leases are denied.

   d. You need to set leases so that they don't expire for a longer period of time.

7. Which of the following can you manage from the Internet Information Services tool? (Choose all that apply.)

   a. Web service extensions

   b. DNS setup for Web services

   c. the Default Web site

   d. application pools

8. What is the advantage of choosing to integrate DNS with Active Directory?

   a. It is not necessary to have a DHCP server on the network.

   b. You can manage DNS entries through an OU under a domain.

   c. DNS registration is handled through Active Directory.

   d. DNS is replicated through Active Directory replication capabilities.

   e. all of the above

   f. only a and b

9. In Microsoft DHCP _____. (Choose all that apply.)

   a. you can exclude one or more addresses out of a range of leased addresses

   b. you use only UNIX commands to configure it, because DHCP was originally a UNIX application

   c. leases for Windows 2003 servers should always be set at 15 days

   d. security for a DHCP server is the same as the security for the user account used to manage it

10. Which of the following are supported by Microsoft Internet Information Services? (Choose all that apply.)

   a. File Transfer Protocol

   b. Open Database Connectivity

   c. HTML

   d. NTFS

11. When you create a DNS server, what type of record would you most likely find in a reverse lookup zone?

   a. pointer resource record

   b. IPv6 host address (AAAA) resource record

   c. host address (A) resource record

   d. reverse host (R) resource record

12. What tool do you use to install IIS?

   a. Computer Management tool

   b. Administrative Tools IIS Install option

   c. Control Panel's Add or Remove Programs option

   d. IIS can only be installed when Windows Server 2003 is initially installed.

13. You have determined that your Web site handles about 2,000 connections at a given time. This is a lot of traffic, and the Web site seems sluggish. Which of the following should you try first?

   a. Install more RAM.

   b. Set the foreground applications to get most of the CPU time.

   c. Tune the Web server performance parameter to lower the connections to 1,500 or 1,000.

   d. Decrease the page file size to reduce the amount of disk writing.

14. Which of the following are permissions that can be set on a virtual directory via the Internet Information Services tool? (Choose all that apply.)

   a. Execute

   b. Write

   c. Modify

   d. List folders

15. You have set up a Web server and now the management in your company wants to use it for multimedia training presentations. What should you install on the Web server?

   a. Just In Time Web Services

   b. Windows Media Services

   c. Windows Media Browser

   d. IIS Performance Enhancer

16. One of your network's DNS servers does not seem to be providing DNS lookup services, even though the server is running and there is no apparent problem. What should you try? (Choose all that apply.)

   a. Reinstall the TCP/IP Resolver.

   b. Make sure the DNS Client service is started.

   c. Stop the Remote Procedure Call service, because it works in conflict with DNS.

   d. Make sure the DNS Server Service is started.

17. You are setting up a DHCP scope in which all of the clients are portable computers. For how long should you establish leases?

    a. one to two months

    b. seven days

    c. three to four days

    d. eight to 24 hours

18. If you want to use dynamic IP address updating, which of the following should you do?

    a. Configure dynamic updating on the DHCP server.

    b. Configure dynamic updating on the DNS server.

    c. Make sure that neither of the DHCP or DNS servers are also domain controllers.

    d. all of the above

    e. only a and b

    f. only b and c

19. Which of the following is an authoritative DNS server?

    a. primary DNS server

    b. secondary DNS server

    c. stationary DNS server

    d. remote DNS server

20. Your boss has worked on computer systems that support using a hashing algorithm for security and prefers this method. Can IIS Web security be configured for this security method?

    a. Yes, by configuring to use integrated Windows authentication.

    b. Yes, by configuring to use basic authentication.

    c. Yes, by configuring to use digest authentication.

    d. A Web server does not support hashing for authentication.

21. When you are planning the installation of a DNS server, which of the following is important to include in your planning?

    a. The DNS server should have a static IP address and not one leased by DHCP.

    b. The DNS server must have an IP address that ends in "1," such as 129.70.88.1, because it must be the first server seen on the network.

    c. The DNS server must also be the Schema Master for the forest.

    d. all of the above

    e. only a and b

    f. only a and c

22. Users are not able to access your Web server, and when you try accessing it from your office you cannot either. Which of the following might you do?

    a. Use the Internet Information Server management tool to restart IIS.

    b. Make sure that the Server Service is started and running.

    c. Take the WINS server off line because WINS can interfere with network access to IIS.

    d. all of the above

    e. only a and b

    f. only a and c

23. How can you configure a server as a Telnet server?

    a. Use the net start tlntsvr command in the Command Prompt window.

    b. Configure it from the All Programs Accessories menu by selecting the System Tools option.

    c. Configure it from the Telnet option in the Administrative Tools menu.

    d. Use the Start menu's Run option, and type telconfig.

24. The research group in your organization is setting up a Web server for a VPN that must have very restricted access. In a committee meeting, they are asking you to list methods that can be used to restrict access. Which of the following are possible?

    a. Restrict access by using VPN encryption.

    b. Restrict access through IP addressing.

    c. Restrict access through the Active Directory Users and Computers tool.

    d. You cannot restrict access, because Web servers are meant to be available to all users.

25. How many scopes can be configured in Microsoft DHCP, per Microsoft's recommendation?

    a. 1

    b. 10

    c. 100

    d. 1,000

    e. none of the above, because the number of scopes is unlimited

CASE PROJECTS

Case Project Background

Brighton Community College is a new college and is in the process of designing and implementing a new network that primarily consists of Windows 2003 servers. They have purchased 22 server computers that will run Windows Server 2003, Standard Edition. The campus network will have Internet access and offer a Web server on the Internet. They also plan to set up DNS and DHCP servers for the network. To help the newly formed IT Department, the college has hired Bayside IT Services to help plan and implement the new network.

Case Project 8-1: Planning the Web, DNS, and DHCP Servers

Develop a document explaining to the IT Department how to plan the implementation of the Web, DNS, and DHCP servers. In that document address the following issues, as well as others that you think are important:

❑ In what order should the Web, DNS, and DHCP services be implemented for network use? Should all of these services be implemented on one server or on different servers?

❑ What setup elements should be planned in advance, such as DHCP scopes, DNS lookup zones, and Web services? What factors should go into their planning?

❑ What security issues should be addressed in the setup of these services?

Case Project 8-2: Web Server Deployment

The IT Department needs training in how to deploy a Web server. Create a general training document that explains the following:

❑ How to install a Web server

❑ How to set up a virtual directory

❑ How to configure the Web server

Case Project 8-3: DNS Server Setup Issues

The IT Department has set up a DNS server, but the server has no reverse lookup zone. The IT Department has sent you an e-mail message asking you to prepare for them a short document that answers the following questions about DNS setup:

❑ What is the purpose of a reverse lookup zone and how can it be set up?

❑ Can more than one DNS server be configured when Active Directory is deployed and, if so, what is the advantage?

❑ Can DHCP be configured to automatically update DNS records, and if so, how?

Case Project 8-4: Solving a DHCP Server Problem

The IT Department has installed DHCP and configured it, but for some reason it is not communicating on the network. What troubleshooting steps should they try in order to solve the problem?

CHAPTER 9

CONFIGURING REMOTE ACCESS SERVICES

After reading this chapter and completing the exercises, you will be able to:

♦ Understand Remote Access Services in Windows Server 2003

♦ Configure Remote Access Services

♦ Implement a virtual private network

♦ Troubleshoot Remote Access Services and virtual private network installations

♦ Connect remote users through Terminal Services

Millions of computer users telecommute from home or while traveling. People who telecommute represent one of the fastest growing populations of network users. Also, there are times when is it important for business partners, vendors, and financial auditors to be able to remotely access their network's resources. To meet these needs, Windows Server 2003 comes equipped with a variety of services, such as Remote Access Services and virtual private network services. Another form of access that is popular in some organizations is the ability to run applications directly on a Windows 2003 server through Terminal Services, which can save money on client computers and increase security.

In this chapter you'll learn how to install, configure, and troubleshoot Windows 2003 Remote Access and virtual private network server services. You will learn to set up security to protect the network that is accessed remotely and to protect its clients. Further, you'll learn how to install and configure Terminal Services for users who need to run programs on a server.

INTRODUCTION TO REMOTE ACCESS

There are several ways to remotely access a server on a network. If you use public telephone lines to dial in to your local Internet service provider (ISP), you have already experienced one method of remote access. That method requires that you have a computer with a **modem**, a computer operating system, and software to use the Internet, such as an e-mail program or Web browser. The servers you access may be Windows Server 2003, UNIX, or other servers that offer a special interface such as Microsoft Internet Information Services (IIS). The files and information that you access are strictly controlled by the capabilities of the interface on the server and the Internet site manager or Webmaster.

Before widespread use of the Internet, many people accessed their organization's network by dialing into a network workstation running remote access software such as PCAnywhere. That workstation was left running most of the time so that a single user could dial in to it from a remote computer, such as one at home (see Figure 9-1). The user dialing in took control of the network computer and gained access to the resources available through the network. When this method was first used, access was frustrating because modems were slow, and someone might inadvertently turn off the computer connected to the network, which is still a problem.

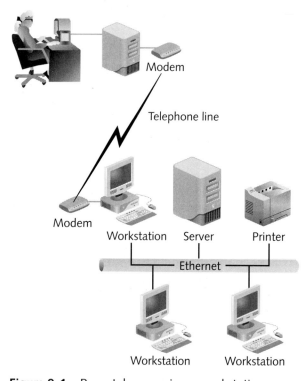

Figure 9-1 Remotely accessing a workstation on a network

Microsoft dramatically improved remote access in Windows NT Server—and now even more in Windows Server 2003—by enabling a server to double as a remote access server. A computer running Windows Server 2003 can have **Routing and Remote Access Services (RRAS)** installed to turn it into a Remote Access Services (RAS) server capable of handling hundreds of simultaneous connections (see Figure 9-2). Performing a variety of roles, the Windows 2003 server performs its normal functions as a server, but serves remote access needs at the same time. A user dials in to the RAS server, providing her or his user credentials. Another way for a client to access the RAS server is through the Internet or an intranet, using specialized tunneling protocols (discussed later in this chapter).

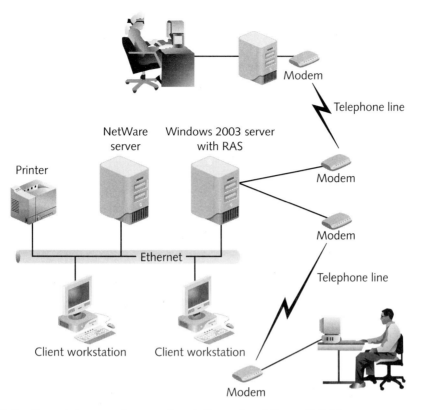

Figure 9-2 Remotely accessing a network through a Microsoft RAS server

Using Microsoft Remote Access Services

A Windows 2003 server configured as a RAS server offers secure, flexible, and remote access to a private network. A computer running Windows Server 2003 with one or more modems can be configured as a RAS server using the Routing and Remote Access tool. Windows Server 2003 enables up to 256 dial-up remote callers and a nearly unlimited number (depending on the hardware) of Internet-based clients to connect at the same time. A RAS server offers remote connectivity to the following client operating systems:

- MS-DOS
- Windows 3.1 and 3.11 (Windows for Workgroups)
- Windows NT (all platforms)
- Windows 95
- Windows 98
- Windows Millennium Edition
- Windows 2000 (all platforms)
- Windows Server 2003 and XP Professional

Not only is it designed to work with many kinds of clients, but a RAS server also supports the following types of connections:

- Asynchronous modems (such as the modem you may already use in your PC)
- Synchronous modems through an access or communications server
- Null modem communications
- Regular dial-up telephone lines

- Leased telecommunication lines, such as a T-carrier
- ISDN lines (and digital "modems")
- X.25 lines
- DSL lines
- Cable modem lines
- Frame Relay lines

Besides supporting different types of modems and communications equipment, Windows Server 2003 RAS is compatible with the following network transport and remote access protocols:

- TCP/IP
- IPX (or Microsoft NWLink IPX/SPX/NetBIOS Compatible Transport Protocol)
- NetBEUI
- Serial Line Internet Protocol (SLIP) and Compressed Serial Line Internet Protocol (CSLIP)
- Point-to-Point Protocol (PPP)
- Point-to-Point Tunneling Protocol (PPTP)
- Layer Two Tunneling Protocol (L2TP)

Implementing Remote Access Protocols

Remote access protocols are used to carry network packets over a WAN link. One of their functions is to encapsulate a packet formatted for a network transport protocol so that it can be transmitted from a point at one end of a WAN to another point—such as between two computers with internal modems connected by a telecommunications line. TCP/IP is the most commonly used transport protocol, and so it is most typically encapsulated in a remote access protocol for transport over a WAN. Two other transport protocols that are sometimes encapsulated in a remote access protocol are IPX (or Microsoft IPX/SPX/NetBIOS Compatible Transport Protocol) and NetBEUI.

There are two remote access protocols, both supported by Microsoft Windows Server 2003, that are used most frequently in remote communications: SLIP and PPP. **Serial Line Internet Protocol (SLIP)** was originally designed for UNIX environments for point-to-point communications among computers, servers, and hosts using TCP/IP. SLIP is an older remote communications protocol with relatively high overhead (larger packet header and more network traffic). **Compressed Serial Line Internet Protocol (CSLIP)** is a newer version of SLIP that compresses header information in each packet sent across a remote link. CSLIP, now usually referred to as SLIP, reduces the overhead of a connection so that it is less than that of PPP by decreasing the header size and thus increasing the speed of communications. However, the header still must be decompressed at the receiving end. The original SLIP and the newer SLIP (CSLIP) are limited in that they do not support network connection authentication to prevent someone from intercepting a communication. They also do not support automatic negotiation of the network connection through multiple network connection layers at the same time. Another disadvantage of both versions of SLIP is that they are intended only for asynchronous communications, such as through a modem-to-modem type of connection.

 At this writing, Microsoft NWLink IPX/SPX/NetBIOS Compatible Transport Protocol is not supported in the 64-bit versions of Windows Server 2003.

Point-to-Point Protocol (PPP) is used more commonly than either version of SLIP for remote communications because it has lower overhead and more capability. PPP supports more network protocols, such as IPX/SPX, NetBEUI, and TCP/IP (although not in all operating systems). It can automatically negotiate communications with several network communications layers at once, and it supports connection authentication. PPP is supplemented by the newer **Point-to-Point Tunneling Protocol (PPTP)**, which enables remote communications to RAS and a **virtual private network (VPN)** through the Internet. Using PPTP, a company manager can access a report housed on that company's in-house intranet by dialing in to the Internet from a remote location. A VPN is a private network that is like a tunnel through a larger network—such as the Internet, an enterprise network, or both—that is restricted to designated member clients only (you'll learn more about VPNs later in this chapter). Microsoft VPN networks also use **Layer Two Tunneling Protocol (L2TP)**, which works similarly to PPTP. Both protocols encapsulate PPP and create special tunnels over a public network, such as the Internet, for VPN and intranet communications. Unlike PPTP, L2TP uses an additional network communications standard, called Layer Two Forwarding, that enables forwarding on the basis of MAC addressing in addition to IP addressing. PPP, PPTP, and L2TP all support the security measures described later in this chapter.

PPP and PPTP both support synchronous and asynchronous communications, enabling connectivity through synchronous and asynchronous modems, cable modems, dial-up and high-speed leased telecommunication lines, T-carrier lines, DSL, ISDN, Frame Relay, and X.25 lines. **T-carrier** lines are dedicated leased telephone lines that can be used for data communications over multiple channels for speeds of up to 44.736 Mbps. **Digital subscriber line (DSL)** is a technology that uses advanced modulation techniques on regular telephone lines for high-speed networking at speeds of up to 60 Mbps between subscribers and a telecommunications company. **Integrated Services Digital Network (ISDN)** is a telecommunications standard for delivering data services over digital telephone lines with a current practical limit of 1.536 Mbps and a theoretical limit of 622 Mbps. **Frame Relay** is a WAN communications technology that relies on packet switching and virtual connection techniques to transmit at speeds from 56 Kbps to 45 Mbps. **X.25** is an older packet-switching protocol for connecting remote networks at speeds up to 2.048 Mbps.

On the client side, PPP is available in Windows 95, Windows 98, all versions of Windows NT, all versions of Windows 2000, all versions of Windows XP, and all versions of Windows Server 2003. PPP configuration is well suited on networks in which users perform remote access through computers running Windows 95/98/NT/2000/XP/2003.

 Windows NT Server 4.0 supports either SLIP or PPP when configured as a RAS server. If you convert Windows NT Server 4.0, set up with RAS and using SLIP, to Windows Server 2003, plan to convert the RAS implementation and all RAS clients to use PPP for more versatility and better security.

CONFIGURING REMOTE ACCESS SERVICES

There are several essential steps to configuring RAS communications on a Windows Server 2003 network:

1. Configure a Microsoft Windows server as a network's RAS server, including configuring the right protocols to provide RAS access through dial-up connectivity.

2. Configure a DHCP relay agent for TCP/IP communications.

3. Configure Multilink and Bandwidth Allocation Protocol.

4. Configure RAS security.

5. Configure a dial-up and remote connection.

6. Configure RAS on client workstations.

Configuring a Remote Access Server

There are two components to making a Windows 2003 server double as a RAS server. You already have learned the first component, which is to implement a way to connect multiple modems to a network. On a very small network you may need to install only one or two modems directly into an existing networked computer running Windows Server 2003. For a larger network, you can install an **access server**, which is a single network device that can house multiple modems, ISDN connections, T-carrier line connections, and other types of connections.

Choose an access server that is designed to be compatible with Windows Server 2003. A compatible access server includes software and drivers that can be used to coordinate communications between the Windows 2003 server and the access server, including IP routing capabilities.

The second component is to install the software needed to turn the Windows 2003 server into a RAS server. (As for most other administrative functions, you must be logged on as Administrator or with Administrator privileges.) You install RAS using the Routing and Remote Access tool, which is opened from the Administrative Tools menu or as an MMC snap-in.

Activity 9-1: Installing a RAS Server

Time Required: Approximately 15 minutes

Objective: Learn how to install RAS.

Description: In this activity, you turn a Windows 2003 server into a RAS server for access by remote users.

1. Click **Start**, point to **Administrative Tools**, and click **Routing and Remote Access**. What access services are provided by Routing and Remote Access, as listed in the right pane?

2. Make sure your server is listed under Routing and Remote Access. If the server you want to configure is not listed, click **Routing and Remote Access**, click the **Action** menu, click **Add Server**, select the option button for **This computer** (or select a different server by using The following computer option and providing the name of the server), and click **OK**.

3. In the left pane, right-click the server, and click **Configure and Enable Routing and Remote Access**.

4. Click **Next** after the Routing and Remote Access Server Setup Wizard starts.

5. There are five options from which to select. Table 9-1 summarizes the available options. Click **Remote access (dial-up or VPN)** to make this a RAS server (see Figure 9-3), if it is not already selected, and then click **Next**.

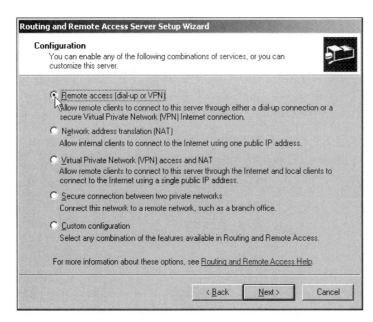

Figure 9-3   Selecting to install RAS

Table 9-1   Routing and Remote Access options

Option	Description
Remote access 2003 (dial-up or VPN)	Use this option to set up remote access services to the network through a Windows 2003 server, using either dial-up modems or a VPN network connection
Network address translation (NAT)	Enables Internet access by employing **network address translation (NAT)**. Sometime used by firewalls, NAT translates IP addresses on an internal network so that the actual IP addresses cannot be determined on the Internet, because each address seen on the Internet is a decoy address used from a pool of decoy addresses. The advantages of using NAT include (1) addresses on the internal network do not have to be registered on the Internet because they are only seen on the local internal network, and (2) users on the internal network gain some measure of protection from Internet intruders.
Virtual Private Network (VPN) access and NAT	Use this option when you want to configure the server so that users can access it using a VPN with NAT address translation
Secure connection between two private networks	Use this option for secure communications between two servers over the Internet, such as one server at a branch location in St. Louis and another at the headquarters in Chicago (both servers must be configured with this option)
Custom configuration	Use this option when you want to customize the routing and remote access capabilities

6. Click the box for **Dial-up**. What other option is on this screen? Click **Next**. (If you have more than one network connection defined, you'll see the Network Selection dialog box in which to select the appropriate network and then click Next.)

7. For this activity, assume there is a DHCP server on the network, and click **Automatically** as the method for assigning IP addresses to remote clients. When you select this option, a DHCP server assigns addresses; or if there is no DHCP server, the RAS server uses Automatic Private IP Addressing (APIPA), as described in Chapter 1, to assign addresses to remote clients. The other option, From a specified range of addresses, enables you to manually (statically) create a range of addresses to assign to remote clients. If you were to choose this option, the next screen you would see after clicking Next is the Address Range Assignment screen.

8. Click **Next**.

9. In the Managing Multiple Remote Access Servers dialog box, you have the option to have this server work with a **Remote Authentication Dial-in User Service (RADIUS)** server. In order to use a RADIUS server, one must already be set up. A RADIUS server might be used if you plan to set up two or more RAS servers and want to standardize access policies and authentication, or if you want to use a RADIUS server's access accounting features. For this activity, click **No, use Routing and Remote Access to authenticate connection requests**, if necessary. (If you were to click Yes, set up this server to work with a RADIUS server, then the next dialog box would request the names of the primary and alternate RADIUS servers and a shared secret (a password) to use for communications with those servers).

10. Click **Next**.

11. Click **Finish**. (Click **OK**, if you see a message box that says you must next configure the DHCP relay agent properties.) You now see the Routing and Remote Access window with features set up for RAS, including Ports, Remote Access Clients, IP Routing, Remote Access Policies, and Remote Access Logging, as shown in Figure 9-4. Leave the window open for the next activity.

In Step 7, if you chose to automatically assign IP addresses and are using a DHCP server, configure the **DHCP relay agent** so that it contains the IP address of the DHCP server. A DHCP relay agent passes IP configuration information between the DHCP server and the client acquiring an address when they are on different networks.

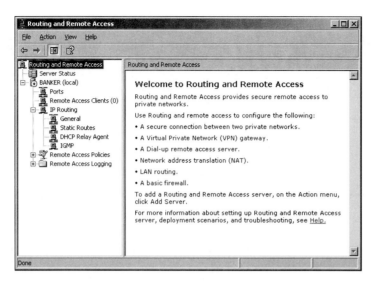

Figure 9-4 Routing and Remote Access window for a RAS setup

After the RAS server is set up, you can further configure it from the Routing and Remote Access tool by right-clicking the RAS server in the tree, and clicking Properties (see Figure 9-5). Table 9-2 summarizes the different property tabs available when only TCP/IP is installed. If your server is configured to use additional protocols, such as NWLink, then you see tabs for those protocols (an IPX tab is used for NWLink).

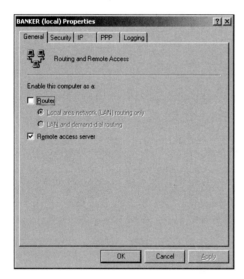

Figure 9-5 RAS server properties

The General tab in Figure 9-5 enables you to configure the server as a router. Some network and server administrators prefer to avoid using a server as a router, because handling routing can create an extra burden on the server, slowing other services. Also, generally it is better to purchase a dedicated router that is connected between the RAS server and the Internet, WAN, or telecommunications connection. A dedicated router has an operating system designed for routing, including a full range of routing features and sophisticated firewall protection. However, if there is no router between your server and the Internet or WAN (or if you are configuring a VPN server) consider using the routing option in Figure 9-5. You would do this if your server directly connects to the Internet or WAN using an ISDN terminal adapter or a DSL adapter, for instance, and has a regular NIC to connect to the local network. A **terminal adapter (TA)**, popularly called a digital modem, links a computer or a fax to an ISDN line; a **DSL adapter** is a digital communications device that links a computer (or sometimes a router) to a DSL telecommunications line.

Table 9-2   RAS server property tabs

Property Tab	Description
General	Allows you to enable the server as a router and/or a remote access server
Security	Allows you to configure an authentication provider and accounting provider (such as a RADIUS server); selecting the Authentication Methods button allows you to enable authentication protocols on the RAS server or enable unauthenticated access
IP	Allows you to enable IP routing and whether IP-based connections are permitted; from this tab you can also change how IP addresses are assigned to clients using either a DHCP server or a static address pool
PPP	Allows you to enable PPP options such as **Multilink** or **Multilink PPP (MPPP)** connections; Multilink enables you to aggregate multiple incoming lines, such as ISDN lines into one logical connection (if Multilink is used, the lines must be aggregated at the server and at the remote connection or device)
Logging	Allows you to enable PPP logging and specify what type of events to log

Configuring a DHCP Relay Agent

When a RAS server is configured so that the IP addresses of RAS clients are obtained automatically via a DHCP server, the RAS server must be designated as a DHCP relay agent. A DHCP relay agent sends IP configuration information between the DHCP server on a network and the client acquiring an address.

Activity 9-2: Configuring a DHCP Relay Agent

Time Required: Approximately 5 minutes

Objective: Configure a DHCP relay agent.

Description: In this activity, you configure a DHCP relay agent for the RAS server you configured in Activity 9-1. If you do not know the IP address of the DHCP server on your network, ask your instructor for the address.

1. Open the **Routing and Remote Access** tool, if it is not still open.

2. Double-click the **RAS server** in the tree, if the objects under it are not already displayed.

3. Click **IP Routing** in the tree.

4. In the right pane, right-click **DHCP Relay Agent**, and click **Properties** (see Figure 9-6).

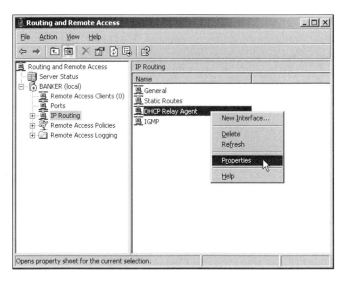

Figure 9-6   Configuring a DHCP Relay Agent

5. If the IP address of the DHCP server is not already entered in the list box, type the IP address of the DHCP server, and click **Add** (see Figure 9-7).

6. Click **OK**.

7. Leave the Routing and Remote Access tool open for the next activity.

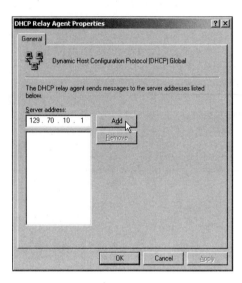

Figure 9-7   Entering the IP address of the DHCP server

You can further configure the DHCP relay agent by specifying the maximum number of routers, called the hop count, that an IP configuration broadcast can pass through between the client, RAS server, and DHCP server (see Step 5 in Activity 9-30). You do this by configuring the interface on the RAS server, such as the internal NIC.

Activity 9-3: Additional DHCP Relay Agent Configuration

Time Required: Approximately 5 minutes

Objective: Configure the DHCP relay agent hop count.

Description: In this activity, you configure hop count routing information for the DHCP relay agent.

1. Make sure the **Routing and Remote Access** tool is open and that you see DHCP relay agent in the tree under the RAS server and IP Routing.

2. Click **DHCP Relay Agent** in the tree.

3. In the right pane, right-click the interface, such as **Internal**.

4. Click **Properties**.

5. Be certain that the Relay DHCP packets box is checked. What is the default value in the Hop-count threshold box?

6. In the Hop-count threshold text box, enter **1** for this activity. Note that the maximum number you can enter is 16.

7. Set the Boot threshold (seconds) value at **4** (the default). This parameter is used to give the DHCP server on the local network time to respond (in this case, four seconds), before a DHCP server on a remote network is contacted.

8. Click **OK**, as shown in Figure 9-8.

9. Leave the Routing and Remote Access tool open for another activity.

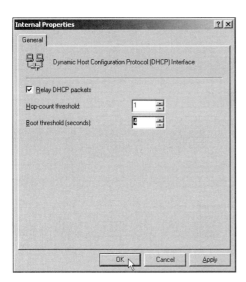

Figure 9-8   Configuring the interface properties

Configuring Multilink and Bandwidth Allocation Protocol

A RAS server can be configured to support Multilink (also called Multilink PPP). If your RAS server has more than one connection that can be used for remote access, Multilink can be enabled to combine or aggregate two or more communications channels so they appear as one large channel. For example, Multilink can combine two 64-Kbps ISDN channels and one 16-Kbps signaling channel in the ISDN basic rate interface service to appear as one 144-Kbps channel; or, multiple 64-Kbps primary rate interface channels and one 64-Kbps signaling channel can be aggregated into a total speed of 1.536 Mbps. Another example is combining two 56-Kbps modems into an aggregate speed of 112 Kbps. The limitation of using Multilink is that it must be implemented in the client as well as in the server, so that the client can take full advantage of the **aggregated links**. For instance, if you use Multilink to aggregate two 56-Kbps modems for one 112-Kbps link at the server, the client, such as Windows XP Professional, must have a communications link set up using Multilink to aggregate the two links.

On its own, Multilink cannot change the bandwidth, or drop or add a connection as needed. This is why it is often used with **Bandwidth Allocation Protocol (BAP)** to ensure that a client's connection has enough speed or bandwidth for a particular application. BAP helps ensure that the amount of bandwidth increases to the maximum for the aggregated channels as needed, and reciprocally contracts as the need becomes less. Links are dynamically dropped or added as needed. For example, consider a connection in which the remote client begins by accessing a relatively low-bandwidth application such as e-mail over an aggregated link of two 56-Kbps modems. BAP might determine that only 56 Kbps is needed for the application. However, when the client accesses a voice and video presentation in a multimedia application, such as a physics lesson or a movie clip, BAP can increase the bandwidth to the full aggregated speed of 112 Kbps by adding the line from the second modem for the duration of the multimedia presentation. BAP matches bandwidth utilization to the need, so that unused bandwidth can be given to another client whenever possible. Besides adding a line for use by a client, BAP can hang up a line so that another client can use it. The Windows Server 2003 version of Multilink PPP also supports **Bandwidth Allocation Control Protocol (BACP)**, which is similar to BAP, but it selects a preferred client when two or more clients vie for the same bandwidth.

To configure Multilink and BAP, right-click the RAS server in the Routing and Remote Access tool, click Properties, and then click the PPP tab (see Figure 9-9). After you enable Multilink, the option to use Link control protocol (LCP) extensions should be selected when you want to use callback security (discussed later in this chapter). Also, select the Software compression option to compress data over a remote link for faster transport. This option enables the use of the Microsoft Point-to-Point Compression Protocol.

Activity 9-4: Using Multilink

Time Required: Approximately 5 minutes

Objective: Configure a RAS server to use Multilink.

Description: This activity enables you to configure your RAS server to use Multilink. (You do not need two modems or multiple ISDN terminal adapters to practice the Multilink configuration.)

1. Open the **Routing and Remote Access** tool, if it is not already open.

2. Right-click the RAS server in the tree in the left pane.

3. Click **Properties**.

4. Click the **PPP** tab.

5. Click all of the following, if they are not selected: **Multilink connections**, **Dynamic bandwidth control using BAP or BACP**, **Link control protocol (LCP) extensions**, and **Software compression** (see Figure 9-9).

6. Click **OK**.

7. Leave the Routing and Remote Access window open to perform more configuration activities.

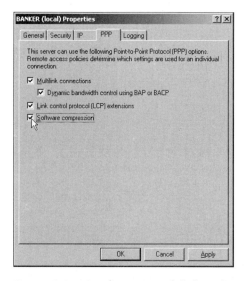

Figure 9-9 Configuring Multilink and BAP

Configuring RAS Security

When a user accesses a RAS server through his or her account, that access is protected by the account access security that already applies, as performed through a Group Policy or the default domain security policy. For instance, if account lockout is set up in a Group Policy, the same account lockout settings apply when a RAS user enters her or his account name and password (see Chapter 10 for more about security policies). Besides the security policies already in place, you can set up RAS security through several other techniques, which include the following:

- Configuring a remote access policy

- Configuring dial-up security

- Configuring clients and client protocols

Remote Access Policy

Prior to Windows 2000 Server and Windows Server 2003, remote access was controlled through the properties of user accounts by enabling the Grant Dial-in permission option. One of the main problems with this is that each user account needed to be manually configured and if there were a large number of user accounts, administrative overhead was drastically increased. This method also did not offer much flexibility in controlling remote access. Windows Server 2003 uses a remote access policy plus the dial-in properties of user accounts to grant users the ability to dial in to RAS server. The use of a remote access policy greatly reduces administrative overhead and offers more flexibility and control for authorizing connection attempts.

Granting remote access permission can still be configured strictly by configuring the properties of a user account using the Active Directory Users and Computers tool, as you learn later. The best practice, though, is to configure a remote access policy and then the remote access properties (through a profile) for accounts.

Elements of a Remote Access Policy   A remote access policy consists of several elements that must be evaluated before a user is granted remote access, which are:

- Conditions
- Permissions
- Profile

The conditions of a remote access policy are a set of attributes that are compared to the attributes of the connection attempt. Conditions can include attributes such as day and time restrictions and the group to which the connecting user must belong. Each connection attempt is evaluated against the conditions of the remote access policy. The connection attempt must match all of the conditions of the policy or it is rejected. If there are multiple policies configured, the conditions of each policy are evaluated until a match is found.

One way to manage users' access to RAS and VPN servers (you learn about VPN servers later in this chapter) is to set up only specific user accounts to grant dial-in access or to control access through the remote access policies. If you control access through the remote access policies, consider fine-tuning the management of user account access by creating groups. For example, create a universal or domain local group that has access to one or more RAS or VPN servers, and create a global group of the user accounts that you want to have the access. Make the global group a member of the universal or domain local group.

If the connection attempt matches the conditions of a remote access policy, the permissions are then evaluated. The permissions of a remote access policy are a combination of those configured under the user account and the remote access policy. If the user has been denied access under the properties of their user account, the connection attempt is rejected. If the user has been granted access, the policy evaluation continues. If the dial-in permission for the user's account is set to Control access through Remote Access Policy, the permissions of the policy are evaluated and the connection attempt is either accepted or rejected.

Once Routing and Remote Access is enabled, a default policy is created. The default permission for this policy is set to Deny remote access permission. Make sure you change the default permission to Grant remote access permission.

If the user has been allowed access, the connection attempt is then evaluated against the profile setting of the remote access policy. The profile consists of settings such as day and time restrictions, Multilink properties, authentication methods, and encryption settings. In order for the user to be granted remote access, the connection attempt must match all of the settings configured in the profile.

The following steps outline what occurs when a user attempts to connect to a RAS server via a remote access policy:

1. When a user attempts to connect to a RAS server, the remote access policy is evaluated. If there is no policy, the connection attempt is rejected. The connection attempt must match the conditions of the policy or the connection attempt is rejected. If there are multiple policies they are evaluated in the order that they appear under the Remote Access Policies container in the Routing and Remote Access tool.

2. If the conditions of one of the policies match the connection attempt, the permissions are then evaluated.

3. If the user has been denied access, the connection attempt is rejected. If the user has been granted dial-in access, the settings configured for the user account and those in the profile are evaluated. If the settings match those of the connection attempt, remote access is granted. If the connection attempt does not match the settings, the connection is rejected.

4. If remote access permission is configured to be controlled through a remote access policy, the permissions of the policy are evaluated and the user is either granted or denied access. If the policy is set to Grant remote access permission, the dial-in settings configured for the user account and the settings of the profile are evaluated. Remote access is granted if the connection attempt matches the settings.

Creating and Configuring a Remote Access Policy and Profile   Once Routing and Remote Access is enabled, plan to create a remote access policy and profile. You can use the Routing and Remote Access tool (accessed via Administrative Tools or as an MMC snap-in) to create and configure remote access policies. To create a new remote access policy, right-click the Remote Access Policies container in the tree under the RAS server, and click the New Remote Access Policy option to start the New Remote Access Policy wizard.

Activity 9-5: Configuring a Remote Access Policy and Profile

Time Required: Approximately 15 to 20 minutes

Objective: Configure a remote access policy.

Description: In this activity, you configure a remote access policy for the RAS server you have installed.

1. Open the **Routing and Remote Access** tool, if it is not already open. Next, in the Routing and Remote Access window, make sure that you can view the elements under the RAS server, particularly Remote Access Policies (double-click the server, if necessary).

2. Right-click **Remote Access Policies**, and click **New Remote Access Policy** as shown in Figure 9-10.

3. Click **Next** after the New Remote Access Policy Wizard starts.

4. Enter a name for the Remote Access Policy, such as **Domain-wide RAS Policy**. Also, select the option to **Set up a custom policy**. Click **Next**.

5. Click the **Add** button to customize your selections for the Policy conditions text box. Scroll through the options in the Attribute types list box. What are the first and last options listed?

6. Click **Authentication-Type**, and click the **Add** button.

7. For this activity, select **MS-CHAP v1** (or **MS-CHAP v1 CPW**), which is compatible with most versions of Windows operating systems. Click **Add**. How can you add MS-CHAP v2 (or MS-CHAP v2 CPW) and EAP as other authentication types? Add both MS-CHAP v2 (or MS-CHAP v2 CPW) and EAP. Table 9-3 summarizes the main types of authentication for a RAS or VPN server.

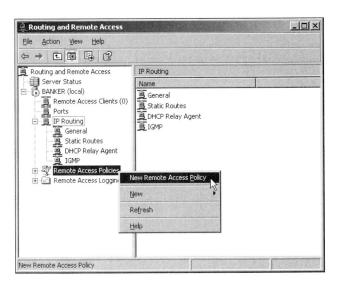

Figure 9-10   Configuring a new remote access policy

8. Click **OK**.

9. In the Policy Conditions dialog box, click the **Add** button.

10. Double-click **Day-And-Time-Restrictions**.

11. Notice that all of the times are blocked out as Denied. Click and drag your pointing device to block 6 to 10 p.m. on Monday through Thursday. Click the option button for **Permitted**, as shown in Figure 9-11. Click **OK**.

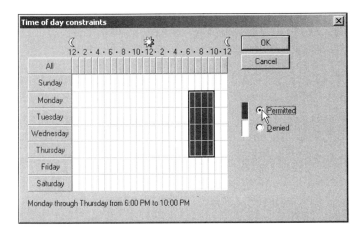

Figure 9-11   Restricting the times and days of the week

12. Click the **Add** button in the Policy Conditions box.

13. Double-click **Framed-Protocol**. Use the scroll bar to view the remote access protocols from which to choose in the Available types list box. How many protocols are available?

14. Click **PPP**, and click the **Add** button. What protocol would you use to enable older UNIX computers to connect through RAS? What protocol would you use for Macintosh computers that are configured for AppleTalk?

15. Click **OK**. The Policy Conditions dialog box should now look similar to Figure 9-12.

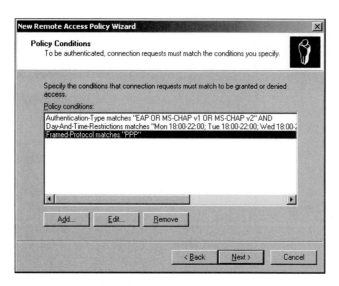

Figure 9-12   The selected policy conditions

16. Click **Next**.

17. Click the option button for **Grant remote access permission**. Click **Next**.

18. Click the **Edit Profile** button to configure the remote access profile. What tabs are available to configure? Click each tab to view the parameters that you can configure. Also, see Table 9-4 for an explanation of these tabs.

19. Click the **Authentication** tab.

20. Click the **EAP Methods** button.

21. Click the **Add** button, and click **Smart Card or other certificate**, if necessary. Click **OK**.

22. Click **OK** in the Select EAP Providers dialog box.

23. In the Edit Dial-in Profile dialog box, ensure that **Microsoft Encrypted Authentication version 2 (MS-CHAP v2)** and **Microsoft Encrypted Authentication (MS-CHAP)** are selected.

24. Click the **Encryption** tab.

25. Select to use only **Strong encryption (MPPE 56 bit)** and **Strongest encryption (MPPE 128 bit)**. Deselect any of the other options that are selected by default (see Figure 9-13). Table 9-5 explains the types of encryption.

26. Click **OK**.

27. Click **No**, if you see an information box about obtaining help for configuring protocols for remote access.

28. Click **Next**. Review your selections. How would you go back to change a selection? Click **Finish**.

29. Close the **Routing and Remote Access** tool.

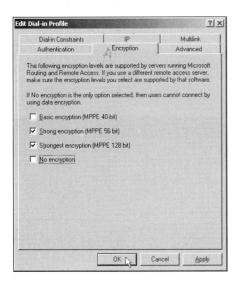

Figure 9-13   Configuring encryption in the profile

As you saw in Step 7 of Activity 9-5, there are several types of authentication that you can configure for a RAS server. You can use one or a combination of these authentication protocols, and if you use a combination, then the RAS server negotiates with the client until it finds an authentication method that works. Table 9-3 summarizes the authentication options.

Table 9-3   Authentication types

Authentication Protocol	Description
Challenge Handshake Authentication Protocol (CHAP)	CHAP requires encrypted authentication between the server and the client, but uses a generic form of password encryption, which enables UNIX computers and other non-Microsoft operating systems to connect to a RAS server.
Extensible Authentication Protocol (EAP)	EAP is used for clients who access RAS through special devices such as smart cards, token cards, and others that use certificate authentication. If you click this option, then Certificate Services should be installed so that you can configure them for a particular device or certificate type. The Certificate Services component is installed as a Windows component by using Control Panel's Add or Remove Programs tool.
Extension	Enables the use of specialized authentication extensions
MS-CHAP v1 (also called CHAP with Microsoft extensions)	MS-CHAP v1 and MS-CHAP v2 are set as the defaults when you install a RAS server, which means that clients must use MS-CHAP with PPP. MS-CHAP is a version of CHAP that uses a challenge-and-response form of authentication along with encryption. Windows 95/98/NT/2000/XP/2003 support MS-CHAP v1.
MS-CHAP v1 CPW	The same as MS-CHAP v1, but enables the user to change his or her password if it has expired
MS-CHAP v2 (also called CHAP with Microsoft extensions version 2)	Developed especially for VPNs, MS-CHAP v2 provides better authentication than MS-CHAP v1, because it requires the server and the client to authenticate mutually. It also provides more sophisticated encryption by using a different encryption key for receiving than for sending. Windows 2000/XP/2003 clients support MS-CHAP v2, and clients such as Windows 95 and Windows 98 can be updated to support this protocol. VPNs attempt to use MS-CHAP v2 with a client, and then use MS-CHAP v1 if the client does not support version 2.
MS-CHAP v2 CPW	The same as MS-CHAP v2, but enables the user to change his or her password if it has expired
Password Authentication Protocol (PAP)	PAP can perform authentication, but does not require it, which means that operating systems without password encryption capabilities, such as MS-DOS, are able to connect to RAS.
Unauthenticated	This option is not recommended, because it means that no authentication takes place.

When you configure a remote access profile in Step 18 of Activity 9-5, there are six tabs of configuration parameters. As a first step, always configure the options on the Authentication and Encryption tabs. Configure other tabs to customize the profile for your particular situation, such as the Multilink tab, if you are using Multilink to aggregate ISDN lines. Table 9-4 describes the options associated with each tab.

Table 9-4   Edit Dial-in Profile tabs

Tab	Description
Dial-in Constraints	Used to configure the idle and session timeouts, the day and time restrictions, whether access is restricted to a single number, and whether access is restricted based on the media used
IP	Used to configure how the client dialing in receives an IP address; IP filters also can be created to determine the protocols that clients can use
Multilink	Configures whether a client can use Multilink, the number of connections they can use, and at what point a link is dropped; BAP also can be enabled using this tab
Authentication	Configures the authentication protocols available
Encryption	Configures the encryption level
Advanced	Used to set RADIUS-specific attributes that can further restrict access

The Encryption tab configured in Step 25 of Activity 9-5 contains four data encryption options. The data encryption options specify the types of data encryption, which include **IP Security (IPSec)**, **Microsoft Point-to-Point Encryption (MPPE)**, and **Data Encryption Standard (DES)**. IPSec is a set of IP-based secure communications and encryption standards created through the Internet Engineering Task Force (IETF). MPPE is an end-to-end encryption technique that uses special encryption keys varying in length from 40 to 128 bits. DES was developed by IBM and the National Security Agency in cooperation with the National Bureau of Standards as an encryption technique using a secret key between the communicating stations. Triple DES employs three secret keys combined into one long key. As is true for authentication protocols, you can select to use one or a combination of encryption options to match what the client is using. Table 9-5 describes the encryption options available to a RAS server.

Table 9-5   RAS encryption options

Encryption Option	Description
Basic encryption (MPPE 40-bit)	Enables clients using 40-bit encryption key MPPE (available in Windows operating systems sold throughout the world); or clients can use 56-bit IPSec or DES encryption
No encryption	Enables clients to connect and not employ data encryption
Strong encryption (MPPE 56-bit)	Enables clients using 56-bit encryption key MPPE, 56-bit IPSec encryption, or DES
Strongest encryption (MPPE 128-bit)	Enables clients using 56-bit IPSec, Triple DES, or MPPE 128-bit encryption

Once a remote access policy is created, it is listed under the Remote Access Policies container. The policies are evaluated in the order in which they appear. To change the order in which they are evaluated, right-click a policy and use the Move Up or Move Down options.

You can change the settings of a policy by right-clicking the policy and clicking the Properties option (see Figure 9-14). Use the Add and Edit buttons to add a new condition to the policy or edit the settings of an existing one. To edit the profile, click the Edit Profile button.

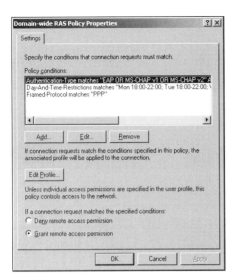

Figure 9-14   Remote access policy properties

Configuring Dial-up Security

After you have configured the remote access policy, you can also configure dial-up security at the user account, which enables you to employ callback security. This security is set on each user's Windows Server 2003 or domain account. With callback security set up, the server calls back the remote computer to verify its telephone number, in order to discourage a hacker from trying to access the server. The callback options available in Windows Server 2003 are:

- *No Callback*—The server allows access on the first call attempt.

- *Set by Caller (Routing and Remote Access Service only)*—The number used for the callback is provided by the remote computer.

- *Always Callback to*—The number to call back is already permanently entered into Windows Server 2003. (This option provides the most security.)

You can configure these and other properties for an individual account by finding the specific user account in the Active Directory Users and Computer tool, right-clicking the account, clicking Properties, and clicking the Dial-in tab.

Configuring a Dial-up Connection for a RAS Server

After RAS is installed and configured and you have created a remote access policy, you may need to create one or more ways for the RAS server to connect to the network so clients can access it. Besides the Local Area Connection that you set up when installing Windows Server 2003, you can also create other connections to match your particular connectivity needs, by configuring a dial-up connection to a private network or ISP through a phone line, for example, or by enabling clients to connect through a telecommunications line or the Internet. You can create any of these connections by opening Control Panel's Network Connections tool.

Activity 9-6: Configuring a Dial-up Network Connection

Time Required: Approximately 10 minutes

Objective: Configure a dial-up connection for a RAS server.

Description: In this activity, you configure a dial-up connection for a RAS server that is connected through a modem and telephone line.

1. Click **Start**, point to **Control Panel**, and point to **Network Connections**.
2. Click **New Connection Wizard**, and click **Next**.
3. Click **Connect to the network at my workplace**, and click **Next**.
4. Choose **Dial-up connection**. Click **Next**.
5. Enter the name of your company, such as **JP's Company**, and click **Next**.
6. Type the telephone number of the ISP to which to connect, and click **Next**.
7. Click **Anyone's use** so that other users can connect through this connection, and click **Next**.
8. Click **Finish**.

Configuring Clients to Connect to RAS through Dial-up Access

Common RAS clients include Windows 98/NT/2000/XP. You have already learned how to install RAS in Windows Server 2003 and to set up a dial-up connection. To access a RAS server from the other operating systems, you must configure a dial-up connection on those clients. For example, the steps for creating a dial-up connection in Windows XP Professional are very similar to those for creating a dial-up connection in Windows Server 2003. The general steps for creating a dial-up connection in Windows XP Professional (using the new experiential or Category View desktop theme) are:

1. Click **Start** and click **Control Panel**.
2. Click **Network and Internet Connections**.
3. Click **Create a connection to the network at your workplace**.
4. Choose **Dial-up connection**. Click **Next**.
5. Enter the name of your company, such as **JP's Company**, and click **Next**.
6. Type the telephone number of the ISP to which to connect, and click **Next**.
7. Click **Finish**.

IMPLEMENTING A VIRTUAL PRIVATE NETWORK

Another method in Windows Server 2003 that can be used to provide remote access to users is a virtual private network (VPN). A VPN can use a public Internet connection or an internal network connection as a transport medium to establish a connection with a VPN server. A VPN uses LAN protocols as well as tunneling protocols to encapsulate the data as it is sent across a public network such as the Internet. One of the benefits of using a VPN for remote access is users can connect to a local ISP and then connect to the local network, thus avoiding the charges of dialing into a server long distance. A VPN is used to ensure that any data sent across the public network, such as the Internet, is secure. Security is achieved by having the VPN create an encrypted tunnel between the client and the RAS server.

To create this tunnel, the client first connects to the Internet by establishing a PPP connection with an ISP. Once connected to the Internet, the client establishes a second connection with the VPN server. The client and the VPN server agree on how the data will be encapsulated and encrypted across the virtual tunnel. Information can then be sent securely between the two computers.

General Steps for Setting Up a VPN Server

A Windows 2003 server can be configured as a VPN server for access through the Internet, through routers, and through telecommunications lines, such as DSL, ISDN, and Frame Relay. After you physically connect the computer that acts in the role as VPN server through one of these methods, the general steps for setting up the VPN server are as follows:

1. Install and configure a VPN server in the Routing and Remote Access tool (a process that is nearly identical to configuring a RAS server).

2. Establish the VPN server properties, a VPN policy, and a VPN profile (a process that is identical to configuring these elements for a RAS server).

3. Configure the number of ports (which is done for either a RAS server, a VPN server, or a server offering both RAS and VPN).

Installing and Configuring a VPN Server

When you configure a VPN server, Windows Server 2003 requires that there are at least two interfaces in the computer, one for the connection to the LAN and one for a connection to the physical VPN network, such as a DSL connection (configuring a RAS server does not have the same requirement, because you can implement it strictly over the local area network connection).

To install and configure a VPN server, you begin by opening the Routing and Remote Access tool. Create the VPN server using the same steps as you used in Activity 9-1, except that in Step 6 select VPN (see Figure 9-15), or select both VPN and RAS to have a combined server.

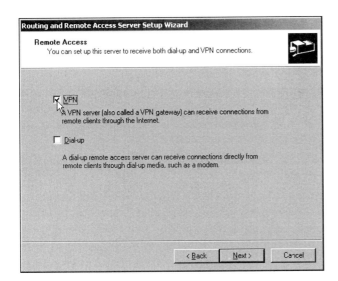

Figure 9-15   Configuring a VPN server

Establishing VPN Server Properties, a VPN Policy, and a VPN Profile

You can further configure a VPN server in the same way as for RAS, by configuring its properties, remote access policies, and profile. After the VPN server installation is complete, right-click the server in the tree, and click Properties to configure the server properties. Make certain that the VPN server is configured on the General tab as a router (see Figure 9-5) by checking the Router box and then clicking LAN and demand-dial routing. The other tabs in the Properties dialog box enable you to modify the configuration, as with using the IP tab to add or remove static IP addresses from the address pool. If you are using Multilink, configure the Multilink connectivity by clicking the PPP tab in the server's properties.

After you examine and configure the VPN server properties, set up the remote access policies and profile. You can configure the remote access policies and profile by right-clicking Remote Access Policies in the tree, and then clicking New Remote Access Policy. Complete the configuration steps using the New Remote Access Policy Wizard, just as you did in Activity 9-5. The remote access policy and profile settings are identical to those already discussed for a RAS server.

Configuring the Number of Ports for a RAS or VPN Server

Consult with your WAN provider on the number of ports that are available through your WAN connection. Once you have this information, configure the number of WAN ports in the RAS/VPN server. To configure the number of ports, right-click Ports in the tree under the server, and click Properties. Double-click WAN Miniport (PPTP), and set the appropriate number of ports (see Figure 9-16). Also, double-click WAN Miniport (L2TP), and configure the same number of ports.

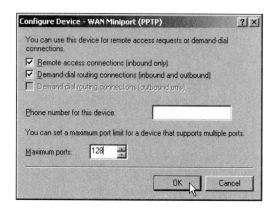

Figure 9-16   Configuring the number of ports

TROUBLESHOOTING RAS AND VPN INSTALLATIONS

Troubleshooting a RAS or VPN server communications problem can be divided into hardware and software troubleshooting tips.

Hardware Solutions

If no one can connect to the RAS or VPN server, try these hardware solutions:

- Use Control Panel's Add or Remove Hardware option or Device Manager to make sure modems and WAN adapters are working properly. Also, use Device Manager to make sure that a modem or WAN adapter has no resource conflicts. If there is a conflict, fix it immediately.

- If you are using one or more internal or external modems connected to the server, make sure the telephone line(s) is (are) connected to the modem(s) and to the wall outlet(s).

- For external modems, make sure the modem cable is properly attached, that you are using the right kind of cable (do not use a null modem cable), and that the modem has power.

- For internal modems or adapter cards (such as DSL or ISDN), make sure they have a good connection inside the computer. Reseat a card, if necessary.

- For a modem connection, test the telephone wall connection and cable by temporarily attaching a telephone to the cable instead of the modem and making a call.

- For an external DSL adapter or a combined DSL adapter and router, make sure the device is properly configured and connected, and check its monitor lights for problems.

Software Solutions

Try the following software solutions if no one can access the RAS or VPN server:

- Use the Computer Management tool to make sure the Remote Access Auto Connection Manager and the Remote Access Connection Manager services are started.

- Make sure that a RAS or VPN server is enabled. To check, right-click the server in the Routing and Remote Access tool, click Properties, and make sure that the Remote access server box is checked on the General tab (for a RAS or VPN server).

- Use the Ports option under the RAS or VPN server name to check the status of configured ports. Check to determine if all ports are being used. Double-click a port to view its connection statistics and information if you think there might be a problem with a specific port.

- If TCP/IP connectivity is used, make sure that the IP parameters are correctly configured for providing an address pool for either a RAS or VPN server. If IP configuration depends on DHCP, make sure that the DHCP server is working on the network and that you have configured a DHCP relay agent (with the correct hop-count threshold).

- If you are using a RADIUS server, make sure that it is connected and working properly and that **Internet Authentication Service (IAS)** is installed. IAS is used to establish and maintain security for RAS, Internet, and VPN dial-in access, and can be employed with RADIUS. IAS can use certificates to authenticate client access.

- If you have configured a remote access policy and profile, check to be sure that both are consistent with the users' access needs. For example, users may not be able to access a RAS or VPN server because the server is set to prevent access at certain times, or because certain users are not in a group that has access to the server.

If only certain clients, but not all, are having connection problems, try these solutions:

- Check the dial-up networking setup on the clients.

- Make sure the clients are using the same communications protocol as the server, for example PPP, and that they are using an authentication and encryption method that is supported by the RAS or VPN server.

- Make sure that each client has a server account and that each knows the correct account name and password. Also, make sure that accounts have the necessary rights and permissions to access files and folders on the server.

- If you manage access to a RAS or VPN server by using groups, make sure that each user account that needs access is in the appropriate group.

- Make sure the client accounts have been granted dial-up access capability and have the correct callback setup.

- For a dial-up RAS connection, determine if the clients' modems are compatible with the modems on the RAS server.

CONNECTING THROUGH TERMINAL SERVICES

Besides using Windows Server 2003 as a RAS or VPN server, you can also use it as a terminal server. A **terminal server** enables clients to run services and software applications on the Windows 2003 server instead of at the client, which means nearly any type of operating system can access Windows Server 2003. The Windows 2003 Terminal Services are used for two broad purposes: to support thin clients and to centralize program access. One of the main reasons for using a terminal server is to enable **thin clients**, such as specialized PCs that have minimal Windows-based operating systems, to access a Windows 2003 server so that most CPU-intense operations, such as creating a spreadsheet, are performed on the server. Some examples of thin client computers are Hewlett-Packard's Netstation, Maxspeed's MaxTerm, Neoware's NeoStation, and Wyse Technologies Winterm terminals. These function similarly to a basic **terminal** that has no CPU and that accesses a mainframe computer to perform all program execution and processing on the mainframe. Thin client network implementations are generally used to save money and reduce training and support requirements. Also, they are used for portable field or handheld remote devices, such as remote hotel reservation terminals and inventory counting devices. Thin client computers typically cost hundreds of dollars less than a full-featured PC, and because the operating system is simpler, it is easier to train users. Thin client field devices can be made inexpensively and tailored for a particular use, such as taking inventory in warehouses.

Another reason for using a terminal server is to centralize control of how programs are used. Some organizations need to maintain tight control over certain program applications, such as sensitive financial applications, top-secret program development, word-processed documents, and spreadsheets. For example, a network equipment company that invents a switch that is 100 times faster than any other on the market can use a terminal server to closely guard access to design documents and programs. These are stored and modified only on the server, which can be configured to provide a high level of security.

Windows 2003 Terminal Services not only support thin clients, but other types of client operating systems, including Windows 98/NT/2000/XP/2003, UNIX, UNIX-based X-terminals, and Macintosh. There are four main components that enable terminal server connectivity, which are shown in Table 9-6.

Table 9-6   Terminal services components

Component	Description
Windows 2003 multiuser Terminal Services	These services enable multiple users to simultaneously access and run standard Windows-based applications on a Windows 2003 server
Terminal server client	This client software runs on Windows 98, Windows NT 4.0, Windows 2000, Windows XP, and Windows 2003 to enable the client to run the Windows graphical user interface which looks like a regular 32-bit version of Windows
Remote desktop protocol (RDP)	This protocol is used for specialized network communications between the client and the server running Terminal Services; RDP follows the International Telecommunications Union (ITU) T.120 standard to enable multiple communication channels over a single line
Terminal services administration tools	These tools are used to manage Terminal Services

Installing Terminal Services

When you install Terminal Services you also need to install Terminal Services licensing to reflect the number of terminal server user licenses you have obtained from Microsoft. If you have several Terminal Services servers, there must be at least one Terminal Services licensing server. Terminal servers and licensing are installed through Control Panel's Add or Remove Programs option.

Activity 9-7: Installing Terminal Services

Time Required: Approximately 10-15 minutes

Objective: Install Terminal Services in Windows Server 2003.

Description: In this activity, you install a Terminal Services application server.

1. Click **Start**, point to **Control Panel**, and click **Add or Remove Programs**.

2. Click **Add/Remove Windows Components**.

3. Select **Terminal Server**. Read the Configuration Warning box and click **Yes**.

4. If this is the first or only Windows 2003 server configured as a terminal server, also select **Terminal Server Licensing** in order to license clients to use Terminal Services.

5. Click **Next** in the Windows Components Wizard dialog box.

6. Read the setup and licensing information, and click **Next**.

7. If your server is using modern applications designed to take advantage of Windows Server 2003 security, click **Full Security**. Or, if your server has older applications, click **Relaxed Security** (consult with your instructor about which to select). Figure 9-17 shows this dialog box. Click **Next**.

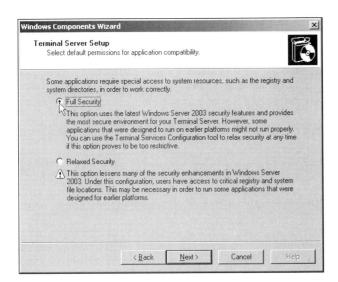

Figure 9-17 Configuring Terminal Services security

9

8. If you are installing a license server, you need to configure its role from two options, which are to make licenses available to Your entire enterprise or to Your domain or workgroup. For this activity, select **Your domain or workgroup**. Click **Next**.

9. If requested, insert the Windows Server 2003, Standard Edition, CD-ROM. Click **OK** or wait for the system to detect the CD-ROM. Also, if the autorun program starts, exit out of it.

10. Click **Finish**.

11. Close the **Add or Remove Programs** tool.

12. Make sure all programs are closed and any work is saved. Click **Yes** to reboot the server. Log back in after the server reboots.

 After you reboot you may see a Terminal Server help window that provides information about Terminal Services.

Managing Terminal Services

After the Terminal Services are installed, two management tools are available in Windows Server 2003: Terminal Services Configuration and Terminals Services Manager. When you install the Terminal Server Licensing component, a third tool also is available, Terminal Server Licensing. Table 9-7 lists these tools, including a description of their functions and how to access them.

Table 9-7 Terminal Services management tools

Management Tool	Function	Tool Location
Terminal Services Configuration	Used to configure terminal server settings and connections	Administrative Tools menu and an MMC snap-in
Terminal Server Licensing	Used to administer client licenses for terminal server in an enterprise or in a single domain	Administrative Tools menu
Terminal Services Manager	Used to control and monitor clients who are connected to Terminal Services on one or more servers	Administrative Tools menu

Configuring Terminal Services

Begin by using the Terminal Services Configuration tool to configure the remote connection properties. Only one connection is configured for each NIC in the server (each NIC can handle multiple clients).

Activity 9-8: Configuring Terminal Services

Time Required: Approximately 10-15 minutes

Objective: Configure a terminal server.

Description: In this activity you configure the terminal server that you set up in Activity 9-7.

1. Click **Start**, point to **All Programs**, point to **Administrative Tools**, and click **Terminal Services Configuration**.

2. Click **Connections**, if necessary. You see the default connection for the NIC installed in the server, such as RDP-Tcp. (If you install additional NICs later on, you can configure additional connections by right-clicking **Connections** and clicking **Create New Connection**.)

3. Right-click the connection in the right pane, such as RDP-Tcp, and click **Properties**. You should see a dialog box similar to the one in Figure 9-18. Table 9-8 describes the properties that can be configured on each tab.

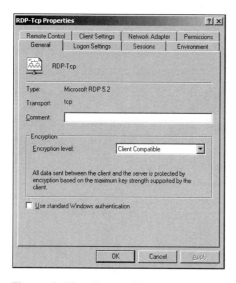

Figure 9-18   Connection properties

4. Click the **Permissions** tab (see Figure 9-19). Immediately after you have installed Terminal Services, make sure you examine the existing permissions and make any changes that are needed for your organization. What are the default permissions set up for each group? Note that the allow and deny permissions are:

   - *Full Control*—Enables access that includes query, set information, remote control, logon, logoff, message, connect, disconnect, and virtual channel use

   - *User Access*—Enables access to query, connect, and send messages

   - *Guest Access*—Enables access to logon

   - *Special Permissions*—Indicates if any special permissions have been configured and is deactivated by default

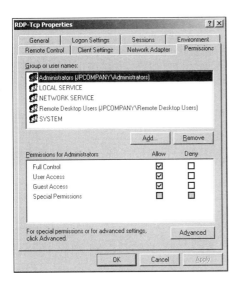

Figure 9-19   Permissions

5. Another property that should be checked is the implementation of encryption and authentication. Click the **General** tab to check these properties. Authentication can be set to use either no authentication or standard Windows authentication when the clients are Windows 95, 98, NT, 2000, XP, and 2003. The encryption options are:

- *Client Compatible*—Data sent from the client to the server and from the server to the client is encrypted using the highest encryption that the client can employ; this is used for Windows 95 or Windows 98 clients, for example.

- *FIPS Compliant*—Client and server data transmission employ Federal Information Processing Standard (FIPS) 140-1 encryption.

- *High*—Data sent from the client to the server and from the server to the client is encrypted using the highest encryption level at the server, which is 128-bit encryption. Only clients that support this encryption level are permitted to connect.

- *Low*—56-bit key encryption is used for data transmitted between the client and the server.

6. Click each of the tabs you have not yet viewed to see their contents.

7. Click **OK** when you are finished examining the tabs.

8. Close the Terminal Services Configuration window.

Table 9-8   Terminal Services connection properties

Tab	Description
Client Settings	Enables you to configure client connection settings, such as whether to use client settings, connect to client drives, or to connect to a default printer; also drive features can be enabled or disabled, such as drive mapping, printer and printer port mapping, clipboard mapping, and audio mapping
Environment	Enables you to establish a program that runs automatically when the client logs on and overrides user profile, remote desktop, or Terminal Services client settings
General	Used to set up encryption and authentication
Logon Settings	Used to determine how the client logs on by using information provided by the client or by using a previously set logon account setup
Network Adapter	Enables you to specify a NIC to use and to control the number of simultaneous connections
Permissions	Used to set up access permissions by user and by group

Table 9-8   Terminal Services connection properties (continued)

Tab	Description
Remote Control	Enables you to remotely control a client or to observe a client's session while that session is active, such as to watch the user's key and mouse strokes to help diagnose a problem without having to go to the client's site
Sessions	Used to establish disconnect settings and how clients can reconnect to the server if a session is interrupted

Configuring a Remote Desktop Connection

Computers that access the terminal server need to use either the Remote Display Protocol (RDP) Client or the Terminal Services Advanced Client software. For computers running Windows operating systems, there are two sets of steps to make the appropriate software available. The first set of steps is to create a shared folder from which to access the setup files, and the second step is for the client to access the shared folder and run the software to install the remote desktop connection capability.

Activity 9-9: Creating a Shared Folder

Time Required: Approximately 5 minutes

Objective: Create a shared folder from which clients can install the client-side Terminal Services software.

Description: This activity enables you to create a shared folder from which a client can install the Terminal Services software in order to use a remote desktop connection.

1. Open **My Computer** or **Windows Explorer**.

2. Locate the folder: **\Windows\system32\clients\tsclient\win32**. What files are in the folder?

3. Right-click the folder, and click **Sharing and Security**.

4. Click **Share this folder**. Enter **Terminal Services Installation** in the Share name text box.

5. Click **OK**.

6. Close My Computer or Windows Explorer.

After you share this folder, a client running a 32-bit Windows operating system, such as Windows 98 or Windows Millennium, can:

1. Access the shared folder via the network.

2. Double-click the setup.exe program in the shared folder to run it and install the client software.

Windows XP Professional already has the RDP Client installed by default. However, you can use the steps described here, if it is missing RDP Client software.

With the software installed on a client, such as Windows XP Professional, the client can start a remote desktop connection by clicking Start, pointing to All Programs (or Programs in earlier operating systems), pointing to Accessories, pointing to Communications, and clicking Remote Desktop Connection. Enter the name or IP address of the Terminal Services computer (see Figure 9-20), and click Connect. After the computer connects, provide your user name and password.

Figure 9-20   Connecting to a terminal server from a client

Configuring Licensing

When you set up a terminal server, you must activate the server and configure the licensing by using the Terminal Server Licensing tool (make sure the Terminal Server Licensing Windows component is installed at the same time that you install the Terminal Services component). To open the tool, click Start, point to All Programs, point to Administrative Tools, and click Terminal Server Licensing. Double-click All servers in the tree to display the servers that offer Terminal Services. To activate a server, right-click the server in the tree, and click Activate Server. When the Licensing Wizard starts, click Next and complete the instructions for contacting Microsoft to activate the licenses. There are three ways to contact Microsoft: Automatic connection (recommended), Web Browser, and Telephone.

 If the Terminal Services Manager fails to start properly for a terminal server, or if users are unable to connect to the server, check to make sure that you have activated the server using the Terminal Server Licensing tool.

Installing Applications on a Terminal Server

After you configure a terminal server, applications are installed to be compatible with this mode. For this reason, you may need to reinstall some applications. Use Control Panel's Add or Remove Programs tool to install new applications after the Terminal Services are installed and use the same tool to uninstall and reinstall programs that were installed prior to setting up the server for Terminal Services.

CHAPTER SUMMARY

❏ A Windows 2003 server configured for RAS enables clients to remotely dial in to a server or a network of servers.

❏ Remote access to a Windows Server 2003 network can be through regular dial-up telephone lines, special high-speed lines, Internet connections, and routers. Remote traffic over telephone lines is transported through the Point-to-Point Protocol (PPP). Traffic through the Internet or through a VPN is transported via the Point-to-Point Tunneling Protocol (PPTP) and the Layer Two Transport Protocol (L2TP).

❏ When you set up a RAS or VPN server you can manage one or multiple servers through remote access policies and profiles. Remote access policies and profiles are used to establish how a server is available to users and to set up security.

❏ A VPN server is configured using steps similar to those used for configuring a RAS server. In fact, one server can be configured to offer both RAS and VPN services.

❏ When you troubleshoot a RAS or VPN connection, troubleshoot both hardware and software.

❏ Terminal Services enable users to access a server and run applications on that server.

❏ After you install Terminal Services, configure each connection (NIC) for the remote connection characteristics, such as security, logon settings, client settings, and the environment.

❏ Users access a terminal server by installing the client-side software for a remote desktop connection.

KEY TERMS

access server — A device that connects several different types of communications devices and telecommunication lines to a network, providing network routing for these types of communications.

aggregated links — Linking two or more communications channels, such as ISDN channels, so that they appear as one channel, but with the combined speed of all channels in the aggregate.

Bandwidth Allocation Control Protocol (BACP) — Similar to BAP, but is able to select a preferred client when two or more clients vie for the same bandwidth.

Bandwidth Allocation Protocol (BAP) — A protocol that works with Multilink in Windows Server 2003 to enable the bandwidth or speed of a remote connection to be allocated on the basis of the needs of an application, with the maximum allocation equal to the maximum speed of all channels aggregated via Multilink.

Challenge Handshake Authentication Protocol (CHAP) — An encrypted handshake protocol designed for standard IP- or PPP-based exchange of passwords. It provides a reasonably secure, standard, cross-platform method for sender and receiver to negotiate a connection.

CHAP with Microsoft extensions (MS-CHAP) — A Microsoft-enhanced version of CHAP that can negotiate encryption levels and that uses the highly secure RSA RC4 encryption algorithm to encrypt communications between client and host.

CHAP with Microsoft extensions version 2 (MS-CHAP v2) — An enhancement of MS-CHAP that provides better authentication and data encryption and that is especially well suited for VPNs.

Compressed Serial Line Protocol (CSLIP) — A newer version of SLIP that compresses header information in each packet sent across a remote link.

Data Encryption Standard (DES) — A data encryption method developed by IBM and the National Security Agency in cooperation with the National Bureau of Standards as an encryption technique using a secret key between the communicating stations. Triple DES employs three secret keys combined into one long key.

DHCP relay agent — A server, such as a RAS or a VPN server, or computer that broadcasts IP configuration information between the DHCP server on a network and the client acquiring an address.

DSL adapter — A digital communications device that links a computer (or sometimes a router) to a DSL telecommunications line.

digital subscriber line (DSL) — A technology that uses advanced modulation technologies on regular telephone lines for high-speed networking at speeds of up to 60 Mbps between subscribers and a telecommunications company.

Extensible Authentication Protocol (EAP) — An authentication protocol employed by network clients that use special security devices such as smart cards, token cards, and others that use certificate authentication.

Frame Relay — A WAN communications technology that relies on packet switching and virtual connection techniques to transmit at speeds from 56 Kbps to 45 Mbps.

Integrated Services Digital Network (ISDN) — A telecommunications standard for delivering data services over digital telephone lines with a current practical limit of 1.536 Mbps and a theoretical limit of 622 Mbps.

Internet Authentication Service (IAS) — Used to establish and maintain security for RAS, Internet, and VPN dial-in access, and can be employed with RADIUS. IAS can use certificates to authenticate client access.

IP Security (IPSec) — A set of IP-based secure communications and encryption standards created through the Internet Engineering Task Force (IETF).

Layer Two Tunneling Protocol (L2TP) — A protocol that transports PPP over a VPN, an intranet, or the Internet. L2TP works similarly to PPTP, but unlike PPTP, L2TP uses an additional network communications standard, called Layer Two Forwarding, that enables forwarding on the basis of MAC addressing.

Microsoft Point-to-Point Encryption (MPPE) — An end-to-end encryption technique that uses special encryption keys varying in length from 40 to 128 bits.

modem — A modulator/demodulator that converts a transmitted digital signal to an analog signal for a telephone line. It also converts a received analog signal to a digital signal for use by a computer.

Multilink or **Multilink PPP (MPPP)** — A capability of RAS to aggregate multiple data streams into one logical network connection for the purpose of using more than one modem, ISDN channel, or other communications line in a single logical connection.

network address translation (NAT) — Sometime used by firewalls, NAT translates IP addresses on an internal or local network so that the actual IP addresses cannot be determined on the Internet, because the address seen on the Internet is a decoy address used from a pool of decoy addresses.

Password Authentication Protocol (PAP) — A nonencrypted, plaintext password authentication protocol. This represents the lowest level of security for exchanging passwords via PPP or TCP/IP.

Point-to-Point Protocol (PPP) — A widely used remote communications protocol that supports IPX/SPX, NetBEUI, and TCP/IP for point-to-point communication (for example, between a remote PC and a Windows 2003 server on a network).

Point-to-Point Tunneling Protocol (PPTP) — A remote communications protocol that enables connectivity to a network through the Internet and connectivity through intranets and VPNs.

Remote Authentication Dial-In User Service (RADIUS) — A protocol and service set up on one RAS or VPN server, as in a domain for example, when there are multiple RAS or VPN servers to coordinate authentication and to keep track of remote dial-in statistics for all RAS and VPN servers.

Routing and Remote Access Services (RRAS) — Microsoft software services that enable a Windows 2003 server to provide routing capabilities and remote access so that off-site workstations have access to a Windows Server 2003 network through telecommunications lines, the Internet, or intranets.

Serial Line Internet Protocol (SLIP) — An older remote communications protocol that is used by some UNIX computers. The modern compressed SLIP (CSLIP) version uses header compression to reduce communications overhead.

T-carrier — A dedicated leased telephone line that can be used for data communications over multiple channels for speeds of up to 44.736 Mbps.

terminal — A device that consists of a monitor and keyboard to communicate with host computers that run the programs. The terminal does not have a processor to use for running programs locally.

terminal adapter (TA) — Popularly called a digital modem, links a computer or a fax to an ISDN line.

terminal server — A server configured to offer Terminal Services so that clients can run applications on the server, similar to having clients respond as terminals.

thin client — A specialized personal computer or terminal device that has a minimal Windows-based operating system. A thin client is designed to connect to a host computer that does most or all of the processing. The thin client is mainly responsible for providing a graphical user interface and network connectivity.

virtual private network (VPN) — A private network that is like a tunnel through a larger network—such as the Internet, an enterprise network, or both—that is restricted to designated member clients only.

X.25 — An older packet-switching protocol for connecting remote networks at speeds up to 2.048 Mbps.

REVIEW QUESTIONS

1. One of your Terminal Services clients on a Windows 2003 server is having trouble with a client/server program that he runs. How might you help diagnose the problem?
   a. Lengthen the session timeout.
   b. Observe his keystrokes by connecting to view his session.
   c. Observe the applications he is using through the Command Prompt Window command.
   d. Restart the client/server program at the server.

2. About half of your RAS server's clients use smart cards. What authentication protocol must you configure for them?
   a. Password Authentication Protocol (PAP)

b. Extensible Authentication Protocol (EAP)

c. Shiva's Password Authentication Protocol (SPAP)

d. CHAP with Microsoft extensions (MS-CHAP)

3. After you set up a VPN server and test it over a WAN link, you see a message that says it is unable to transport via L2TP (Layer Two Tunneling Protocol). What should you first check to diagnose this problem?

a. Make sure that you have enabled L2TP ports and specified the number of L2TP ports to match the number of ports available over a WAN connection.

b. Disable PPTP because it is conflicting with L2TP communications.

c. Make sure that the VPN server is configured to transport NetBEUI as well as TCP/IP, because L2TP is a special Microsoft network routing protocol.

d. This message is normal because you have set up a T-1 WAN link and T-1 does not enable use of L2TP.

4. One of your users is trying to connect to a RAS server, but is not able to make the connection. All ports and communications devices at the server end are working. The user, who is running Windows NT 4.0 Workstation, has checked his modem and telephone system and all are working. Which of the following might be the problem? (Choose all that apply.)

a. The user's modem is not compatible with the modem on the RAS server.

b. The user's account is denied dial-in access in the account's properties.

c. The user's dial-up connectivity is set to use SLIP:Internet, but the RAS server is not set up for this access.

d. Windows NT 4.0 Workstation is not supported in Windows Server 2003 RAS.

5. You have installed a RAS server to obtain IP addresses from a DHCP server that is connected to the network. No error messages were displayed during the installation, but for some reason, IP addresses are not being automatically assigned to RAS clients. What step might you have omitted?

a. configuring a DHCP relay agent

b. configuring a hard coded IP address at each client

c. disabling IPX which creates routing problems with TCP/IP

d. creating a pool of addresses in the RAS server

6. Your network is located in Philadelphia, but five employees in your organization telecommute from a shared office that is in Washington, D.C. Each of the telecommuters has her or his own telephone line and dedicated number. How can you set up security so that the RAS server verifies each user by her or his telephone number?

a. Control RAS server access through a remote access policy that contains a list of telephone numbers that the server can call back.

b. Assign a static IP address to each of the five users and set up a telephone number in the RAS server that is assigned to each IP address.

c. Set up callback security on each user's account so that only a specific number is called back.

d. You cannot set up verification on the basis of a specific telephone number, only by area code.

7. How can you make client-side software available for a Terminal Services client?

a. Copy the termserve.exe file to a floppy disk and have each client run it.

b. Simply have a client running any Windows-based operating system run the Terminal program in their own Accessories folder.

c. Have each client purchase the software directly from Microsoft.

d. Share the \Windows\system32\clients\tsclient\win32 folder on the Terminal Services server and have clients run the setup.exe file from the shared folder.

8. The computer committee at your business has been discussing setting up a VPN that includes remote access through high-speed communication lines. The committee has already contacted the local telephone company and found that they can connect using DSL, T-carrier lines, ISDN, and Frame Relay. Which of these is (are) compatible with a Windows 2003 VPN server? (Choose all that apply.)

   a. DSL

   b. T-carrier lines

   c. Frame Relay

   d. ISDN

9. Which of the following is not a permission used by a Terminal Services connection?

   a. Full Control

   b. Modify

   c. Guest Access

   d. User Access

10. You have set up a TCP/IP-based Windows 2003 terminal server and a user calls because she is trying to use the service for the first time by dialing in from home, but is not succeeding. What should she check? (Choose all that apply.)

   a. that her home computer is configured for TCP/IP

   b. that her home computer uses Terminal Services parity check

   c. that her home computer is configured for PPP

   d. that her home computer monitor is the same type of monitor as is used on the terminal server

11. Your VPN server is configured to enable Multilink as a way to aggregate Frame Relay channels when users need more bandwidth, such as for multimedia applications. However, when a user connects, the server does not seem to adjust for the amount of bandwidth needed by a user. How can you fix the problem?

   a. Restrict Multilink to increments of 56 Kbps per port.

   b. Configure the VPN server to limit the maximum number of ports to 1.

   c. Configure the VPN server to dynamically use the Bandwidth Allocation Protocol (BAP) along with Multilink.

   d. A VPN server cannot adjust bandwidth needs, that must be done at the Frame Relay provider site.

12. Which of the following tools enables you to monitor client connections to a RAS or VPN server?

   a. Active Directory Users and Computers tool

   b. IP Routing tool

   c. Security MMC snap-in

   d. Routing and Remote Access tool

13. Which of the following can be Windows 2003 RAS server clients? (Choose all that apply.)

   a. Windows NT 4.0

   b. Windows 98

   c. Windows XP

   d. Windows 2000

14. Which authentication method provides the best security?

   a. CHAP

   b. MS-CHAP v1

    c. MS-CHAP v2

    d. PAP

15. Which encryption method is 128-bit and compatible with IPSec?

    a. Basic

    b. Strong

    c. Strongest

    d. IPP v9

16. Which of the following protocols can be transported by PPP?

    a. IPX

    b. NetBEUI

    c. TCP/IP

    d. all of the above

    e. only a and c

17. A _____ server can disguise IP addresses on an internal network.

    a. network address translation

    b. network proxy decoy

    c. IP authoritative

    d. reverse code IP

18. You have installed Terminal Services and several remote clients have called to say that an older spreadsheet application is not working properly. What should you do to solve the problem?

    a. Increase the channel bandwidth for that application.

    b. Reinstall the application because it was installed prior to installing Terminal Services.

    c. Increase the Terminal Services Buffer parameter used at those clients.

    d. Run the Terminal Services Capability tool on that application.

19. When you set up Routing and Remote Access services, which of the following is not an option?

    a. security connection between two private networks

    b. remote access

    c. custom configuration

    d. remote telecommunications switching

20. You are configuring four terminal servers in a domain. At least one of those servers must be a _____.

    a. license server

    b. DNS server

    c. connection manager moderator

    d. smart card server

CASE PROJECTS

Case Project Background

The International Wheat Association is a nonprofit association of wheat growers, researchers, and bakers that provides a wide range of information about growing, processing, and using wheat and wheat-based products. The association is located in Toronto and has member groups throughout the world. One of the

International Wheat Association's most popular services is maintaining a database of research information for all members. The database has been on a Windows NT 4.0 RAS server, but the association has hired you, through Bayside IT Services, to help them convert this vital service to a new Windows 2003 server set up as a RAS server.

Case Project 9-1: Planning the Windows 2003 RAS Implementation

The association's small IT staff asks you to describe the general issues involved in working with Windows 2003 RAS. Prior to upgrading the Windows NT 4.0 RAS server, they would like you to present a brief paper that discusses the following elements associated with creating a Windows 2003 RAS server:

❐ Remote access protocols

❐ IP addressing

❐ Remote access policies

❐ Authentication

❐ Encryption

❐ Multilink connectivity

Case Project 9-2: Managing a RAS Server

The IT staff of four people wants you to train them in how to manage the RAS server after it is installed. Provide a preliminary training paper that discusses the tools available to them for configuring, managing, monitoring, and troubleshooting the server.

Case Project 9-3: Configuring a VPN Server

The association's research group has received funding from management to set up a VPN server that can be remotely accessed over the Internet by top-level researchers all over the world. Create a document for the IT staff that explains any special configuration and setup steps of which the IT staff needs to be aware for the VPN server setup.

Case Project 9-4: The Order Entry Program

The association sells many practical and scientific publications through its Customer Service Department, which consists of eight people who use the same specialized customer service order entry program and database. Currently, the program runs on each user's client computer, but it was really designed to work best from one server. Is there a way for the association to enable all eight customer service representatives to run this program on a server, rather than on multiple computers? Create a short document to explain your answer and its benefits, if any.

10

SECURING WINDOWS SERVER 2003

After reading this chapter and completing the exercises, you will be able to:

♦ Understand the use of Group Policy

♦ Secure Windows Server 2003 using security policies

♦ Manage security by using the Security Templates Snap-in

♦ Configure client security by using Windows Server 2003 policies

♦ Configure the Encrypting File System

Good security is critical for all server operating systems and networks. Fortunately, Windows Server 2003 incorporates many security options and configuration tools. In Chapter 5, you learned about some of these tools in the form of attributes, NTFS permissions, and share permissions. There are many additional security options in the form of Group Policies that can be applied to local computers and to Active Directory containers, such as domains.

In this chapter, you'll begin by learning about Group Policies and how they are generally applied. You'll learn to configure policies that specifically focus on security, including polices that govern user accounts. You will learn how to work with the Security Templates Snap-in to configure security templates on networks that use different Group Policies for multiple organizational units (OUs, see Chapter 4) and domains. Group Policies can be configured on servers so that they control server clients, such as through controlling desktop options on the client computer. You'll learn how to establish all kinds of policies that affect how clients access software, their desktops, the network, and windows components at their workstations. Finally, you will learn about managing the Encrypting File System by using the cipher command.

INTRODUCTION TO GROUP POLICY

The use of **Group Policy** in Windows Server 2003 enables you to standardize the working environment of clients and servers by setting policies in Active Directory. There are hundreds of policies that can be configured through Group Policy, so that you can manage desktop configurations, logon security, resource auditing, software availability, and many other functions.

Group Policy has evolved from the Windows NT Server 4.0 concept of system policy. **System policy** is a set of basic user account and computer parameters that can be configured using the **system policy editor**, Poledit.exe. Parameters that are established in the system policy editor can apply domainwide or just to specific groups of users. There are important differences between using system policy and Group Policy. For example, the largest range for system policy is the domain, whereas Group Policy can extend to cover multiple domains in one site. There are fewer objects to configure in a system policy than in a Group Policy. Also, the system policy parameters focus mainly on the clients' desktop environment as controlled by registry settings. Group Policy is set for more environments, ranging from client desktops to account policies to remote installation of Windows XP Professional on clients. System policy is less secure because it is possible for users to change system policy parameters that apply to them by accessing the Registry Editors in their client operating systems (such as in Windows 98). Group Policies are secured so that they cannot be changed by individual users. Another problem with system policies is that because they are applied to the clients' registries, the system policies can live on after they are no longer needed. This is not a problem with Group Policy because a Group Policy is dynamically updated and configured to represent the most current needs.

The defining characteristics of Group Policy are:

- *Group Policy can be set for a site, domain, OU, or local computer*—Group Policy can be linked to any site, domain, OU, or local computer. An OU is the smallest Active Directory container with which a Group Policy is linked. Group Policy is not linked to security groups directly, but it can be filtered through these groups. Also, when the first domain is created, a default domain policy is automatically associated with that domain. The default domain policy is, by default, inherited by child domains, but can be changed so that a child domain has a different Group Policy than its parent domain.

- *Group Policy cannot be set for non-OU folder containers*—Default containers that are folders instead of OUs, such as the Builtin, Computers, ForeignSecurityPrincipals, and Users folders, are not truly OUs, and therefore you cannot link Group Policy with these containers. You can verify this by opening the Active Directory Users and Computers tool, right-clicking Users, and clicking Properties. There is no Group Policy tab in the Users Properties dialog box. Compare this to right-clicking the Domain Controllers OU and clicking Properties. The Domain Controllers OU does have a Group Policy tab.

- *Policy settings for groups are stored in Group Policy objects*—A **Group Policy object (GPO)** is an Active Directory object that contains policy settings for groups for a site, domain, OU, or local computer. Each GPO has a unique name and globally unique identifier (GUID). When Active Directory is installed, there is one local GPO for every Windows 2003 server. A server can also be governed by Active Directory GPOs for sites, domains, and OUs.

- *There are local and nonlocal GPOs*—The local GPO applies to the local computer. Nonlocal GPOs apply to sites, domains, and OUs. When there are multiple GPOs, their effect is incremental (local GPO first, default domain GPO next, site GPO next, and the GPOs for OUs next).

- *Group Policy can be set up to affect user accounts and computers*—Group Policy is set up to affect user configuration, computer configuration, or both, as illustrated in the Default Domain Policy shown in Figure 10-1. If a policy is set up for one, but is not the same as a policy set up for the other, then the policy set up for computers prevails over the policy for user accounts.

- *When Group Policy is updated, old policies are removed or updated for all clients*—Each time you update Group Policy, the new information is updated for clients and the old information that no longer applies is removed.

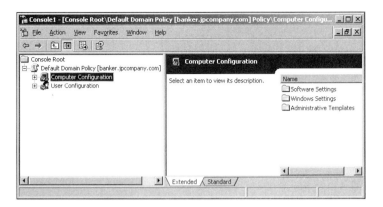

Figure 10-1   Default domain security policy

SECURING WINDOWS SERVER 2003 USING SECURITY POLICIES

Security policies are a subset of individual polices within a larger Group Policy for a site, domain, OU, or local computer. Before you release a server for use, always make sure you configure the security policies on the local computer and the default domain security policies. There are many individual security policies that you can configure, and this chapter is designed to simply give you a taste of some of the most important ones. In the next sections, you learn how to establish the following security policies:

- Account Policies
- Audit Policy
- User Rights
- Security Options
- IP Security Policies

Activity 10-1: Using the Domain Security Policy Tool

Time Required: Approximately 10 minutes

Objective: Learn how to access the Domain Security Policy tool.

Description: The basic security policies for a domain and for a local computer can be configured from the Domain Security Policy tool that is accessed from the Administrative Tools menu. In this activity, you open this tool and briefly examine its contents.

1. Click **Start**, point to **All Programs**, point to **Administrative Tools**, and click **Domain Security Policy**. Make sure that the elements under Security Settings are displayed in the tree. What elements do you see?

2. Double-click **Account Policies** to view its associated elements.

3. Double-click **Local Policies** to view the elements you can configure.

4. Double-click **System Services** and note the services that you can configure. Double-click a service, such as **Alerter**, to see what can be configured. What options do you see? Click **Cancel**.

5. Double-click each of the other options under Securty Settings that you have not yet viewed.

6. Close the **Default Domain Security Settings** window.

An alternative way to configure security policies is to use the Group Policy Object Editor Snap-in through the MMC. The advantage of using the Group Policy Object Editor is that you can configure many more group policies and security settings than you can by using the Domain Security Policy tool. Also, you can select from different Group Policy objects to configure, such as one for a domain or one for an OU.

10

Activity 10-2: Using the Group Policy Object Editor Snap-in

Time Required: Approximately 5 minutes

Objective: Learn how to access the Group Policy Object Editor Snap-in.

Description: In this activity you learn how to open the Group Policy Object Editor Snap-in for modifying security policies and other Group Policies.

1. Click **Start** and click **Run**.

2. Enter **mmc** in the Open box, and click **OK**.

3. Maximize the console windows, if necessary.

4. Click the **File** menu, and then click **Add/Remove Snap-in**.

5. Click the **Add** button.

6. Double-click **Group Policy Object Editor** under Available Standalone Snap-ins. Notice that the Group Policy Object you configure is stored on the Local Computer by default.

7. Click the **Browse** button. Now notice that you can select to edit the Group Policy for existing domains and OUs, as shown in Figure 10-2.

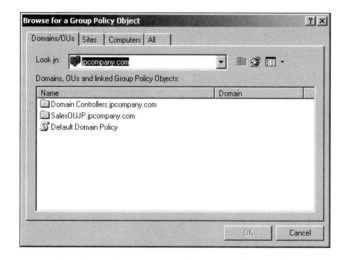

Figure 10-2   Selecting which Group Policy to edit

8. Click **Default Domain Policy**.

9. Click **OK**.

10. Click **Finish**.

11. Click **Close**.

12. Click **OK**.

13. Double-click **Default Domain Policy** [*computer and domain name*] **Policy** to view the elements under it.

14. Close the console window.

15. Click **Yes** to save the console settings. In the File name box, enter Domain Policy plus your initials, and use .msc as the extension, such as **Domain PolicyJP.msc**. Click **Save**.

Yet another way to edit a Group Policy for a domain or OU is to open the Active Directory Users and Computers tool, right-click the domain or OU, click properties, click the Group Policy tab, and click Edit.

Establishing Account Policies

Account policies are security measures set up in a Group Policy that apply to all accounts or to all accounts in a container, such as a domain, when Active Directory is installed. The account policies are located in the following path in the tree of a Group Policy: Computer Configuration, Windows Settings, Security Settings. This is what you observed in Step 1 of Activity 10-1, using the Domain Security Policy Tool. The account policy options that you can configure affect three main areas:

- Password security
- Account lockout
- Kerberos security

Each of these is described in the next sections.

Password Security

The first line of defense for Windows Server 2003 is password security. One option is to set a password expiration period, requiring users to change passwords at regular intervals. Many organizations use this feature, requiring users to change their passwords every 45 to 90 days.

Server administrators should consider changing passwords every month or sooner for the Administrator account and other accounts that can access sensitive information.

Some organizations require that all passwords have a minimum length, such as six or seven characters (for a "strong password" Microsoft recommends a minimum of seven characters). This requirement makes passwords more difficult to guess. Another option is to have the operating system "remember" passwords that have been previously used. For example, the system might be set to recall the last five passwords, preventing a user from repeating one of these. Password recollection forces the user to change to a different password instead of reusing the same one when a new one is set. An account lockout option can also be configured. The specific password security options that you can configure are as follows:

- *Enforce password history*—Enables you to require users to choose new passwords when they make a password change, because the system can remember the previously used passwords

- *Maximum password age*—Permits you to set the maximum time allowed until a password expires

- *Minimum password age*—Permits you to specify that a password must be used for a minimum amount of time before it can be changed

- *Minimum password length*—Enables you to require that passwords are a minimum length

- *Passwords must meet complexity requirements*—Enables you to create a filter of customized password requirements that each account password must follow

- *Store passwords using reversible encryption*—Enables passwords to be stored in reversible encrypted format

Activity 10-3: Configuring Password Security

Time Required: Approximately 5 to 10 minutes

Objective: Configure the password security in the default domain security policy.

Description: In this activity, you configure the password security for a domain.

1. Open the Domain Policy console window you saved in Activity 10-2 by clicking **Start**, pointing to **All Programs**, pointing to **Administrative Tools**, and clicking **Domain PolicyJP.msc**.

2. Double-click **Account Policies** in the tree (under Computer Configuration, Windows Settings, and Security Settings).

3. Click **Password Policy** in the tree. In the right pane, notice the policies that you can configure.

4. Double-click **Enforce password history** in the right pane. Be certain that **Define this policy setting** is checked. Set the password history to remember the last **7** passwords, and click **OK**, as shown in Figure 10-3.

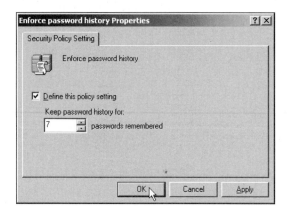

Figure 10-3   Configuring the password history

5. Double-click **Maximum password age**. Ensure that **Define this policy setting** is checked, and change the days text box to **60**. Click **OK**.

6. Double-click **Minimum password length**. Be sure that **Define this policy setting** is checked, and set the characters text box to **7**. Click **OK**. The console window should now look similar to the one in Figure 10-4.

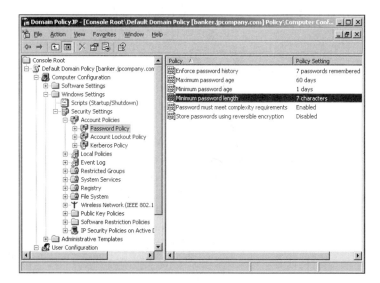

Figure 10-4   Password Policy configurations

7. Close the console window and click **Yes**.

Account Lockout

The operating system can employ account lockout to lock out an account (including the true account owner) after a number of unsuccessful tries. The lockout can be set to release after a specified period of time or by intervention from the server administrator.

A common policy is to have lockout go into effect after five to 10 unsuccessful logon attempts. Also, an administrator can set lockout to release after a designated time, such as 30 minutes. The 30 minutes creates enough delay to discourage intruders, while giving some leeway to a user who might have forgotten a recently changed password. The following are the account lockout parameters that you can configure in the account lockout policy:

- *Account lockout duration*—Permits you to specify in minutes how long the system keeps an account locked out after reaching the specified number of unsuccessful logon attempts

- *Account lockout threshold*—Enables you to set a limit to the number of unsuccessful attempts to log on to an account

- *Reset account lockout counter after*—Enables you to specify the number of minutes between two consecutive unsuccessful logon attempts, to make sure that the account is not locked out too soon

Activity 10-4: Configuring Account Lockout Policy

Time Required: Approximately 5 minutes

Objective: Configure the account lockout policy in the default domain security policy.

Description: In this activity, you configure the account lockout policy settings.

1. Open the Domain Policy console window you created earlier by clicking **Start**, pointing to **All Programs**, pointing to **Administrative Tools**, and clicking **Domain PolicyJP.msc**.

2. Click **Account Lockout Policy** in the tree under Computer Configuration, Windows Settings, Security Settings, and Account Policies.

3. Double-click **Account lockout duration** in the right pane.

4. Check the box for **Define this policy setting**, if it is not already checked. Enter **40** in the minutes text box, and click **OK**.

5. If this is the first time that the Account Lockout Policy has been configured, or if the values for the lockout parameters were not previously defined, you will see the Suggested Value Changes box. Click **OK** in the Suggested Value Changes box. How did the other settings change?

6. Close the console window and click **Yes**.

Kerberos Security

Kerberos security involves the use of tickets that are exchanged between the client who requests logon and network services access and the server or Active Directory that grants access. On a network that does not use Active Directory, each standalone Windows 2003 server can be designated as a Kerberos key distribution center, which means that the server stores user accounts and passwords. When Active Directory is used, then each domain controller is a key distribution center. When a user logs on, the client computer sends an account name and password to the key distribution center. The key distribution center responds by issuing a temporary ticket that grants the user access to the Kerberos ticket-granting service on a domain controller (or standalone server), which then grants a permanent ticket to that computer. The permanent ticket, called a **service ticket**, is good for the duration of a logon session (or for another period of time specified by the server administrator in the account polices) and enables the computer to access network services beginning with the Logon service. The permanent ticket contains information about the account that is used to identify the account to each network service it requests to use. You might think of a Kerberos ticket as similar to one you would purchase to enter a concert; the ticket is good for the duration of that event and for entry to refreshment and merchandise booths, but you must purchase a new ticket to attend a concert on another date.

When Active Directory is installed, the account policies enable Kerberos, which is the default authentication. If Active Directory is not installed, Kerberos is not included by default in the account policies because the default authentication is through **Windows NT LAN Manager (NTLM)**. NTLM is the authentication used by all versions of Windows NT Server prior to Windows 2000 Server.

The following options are available for configuring Kerberos:

- *Enforce user logon restrictions*—Turns on Kerberos security, which is the default

- *Maximum lifetime for a service ticket*—Determines the maximum amount of time in minutes that a service ticket can be used to continually access a particular service in one service session

- *Maximum lifetime for a user ticket*—Determines the maximum amount of time in hours that a ticket can be used in one continuous session for access to a computer or domain

- *Maximum lifetime for user ticket renewal*—Determines the maximum number of days that the same Kerberos ticket can be renewed each time a user logs on

- *Maximum tolerance for computer clock synchronization*—Determines how long in minutes a client waits until synchronizing its clock with that of the server or Active Directory it is accessing

 If getting users to log off when they go home at night is a problem, limit the maximum lifetime for service ticket or maximum lifetime for user ticket values to a certain number of hours, such as 10 or 12.

 ## Activity 10-5: Configuring Kerberos Security

Time Required: Approximately 10 minutes

Objective: Configure Kerberos in the default domain security policy.

Description: In this activity, you configure the Kerberos policy settings for a company in which people work 10- and 12-hour shifts (setting Kerberos for up to 12 hours).

1. Open the Domain Policy console you created earlier, such as **Domain PolicyJP.msc**.

2. Click **Kerberos Policy** in the tree under Computer Configuration, Windows Settings, Security Settings, and Account Policies.

3. Double-click **Maximum lifetime for service ticket**. Ensure the box for **Define this policy setting** is checked. Enter **720** in the minutes text box. Click **OK**.

4. Click **OK** in the Suggested Value Changes dialog box to also set Maximum lifetime for user ticket to 12 hours. When you are finished, the right pane should look similar to Figure 10-5.

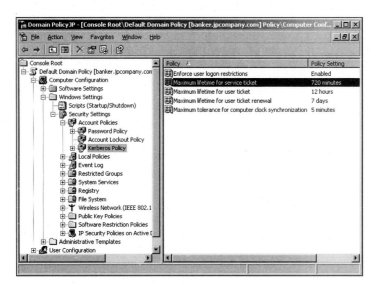

Figure 10-5 Configuring Kerberos Policy

5. Close the console window and click **Yes**.

Establishing Audit Policies

After accounts are set up, you can specify account auditing to track activity associated with those accounts. For example, some organizations need to track security changes to accounts, while others want to track failed logon attempts. Many server administrators track failed logon attempts for the Administrator account, to be sure an intruder is not attempting to access the server. Accounts that access an organization's financial information often are routinely audited to protect their users as well as the information they access. Examples of events that an organization can audit are:

- Account logon (and logoff) events
- Account management
- Directory service access
- Logon (and logoff) events at the local computer
- Object access
- Policy change
- Privilege use
- Process tracking
- System events

10

Each listed activity is audited in terms of the success or failure of the event. For example, if account logon attempts are audited, a record is made each time someone logs on to an account successfully or unsuccessfully (for attempted logons).

 Use auditing sparingly. Each audited event causes a record to be made in the security event log. For example, if you audit all logon attempts of 200 domain accounts, the server log quickly becomes loaded down just from auditing events.

Activity 10-6: Configuring Auditing

Time Required: Approximately 5 minutes

Objective: Configure an audit policy.

Description: Assume that the IT manager in your organization wants to track the logon activity of all accounts in the domain over a 24-hour period. In this activity, you enable account logon auditing to facilitate that request.

1. Open the Domain Policy console you created earlier, such as **Domain PolicyJP.msc**.

2. Click **Audit Policy** in the tree under Computer Configuration, Windows Settings, Security Settings, and Local Policies.

3. Double-click **Audit account logon events**.

4. Click the box for **Define these policy settings**, if it is not already selected.

5. Ensure that both the Success and the Failure boxes are checked, as shown in Figure 10-6.

6. If you make new selections in Steps 4 and 5, click **Apply** to have these take effect immediately, and then click **OK**. If you were concerned about tracking changes to Group Policy, what would you audit?

7. Close the console window and click **Yes**.

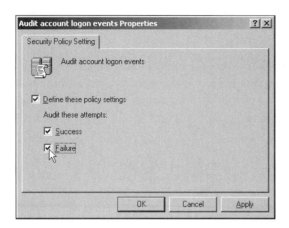

Figure 10-6   Configuring account logon auditing

 If you want to audit activity on a particular object, such as a folder, file or printer, enable Audit object access. Next, in the object's properties, such as the properties for a folder, specify the accounts or groups you want to audit. For a folder, you would do this by right-clicking the folder in My Computer or Windows Explorer and clicking Properties. Click the Security tab, the Advanced button, and the Auditing tab. (See the section "Configure Folder and File Auditing" in Chapter 5).

Configuring User Rights

User rights enable an account or group to perform predefined tasks. The most basic right is the ability to access a server. More advanced rights grant authority to create accounts and manage server functions. User rights are established through setting up the user rights assignment in a Group Policy. You'll have an opportunity to view the actual user rights in Activity 10-7.

The most efficient way to assign user rights is to assign them to groups instead of to individual user accounts. When user rights are assigned to a group, then all user accounts (or groups) that are a member of that group inherit the user rights assigned to the group, making these **inherited rights**.

Activity 10-7: Configuring User Rights

Time Required: Approximately 10 minutes

Objective: Learn how to configure user rights.

Description: This activity enables you to view the existing user rights and restrict local logon access to this server to the Administrator account, the Administrators group, and the Server Operators group. Also, you restrict the ability to shutdown the server to the Administrators group.

1. Open the Domain Policy console you created earlier, such as **Domain PolicyJP.msc**.

2. Click **User Rights Assignment** in the tree under Computer Configuration, Windows Settings, Security Settings, and Local Policies.

3. Scroll through the right pane to view the rights that can be configured, as shown in Figure 10-7.

4. Double-click **Allow log on locally**.

5. Check the box for **Define these policy settings**, if it is not already selected.

6. Click **Add User or Group**.

7. Click the **Browse** button.

8. Click the **Advanced** button.

9. Click **Find Now**.

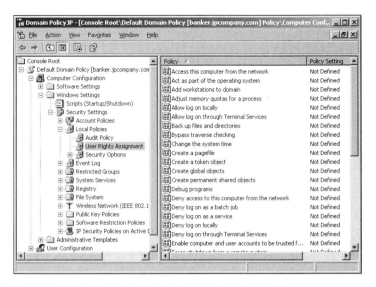

Figure 10-7 User Rights Assignment policy options

10. Hold down the **Ctrl** key and click **Administrator**, **Administrators**, and **Server Operators**. Click **OK**.

11. Click **OK,** and click **OK** again. What now appears in the text box on the Allow log on locally Properties dialog box?

12. Click **OK**. Notice that the Policy Setting column for Allow log on locally now reflects your changes.

13. Double-click **Shut down the system**. Check **Define these policy settings**.

14. Click **Add User or Group**.

15. Click the **Browse** button.

16. Click the **Advanced** button.

17. Click **Find Now**.

18. Double-click **Administrators**, and click **OK**.

19. Click **OK**, and click **OK** again.

20. Close the console window and click **Yes**.

Configuring Security Options

There are over 65 specialized security options that you can configure in the security policies. These options are divided into the following categories:

- Accounts
- Audit
- Devices
- Domain controller
- Domain member
- Interactive logon
- Microsoft network client
- Network access

- Network security
- Recovery console
- Shutdown
- System cryptography
- System objects
- System settings

The options in each of these categories are specialized to the category. For example, if you are concerned about intruders attempting to access the Administrator account, you can use the Accounts: Rename administrator account policy to disguise the Administrator account with another name. In another example, you enforce the use of signed drivers by configuring Devices: Unsigned driver installation behavior. Or, if you have configured specific logon hour controls so that users cannot log on during certain times, then you can force off users who have not logged off after hours by configuring Network security: Force logoff when logon hours expire.

Activity 10-8: Configuring Security Options

Time Required: Approximately 10 minutes

Objective: Examine the Security Options and configure an option.

Description: In this activity, you view all of the Security Options that can be set up as policies. Next, you rename the Guest account to designate it for use by vendors who visit your organization, and then you create a message for users who log on to the server or network.

1. Open the Domain Policy console you created, such as **Domain PolicyJP.msc**.

2. Click **Security Options** in the tree under Computer Configuration, Windows Settings, Security Settings, and Local Policies. You should see a window similar to Figure 10-8.

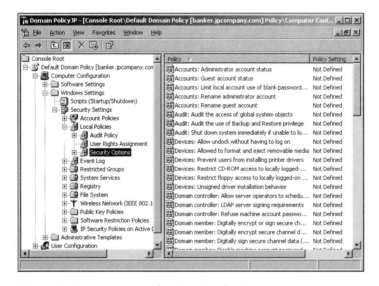

Figure 10-8   Accessing the Security Options

3. Scroll through the options. What option would you use to restrict access of the CD-ROM in the computer so that it can only be accessed by someone logged on locally? How can you set up the system so that it can be shut down without first having someone logged on locally?

4. Double-click **Accounts: Rename guest account**.

5. Check the box for **Define this policy setting**.

6. Enter the name **Vendors** in the text box. Click **OK**.

7. Double-click **Interactive logon: Message text for users attempting to log on**.

8. Check the box for **Define this policy setting in the template**, if it is not already selected.

9. Enter a message in the text box, such as **Welcome to our school's network** (see Figure 10-9).

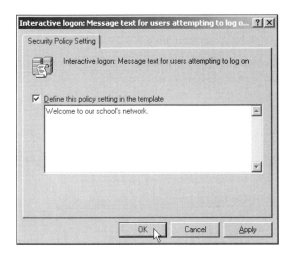

Figure 10-9   Configuring a logon message

10. Click **OK**. Notice how the Policy Setting column is changed for both of the policies you configured.

11. Close the console window and click **Yes**.

Using IP Security Policies

Windows Server 2003 supports the implementation of **IP security (IPSec)**, which is a set of IP-based secure communications and encryption standards created through the Internet Engineering Task Force (IETF). When an IPSec communication begins between two computers, the computers first exchange certificates to authenticate the receiver and sender. Next, data is encrypted at the NIC of the sending computer as it is formatted into an IP packet, which consists of a header containing transmission control information, the actual data, and a footer with error-correction information. IPSec can provide security for all TCP/IP-based application and communications protocols, including FTP and HTTP, which are used in Internet transmissions. IPSec policies for a domain can be managed from the Domain Security Policy tool on the Administrative Tools menu or through the IP Security Policy Management Snap-in in the MMC (for sites, domains, OUs, and the local computer). A computer that is configured to use IPSec communication can function in any of three roles:

- *Client (Respond Only)*—When Windows Server 2003 is contacted by a client using IPSec, it responds by using IPSec communication.

- *Server (Request Security)*—When Windows Server 2003 is first contacted or when it initiates a communication, it uses IPSec by default. If the responding client does not support IPSec, Windows Server 2003 switches to the clear mode, which does not employ IPSec.

- *Secure Server (Require Security)*—Windows Server 2003 only responds using IPSec communication, which means that communication via any account and with any client is secured through strict IPSec enforcement.

IPSec security policies can be established through the IP Security Policies Management Snap-in so that specific security standards apply to all computers that log on to a domain in Active Directory. When you right-click IP Security Policies in the MMC and click Create IP Security Policy, Windows Server 2003 starts the IP Security Policy Wizard to help guide you through the steps in creating a security policy. A security policy consists of your specifications for what security methods to use for client and server communication, what IP filters to apply to communications, and which domain or domains are affected by the policy.

Activity 10-9: Configuring IPSec

Time Required: Approximately 5 minutes

Objective: Configure IPSec.

Description: In this activity, you learn how to configure a server to use IPSec.

1. Open the Domain Policy console you created, such as **Domain PolicyJP.msc**.

2. Click **IP Security Policies on Active Directory (*domainname*)** in the tree under Computer Configuration, Windows Settings, and Security Settings (see Figure 10-10).

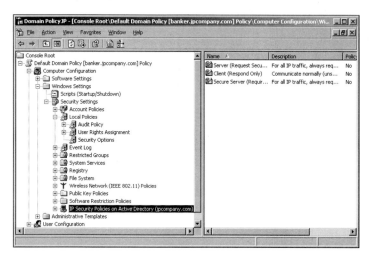

Figure 10-10   Configuring IPSec

3. In the right pane, double-click **Server (Request Security)**. On the Rules tab are listed the IP Security rules already configured (see Figure 10-11). To create a new rule, you would click the Add button to start the Create IP Security Rule Wizard.

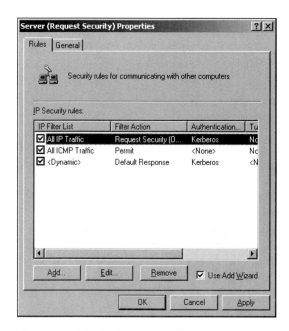

Figure 10-11   IP Security rules

4. Double-click **All IP Traffic** to view the properties of a rule that is already created.

5. Click each tab to view the properties. When you view the Filter Action tab, what Filter Action is selected? On the Connection Type tab, what connection types can be selected? What tab would you use to configure IPSec for tunneling, such as over a VPN? What Authentication Methods are used?

6. Click **Cancel**.

7. Click the **General** tab on the Server (Request Security) Properties dialog box.

8. Notice the description text box.

9. Click **Cancel**.

10. In the console window, right-click **Server (Request Security)**, point to **All Tasks**, and click **Assign**. This policy is now assigned so that it takes effect on this server. (Check with your instructor about whether to leave it assigned. You can follow similar steps to unassign the policy.)

11. Close the console window and click **Yes**.

MANAGING SECURITY USING THE SECURITY TEMPLATES SNAP-IN

Windows Server 2003 offers the Security Templates Snap-in for the MMC, which enables you to create one or more security templates to house in Active Directory. This snap-in enables you to set up security to govern the following:

- Account policies
- Local policies
- Event log tracking policies
- Group restrictions
- Service access security
- Registry security
- File system security

This tool is particularly useful when you have multiple Group Policies to maintain or when you have multiple OUs, but many of those OUs share the same Group Policy. For example, if you have 20 OUs set up in a domain and use one security policy for eight OUs, a different one for eight OUs, and still another one for four OUs, then you would create three security templates.

When you are ready to create a new security template, use these general steps:

1. Make sure there is no default security template that already matches what you want to do (if there is, use the default security template).

2. Make sure that the **Group Policy Object Editor** and **Security Templates** Snap-ins are installed in the MMC.

3. Create a security template by clicking the main folder under Security Templates in the MMC (such as \Windows\security\templates), clicking the Action menu, and clicking New Template. Enter a name for the new template, and click **OK**. Double-click the template, and configure the settings you want.

4. Import your newly created template to an existing Group Policy by installing the MMC's **Security Configuration and Analysis** Snap-in, right-click that snap-in, open a database or create a new one, right-click **Security Configuration and Analysis** in the tree, click **Import Template**, click the template configuration file you created, and click **Open**. (If you create a

new database, you will automatically be prompted to import a template.) Right-click the **Security Configuration and Analysis** Snap-in again, click **Configure Computer Now**, and click **OK**.

When you apply a security template, it incrementally updates the Group Policy object to which it is applied.

There are several default security templates that come with Windows Server 2003, which you can import to an existing Group Policy, instead of creating a new security template:

- *compatws*—Provides compatible workstation or server security settings for computers running Windows Server 2003 and Windows NT

- *DC security*—Default security for DCs that is updated beyond basic domain controller security

- *hisecdc*—Sets maximum (high security) protection for domain controllers running Windows Server 2003

- *hisecws*—Sets maximum (high security) protection for workstations accessing Windows Server 2003

- *rootsec*—Consists of the default security settings used by the root domain in a tree

- *securedc*—Provides the recommended security on DCs, excluding files, folder, and registry key security

- *securews*—Provides the recommended security on client workstations, excluding files, folder, and registry key security

- *setup security*—Provides "out of the box" security which leaves most security settings undefined.

CONFIGURING CLIENT SECURITY USING POLICIES IN WINDOWS SERVER 2003

You can customize desktop and other settings for client computers that access Windows Server 2003 networks. There are several advantages for customizing settings used by clients, including improvements in security and providing a consistent working environment in an organization. The settings are customized by configuring policies on the Windows 2003 servers that the clients access. When the client logs onto the server or the network, the policies are applied to the client.

For example, you can configure a policy that disables Control Panel or specific Control Panel options on particular clients or all clients. Another policy might be configured to ensure that all clients have an icon on their desktop that starts the same application in the same way. If a client inadvertently deletes the icon, it is reapplied the next time the client logs on. In some organizations it is important to store sensitive information on a server to enhance security and conformity of use. If this is the case, you can use folder redirection, so that a folder appears on the clients' desktops that really points to a secure folder on the server. There are literally hundreds of ways to configure clients through modifying group policies in Windows Server 2003.

Manually Configuring Policies for Clients

You always have the option to manually configure policies that apply to clients, in order to accomplish specific purposes. For example, sometimes the management of an organization makes a decision to standardize a specific item, such as the use of certain printers or the implementation of specific software. In other cases, there may be a decision to prevent users from having access to specific functions, because they are a security risk or a distraction.

You can manually configure one or more policies that apply to clients by using the Group Policy Object Editor Snap-in. With this tool, you customize the desktop settings for client computers by using the Administrative Templates object under User Configuration in a Group Policy object (see Figure 10-12).

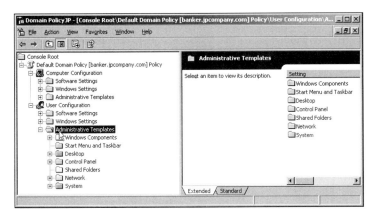

Figure 10-12   Group Policies for clients

Table 10-1 presents very general descriptions of the Administrative Templates options under User Configuration.

10

Table 10-1   Options for configuring administrative templates settings under user configuration

Component	Description
Windows Components	Controls access to installed software such as NetMeeting, Internet Explorer, Windows Explorer, MMC, Task Scheduler, Windows Installer, Windows Media Player, and many others
Start Menu & Taskbar	Controls the ability to configure the Start menu and Taskbar, the ability to access program groups from the Start menu, and the ability to use Start menu options including Run, Search, Settings, and Documents
Desktop	Controls access to desktop functions including the icons for My Network Places, Internet Explorer, the ability to configure the Active Desktop, and the ability to configure Active Directory searches
Control Panel	Controls access to Control Panel functions such as Add/Remove programs, Display, Printers, and Regional Settings; plus the ability to disable Control Panel altogether, or to hide or display only specific Control Panel icons
Network	Controls access to offline files and the ability to configure network access via Network and Dial-up Connections (Windows 2003) or Network Connections (Windows XP and Server 2003)
System	Controls access to Logon/Logoff capabilities, scripts, Task Manager functions, Change Password, Group Policy refresh rate, slow link dettection, and other system functions

Activity 10-10: Configuring Policies to Apply to Clients

Time Required: Approximately 10 minutes

Objective: Learn how to configure a Group Policy to apply to Windows Server 2003 clients.

Description: This activity gives you experience configuring policies to apply to clients. For this project, assume that your organization has decided that its home page should appear in Internet Explorer for every user. Also, there have been problems as a result of users configuring their own computers, causing the user support group to work overtime on unnecessary problems, plus this has caused some security breaches. In response, the organization's management has decided to prohibit access to Control Panel on every client computer.

1. Open the Domain Policy console you created, such as **Domain PolicyJP.msc**.

2. Double-click **User Configuration** in the tree to display the elements under it.

3. Double-click **Administrative Templates** in the tree to display its contents.

4. Click **Windows Components**. What folders appear in the right pane?

5. Double-click **Internet Explorer** in the right pane to view the settings you can configure (see Figure 10-13).

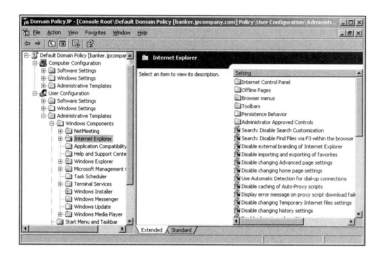

Figure 10-13   Internet Explorer policies

6. Double-click "**Disable changing home page settings**". Click the **Explain** tab to see what this setting does. Click the **Setting** tab. Click the option button for **Enabled**, and click **OK**.

7. In the left pane under User Configuration and Administrative Templates, click **Control Panel**.

8. In the right pane, double-click **Prohibit access to the Control Panel**.

9. Click the option button for **Enabled**, and click **OK**.

10. In the left pane, click each of the following folders under Administrative Templates that you have not yet opened to view their contents: **Start Menu and Taskbar**, **Desktop**, **Shared Folders**, **Network**, and **System**.

11. Close the console window and click **Yes**.

Using Preconfigured Administrative Templates

The settings in Table 10-1 can be set as a group through the use of preconfigured administrative templates already provided in Windows Server 2003. Table 10-2 describes the templates that are preconfigured.

Table 10-2   Administrative templates included with Windows Server 2003

Template	Purpose
Common.adm	Manages desktop settings that are common to all of Windows 95/98/NT
Conf.adm	Used to standardize NetMeeting setups on clients for common communications
Inetcorp.adm	Used for dial-up, language, and temporary Internet files settings in Internet Explorer
Inetres.adm	Default for managing Internet Explorer in Windows 2000 Professional clients

Table 10-2   Administrative templates included with Windows Server 2003 (continued)

Template	Purpose
Inetset.adm	Used for advanced settings and additional Internet properties in Internet Explorer
System.adm	Default for managing Windows 2000 Professional and Windows XP Professional clients
Windows.adm	Manages Windows 95 and 98 clients
Winnt.adm	Manages Windows NT 4.0 clients
Wmplayer.adm	Used to standardize Windows Media Player client configurations
Waua.sam	Manages how Windows Updates are performed through the Internet

If there is a combination of Windows 95/98/NT/2000/XP clients, then you likely want to use a matching combination of administrative templates, such as Common.adm and System.adm, for example. Common.adm provides desktop configuration for Windows 95/98/NT clients and System.adm provides desktop configuration for Windows 2000 and Window XP clients. You can do this because the Administrative Templates setting under User Configuration enables you to add or remove multiple templates in one Group Policy (see Figure 10-14).

Figure 10-14   Adding or removing administrative templates

Activity 10-11: Installing an Administrative Template

Time Required: Approximately 5 minutes

Objective: Learn how to install an administrative template.

Description: In this activity, you learn how to add the Winnt.adm administrative template to the default domain Group Policy.

1. Open the Domain Policy console you created, such as **Domain PolicyJP.msc**.

2. Under User Configuration in the tree, right-click **Administrative Templates**.

3. Click **Add/Remove Templates** (see Figure 10-14). What templates are already added? Record your observations.

4. Click the **Add** button in the Add/Remove Templates dialog box.

5. Double-click **winnt.adm**. (Click **Yes**, if you see a confirmation box because the template is already installed.) For what clients does this template apply?

6. Click **Close**.

7. Close the console window and click **Yes**.

Publishing and Assigning Software

For some organizations, one of the most important concerns is that their users employ the same software with the same software settings for the sake of productivity and security. This can be particularly important for applications that have frequent version changes, such as Microsoft Word or Excel. Another important element of this issue is to make it possible for users to deploy this software without sending a user support professional to configure each workstation. There are several advantages to this approach. One is that users can be more productive, because they use the same software in the same way, whether they are on their own computer or someone else's. Also, because all users have the same software setup, there is a large body of individuals who can support their colleagues. These factors are great for ensuring user productivity. Another advantage is that data security weaknesses caused by users installing and configuring their own software are reduced. Further, the load on user support professionals is eased, because these professionals do not have to individually install software or troubleshoot problems created by users who install their own software.

Windows Server 2003 addresses all of these issues through the ability to configure polices for client software use. There are two very effective ways to control client software use: publishing applications and assigning applications. **Publishing applications** (or software) involves setting up software through a Group Policy so that clients install the software from a central distribution server using the Add or Remove Programs (in Windows XP or Windows Server 2003) or the Add/Remove Programs (in Windows 2000) option in Control Panel. **Assigning applications** involves configuring a policy so that a particular software application is started automatically through a desktop shortcut, through a menu selection, or by clicking a file that has a specific file extension (such as starting Microsoft Excel when the user opens a file with the .xls extension).

Activity 10-12: Configuring Software Installation

Time Required: Approximately 5 minutes

Objective: Learn where to set up software installation in a Group Policy.

Description: In this activity, you view where to configure software to be published or assigned.

1. Open the Domain Policy console you created, such as **Domain PolicyJP.msc**.

2. Under User Configuration in the tree, double-click **Software Settings**.

3. Right-click **Software Installation**, and then click **Properties**.

4. Make sure that the **General** tab is displayed (see Figure 10-15). Notice that you can use the Default package location box to specify the location of the software that users install, which can be on this server or on a different server in the network. Also, among the New packages parameters, there are options to Publish or Assign software.

5. Click each of the **Advanced**, **File Extension**, and **Categories** tabs to view the properties that can be configured on those tabs.

6. Click **Cancel**.

7. To view from where to set up published or assigned software, right-click **Software Installation** (under User Configuration, Software Settings) point to **New**, and notice the **Package** option. If you were publishing or assigning software, you would click **Package**, use the Open dialog box to locate the installer package for the software, click **Open**, select **Publish** or **Assigned**, click **OK**, and complete the setup steps. (Besides Publish and Assigned, you can also select the Advanced option to configure specialized Published or Assigned options as well as specialized options in the software.)

8. Click in an open location on your desktop to close the shortcut menus.

9. Close the console window and click **Yes**.

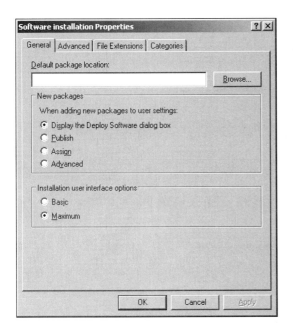

Figure 10-15   Software installation Properties dialog box

Resultant Set of Policy

A new feature included with Windows Server 2003, called **Resultant Set of Policy (RSoP)** is used to make the implementation and troubleshooting of Group Policies much simpler for an administrator. When multiple Group Policies are applied, configuration settings and conflicts can be difficult to track. RSoP can query the existing policies that are in place and then provide the results.

RSoP supports two modes: planning and logging. Planning mode generates a report and provides the result of proposed policy changes. Logging mode generates a report based on the current policies in place and provides the resulting policy settings.

Activity 10-13: Using the Resultant Set of Policy Tool

Time Required: Approximately 10 minutes

Objective: Learn how to use the Resultant Set of Policy tool.

Description: In this activity, you create an RSoP report using the logging mode to review the policies you have set in this chapter.

1. Click **Start** and click **Run**.

2. Enter **mmc** in the Open box, and click **OK**.

3. Maximize the console windows, if necessary.

4. Click the **File** menu, and click **Add/Remove Snap-in**.

5. Click the **Add** button.

6. Double-click **Resultant Set of Policy** in the Snap-in text box.

7. Click **Close**, and then click **OK**.

8. Right-click **Resultant Set of Policy** in the tree, and click **Generate RSoP Data**.

9. Click **Next** after the Resultant Set of Policy Wizard starts. What two modes can you select to use on the Mode Selection dialog box?

10. Click the option button for **Logging mode**, if it is not selected already. Click **Next**.

11. Ensure the option button for **This computer** is selected, and click **Next**.

12. For this activity, use the default settings for User Selection, which are **Display policy settings for** and **Current user**. Click **Next**.

13. Review the summary of the selections you have made, and click **Next**. It takes a few moments for the tool to create the report.

14. Click **Finish**. What are the options now displayed in the right pane?

15. In the right pane, double-click **Computer Configuration**.

16. Double-click **Windows Settings**.

17. Double-click **Security Settings**. You see the security settings options displayed in the right pane as shown in Figure 10-16.

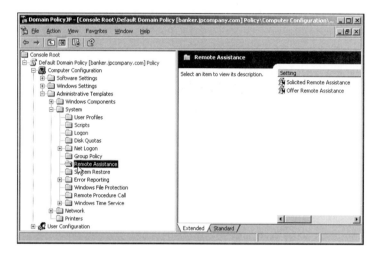

Figure 10-16   RSoP report for security settings

18. Double-click **Account Policies,** and then double-click **Password Policy**. You should see a report of the same policies you configured earlier in this chapter for the domain, with no conflicts.

19. Close the console window, and click **No** (to not save the settings).

CONFIGURING THE ENCRYPTING FILE SYSTEM

As you learned in Chapter 5, when you deploy NTFS you can use the encrypt attribute to protect folders and files, enabling only the user who encrypts the folder or file to read it. An encrypted folder or file uses Microsoft's Encrypting File System (EFS), configuring a unique private encryption key that is associated with the user account that encrypted the folder or file. This capability might be used at a government facility that has servers that house top-secret data. If a hard drive is stolen or discarded because it is malfunctioning, data on the hard drive is protected from unauthorized users.

In Chapter 5, you learned that you can set the encrypt attribute on a folder or file through working with that folder's or file's properties. Another option that you learn in this section is to use the cipher command from the Command Prompt window. You can use the cipher command with the parameters listed in Table 10-3. If you do not specify any parameters with the command, it displays the encryption status of the current folder.

Table 10-3 Cipher command-line parameters

Parameter	Description
/?	Lists the cipher commands
/e	Encrypts the specified folder so any files added to the folder are encrypted
/d	Decrypts the contents of the specified folder and sets the folder so that any files added to the folder are not encrypted
/s	Used with other cipher options so that they are applied to the contents of the current folder and the contents of subfolders under it
/a	Executes the specified operation on all files and folders
/i	Proceeds with the encryption, ignoring reported errors
/f	Forces the encryption operation on all folders and files (ignores folders and files currently encrypted)
/q	Generates a short-version encryption report
/h	Enables you to view which folders and files use the hidden or system attributes
/k	The account employing cipher is provided a new encryption key, meaning that previous keys associated with other accounts are no longer valid—use with extreme caution
/n	Use with the /u option so that encryption keys are not modified, but so that you can view the currently encrypted folders and files
/u	Updates the cipher user's encryption key
/r	Used to invoke a recovery agent key so that the server administrator can set up a recovery policy
/w	Purges data from disk space that is flagged as unused (but which still contains data that could be recovered)
/x	Copies encryption key and certificate data to a file that is encrypted for use by the cipher user

10

Activity 10-14: Using the Cipher Command

Time Required: Approximately 10 minutes

Objective: Use the cipher command in the Command Prompt window.

Description: This activity enables you to use the cipher command to view which folders and files are encrypted on your system. Use the cipher command on a volume formatted with NTFS.

1. Click **Start** and click **My Computer**.

2. Double-click an NTFS-formatted volume on which you can create a folder, such as **Local Disk (C:)**.

3. Click the **File** menu, point to **New**, and click **Folder**.

4. Type Encrypt plus your initials, such as **EncryptJP**. Press **Enter**.

5. Right-click the folder you created, and then click **Properties**.

6. On the **General** tab, click **Advanced**.

7. Click **Encrypt contents to secure data**. Click **OK**.

8. Click **OK** in the folder's Properties dialog box, and close the drive window, such as C:\.

9. Click **Start**, point to **All Programs**, point to **Accessories**, and click **Command Prompt**.

10. At the prompt, type **cd ** and press **Enter** to change to the root directory, if necessary.

11. Type **cipher** and press **Enter**. Do you see any files or folders that are encrypted, as signified by a capital "E"? How do you know if a file or folder is not encrypted?

12. Type **exit** and press **Enter** to close the Command Prompt window. (Ask your instructor about whether or not to delete the folder you created.)

CHAPTER SUMMARY

❏ A Group Policy enables you to standardize how people use server and client computers on a network.

❏ Security policies are part of a Group Policy and are configured to protect users and resources.

❏ Configure account policies to apply to OUs, domains, sites, or local computers, such as password policies, account lockout policies, and Kerberos authentication policies.

❏ Use audit policies to track how resources are accessed, such as folders, files, or user accounts.

❏ User rights policies enable you to create specific security controls over privileges and logon access.

❏ Security options are specialized policies for accounts, auditing, devices, domain controllers, logon, clients, network access, network security, and other activities.

❏ Use the Security Templates Snap-in to apply default security settings or to create different Group Policy objects for different OUs, domains, or sites.

❏ For better control over the activities of clients, manually configure administrative templates or apply preconfigured administrative templates (or both).

❏ Publish and assign applications to manage how clients use them.

❏ Use the Resultant Set of Policy Snap-in to plan and troubleshoot Group Policies.

❏ Fine-tune the use of the Encrypting File System by using the cipher command in the Command Prompt window.

KEY TERMS

assigning applications (or software) — Involves configuring a Group Policy so that a particular software application is automatically started through a desktop shortcut, through a menu selection, or by clicking a file that has a specific file extension.

Group Policy — A set of policies that govern security, configuration, and a wide range of other settings for objects within containers in Active Directory.

Group Policy object (GPO) — An object in Active Directory that contains Group Policy settings for a site, domain, OU, or local computer.

Kerberos — A security system developed by the Massachusetts Institute of Technology to enable two parties on an open network to communicate without interception from an intruder, by creating a unique encryption key for each communication session.

inherited rights — User rights that are assigned to a group and that automatically apply to all members of that group.

IP security (IPSec) — A set of IP-based secure communications and encryption standards created through the Internet Engineering Task Force (IETF).

publishing applications (or software) — Involves setting up specific software through a Group Policy so that Windows 2000/XP/2003 clients install the software from a central distribution server using the Add or Remove Programs or the Add/Remove Programs option in Control Panel.

Resultant Set of Policy (RSoP) — A Windows Server 2003 tool that enables you to produce reports about proposed or current Group Policy settings for the purpose of planning and troubleshooting, when there are multiple Group Policies in use (such as for OUs and domains).

service ticket — In Kerberos security, a permanent ticket good for the duration of a logon session (or for another period of time specified by the server administrator in the account polices) that enables the computer to access network services beginning with the Logon service.

system policy — A grouping of user account and computer parameters that can be configured in Windows NT 4.0 enabling some control of the desktop environment and specific client configuration settings.

system policy editor — Used to configure system policy settings in Windows NT 4.0 and is also available in Windows 2000 Server, but not in Windows Server 2003.

Windows NT LAN Manger (NTLM) — An authentication protocol used in Windows NT Server 3.5, 3.51, and 4.0 that is retained in Windows 2000 Server and Windows Server 2003 for backward compatibility for clients that cannot support Kerberos, such as MS-DOS and Windows 3.1x.

REVIEW QUESTIONS

1. In your organization, the creation of accounts is performed by administrative assistants in each department. Account holders in one of the departments report that properties of their accounts sometimes change without notice and the financial auditors are concerned. Which of the following is the best course of action for now?

   a. Reconfigure the account policies once a week.

   b. Set up a policy for auditing logon and logoff events.

   c. Configure a policy to audit account management.

   d. Change the administrative templates of each department's administrative assistant.

2. One of your server operators has an account that does not enable her to log on to servers. What might you troubleshoot?

   a. the length of that server operator's password

   b. the authentication protocol associated with the server operator's user account

   c. whether or not EAP is configured on that server

   d. whether the server operator's account has the right log on locally

3. Your management has decided that users should change their passwords every month. Is there a way you can enforce this?

   a. Configure all client's desktops to Require a new password every month.

   b. Configure the Maximum password age policy in the password policies.

   c. Set up an expiration date on each account's properties.

   d. There is no way to honor this decision; management should have first consulted with you prior to their meeting.

4. Which of the following are preconfigured templates? (Choose all that apply.)

   a. System.adm

   b. Win98.adm

   c. WinXP.adm

   d. Internetsecure.adm

5. One department in your organization has several users who reconfigure an authoring program or sometimes uninstall it altogether. These actions cause a lot of needless extra work on the part of the organization's user support professionals. What can you do?

   a. Create a Group Policy for the OU in which that department's accounts are located, and assign the authoring program.

   b. Use the Windows Server 2003 time accounting software to track the user support calls to that department and charge them for each call.

   c. Disable Control Panel for all of that department's users.

   d. Change the attribute on each user's Programs Folder, so it is read-only.

10

6. Use the _____ tool to configure security for the domain.

   a. Domain Security Policy

   b. Security Configuration

   c. Active Directory Domain Security

   d. Dcpromo

7. Which of the following is (are) a mode that you can select when using the Resultant Set of Policy Tool? (Choose all that apply.)

   a. temp

   b. configure

   c. logging

   d. planning

8. How can you discourage intruders from trying to access users' accounts?

   a. Set up an account firewall.

   b. Configure account lockout.

   c. Turn off Kerberos and use NTLM instead.

   d. Configure the user's NIC for the monitor policy.

9. When you configure the maximum lifetime for a service ticket in the Kerberos policies, what else should you configure?

   a. start/stop time

   b. maximum tolerance for clocking certification

   c. ticket ID

   d. maximum lifetime for user ticket

10. A Kerberos policy is a example of a(n) _____.

    a. account policy

    b. audit policy

    c. permission

    d. access list attribute

11. _____ is used instead of Group Policy in Windows NT Server to configure basic computer and account controls.

    a. The Domain Users tool

    b. System policy

    c. WINS

    d. The Autoexec.bat file

12. For which of the following can you set a Group Policy? (Choose all that apply.)

    a. folder

    b. subfolder

    c. site

    d. administrative tool

13. You have lectured users about reusing the same passwords, but no on seems to be listening. This is a major security problem, because users have often shared their passwords with other users in the past. How can you best solve this problem?

    a. Randomly rename user accounts.

    b. Enable the password encryption policy.

    c. Fine users for sharing their passwords.

    d. Deploy the enforce password history policy.

14. Which of the following are categories of security options policies? (Choose all that apply.)

    a. Devices

    b. Network security

    c. Configuration tools

    d. Startup

15. Sometimes members of the Server Operators group decide to connect printers to certain servers for their convenience and load drivers for those printers to make them work. What steps might you take, so that only the Administrators group has this option?

    a. Configure the block serial ports policy.

    b. Configure the load and unload device drivers user rights policy so that it is only enabled for the Administrators group.

    c. Configure the share objects sharing policy so that it is only enabled for the Administrators group.

    d. Set the serial ports policy so that only the Administrators group is the owner of the policy.

16. Your assistant wants to audit all kinds of activities on a server, from every time someone accesses the server to every time a file or printer is used. What is your opinion?

    a. Auditing all of these activities is vital for good server security.

    b. Use auditing sparingly; it creates high maintenance for the security logs.

    c. It is not possible to audit logon events.

    d. Auditing access to all processes should be added to the list.

17. How often should server administrators consider changing their passwords?

    a. These particular passwords do not need to be changed, because there is a default policy to change them automatically and then notify the administrators.

    b. Because it is so important to remember an administrator's password there is a fixed policy that prevents these passwords from being changed.

    c. About every month or sooner.

    d. Each time a Group Policy is modified.

18. Which of the following is a Group Policy category above Software Settings? (Choose all that apply.)

    a. Computer Configuration

    b. Network Security

    c. Certificate Key Security

    d. Software Installation

19. Group Policy settings are stored in _____.

    a. GUIDs

    b. access containers

    c. GPOs

    d. the forest controller (FC) only

20. Which of the following are choices for configuring IPSec policies? (Choose all that apply.)

    a. Server (Request Security)

    b. OS (Demand Security)

    c. Client (Respond Only)

    d. Active Directory (Authenticate)

10

21. The _____ Command Prompt window command is used to configure the Encrypting File System.

    a. encode

    b. encrypt

    c. secure

    d. cipher

22. The Administrative Templates policies in User Configuration enable you to _____.

    a. permanently set the home page when users access Internet Explorer

    b. configure Kerberos policies

    c. secure system services

    d. configure user rights policies

23. With which file system can you use the Encrypting File System?

    a. NTFS

    b. FAT64

    c. CDFS

    d. OS/10

24. Which of the following is (are) a security template that comes with Windows Server 2003? (Choose all that apply.)

    a. hisecws

    b. compatws

    c. dc security

    d. securedc

25. Use the _____ Snap-in to import a newly created security template to an existing Group Policy.

    a. Resultant Set of Policy

    b. Security Configuration and Analysis

    c. Set Template

    d. Domain Controller Policy

CASE PROJECTS

Case Project Background

Anderson Elevators is an Atlanta-based company that designs, manufactures, and installs elevators for all types of buildings. They have converted their computer operations from a mainframe computer to using 10 computers deploying Windows Server 2003. Their Information Systems Department has installed the servers in a test environment, but plan to go live soon. There will be over 500 users accessing these servers in four departments: Administration, Marketing, Operations/Warehousing, and Research. They have already created OUs for each department and have installed Active Directory. They are using you, through Bayside IT Services, to provide assistance in addressing security issues.

Case Project 10-1: Understanding Security Policies

The Information Systems Department has heard of security policies, but is not sure what these entail. They ask you to create a report that can be used as a resource by the department that explains the main components of security policies.

Case Project 10-2: Tools for Configuring Security Policies

After you begin work on your report, the Information Systems Department asks that you include information about the Windows Server 2003 tools that can be used to configure security policies. Write this into your report so that members of the department can use it as a resource when they are configuring security policies.

Case Project 10-3: Configuring Clients from the Server

The management of Anderson Elevators wants to use the Windows Server 2003 environment to enforce certain client access issues on their Windows XP Professional clients who will access the servers. Specifically, the Information Systems Department wants you to prepare a supplementary report on whether or not it is possible to:

❑ Prevent Windows XP Professional clients from using Control Panel's Add or Remove Programs option on their computers.

❑ Ensure that all Windows XP Professional clients start the most recent version of Microsoft Excel when they click on a file with an .xls extension.

❑ Prevent users from changing information about their Network Connections.

❑ Remove the My Music icon from the Start menu.

For any of these that are possible, include general instructions for the Information Systems Department about how to accomplish them.

10

Case Project 10-4: Solving an Encryption Problem

One of the server administrators, a member of the Information Systems Department, was playing around with features and managed to invoke the Encrypting File System on some of the folders in the root directory. They send you a frantic e-mail asking you to respond with an e-mail explaining how they can: (1) determine which folders are encrypted and (2) unencrypt the folders.

11

SERVER AND NETWORK MONITORING

After reading this chapter and completing the exercises, you will be able to:

♦ Understand the importance of server monitoring

♦ Monitor server services

♦ Use Task Manager to monitor processes and performance

♦ Use System Monitor to monitor all types of system elements

♦ Configure performance logs and alerts to monitor a system

♦ Use Network Monitor to monitor network performance

♦ Use the SNMP Service for network monitoring and management

The best approach to server and network management is prevention through good practices. Besides careful installation and configuration, one of the best practices for keeping a server and network in top condition is deploying monitoring tools. There are several advantages to monitoring. One is that through monitoring you gain a solid idea of what conditions are typical for your server and network, so you are quickly aware if a problem develops. Another advantage is that monitoring enables you to take steps early to address a problem before it affects how users conduct business. If you have a server that needs more memory, for instance, monitoring enables you to spot the problem and add memory as a preventative measure.

In this chapter you'll learn why server monitoring is important and how to develop a strategy for establishing a baseline of performance. You will learn about important system services and how to monitor the services. You'll use Task Manager for monitoring applications, processes, and server performance information. Also, you will find out about the robust system monitoring features of System Monitor, enabling you to generate all types of server performance statistics and information. Next, you'll learn how to monitor a network using the Network Monitoring tool. Finally, you will learn how to install and configure Simple Network Management Protocol (SNMP) for network management and performance monitoring.

INTRODUCTION TO SERVER MONITORING

Server monitoring is performed for several reasons. One reason is to establish a baseline of performance so problems are more easily identified when they occur. It may be difficult to diagnose a problem or determine if there is a resource shortage unless you first know what performance is typical for your server. Other reasons to monitor are to prevent problems before they occur and to diagnose existing problems to resolve them. Monitoring enables you to pinpoint problems and identify solutions, such as when tracking disk errors and replacing a hard disk before it fails.

The most important way to get to know your server is to use monitoring tools to establish normal server performance characteristics. This is a process that involves establishing benchmarks. **Benchmarks**, or **baselines**, provide a basis for comparing data collected during problem situations with data showing normal performance conditions. This creates a way to diagnose problems and identify components that need to be upgraded or replaced.

The best way to get a feel for a server's performance is to establish a baseline, and then frequently monitor server performance by comparing the data collected to that in the baseline. Performance indicators can be confusing at first, so the more time you spend observing them, the better you'll understand them.

Sample benchmarks that you might acquire are:

- Benchmarks of disk, CPU, memory, and network response before releasing a new operating system, server hardware, or a complex application to users
- Slow, typical, and heavy usage of disk, CPU, memory, and other server resources for each server
- Slow, typical, and heavy usage of the combined network and server resources
- Increase in use of network and server resources at specific intervals, such as every six to twelve months

In the sections that follow, you'll explore all types of techniques to monitor resources for benchmarks, to help avoid problems, and to fix problems as they occur.

MONITORING SERVER SERVICES

Servers are always running a number of services. The exact number of services depends on the number and types of components you have installed. Table 11-1 describes some of the services typically in use in Windows Server 2003.

Table 11-1   Sample Windows Server 2003 services

Service	Description
Alerter	Sends notification of alerts or problems on the server to users designated by the network administrator
Computer Browser	Keeps a listing of computers and domain resources to be accessed
Event Log	Enables server events to be logged for later review or diagnosis in case problems occur
File Replication Service	Replicates the Active Directory elements on multiple DCs when Active Directory is installed
Intersite Messaging	Transfers messages between different Windows Server 2003 sites
IPSec Services	Enables IPSec security
Kerberos Key Distribution Center	Enables Kerberos authentication and the server as a center from which to issue Kerberos security keys and tickets
License Logging	Enables the monitoring of server and other licensing

Table 11-1   Sample Windows Server 2003 services (continued)

Service	Description
Logical Disk Manager	Monitors for disk problems, such as a disk that is nearly full
Messenger	Handles messages sent for administrative purposes
Net Logon	Maintains logon services such as verifying users who are logging onto the server or a domain
Plug and Play	Enables automatic detection and installation of new hardware devices or devices that have changed
Print Spooler	Enables print spooling
Protected Storage	Enables data and services to be stored and protected by using private key authentication
Remote Procedure Call (RPC)	Provides Remote Procedure Call Services
Remote Procedure Call (RPC) Locator	Used in communications with clients using remote procedure calls to locate available programs to run
Remote Registry	Enables the registry to be managed remotely
Removable Storage	Enables management of removable storage media, such as tapes, CD-RWs, and Zip and Jaz drives
Security Accounts Manager	Keeps information about user accounts and their related security setup
Server	A critical service that supports shared objects, log on services, print services, and remote procedure calls
System Event Notification	Enables the detection and reporting of important system events, such as a hardware or network problem
Task Scheduler	Used to start a program at a specified time and works with the software Task Scheduler
TCP/IP NetBIOS Helper	Activated when TCP/IP is installed and used to enable NetBIOS name resolution and NetBIOS network transport
Uninterruptible Power Supply	Used with a UPS to supply power to the server during power failures
Windows Time	Enables updating the clock
Workstation	Enables network communications and access by clients over the network

11

Accessing Server Services

You can access server services as one of the elements in the tree of the Computer Management tool (see Figure 11-1), which is opened in several ways:

- From the Administrative Tools menu on Control Panel
- As an MMC snap-in
- By right-clicking My Computer (in the Start menu) and clicking Manage

Services are displayed in the right pane of the window, which contains five columns. The Name column shows services listed alphabetically. A short description of each service is provided in the Description column. The Status column indicates the current status of the service as follows:

- Started shows that the service is running.
- Paused means that the service is started, but is not available to users.
- A blank means that the service is halted or has not been started.

The Startup Type column shows how a service is started when the computer boots. Most services are started automatically when the server is booted. Some services are started manually because they may not be needed until a given time. Services that are not set to start automatically or manually are disabled. The Log On As column specifies the account that the service is running under. Most services log on to a Local System account.

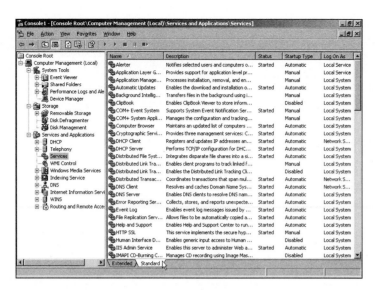

Figure 11-1   Computer Management Snap-in

Solving a Problem with a Service

When you experience a problem on a server that is associated with a service, check the status of the service to make sure that it is started or set to start automatically. You can start, stop, pause, resume, or restart a service by right-clicking it and clicking any of these options. For example, occasionally a service does not start properly when the server is booted or hangs while the server is running, such as the Print Spooler Service. The Services tool provides a way to monitor this situation. If the Print Spooler shows that it is started, but you decide to restart it, right-click the service, and click Restart (keep in mind, though, that you will lose print jobs in the print queue).

Use the Stop option carefully, because some services are linked to others. Stopping one service stops the others that depend on it. For instance, stopping the Workstation Service affects these other services: Alerter, Computer Browser, Distributed File System, Messenger, Net Logon, and Remote Procedure Call (RPC) Locator. The system gives you a warning when other services are affected by stopping a particular service.

You can check dependencies by double-clicking a service and clicking the Dependencies tab (see Figure 11-2).

 Many services are linked to the Server and Workstation services, including services such as Net Logon that enable users to log onto and remain logged on to a network or server. If it is necessary to stop one of these services—for example, to diagnose a problem—give the users advance warning or stop the service after work hours.

Pausing a service takes it offline to be used only by Administrators or Server Operators. A paused service is restarted by right-clicking it and clicking Restart.

Another way to manage a service is to double-click it to view that service's properties (see Figure 11-2). For example, you can set a service to start automatically by double-clicking the service, accessing the General tab, and setting the Startup type box to Automatic.

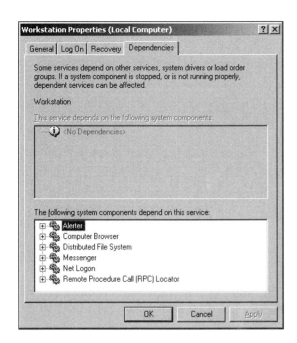

Figure 11-2   Workstation Service dependencies

Activity 11-1: Monitoring and Managing a Service

Time Required: Approximately 10 minutes

Objective: Use the Computer Management tool to monitor and manage a Windows Server 2003 service.

Description: In this activity, you practice monitoring, starting, and stopping a service. You also view a service's dependencies.

1. To open the Computer Management Snap-in, click **Start**, click **Run**, enter **mmc**, click **OK**, click the **File** menu, click **Add/Remove Snap-in**, click **Add**, and double-click **Computer Management**. In the Computer Management dialog box, notice that you can select to manage the local computer or another computer on the network. Leave **Local computer: (the computer this console is running on)** selected, and click **Finish**. Click **Close**, and click **OK**. Maximize the console windows.

2. Open the tree, if necessary, so that you can click **Services** under Services and Applications. Notice that you can change the display in the right pane (see the bottom left corner of the right pane below the slider bar) by clicking **Extended** or **Standard**. Click each selection to see how it changes the display.

3. Scroll through the right pane to survey the services and notice the status of each one.

4. Make sure that the Extended display is selected by clicking **Extended**.

5. Click the **Server** Service. Read the description of this service in the right pane. What would happen to file sharing if this service was stopped or experiencing problems?

6. Double-click the **Server** Service.

7. Click the **Dependencies** tab and wait a few moments. What services depend on the Server Service? Record your observations. Click **Cancel**.

8. Click the **Workstation** Service to view its description in the right pane. Why is this service important?

9. Double-click the **Network DDE DSDM** Service.

10. Set this service to start when the server is booted by selecting **Automatic** in the Startup type list box (it is disabled by default). Click **Apply**. Notice that the Start button is now activated.

11. Click the **Dependencies** tab to determine if any other service(s) must be started prior to starting this service. Notice that this service does not depend on any other services, but the Network DDE Service is dependent on it. (For example, if you want to make the ClipBook Service available to clients, you would first have to start Network DDE DSDM, then start Network DDE, and then start ClipBook).

12. Click the **General** tab, and then click **Start** (see Figure 11-3).

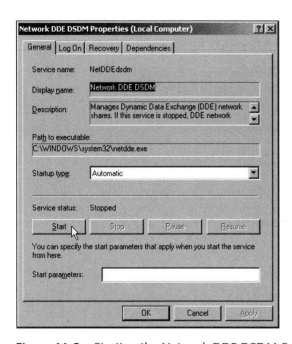

Figure 11-3   Starting the Network DDE DSDM Service

13. Click **OK**. Notice that the Network DDE DSDM Service is now started and set to start automatically.

14. Double-click **Network DDE DSDM**.

15. Click **Stop** to practice stopping the service. Click **OK**. Even though the service is stopped now, what will happen when you reboot the computer?

16. Close the **Computer Management** console window.

17. Click **No** so as to not save the console settings.

USING TASK MANAGER

Windows Server 2003 includes a tool that can be used to monitor applications and processes running on a server. Sometimes one of these components may hang or consume server resources slowing overall performance of the server. One tool that you can use to monitor and manage applications and processes is Task Manager.

Monitoring Applications

You can use Task Manager to view applications running on the server by pressing Ctrl+Alt+Del while logged on as Administrator or as a member of the Administrators group. Click the Task Manager button, which displays a dialog box with five tabs: Applications, Processes, Performance, Networking, and Users (an alternate way to start Task Manager is to right-click an open space on the taskbar and click Task Manager).

When you select the Applications tab, shown in Figure 11-4, you see all of the software applications running from the server console, including 16-bit applications. To stop an application, highlight it, and click the End Task button. If an application is hung (no longer responding to user input), you can select that application, and press End Task to stop the application and release server resources. The Switch To button brings the highlighted application to the front so you can work in it, and the New Task button enables you to start another application at the console, using the Run option, which is the same option that you would access from the Start button. The status bar at the bottom of the screen shows information about the total number of processes, the CPU usage, and minimum/maximum available memory.

Figure 11-4   Task Manager Applications tab

If you right-click a task, several active options appear in a shortcut menu, as follows:

- *Switch To*—Takes you into the highlighted program
- *Bring To Front*—Maximizes and brings the highlighted program to the front, but leaves you in Task Manager
- *Minimize*—Causes the program to be minimized
- *Maximize*—Causes the program to be maximized, but leaves you in Task Manager
- *End Task*—Stops the highlighted program
- *Go To Process*—Takes you to the Processes tab and highlights the process associated with the program

Activity 11-2: Working with Applications in Task Manager

Time Required: Approximately 10 minutes

Objective: Use Task Manager to monitor and manage applications.

Description: In this activity, you start an application and then use it to learn about Task Manager functions for controlling applications, including ending the application.

1. Click **Start**, point to **All Programs**, point to **Accessories**, and click **Calculator**.
2. Press the **Ctrl+Alt+Del** keys at the same time. Click **Task Manager**.
3. Click the **Applications** tab, if it is not displayed already.

4. Right-click **Calculator** and notice the active options on the shortcut menu (see Figure 11-5).

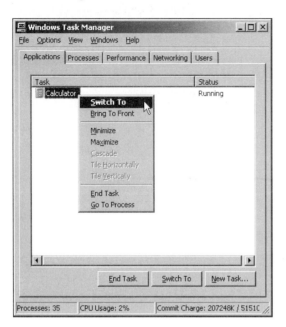

Figure 11-5 Shortcut menu options

5. Click **Switch To**. What happens?

6. Click **Windows Task Manager** in the taskbar.

7. Click **Calculator**, if it is not still selected. Click **End Task** to close the Calculator application.

8. Leave Windows Task Manager open for the next activity.

Monitoring Processes

The Processes tab lists the processes in use by all running applications (see Figure 11-6). If you need to stop a process, simply highlight it, and click End Process. The Processes tab also shows information about each started process, as summarized in Table 11-2.

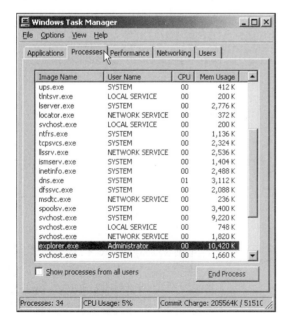

Figure 11-6 Processes tab

Table 11-2   Task Manager information on processes

Process Information	Description
Image Name	The process name, such as winword.exe for Microsoft Word
User Name	The user account under which the process is running
CPU	The percentage of the CPU resources used by the process
Mem Usage	The amount of memory the process is using

Table 11-2 lists only the default information that is displayed on the Processes tab. You can change the display to view other information, such as page faults, base priority, and thread count (all described later in this chapter) by clicking the View Menu and then clicking Select Columns.

Setting Priorities

Using the Processes tab within Task Manager you can also increase the priority of a process (or processes) in the list so that it has more CPU priority than what is set as its default. Suppose, for example, that you want to increase the priority for Windows Explorer, which is process explorer.exe. To start, right-click explorer.exe, which displays a shortcut menu in which you can end the process, end the process tree (end that process and all subprocesses associated with it), or reset the priority. Point to Set Priority and then select the priority you want to set (see Figure 11-7).

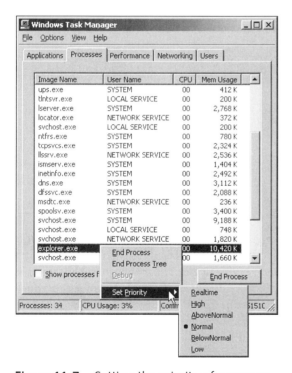

Figure 11-7   Setting the priority of a process

Normally, the priority at which a process runs is set in the program code of the application, which is called the **base priority class**. If the base priority class is not set by the program, a normal (average) priority is set by the system. The server administrator always has the option to set a different base priority. As shown in Figure 11-7, the administrator can change the priority to any of six options: Low, BelowNormal, Normal, AboveNormal, High, or Realtime. You might think of these processes as being on a continuum, with

Normal as the midpoint, which is 0. Low is -2, BelowNormal is -1, AboveNormal is +1, or High is +2. Realtime is given an extra advantage at +15. For example, a Low priority means that if a process is waiting in a queue—for example, for processor time, disk access, or memory access—all processes with a higher priority go first. The same is true for BelowNormal, except that processes with this priority run before those set at Low, and so on.

> Use the Realtime priority with great caution. If assigned to a process, that process may completely take over the server, preventing work by any other processes. For instance, you might want to assign a Realtime priority when you detect a disk drive that is about to fail and you want to give all resources over to the backup process so you can back up files before the disk fails.

Activity 11-3: Working with Processes in Task Manager

Time Required: Approximately 10 minutes

Objective: Use Task Manager to monitor processes and to reset the priority of a process.

Description: In this activity, you use Task Manager to learn about how a process is functioning and then to reset the priority of that process.

1. Start the **Calculator** program, as you did in Activity 11-2.
2. Open **Task Manager**, if it is closed, and, if necessary, click the **Applications** tab.
3. Right-click **Calculator**, and click **Go To Process**. What happens when you do this?
4. Right-click **calc.exe**, and notice the options.
5. On the shortcut menu, point to **Set Priority**.
6. Click **AboveNormal** (see Figure 11-7).
7. Click **Yes** in the information box.
8. Position the Calculator program and Task Manager so that you can view both. Click several numbers on the Calculator and watch the CPU column for calc.exe. If you watch carefully, you notice a temporary change in the CPU use, such as between 01 to about 04.
9. Click **calc.exe**, and click **End Process**. Click **Yes** in the information box.
10. Close **Task Manager**.

Monitoring Real-time Performance

The Performance tab shows vital CPU and memory performance information through bar charts, line graphs, and performance statistics (see Figure 11-8). The CPU Usage and PF Usage bars show the current use of CPU and page file use. To the right of each bar is a graph showing the immediate history statistics. The bottom of the Performance tab shows more detailed statistics, such as those for handles and threads, which are described in Table 11-3. A **handle** is a resource, such as a file, used by a program that has its own identification so the program is able to access it. **Threads** are blocks of code within a program.

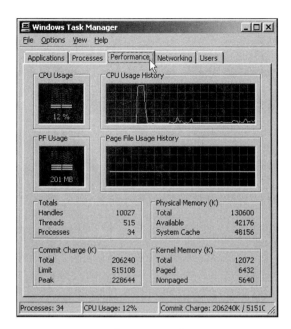

Figure 11-8 Performance tab

Table 11-3 Task Manager performance statistics

Statistic	Description
Handles	The number of objects in use by all processes, such as open files
Threads	The number of code blocks in use, in which one program or process may be running one or more code blocks at a time
Processes	The number of processes that are active or sitting idle
Physical Memory Total	The amount of RAM installed in the computer
Physical Memory Available	The amount of RAM available to be used
System Cache	The amount of RAM used for file caching
Commit Charge Total	The size of virtual memory currently in use
Commit Charge Limit	The maximum virtual (disk) memory that can be allocated
Commit Charge Peak	The maximum virtual memory that has been used during the current Task Manager monitoring session
Kernel Memory Total	The amount of memory used by the operating system
Kernel Memory Paged	The amount of virtual memory used by the operating system
Kernel Memory Nonpaged	The amount of RAM memory used by the operating system

Monitoring Network Performance

The Networking tab in Task Manager enables you to monitor network performance on all of the NICs installed in the server. A graphical representation shows the total network utilization, which is roughly the percentage of the network bandwidth in use.

The lower portion of the tab shows (see Figure 11-9) the network performance data across each NIC. It lists the name of the adapter (or connection), the network utilization detected by the adapter (from 0% to 100%), the speed of the network link, such as 100 Mbps, and the operational state of the adapter. This information can be valuable if you suspect there is a problem with a NIC in the server and you want an immediate determination if it is working. The information on the tab also can be an initial warning that something is causing prolonged high network utilization—80% to 100%, for instance.

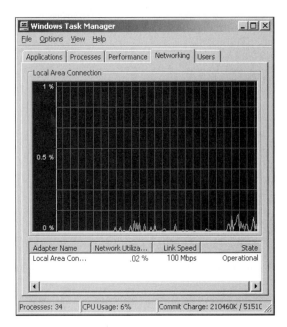

Figure 11-9   Networking tab

Monitoring Users

The Users tab simply provides a listing of the users currently logged on. You can log off a user by clicking that user and clicking the Logoff button, which ensures that any open files are closed before the user is logged off. Another option is to Disconnect a user, which you might use if the Logoff action does not work because the user's connection is hung.

Using System Monitor

One of the most versatile tools used to help detect and troubleshoot performance issues on a Windows Server 2003 is **System Monitor**. System Monitor can be used to monitor components such as hard disks, memory, the processor, disk caching, a started process, and the page file. For example, you might monitor memory and paging to determine if you have fully tuned the page file for satisfactory performance and to determine if you have adequate RAM for the server load.

Capturing Data Using System Monitor

System Monitor is opened from the Administrative Tools menu by clicking Performance to view the console screen, which offers two main choices. System Monitor is the top selection in the tree, and Performance Logs and Alerts (discussed later in this chapter) is the other option. Make sure that System Monitor is selected in the tree to view the screen as shown in Figure 11-10. The default view is in the graph mode, showing a grid that you use for graphing activities on the server. To begin gathering data for your analysis, select one or more objects to monitor. A System Monitor object may be memory, the processor, or another part of the computer. Other objects are added as you install services and applications.

For each object, there are one or more counters that can be monitored. A **counter** is an indicator of a quantity of the object that can be measured in some unit, such as percent, rate per second, or peak value, depending on what is appropriate to the object. For example, the % Processor Time counter for the Processor object measures the percentage of processor time that is in use by non-idle processes. (It is not uncommon for % Processor Time to occasionally be very high, but this often just means that an application is using the processor very efficiently.) Pages/sec is an example of a counter for the Memory object that measures the number of pages written to or read from virtual memory per second. The processor is one of the common objects to monitor when a server is slow. Table 11-4 gives examples of some of the most frequently used counters for the Processor object.

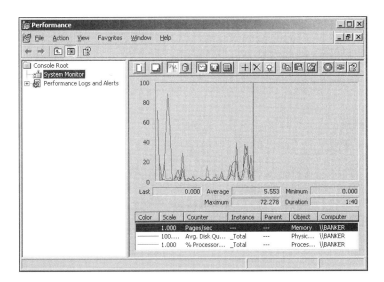

Figure 11-10   System Monitor

Table 10-4   Sample processor counters in System Monitor

Counter	Description
% DPC Time	Processor time used for deferred procedure calls, for example for hardware devices
% Interrupt Time	Time spent on hardware interrupts by the CPU
% Privileged Time	Time spent by the CPU for system activities in privileged mode, which is used for the operating system
% Processor Time	Time the CPU is busy on all non-idle activities
% User Time	Time spent by the CPU in user mode running software applications and system programs
Interrupts/sec	Number of device interrupts per second

Sometimes there are instances associated with a counter. An **instance** exists when there are different elements to monitor, such as individual processes when you use the Process object, or when a process contains multiple threads or runs subprocesses under it for the Thread object. Other examples are when there are two or more disks or multiple processors to monitor. In many cases, each instance is identified by a unique number for ease of monitoring.

System Monitor offers several buttons from which to operate it and to set up the display options. After the tool is opened, click the Add button (represented by a plus sign) on the button bar just above the tracking window (refer to Figure 11-10). This opens the Add Counters dialog box (see Figure 11-11) from which to select objects to monitor, counters, and instances.

You can monitor one or more objects at a time as a way to get a better understanding of how particular objects interact, for example by monitoring both memory and the processor. Also, you can monitor the same object using different combinations of counters. You stop monitoring by clicking the Delete button (represented by an X) on the button bar.

There are three views you can use when monitoring objects: graph, histogram, and report.

- A graph is a running line chart of the object that shows distinct peaks and valleys. For example, when you use the graph mode and monitor for different objects, a line with a unique color, such as red or green, represents each object.

- A histogram is a running bar chart that shows each object as a bar in a different color.

- The report mode simply provides numbers on a screen, which you can capture to put in a report.

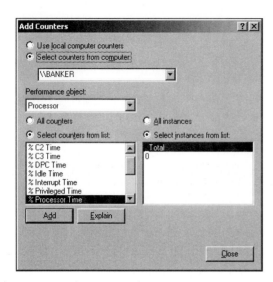

Figure 11-11   Add Counters dialog box

Each of these options is set from a button on the button bar just above the tracking window, and the buttons are titled: View Graph, View Histogram, and View Report. You can change the view mode at any time by clicking the appropriate button. Figure 11-12 illustrates the use of the histogram mode to monitor several counters.

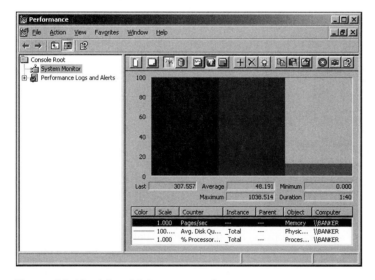

Figure 11-12   View Histogram mode

Each object and counter combination is displayed using a different color, so they are easily identified. If Figure 11-12 were in color you would see that Page/sec is blue, Avg. Disk Queue Length is green, and % Processor Time is red. The counters are shown at the bottom of the screen with a key to indicate the graphing color for each one. When you click one of these counters, the status information just above the counters shows the following for that counter:

- *Last*—The current value of the monitored activity
- *Average*—The average value of the monitored activity for the elapsed time
- *Maximum*—The maximum value of the activity over the elapsed time
- *Minimum*—The minimum value of the activity over the elapsed time
- *Duration*—The amount of time to complete a full graph of the activity

Monitoring System Components

When monitoring the performance of a server there are four objects that are often used: processor, memory, physical disk, and network interface. It is important to monitor other installed components, and as you add different components, other objects and counters are added, but these four are particularly important for monitoring server performance. Table 11-5 provides a sampling of object/counter combinations that you can use initially for monitoring the computer system performance.

Table 10-5   Sample objects and counters for system monitoring

Object	Counters
Processor	% Processor Time—Percentage of time for threads to process % Privileged Time—Time spent by the CPU for system activities in privileged mode % User Time—Percentage of time spent processing user threads
Memory	Available Bytes—Physical memory currently available for use Committed Bytes—Amount of virtual memory currently being used Pages/Sec—Number of hard page faults per second
Physical Disk	% Disk Time—Amount of time the disk spends working Avg. Disk Bytes/Transfer—Average number of bytes transferred between memory and disk during read and write operations Disk Bytes/Sec—The speed at which bytes are transferred Current Disk Queue Length—Number of requests waiting to be processed
Network Interface	Bytes Total/Sec—As measured across the NIC, number of bytes sent and received per second

The Memory column in Table 11-5 refers to the concept of a page fault. **Page faults** occur whenever memory pages must be called from disk (from the paging file).

The next two activities enable you to explore how to use System Monitor and then how to troubleshoot processor difficulties. In the third activity, you'll learn how to enable System Monitor to track disk activity through activating the Disk Performance Statistic Driver.

Activity 11-4: Exploring System Monitor

Time Required: Approximately 10 minutes

Objective: Examine available options in System Monitor.

Description: This activity gives you an opportunity to practice viewing objects, counters, and instances in System Monitor.

1. Click **Start**, point to **All Programs**, point to **Administrative Tools**, and click **Performance**.

2. Double-click **Console Root** to view System Monitor, if it is not displayed.

3. Click **System Monitor**, if necessary. What objects and counters are displayed in the right pane by default?

4. Move your pointer over each of the buttons on the button bar to view its description.

5. Click the **Add** button (a plus sign) in the button bar in the right pane. What computer is selected by default for monitoring? How would you monitor activity on a different computer? Record your observations.

6. Click the **down arrow** in the Performance object box. Scroll through the options and record some of them.

7. Select the default, which is **Processor**. Make sure that the **Select counters from list** option button is selected. Scroll to view the counters associated with the Processor object. What instances are available?

8. Next, select to view **Server** as the object. How many counters and instances are associated with this object?

9. Select to view **Process** as the object. How many counters and instances are associated with the Process object?

10. Choose to view the **TCPv4** object. Click the **Segments/sec** counter, and click the **Explain** button. Notice the description of this counter.

11. Observe two more objects and their associated counters and instances.

12. Click **Close** in the Add Counters dialog box, but leave the Performance console open for the next activity.

Activity 11-5: Monitoring for Processor Problems

Time Required: Approximately 10 minutes

Objective: Learn how to monitor for processor bottlenecks.

Description: In this activity, you use System Monitor to check for processor bottlenecks, such as the processor's ability to handle the server load and possible problems caused by hardware.

1. Make sure that the **Performance** console is already open, and if not, open it to display **System Monitor**.

2. If any object/counter combinations are currently running, stop each one by clicking the object/counter combination in the lower- right part of the console, and then clicking the **Delete** button, as shown in Figure 11-13.

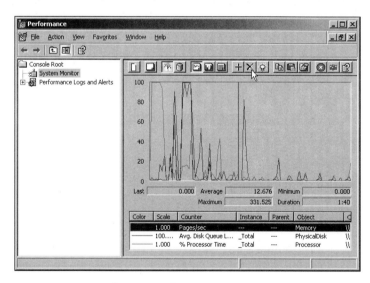

Figure 11-13 Deleting an object/counter

3. Click the **Add** button in the button bar to add counters.

4. If it is not already selected, click **Select counters from computer**, and make sure that the computer you are using is selected.

5. Make sure that **Processor** is selected in the Performance object box.

6. Make sure that **Select counters from list** is selected, and click **% Processor Time**. Leave **_Total** as the default for instances. What information does this counter provide for the Processor object? How would you find out, if you didn't know? Record your observations. Note that when you monitor % Processor Time, sustained values of 80–85% or higher indicate a heavily

loaded machine; consistent readings of 95% or higher may indicate a machine that needs to have its load reduced, or its capabilities increased (with a new machine, a motherboard upgrade, or a faster CPU)

7. Click **Add**.

8. Click **% Interrupt Time** as the counter, and leave **_Total** as the instance. Click **Add**. Note that the % Interrupt Time is useful to monitor because it measures the amount of the processor's time that is used to service hardware requests from devices such as the NIC, disk, and CD-ROM drives, and serial and parallel peripherals. A high rate of interrupts when compared to your baseline statistics indicates a possible hardware problem, such as a malfunctioning NIC.

9. Scroll the counters list, and click **Interrupts/sec**. Leave **_Total** as the instance, and click **Add**. This counter measures the average number of times per second that the CPU is interrupted by devices requesting immediate processing. Network traffic and system clock activity establish a kind of background count against which this number should be compared. Problem levels occur when a malfunctioning device begins to generate spurious interrupts, or when excessive network traffic overwhelms a network adapter. In both cases, this usually creates a count that's five times or more greater than a lightly loaded baseline situation.

10. In the Performance object box, select **System**.

11. Scroll the counters list, and click **Processor Queue Length**. Click **Add**. This counter for the System object measures the number of execution threads waiting for access to a CPU. If this value is frequently over 4 on a single CPU, it indicates a need to distribute this machine's load across other machines, or the need to increase its capabilities, usually by adding an additional CPU or by upgrading the machine or the motherboard. When the value is over 2 per each CPU on multiple-processor systems, you should consider adding processors or increasing the processor speed.

12. Click **Close**.

13. Monitor the system for several minutes to determine if there are any processor problems. Record any problems that you diagnose from using the System Monitor.

14. Click the **View Histogram** button to see this mode.

15. Click the **View Report** button to observe this mode.

16. Click **View Graph** to return to this mode.

17. In the bottom portion of the right pane, click each counter one at a time, and click the **Delete** button.

18. Leave the Performance console open.

Activity 11-6: Verifying the Disk Counters

Time Required: Approximately 5 minutes

Objective: Learn to check the status of Diskperf.

Description: Monitoring disks through System Monitor is accomplished by using the Disk Performance Statistic Driver, which is enabled through the command-line program, Diskperf. Normally, hard disk System Monitor counters are enabled by default. If they are not enabled, you can start them by typing diskperf -y and pressing Enter in the Command Prompt window. Or, to disable the disk counters, you type diskperf -n. In this activity, you use Diskperf to verify the status of the hard disk performance counters to see if they are enabled.

1. Click **Start**, point to **All Programs**, point to **Accessories**, and click **Command Prompt**.

2. In the Command Prompt window, type **diskperf**, and press **Enter**. If the disk counters are enabled, you see a window similar to the one in Figure 11-14.

Figure 11-14   Disk counters status

3. Type **exit**, and press **Enter** to close the Command Prompt window.

CONFIGURING PERFORMANCE LOGS AND ALERTS

Performance Logs and Alerts is another tool that is used to monitor performance. **Performance logs** are used to track performance data over a given period of time, and **alerts** are used to warn you of problems when they occur. There are two kinds of performance logs: **counter logs** and **trace logs**. A counter log traces information on System Monitor objects that you configure, taking a snapshot at intervals that you determine, such as every 15 seconds. Trace logs monitor particular events that you specify, so that the log contains only those instances when the events occur, such as creating a trace to record each time there is disk input/output activity or when there is an Active Directory Kerberos security event. After a log is created, you can open it from System Monitor to view its contents. You can also create a log in a format that can be imported into a spreadsheet, such as Excel.

Creating Counter Logs

In general, the steps to create a counter log are: open the Performance tool from the Administrative Tools menu, double-click Performance Logs and Alerts to display the objects under it in the tree, right-click Counter Logs, and click New Log Settings (see Figure 11-15). Enter a name for the log, click the Add button, click the Add Counters button on the General tab, and complete setting up the monitoring parameters in the Add Counters dialog box (which is similar to the Add Counters dialog box used in System Monitor setup).

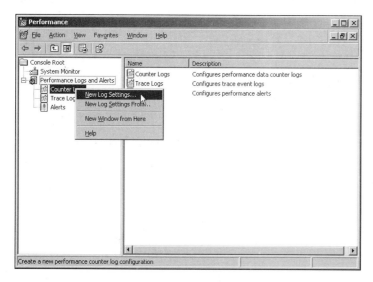

Figure 11-15   Configuring a counter log

Counter logs can quickly grow in size and occupy a significant amount of disk space and can slow system performance. Microsoft recommends that you take a snapshot at 15-second intervals or more frequently, if you plan to monitor for four hours or less. If you plan to monitor for over four hours, increase the interval. For example, if you monitor for eight hours, take a snapshot at about every five minutes or so. Also, adjust the log file size so that it is large enough to hold the information sampled for a specified period of time.

If you need to manually stop the log before the specified stop time, right-click the log in the right pane of the Performance tool, and then click Stop. You can restart the log by right-clicking it, and then clicking Start. Also, you can start a new logging session, for example, each morning, by right-clicking the log, and then clicking Start. To add more objects and counters to monitor, right-click the log, click Properties, and then access the General tab. Click Add Objects or Add Counters to use more objects and counters, or click Remove to delete ones you do not want. Also, each new generation of a log (for instance if you start a log every morning for a week) is automatically labeled according to your specifications, which are set on the Log tab. Or, you can use the default, which is to end the saved log file from each recording session with an incremented number in the form *nnnnnn*, such as 000001 for the first session, 000002 for next session, and so on.

Activity 11-7: Creating a Counter Log

Time Required: Approximately 15 minutes

Objective: Learn how to create a counter log.

Description: This activity gives you practice in creating a counter log. Consider a situation in which you want to monitor paging and memory for a typical workday to help determine if you need to adjust the page file size or to add more RAM. Use the following steps to set up a counter log for monitoring the performance over a period of eight hours.

1. Make sure that the **Performance** console is already open, and if not, open it to display **Performance Logs and Alerts**.

2. Double-click **Performance Logs and Alerts** to display the objects under it in the tree, if necessary.

3. Right-click **Counter Logs**, and click **New Log Settings** (see Figure 11-15).

4. Enter **Mem** plus your initials as a name for the log, and then click **OK**.

5. Click the **Add Counters** button. Compare the options that you see to those you can use in System Monitor and record your observations.

6. Make sure that **Select counters from computer** is selected as well as the computer on which you are working.

7. Choose the performance object **Paging File**, select **%Usage** as the counter, and then select **_Total** as the instance. Click **Add**.

8. Choose the object **Paging File**, select **%Usage Peak** as the counter, and then select **_Total** as the instance. Click **Add**.

9. Choose the object **Memory**, select **Page Faults/sec** as the counter. Are there any instances from which to select? Click **Add**.

10. Click **Close**.

11. Set the Interval box to **5** and the Units box to **minutes**. The dialog box should now look similar to the one in Figure 11-16.

12. Click **OK**.

13. Click **Yes** to create the folder for the log in which to record the information, if a folder has not already been created.

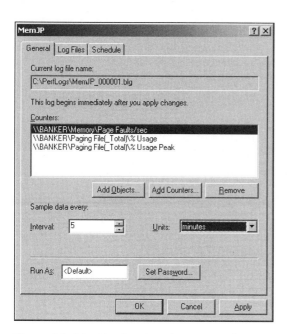

Figure 11-16   Configuring the counter log parameters

14. Click **Counter Logs** in the left pane. There should be a green disk icon in front of the log name in the right pane that shows the log is active and gathering data. Right-click the log, click **Properties**, and click the **Schedule** tab.

15. In the Start log section of the dialog box, make sure that **At** is clicked, and set the start time and date to match the current time and date (the default).

16. Next, in the Stop log section, click **After**, and enter **8** in the After box and **hours** in the Units box (see Figure 11-17).

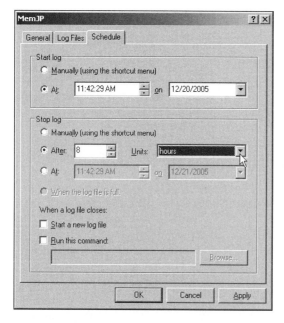

Figure 11-17   Configuring the schedule

17. Click the **Log Files** tab. List the options for Log file type and record them. (Note that any of the file formats can be converted to another format by using the Save As option when you right-click the log in the right pane.)

18. Click **OK**. How would you view the log's contents?

19. After the log has run for a few minutes, right-click it, and click **Delete**.

20. Click **OK**.

21. Leave the Performance console open.

> If your counter log icon is red and you cannot start the logging, make sure that the Performance Logs and Alerts Service is not disabled.

Creating Trace Logs

Trace logs are useful when you do not want to continuously monitor performance, but want to document each instance of a particular event over a period of time. This is especially helpful in finding intermittent problems, such as excessive load on the server or network at certain times of the day or on certain days of the week. The elements that you can monitor in a trace log are more limited than those available to a counter log, as you'll find in Activity 11-8.

Activity 11-8: Creating a Trace Log

Time Required: Approximately 10 minutes

Objective: Learn how to set up a trace log.

Description: In this activity, you set up a trace log to monitor each time a page fault occurs. Because this type of monitoring requires extra system resources, you set up to only monitor for 30 minutes.

1. Make sure that the **Performance** console is already open, and if not, open it to display Performance Logs and Alerts. Make sure that Trace Logs is displayed under it in the tree.

2. Right-click **Trace Logs**, and click **New Log Settings**.

3. Enter **CPU** plus your initials as the log name, and click **OK**. (If no folder has previously been created for log files, click **OK** to create the folder.)

4. On the General tab, click **Events logged by system provider**, and make sure that only **Process creations/deletions** and **Page faults** are checked. Click **OK** when you see the warning about collecting information on page faults. The General tab should look similar to Figure 11-18. Notice the name and location of the log file, which is where you can access it later to obtain its contents. Record this information.

5. Click the **Schedule** tab.

6. Click the **Manually (using the shortcut menu)** option button to start the log manually.

7. In the Stop log area, click **After**, and set the After box to **30** and the Units box to **minutes**.

8. Click **OK**.

9. Click **Trace Logs** in the left pane, and notice the log you have configured in the right pane. The disk icon for the trace log should still be red, because you haven't started it.

10. Right-click the log in the right pane, and click **Start**. Click **OK** to the warning that the log may take a few minutes to start.

11. Whether or not your log has started, right-click it in the right pane, and click **Delete**. (Click **OK** if your log is running.)

12. Leave the Performance console open.

11

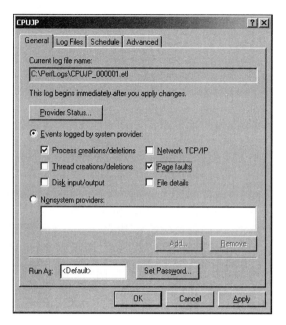

Figure 11-18   Configuring a trace log

Creating Alerts

An alert immediately warns you when a problem occurs. For example, you may want Windows Server 2003 to send you an alert each time the CPU is at 100% utilization. Each alert is sent to specific accounts or groups, such as to the accounts belonging to the Administrators group.

Activity 11-9: Configuring an Alert

Time Required: Approximately 10 minutes

Objective: Learn how to set up an alert.

Description: In this activity, you configure an alert to track 100 % CPU use.

1. Open the **Performance** console, if it is not already open.

2. Double-click **Performance Logs and Alerts** to display the objects under it in the tree, if necessary.

3. Right-click **Alerts**, and click **New Alert Settings**.

4. Enter a name for the alert, such as **Processor** plus your initials. Click **OK**.

5. Make sure you are on the **General** tab. Click **Add**. Notice that you can select from the same object, counters, and instances as in System Monitor.

6. Select to monitor the **Processor** in the Performance object list box (the default). Select **% Processor Time** as the counter (also the default), and select **_Total** as the instance (the default) to monitor all processors. Click **Add**, and then click **Close**. (Click OK if a warning is displayed that you must set the alert limit.)

7. Make sure that the object and counter are highlighted. Select **Over** (the default) in the Alert when the value is box. Enter **99** in the Limit box.

8. Set the Interval and Unit boxes to have the system check for this event every **10 seconds**.

9. Click the **Action** tab. Check **Log an entry in the application event log**, if it is not already checked. Check **Send a network message to**, and specify **Administrators** (for the Administrators group). Notice there also are options to start a performance data log or to run a program when the event occurs.

10. Click **OK**.

11. Click Alerts in the left pane, and notice that the alert you created is displayed in the right pane. (Right-click the alert, and click **Delete**, if your instructor requests that you delete the alert. Click **OK** if requested to confirm the deletion.)

12. Close the **Performance** window.

USING NETWORK MONITOR

Not only is it important to monitor the performance of your server, it's also important to monitor network performance, because this is another area where problems can occur. Regularly monitoring your network is vital, because network conditions can change from moment to moment. Besides System Monitor, Windows Server 2003 provides Network Monitor for creating trace logs of network activity and capturing frames and packets. In the sections that follow, you'll learn how to install the Network Monitor tool, and then use it.

Installing Network Monitor

There are two main steps to installing Network Monitor:

- Installing the Network Monitor Windows component
- Installing Network Monitor Driver

Network Monitor is a Windows component that you install using the Add or Remove Programs option in Control Panel. It is a Microsoft tool that captures and distills network performance information.

Network Monitor Driver can be installed on a server or workstation and it enables that computer's NIC to collect statistics about network performance, such as the number of packets sent and received at that computer. Because Network Monitor Driver is a protocol that works along with the Network Monitor, you install Network Monitor Driver using the Network Connections option in Control Panel.

Activity 11-10: Installing the Network Monitor Windows Component

Time Required: Approximately 10 minutes

Objective: Install Network Monitor.

Description: This activity enables you to install Network Monitor.

1. Click **Start**, point to **Control Panel**, and click **Add or Remove Programs**.

2. Click **Add/Remove Windows Components**.

3. Double-click **Management and Monitoring Tools**.

4. Click **Network Monitor Tools**, and click **OK**.

5. Click **Next** and wait a few moments for the installation to complete. (Insert the Windows Server 2003 CD-ROM, if requested, click **OK** after inserting the CD-ROM, and close the Windows Server 2003 Welcome screen.)

6. Click **Finish**.

7. Close the **Add or Remove Programs** window.

If you cannot access Control Panel because your system has the Group Policy to "Prohibit Access to the Control Panel" still configured from Chapter 10, review Activity 10-10 and disable this policy.

Activity 11-11: Verifying the Installation of Network Monitor Driver

Time Required: Approximately 5 minutes

Objective: Verify that Network Monitor Driver is installed.

Description: When you install Network Monitor, Network Monitor Driver is automatically installed as a protocol. In this activity, you verify that Network Monitor Driver is installed, and you learn how to reinstall it, if it is removed.

1. Click **Start**, point to **Control Panel**, point to **Network Connections**, right-click **Local Area Connection**, and click **Properties**.

2. In the box labeled This connection uses the following items, verify that Network Monitor Driver is installed. (If it is not installed, you can install it manually at this point. Click Install, double-click Protocol, click Network Monitor Driver, and click OK.) As long as you plan to use Network Monitor, make sure that you do not remove Network Monitor Driver from the Local Area Connection properties.

3. Close the **Local Area Connection Properties** dialog box.

Using Network Monitor to Capture Data

After Network Monitor is installed, it enables you to monitor a full range of network activity and to check for possible problems. Network Monitor tracks information such as the following:

- Percent network utilization
- Frames and bytes transported per second
- Network station statistics
- Statistics captured during a given time period
- Information concerning transmissions per second
- Information about broadcast, unicast, and multicast transmissions
- NIC statistics
- Error data
- Addresses of network stations
- Network computers running Network Monitor and Network Monitor Driver

When you run Network Monitor to monitor traffic across a network, the Network Monitor Driver detects many forms of network traffic and captures packets and frames for analysis and reporting by Network Monitor. All packets and frames that pass through the server's NIC are monitored (although not all contents are viewed) so that it is possible to determine basic information about the network, such as the amount of traffic, the types of packets, and the source and destination addresses of computers transmitting data.

 The version of Network Monitor that is included on the Windows Server 2003 CD-ROM is only designed to capture data at the server's NIC. Consider purchasing Microsoft System Management Server, which comes with a version of Network Monitor that can connect to and monitor activity from a NIC on any network computer that has the Network Monitor Driver installed.

Activity 11-12: Using Network Monitor

Time Required: Approximately 15 minutes

Objective: Learn how to use Network Monitor.

Description: In this activity, you start Network Monitor and capture live network data for analysis.

1. Click **Start**, point to **Administrative Tools**, and click **Network Monitor**.

2. Click **OK** if an information box is displayed to remind you to select the network to monitor or to use the local area network as the default. Then, in the Select a network dialog box, click the network you want to monitor. For this activity, click **Local Computer**, click **Local Area Connection**, and click **OK**.

3. Maximize one or both Network Monitor screens if the display is not maximized.

4. Click the **Start Capture** button on the button bar to start capturing network performance data. View the data displayed on the screen, such as % Network Utilization or Network Statistics, as shown in Figure 11-19. Use the scroll bars in each of the four panes to view the information. Table 11-6 explains the information you can view in each of the panes, which are:

   ■ Graph pane (upper-left pane)

   ■ Total pane (upper-right pane)

   ■ Session pane (lower-left pane)

   ■ Station pane (bottom pane)

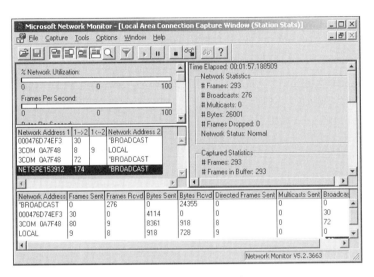

Figure 11-19   Capturing data in Network Monitor

5. If you want to pause capturing data, click the **Pause/Continue Capture** button on the button bar, and click it again to resume capturing. When you are finished, click the **Stop Capture** button on the button bar.

6. Leave Network Monitor open for the next activity.

Table 11-6   Network Monitor panes

Pane	Information Provided in the Pane
Graph	Shows bar graphs of the following: % Network Utilization, Frames per Second, Bytes Per Second, Broadcasts Per Second, and Multicasts Per Second
Total	Provides total statistics about network activity that originates from, or is sent to, the computer (station) that is using Network Monitor, and includes many statistics in each of the following categories: Network Statistics, Capture Statistics, Per Second Statistics, Network Card (MAC) Statistics, Network Card (MAC) Error Statistics
Session	Shows statistics about traffic from other computers on the network which include the MAC (device) address of each computer's NIC and data about the number of frames sent from, and received by, each computer
Station	Provides total statistics on all communicating network stations which include: Network (device) address of each communicating computer, Frames Sent, Frames Received, Bytes Sent, Bytes Received, Directed Frames Sent, Multicasts Sent, and Broadcasts Sent

11

Configuring Network Monitor

Network Monitor supports event management, which enables a server administrator to set up **filters** to capture a certain event or type of network activity. For example, the administrator may want to watch only activity between the server and a specific workstation. Another possibly is to track only IP activity related to Internet traffic into the server.

Network Monitor can filter frames and packets on the basis of two property types, Service Access Point (SAP) or Ethertype (ETYPE). SAP refers to the service access point which specifies the network process that should accept a frame at the destination, such as TCP/IP, BPDU (a frame type used by network bridges), and special manufacturers, including Novell (for IPX/SPX). ETYPE refers to a property of an Ethernet frame that includes a two-byte code for the protocol type and is used in Ethernet communications by some vendors, but is not a part of the Ethernet standard. For some protocols, such as IP, you can choose from either property or you can monitor for both. If you are in doubt, monitor both types or select SAP, which conforms to the Ethernet standard.

Activity 11-13: Creating a Filter in Network Monitor

Time Required: Approximately 15 minutes

Objective: Learn how to create a filter in Network Monitor.

Description: In this activity, assume that your network has an older NetWare server that runs a database application, which uses NetWare's Service Advertising Protocol (SAP—do not confuse this with Service Access Point, which has the same acronym, but is a different network concept). You want to create a filter to monitor only NetWare SAP frames that are received and sent by the NetWare server to determine if they are creating excessive network traffic.

1. Open **Network Monitor**, if it is not already open.

2. Click the **Stop Capture** button, if you are still capturing data.

3. Click the **Edit Capture Filter** button (resembling a funnel) on the button bar.

4. If you are using the Network Monitor version installed from the Windows Server 2003 CD-ROM, you see a warning that this version only captures data coming across the local computer. Click **OK**.

5. Double-click **SAP/ETYPE = Any SAP or Any ETYPE** (remember that here SAP means Service Access Point, see Figure 11-20). What are some of the protocols that you can monitor? Record some examples in your lab journal or in a word-processed document.

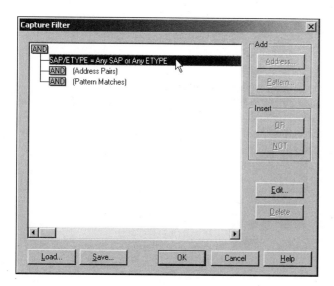

Figure 11-20 Configuring a capture filter

6. Click the **Disable All** button.

7. Click **Netware SAP** (SAP here means Service Advertising Protocol) in the Disabled Protocols box, and click the **Enable** button. Click **OK** (see Figure 11-21).

8. Double-click **(Address Pairs)**. What stations are included in the Station 1 and Station 2 boxes? In what directions can communications be tracked between stations in the two boxes? How would you set up to view all traffic between only a NetWare server and all other stations on the network?

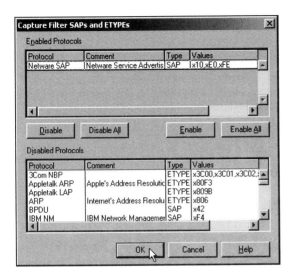

Figure 11-21   Configuring to monitor Netware SAP

9. Although the default settings monitor all traffic, practice setting up a relationship that monitors traffic from "any group" to "*any" address on the network (even though these are already set up). Click the **Include** option button. Click ***ANY GROUP** in the Station 1 box. Click the two-way arrows ←→ in the Direction box, and click ***ANY** in the Station 2 box. Click **OK**. What relationship is now displayed under the (Address Pairs) line?

10. Click **OK**.

11. Click the **Start Capture** button on the button bar (click **No** if asked to save a previous capture session), and monitor for a minute or two.

12. Click the **Stop Capture** button.

13. If the Save File dialog box is displayed, click **Yes** if you want to save the captured data in a file, or click **No** if you do not want to save the data. If you click Yes, specify the filename for saving the captured data, and then click **Save**.

14. Close **Network Monitor**.

Using Network Monitor to Set Baselines

A basic way to establish network baselines from which to diagnose problems is to use information that you obtain from the Graph pane in Network Monitor. The data bars provide useful information that you can collect about network performance under light, medium, and heavy loads. Four of the most helpful statistics are the following:

- *% Network Utilization*—Shows how much of the network bandwidth is in use

- *Frames Per Second*—Shows total traffic in frames for broadcasts, unicasts, and multicasts

- *Broadcasts Per Second*—Shows how much network traffic is the result of broadcasts from servers, workstations, and print servers

- *Multicasts Per Second*—Shows how much network traffic is due to multimedia servers

Begin gathering benchmarks on all four statistics so that you have an immediate understanding of what network load is typical. Also, be prepared to make adjustments in the network when even the typical statistics are high. For example, if % Network Utilization is frequently over 40%, that means the network is experiencing collisions, and there may be bottlenecks due to the network design, possibly indicating the need to create subnets. Network utilization that is regularly over 60% to 70% indicates a serious need to modify the network to address bottlenecks or increase network speed. Network utilization that is over 90% for a sustained period requires immediate attention in terms of locating the network problem or redesigning the network.

USING THE SNMP SERVICE

The **Simple Network Management Protocol (SNMP)** is used for network management on TCP/IP-based networks. It provides administrators with a way of centrally managing workstations, servers, hubs, and routers from a single computer running management software. SNMP can be used for the following:

- Configuring network devices
- Monitoring the performance of a network
- Locating network problems
- Monitoring network usage

SNMP provides network management services through agents and management systems. The SNMP management system (a computer running management software) sends and requests information from an SNMP agent. The SNMP agent (any computer or network device running SNMP agent software) responds to the management system's request for information. The management systems and agents can be grouped into communities for administrative and security purposes. Only those management systems and agents in the same community can communicate with each other.

When there is a network management station set up on a network, the following Microsoft operating systems and components are compatible with SNMP:

- Windows 2003, 2000, and NT servers
- Windows XP, 2000, and NT workstations
- WINS servers
- DHCP servers
- Internet Information Services servers
- Microsoft RAS and IAS servers

One immediate reason to install the SNMP Service in Windows Server 2003, is so that you can monitor the SNMP traffic using Network Monitor. For example, you can set up a Network Monitor filter to monitor SNMP activity. You might do this to make sure that there are no unauthorized users of network management software who are trying to surreptitiously change security on devices such as routers. If you use a network management system to monitor network and SNMP-compliant devices, consider installing the SNMP Service.

Activity 11-14: Installing SNMP

Time Required: Approximately 10 minutes

Objective: Install SNMP in Windows Server 2003.

Description: In this activity, you install the SNMP Service as a Windows component.

1. Click **Start**, point to **Control Panel**, and click **Add or Remove Programs**.
2. Click **Add/Remove Windows Components**.
3. Double-click **Management and Monitoring Tools**.

4. Click the box for **Simple Network Management Protocol**.

5. Click **OK**.

6. Click **Next**. (Insert the Windows Server 2003 CD-ROM, if requested. If necessary, click **OK** after inserting the CD-ROM, and close the Windows Server 2003 Welcome screen.)

7. Click **Finish**.

8. Close the **Add or Remove Programs** window.

After you install the SNMP Service, make sure that it is started, is set to start automatically, and is set up to have a **community** of hosts that share use of the service and a **community name**, which is similar to having a rudimentary password used among the hosts.

Activity 11-15: Configuring the SNMP Service

Time Required: Approximately 10 minutes

Objective: Learn how to configure the SNMP Service.

Description: In this activity, you learn how to configure the SNMP Service and the SNMP Trap Service. Plan to configure both services, particularly for use with Network Monitor and with third-party network management software.

1. Click **Start**, right-click **My Computer**, and click **Manage**.

2. In the tree, click **Services** under **Services and Applications**.

3. In the right pane, double-click **SNMP Service**.

4. On the General tab, make sure the Startup type is set to **Automatic** and that the service is started.

5. Click the **Security** tab (see Figure 11-22). From here you can configure the accepted communities for the agent. For example, Public is a community name that is often accepted by SNMP implementations. You click the Add button in the upper half of the dialog box to configure community names. Also, by default, the SNMP agent is configured to accept SNMP packets from localhost. You can configure the SNMP agent to accept SNMP packets from additional hosts by clicking the Add button in the lower half of the dialog box. Additional hosts are specified by host name, or by the IP or IPX address of the host from which the agent can accept SNMP packets.

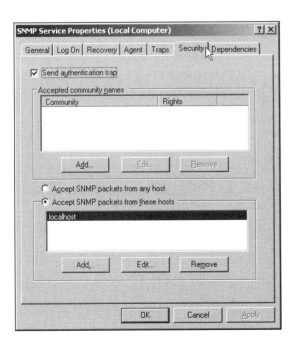

Figure 11-22   SNMP security parameters

11

6. Click the **Traps** tab (see Figure 11-23). When a certain type of event occurs on an SNMP agent (such as the system being restarted), the agent can send a message known as a **trap** to a management system. The management system that receives the trap is known as the trap destination. To configure a trap, you type in the name of the community to which the SNMP agent will send trap messages, and click **Add to list**. Next, you click **Add** in the Trap destinations, and type in the host name, or the IP or IPX address of the management system that will receive the trap messages.

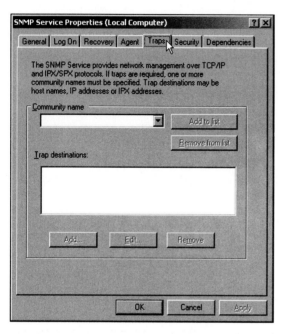

Figure 11-23   SNMP trap parameters

7. Click **OK**.

8. Double-click the **SNMP Trap Service**. If you plan to create traps, you need to configure this service, which is set to start manually by default. Consider setting the Startup type to **Automatic**, so that you do not have to remember to start the service after every reboot of the system.

9. Click **OK**.

10. Close the **Computer Management** tool.

CHAPTER SUMMARY

❏ Use system and network monitoring to thoroughly understand the servers on your network and the network's typical performance.

❏ The Computer Management tool enables you to monitor system services to determine if they are experiencing problems, and it enables you to restart a service, if necessary. It also helps you know what services are dependent on other services.

❏ Use Task Manager to monitor applications, processes, system performance, network performance, and logged on users. If there is a problem with a particular application or process, you can use Task Manager to stop the application or process. Also, use Task Manager to log off a hung user connection.

❏ System Monitor is a powerful tool that enables you to monitor all types of system and network activities. You can customize how information is displayed and save it to a file for later reference and analysis.

❏ Performance logs enable you to gather System Monitor data at specific times or intervals and record information.

❐ Network Monitor is used to gather information about network performance and is installed with Network Monitor Driver.

❐ The SNMP Service enables network agents to gather network performance data for use by network management software. It also provides a way to manage and configure specific network devices.

KEY TERMS

alert — Provides a warning of a specific Windows Server 2003 system or network event. The warning is sent to designated users.

base priority class — The initial priority assigned to a program process or thread in the program code.

benchmark (or **baseline**) — A measurement standard for hardware or software used to establish performance baselines under varying loads or circumstances.

community — A group of hosts that share the same SNMP Services.

community name — In SNMP communications, a rudimentary password (name) used by network agents and the network management station (or software) in the same community so that their communications cannot be easily intercepted by an unauthorized workstation or device.

counter — Used by System Monitor, this is a measurement technique for an object, as when measuring the processor performance by percentage in use.

counter log — Traces information on System Monitor objects that a server administrator configures, taking a snapshot at specified intervals.

Ethertype (ETYPE) — A property of an Ethernet frame that includes a two-byte code for the protocol type and is used in Ethernet communications by some vendors, but is not a part of the Ethernet standard.

filter — A capacity in network monitoring software that enables a network or server administrator to view only designated protocols, network events, network nodes, or other specialized views of the network.

handle — A resource, such as a file, used by a program that has its own identification so the program is able to access it.

instance — Used by System Monitor, when there are two or more types of elements to monitor, such as two or more threads or disk drives.

Network Monitor — A Windows Server 2003 network monitoring tool that can capture and display network performance data.

Network Monitor Driver — Enables a Microsoft-based server or workstation NIC to gather network performance data for assessment by Network Monitor.

page fault — This occurs whenever memory pages must be called from disk (from the paging file).

performance log — Tracks system and network performance information in a log that can be viewed later or imported into a spreadsheet, such as Microsoft Excel.

Service Access Point (SAP) — An access point in network communications, which specifies the network process that should accept a frame at the destination, such as TCP/IP, BPDU (a frame type used by network bridges), and special manufacturers, including Novell (for IPX/SPX).

Simple Network Management Protocol (SNMP) — Used for network management and performance monitoring on TCP/IP-based networks.

System Monitor — The Windows Server 2003 utility used to track system or application objects. For each object type there are one or more counters that can be logged for later analysis, or tracked in real time for immediate system monitoring.

thread — A block of program code executing within a running process. One process may launch one or more threads.

trace log — Monitors particular events (far fewer than offered through System Monitor) specified by a server administrator, so that the log contains only those instances when the events occur, as when creating a trace to record each time there is disk input/output activity or when there is an Active Directory Kerberos security event.

11

REVIEW QUESTIONS

1. You want to use Network Monitor to monitor only NWLink traffic on a network. How can you do this?

   a. Create a trigger.

   b. Use the NWLink object.

   c. Create a trap.

   d. Create a filter.

2. You have purchased a network management system and already have the network management station installed on your network. Today you are reviewing vendor statistics for switches and routers because you plan to buy several new ones for the network. What network management feature should you look for in these devices? (Choose all that apply.)

   a. SNMP compatibility

   b. TCP/IP compatibility

   c. use of service interfaces for HTTP

   d. the built-in WinManage driver

3. Your boss is trying to find some statistics about the network traffic across the Windows 2003 server that processes student degree checks at a college. What tool might you use to determine the number of broadcasts and multicasts seen by that server?

   a. Task Manager

   b. Network Monitor

   c. Broadcast Monitor

   d. DHCP Monitor

4. Your advertising firm is expecting a new client to visit in about 15 minutes. In preparation, you have been printing out reports and graphics for the meeting, but the print process is slow because the server is so busy. What can you do to best help ensure the printouts are finished in time?

   a. Log all other users off, even if there is not time to give them sufficient notification.

   b. Increase the priority of the print spooler process to AboveNormal or High.

   c. Decrease the priority of all processes, except the spooler process, to Low.

   d. Quickly increase the page file size by 1 to 2 MB to handle the printouts.

5. You are about to back up a Windows 2003 server in a small office, and everyone has gone home for the evening. However, you notice through a window in a locked office that a computer is still logged on and seems to have a file open. How can you log off that computer from the server?

   a. Use the System option in the Computer Management console.

   b. Use the Services and Applications option in the Computer Management console.

   c. Use the Users tab in Task Manager.

   d. Right-click that user's account in Local Users and Groups, and click Log Off.

6. Your server is running slowly, and you suspect there is a program or program process that is causing the problem, because you just installed eight new programs on a Windows 2003 server, which are run by you on the server and by clients using Terminal Services. Which of the following tools enable you to monitor for the problem? (Choose all that apply.)

   a. Computer Management tool using the Services option

   b. System Monitor using the Process object

   c. Task Manager using the Processes tab

   d. Dcpromo using the Application Management option

7. Which of the following modes can you use in System Monitor for displaying tracked data?

    a. Histogram

    b. Graph

    c. Report

    d. all of the above

    e. only a and b

    f. only b and c

8. You want to track each communication event associated with a computer for which you know the network address. What monitoring tool enables you to do this type of tracking? (Choose all that apply.)

    a. System Monitor using the View Computers window

    b. System Monitor using the Job Object Details object

    c. Network Monitor using the Station pane

    d. Network Monitor using the Total pane

9. You have opened Network Monitor, but it does not seem to be able to capture data from your server's NIC. Which of the following is the most likely cause?

    a. Network Monitor Driver is not installed.

    b. SNMP Service is not set up to enable traps.

    c. You have not previously run netperf in the Command Prompt window.

    d. all of the above

    e. only a and b

    f. only b and c

10. Your network has several older NetWare servers using IPX that seem to make the network operate more slowly. What should you monitor in this situation?

    a. Use Network Monitor to track traffic from NetWare servers.

    b. Use Network Monitor to track all BPDU traffic.

    c. Use System Monitor to monitor SNMP at those servers, because they are using an older SNMP version that creates congestion.

    d. Use System Monitor to monitor SMTP traffic at those servers, because SMTP can be transmitted with bogus IPX addresses.

11. While you are directly logged onto a Windows 2003 server using Internet Explorer, you discover that the program is not responding to any keystroke you make, including your attempts to close the program. When you go to another window, all functions are normal. How can you close Internet Explorer?

    a. Use the Services tool to stop and restart the Explorer Service.

    b. Use the Computer Management tool to stop and restart the Browser Service.

    c. Use the Performance snap-in to set the priority of the Explorer.exe program to 0.

    d. Use Task Manager to end the Internet Explorer task.

12. You are receiving calls from users that they cannot log onto a Windows 2003 server over the network. You know that the server has a reliable NIC and network connection and that it is running without apparent problems. Which service should you check as one place to start working on the problem?

    a. Plug and Play

    b. System Event Notification

    c. Workstation

    d. RunAs

13. After you install the SNMP Service in Windows Server 2003, what should you configure first in order to guarantee security?

    a. a trap

    b. a community name

    c. set the SNMP version to SNMPv1

    d. the MIB routing table

14. You have been monitoring a network that normally has network utilization at 20% to 30%, but during the past month the typical network utilization has risen to 75%. What should you do?

    a. This percentage represents an acceptable figure, and there is no need to do anything.

    b. This percentage is not a serious problem, but you should plan to examine how to tune network performance during the next couple of months.

    c. This percentage represents a serious problem, and you should begin more intense monitoring to locate problems and possibly upgrade portions of the network.

    d. This percentage means that a majority of your servers are overloaded and should be upgraded immediately.

15. Which of the following is (are) made possible by using SNMP?

    a. managing network devices

    b. monitoring a network and network devices

    c. locating network problems

    d. all of the above

    e. only a and b

    c. only b and c

16. While practicing, your assistant changed the priority of Windows Explorer and now the server response for all users is extremely slow. What priority did he most likely set?

    a. High

    b. Normal

    c. Realtime

    d. Low

17. In Question 16, if you did not already know the process for which the priority was changed, which tool could you use to determine the process?

    a. Task Manager Performance tab

    b. Task Manager Processes tab

    c. System Monitor using the Process object

    d. all of the above

    e. only a and b

    f. only b and c

18. You want to monitor a server while you are in a long morning meeting, because that is the best time for you to capture the data you need. Unfortunately, you are worried that it may slow server performance if it runs for the duration of your meeting. What can you do?

    a. Temporarily excuse yourself in the middle of the meeting, and pause the capture.

    b. For the sake of the server's performance, don't start the capture until you return.

    c. Set the Network Monitor to run as a background process.

    d. Create a counter log to automatically start the capture and stop it after 10 minutes.

19. Your boss has been using System Monitor to exclusively track the Processor object and % Processor time on a single CPU server. She does not have much time to monitor, but has decided that it is time to purchase a faster CPU because % Processor time occasionally reaches 85% to 100%. What is your advice?

    a. You agree it is time to purchase a new CPU.

    b. You recommend adding more RAM instead.

    c. You recommend rebooting the server immediately, because this is a sign of CPU leakage.

    d. You recommend doing nothing for now, because this probably indicates efficient use of the CPU by some programs and services.

20. Network Monitor is installed from which of the following?

    a. Add or Remove Programs option in Control Panel

    b. Network Connections option in Control Panel

    c. Add Hardware option in Control Panel

    d. Monitor tab from the System option in Control Panel

21. Which of the following are Windows Server 2003 services? (Choose all that apply.)

    a. Net Logon

    b. Protected Storage

    c. Remove Procedure Call (RPC) Locator

    d. Alerter

22. One of your server administrator colleagues in another company is struggling to understand the data produced by System Monitor. The servers and network at that company have been in place for about five months, but he has been too busy setting up clients to gather information about server performance. Now he does not know how to interpret the information so as to determine in what areas performance is normal and in what areas it is not. What should he have done in advance?

    a. Gather server and network benchmarks.

    b. Started the System Monitor from day one and left it running continuously to gather data on the ten most critical monitor objects.

    c. Run a trace log at least two full days a week, every week, monitoring system provider events.

    d. Run Task Manager constantly to gather performance information, and then periodically taken screen captures.

23. You want to stop the Network DDE Service, but are not sure what other services depend on it. How can you most easily find out?

    a. Use the Task Manager Applications tab.

    b. View the properties for the Network DDE Service in the Services portion of the Computer Management tool, and access the Dependencies tab.

    c. Stop the services that you think it might depend on, and look for the error messages.

    d. Look in the System Information option under the console tree in the Computer Management tool.

24. Which of the following can you view in the Graph pane in Network Monitor? (Choose all that apply.)

    a. % Network Utilization

    b. Bytes Per Hour

    c. Broadcasts Per Second

    d. Number of Connected Stations

25. You want to create a filter in Network Monitor, but the Edit Capture Filter button is deactivated. What is the problem?

    a. You must set the Network Monitor properties to enable filtering.

    b. You must set the Network Monitor Driver properties to enable filtering.

    c. Network Monitor is already capturing data and you must pause or stop capturing.

    d. You can only create a filter in the Session pane, but you have deactivated that pane.

CASE PROJECTS

Case Project Background

Wild Rivers is a company that manufactures canoes and kayaks for recreational use. The business and manufacturing activities of the company take place in a large industrial building that houses offices, the manufacturing unit, an inventory unit, and a shipping unit. The company supplies products to major sporting goods stores, retail outlets, and outdoor mail-order companies. Its network consists of 18 Windows 2003 servers that are configured to use TCP/IP and four older Novell NetWare servers that are configured for IPX/SPX. They have hired you to advise the server administrators in network monitoring, a task that has largely been ignored as the company has raced to implement servers and software to keep up with business needs.

Case Project 11-1: Server Benchmarks

Wild Rivers has never taken the time to gather server performance benchmarks. Develop a written plan for gathering benchmarks that will help them monitor the server, perform regular tuning maintenance, and diagnose problems.

Case Project 11-2: Tools for Monitoring a Server

The server administrators are very unfamiliar with the basic server monitoring tools. Prepare a brief description of each of the following tools, including how to access each tool:

❑ Computer Management tool for monitoring services

❑ Task Manager

❑ System Monitor

❑ Performance Logs and Alerts

Case Project 11-3: Installing Network Monitoring Tools

The server administrators have never installed any network monitoring tools in Windows Server 2003. Prepare a brief written report explaining how to install the following:

❑ Network Monitor Driver

❑ Network Monitor

❑ SNMP Service

Case Project 11-4: Solving a Network Problem

Wild Rivers gives you a call to report the network seems to be saturated with heavy traffic, but none of the server administrators can determine the source of the problem or if the excessive traffic is TCP/IP-based or IPX-based. How would you explain to them in a fast e-mail how they might use Network Monitor, System Monitor, or both to locate the problem? Can either of these network monitoring tools be used to monitor the NetWare servers in case they are a source of the problem, and if so, how?

CHAPTER
12
MANAGING SYSTEM RELIABILITY AND AVAILABILITY

After reading this chapter and completing the exercises, you will be able to:

♦ Develop general problem-solving strategies
♦ Resolve boot problems
♦ Back up and restore system state data
♦ Restore a failed system volume
♦ Use Event Viewer for solving problems
♦ Troubleshoot security using the Security Configuration and Analysis Snap-in
♦ Troubleshoot connectivity
♦ Remotely administer a server

Many organizations want their servers to be available around the clock, but despite the best laid plans, problems do occur. Your challenge as a server administrator is to reduce the effect of problems by developing solid problem-solving techniques, including how to quickly get a system back on its feet. Even though you use fault-tolerance methods and prevention through system monitoring, problems may still occur. For instance, a lightning strike may be conducted through a network connection and corrupt the boot sector; or a virus may get through your virus checker.

In this chapter, you'll learn how to effectively address server problems through problem-solving strategies. You will discover how to diagnose problems and use Windows Server 2003 troubleshooting tools, such as safe mode and Recovery Console to address boot problems. You'll learn to back up and restore system state data and the system protected files, and how to restore a failed volume. Also, you will find out how to use Event Viewer as a diagnostic tool, plus use the Security Configuration and Analysis Snap-in to analyze security on a server or in Active Directory. Further, you will learn how to troubleshoot system connectivity problems and how to administer a server remotely.

GENERAL PROBLEM-SOLVING STRATEGIES

The best approach to solving server and network problems is to develop troubleshooting strategies. Four general strategies are:

- Understand how a server and the network interact
- Train your users to help you solve problems
- Solve problems step-by-step
- Track problems and solutions

Understanding How Servers and the Network Interact

There are many steps you can take to better understand the environment in which a server operates. Many server and network administrators create a diagram of the entire network and update the diagram each time an aspect of the network changes. The network diagram should include the following elements:

- Mainframes, minicomputers, and servers
- Workstations and network printers (unless the network is too large to include these)
- Network devices
- Telecommunications links
- Remote links
- Building locations

A server does not exist in a vacuum, but instead is a member of a larger community of networked workstations and their users. Gathering benchmarks, as discussed in Chapter 11, helps you understand your server and how its network context affects it. For example, slow server performance can look like a network problem, and slow network performance can look like a server problem. The more you know about the server's network context, the faster you can resolve a problem such as slow server performance.

Training Users to Help

Another valuable strategy is to train network users to be your partners in reporting problems. If you encourage users to be troubleshooting allies, they are more likely to feel they can take action to deal with a problem, rather than wait impatiently for you to detect and solve it. When you train users to gather information and report it to you, they become troubleshooting partners who can advance you several steps toward the solution. The following are some actions you can train users to take to help you and themselves. For example, they should:

- Save their work at the first sign of a problem.
- Record information about a problem as the problem is occurring.
- Report any protocol information, such as error messages about a protocol or an address.
- Quickly report a problem by telephone, or by voice mail if you cannot be reached immediately.
- Avoid sending e-mail about urgent problems.

Solving Problems Step-by-Step

Equipped with knowledge of your network context and help from trained users, you can use the following step-by-step techniques to solve server and network problems:

1. Get as much information as possible about the problem. If a network user reports the problem, listen carefully to his or her description. Even if he or she does not use the right terminology, the information is still valuable. Part of your challenge is to ask the right questions to get as much information as possible.

2. Record the error message at the time it appears or when a user reports it to you. This is an obvious, but sometimes overlooked step. If you try to recall the message from memory, you may lose some important information. For example, the error "Network not responding" can lead you to a different set of troubleshooting steps than the message "Network timeout error." The first message might signal a damaged NIC, whereas the second message could mean that a database server is overloaded and the application is waiting to obtain data.

3. Start with simple solutions. Often the solution to a problem is as simple as connecting a cable or power cord.

4. Determine if anyone else is experiencing the problem. For example, several people may report they cannot load a word-processing software package. This may be due to a problem at the server they use to load the software. If only one person is experiencing this problem, it may point to trouble on her or his workstation.

5. Regularly check the Windows Server 2003 event logs for signs of a problem (you'll learn how to do this later in the chapter).

6. Use System Monitor and Network Monitor filtering to help you troubleshoot problems.

7. Check for power interruptions. Power problems are a common source of server and network difficulties. Even though the server is on a UPS, its network connection can still be a source of problems because the network cable can carry current to the server's NIC during a lightning storm.

Tracking Problems and Solutions

One effective troubleshooting tool is to keep a log of all network problems and their solutions. Some server administrators log problems in a database created for that purpose. Others build problem logging into help desk systems maintained by their organization. A help desk system is application software designed to maintain information on computer systems, user questions, problem solutions, and other information that members of the organization can reference.

The advantage of tracking problems is that you soon accumulate a wealth of information on solutions. For example, to jog your memory about a solution, you can look up how you handled a similar problem six months ago. The log of problems also can be used as a teaching tool and reference for other computer support staff. Problems that show up repeatedly in the log may indicate that special attention is needed, such as replacing a server that experiences frequent hardware problems.

It is also good practice to keep a change log or record of changes made to the system. Sometimes problems arise when configuration changes are made to a server, such as the installation of new hardware and/or software or a change in settings. Documenting changes provides a reference for troubleshooting if problems should arise later. This is especially important if you are not the only server administrator and someone else is troubleshooting the problem.

12

RESOLVING BOOT PROBLEMS

Sometimes a server encounters a hardware problem and cannot be booted, or it displays an error screen during the boot process, or it simply hangs. Several things can lead to boot problems, such as the installation of new software, new or corrupt driver files, or hardware problems. Some of the common causes of boot failures include:

- Disk failure on the drive or drives containing the system and boot files
- A corrupted partition table
- A corrupted boot file
- A corrupted Master Boot Record
- A disk read error

In most cases, the first step is to power off the computer and try rebooting. Often this will work in instances where there is a temporary disk read error or memory error during the first boot attempt, which is corrected on the second try. Also, one or more data storage registers may be out of synchronization in the CPU, causing a transient problem. Rebooting resets the CPU registers. If there are multiple drives in the computer, a disk controller may need to be reset, which is accomplished by rebooting.

 The best way to reboot for clearing a temporary error is to turn the power off, wait several seconds for the hard disk drives to fully come to a stop, and then turn on the power. This causes all components to completely reset. If, instead, you reboot using a reset button, some components may not fully reset.

Troubleshooting by Using Safe Mode

If a simple reboot does not fix the problem, or if you have installed new software or drivers, or changed the server configuration, and the server still does not properly boot, try using the advanced options for booting—accessed by pressing F8 as soon as the computer boots—which include starting the computer in safe mode. **Safe mode** boots the server using the most generic default settings for the display, disk drives, and pointing device, and only those services needed to boot a basic configuration. After you boot into safe mode, you have the opportunity to further troubleshoot the problem.

For example, if you install software or a driver that causes a problem with the boot process, you can boot into safe mode and remove that software or driver. Or, perhaps you have replaced the mouse with a trackball and installed the new driver for the trackball, but after you reboot, there is no pointer on the screen when you move the new trackball. You can boot into safe mode, reinstall the old driver and mouse, and contact the trackball vendor for a solution or new driver. Or, if you changed the server's configuration, as in setting up an additional paging file or installing a Windows component, and the server does not properly boot, you can restore the original paging file settings or remove the Windows component while in safe mode.

 If you contact a Microsoft technician for help with a server problem, often she or he will ask you to boot in safe mode in order to execute troubleshooting steps.

Table 12-1 lists the advanced booting options that are available when you press F8 at the beginning of the boot process. Also, Figure 12-1 illustrates these options.

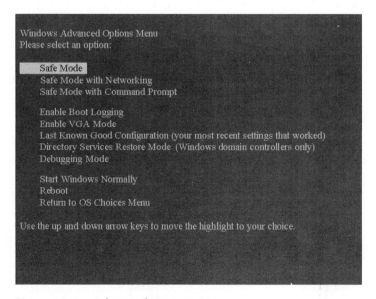

Figure 12-1 Advanced Options Menu

To access the advanced options menu:

1. Reboot the computer. (Be sure all users are logged off before doing this.)

2. Press **F8** as soon as the computer boots.

3. Select the option you want to use, and press **Enter**.

4. Highlight **Windows Server 2003, Standard** as the operating system option, and press **Enter**. (Make sure the option you selected in Step 3 is displayed at the bottom of the screen; if it is not, press F8 to return to the Advanced Options Menu.)

Table 12-1   Advanced Options Menu

Booting Option	Description
Safe Mode	System boots using the minimum configuration of devices and drivers, and does not have network connectivity
Safe Mode with Networking	System boots using the minimum configuration of devices and drivers, and does have network connectivity
Safe Mode with Command Prompt	System boots into the command mode using the minimum configuration of devices and drivers, and does not have network connectivity
Enable Boot Logging	Used to create a record of devices and drivers that started, so you can check a log for points of failure—look for the log in the \Windows folder with the name ntbtlog.txt
Enable VGA Mode	System boots using a generic VGA setting
Last Known Good Configuration	System boots using the last configuration before any changes to the configuration were made and implemented in the registry
Directory Services Restore Mode	Recreates the Active Directory service and the SYSVOL Restore Mode shared folder
Debugging Mode	Boots the system while transmitting debug data to be viewed at another computer over a serial connection, which can be used by Microsoft technicians to troubleshoot problems
Start Windows Normally	Starts the system without any special options
Reboot	Reboots the system
Return to OS Choices Menu	Returns to the regular operating system menu from which to select to boot into Windows Server 2003 (or another operating system on a dual-boot system)

12

Use the advanced option that is the most appropriate for the kind of problem you are troubleshooting. For example, if your only problem is that you have installed a new monitor driver and cannot use or see the display when you boot, select Enable VGA Mode. If the problem is related to the most recent software or configuration change you have made, such as installing an additional SCSI adapter or a new modem, boot using the Last Known Good Configuration. The **Last Known Good Configuration** is the Windows Server 2003 configuration that is stored in the registry (HKEY_LOCAL_MACHINE\System\ CurrentControlSet) and is the configuration in effect prior to making a system, driver, or configuration change since the last time the computer was booted. For those times when you are not sure why the system is having problems, or you have installed multiple new drivers or several new software programs, use the Safe Mode or the Safe Mode with Networking option so that you can access the Windows Server 2003 desktop to work on the problem.

If you use safe mode, but are unable to troubleshoot the problem, or a failed driver message is displayed during the boot process, use the Enable Boot Logging option so that you can create a log that you can check later for problems. For example, you might boot so that the log is created, and then boot again into safe mode so that you can view the contents of the log.

The Safe Mode with Command Prompt option is particularly useful when you can solve a problem by executing a command, such as by running chkdsk to repair damaged files or by running sfc to locate critical system files that have been overwritten and then restore them.

If you have Active Directory installed and suspect that it is damaged, or that the **SYSVOL** shared volumes (see the following Note) are corrupted, use the Directory Services Restore Mode to restore damaged files and folders.

When you set up Active Directory, a domain controller is automatically set up with the SYSVOL shared volume, which contains publicly available files that users and domain controllers (DCs) need for domain access. The SYSVOL shared folder exists on all DCs, and when the contents change on one DC, the change is replicated to all DCs.

Activity 12-1: Booting into Safe Mode

Time Required: Approximately 15 minutes

Objective: Learn how to boot into safe mode.

Description: In this activity, you practice accessing the advanced menu options on a server, and then you boot into the safe mode.

1. Make sure all users are logged off Windows Server 2003. What tool would you use to check?

2. Shut down and then reboot the computer (click **Start**, click **Shut Down**, select **Restart** in the What do you want the computer to do? box, select **Hardware: Maintenance (Planned)** in the Options box, and click **OK).**

3. Press **F8** as soon as the computer boots. (You may need to press F8 several times.) What are the options that you see on the screen? What option do you use to boot to fix a monitor driver problem? Which one do you use to run chkdsk?

4. Select **Safe Mode,** and press **Enter.**

5. Highlight **Windows Server 2003, Standard** as the operating system option, and press **Enter.** What information is displayed as the system boots? How might this information prove helpful in troubleshooting a problem?

6. Press **Ctrl+Alt+Del** and log in with your username and password.

7. Click **OK** when you see the warning that you are in safe mode. How is the Windows Server 2003 desktop display different in safe mode from when you boot normally? Record your observations about safe mode.

8. Shut down the computer, and then reboot.

Using the Automated System Recovery Set to Solve a Boot Problem

If rebooting does not work and you cannot solve the problem using the advanced menu options, then an alternative is to use the Automated System Recovery (ASR) set that you learned how to create in Chapter 2. Before you begin the recovery procedure make sure you have the following:

- The ASR set of disks previously created using the Backup program

- Previously created backup media

- The Windows Server 2003, Standard Edition, CD-ROM

To use the ASR set for a recovery, follow these steps:

1. Shut down (if possible) and power off the computer.

2. Insert the Windows Server 2003, Standard Edition, CD-ROM, and power on the computer.

3. Use the appropriate steps for that computer to boot from the CD-ROM, such as pressing any key.

4. During the text-mode portion of Windows Setup, press **F2** when prompted at the bottom of the screen (do not press F2 until after the text-mode portion of Windows Setup is started). Insert the ASR floppy when prompted.

5. Follow the on-screen instructions.

The ASR recovery process reads the disk configuration information on the ASR set and restores the disk signatures, volumes and partitions, and the system files required to start the computer. Once this is complete, a basic version of Windows Server 2003, Standard Edition, is installed and you can start a restore using the backup media previously created.

Troubleshooting by Using the Recovery Console

The **Recovery Console** enables you to boot into the Windows Server 2003 command line so that you can repair a disk problem or copy a critical file back to the server. Another reason for using the Recovery Console is to start a service or to format a drive.

In Windows NT Server, server administrators sometimes created MS-DOS, Windows 95, or Windows 98 startup disks so that they could boot the system from Drive A using one of these operating systems, and then execute command-line utilities to troubleshoot problems, such as to format a disk. The Recovery Console makes creating this type of disk less important, because it provides a better way to access Windows Server 2003 files and repair utilities directly from Windows Server 2003.

There are two ways to start the Recovery Console:

- Start it from the Microsoft Windows Server 2003 CD-ROM

- Install the Recovery Console as a program that can be run when Windows Server 2003 is booted

The Recovery Console can be installed on the computer by following these general steps:

1. Insert the Windows Server 2003, Standard Edition, CD-ROM.

2. Click **Start**, point to **All Programs**, point to **Accessories**, and click **Command Prompt**.

3. At the prompt, type the CD-ROM drive letter and \i386\winnt32 /cmdcons, such as E:\i386\winnt32 /cmdcons.

After it is installed, the Recovery Console is listed as a startup option from the Advanced Options Menu. When you go into the Recovery Console, the system places you directly into the \Windows folder from which to work in a character mode using command-line commands. To determine what commands are available, type help, and then press Enter. Table 12-2 provides a sampling of many of the commands.

Table 12-2   Sample Recovery Console commands

Command	Description
attrib	Manages folder and file attributes
batch	Executes a batch file of commands that can be run from the command prompt (and select batch file programming commands)
cd (or chdir)	Changes to a different directory (folder), to the parent directory, or shows the directory you are in
chkdsk	Verifies and fixes files (requires access to the Autochk.exe file)
cls	Reinitializes the display
copy	Copies files
del (delete)	Deletes files
dir	Lists the contents of a directory (folder)
disable	Disables a hardware driver or service
diskpart	Partitions a disk and manages multiple partitions on a system

12

Table 12-2   Sample Recovery Console commands (continued)

Command	Description
enable	Enables a hardware driver or service that has been previously disabled
exit	Closes the Recovery Console and reboots the system
expand	Uncompresses a file
fixboot	Repairs the system partition so that you can boot from that partition, because it applies a new boot sector
fixmbr	Fixes a corrupted Master Boot Record
format	Used to format a drive
help	Provides a listing of Recovery Console commands or can be used to view the documentation for a specific command
listsvc	Displays all of the hardware drivers and system services
map	Maps a drive that is accessed through the network
md (mkdir)	Creates a new directory
more	Shows a file's contents
rd (rmdir)	Deletes a directory
ren (rename)	Modifies a file's name
systemroot	Changes to the root directory
type	Shows a file's contents

You can find information about the purpose and syntax of a specific command by typing help and then the command, such as by typing help attrib, and then pressing Enter. Use any of these commands to repair a problem. For example, if you believe that the boot sector is corrupted on the system partition, use the fixboot command to fix it. Use the fixmbr utility to fix a corrupted Master Boot Record.

Activity 12-2: Using Recovery Console

Time Required: Approximately 15 minutes

Objective: Learn how to access and use the Recovery Console.

Description: In this activity, you practice using the Recovery Console. You need the Windows Server 2003, Standard Edition, CD-ROM. Also, obtain the Administrator account password from your instructor, if you do not know it already.

1. If the server is already booted, make sure all users are logged off. Insert the Windows Server 2003, Standard Edition, CD-ROM, and reboot the computer (click **Start**, click **Shut Down**, select **Restart** in the What do you want the computer to do? box, select **Hardware: Maintenance (Planned)** in the Options box, and click **OK**). Boot from the Windows Server 2003, Standard Edition, CD-ROM (do not perform a normal boot, but boot the system as though you plan to install the operating system directly from the installation CD-ROM).

2. After the Windows Setup program starts, continue with the installation process until you reach the Welcome to Setup screen. On the Welcome to Setup screen, press **R** to access the Recovery Console (see Figure 12-2).

3. Select the drive containing the \Windows folder you want to access, such as by typing 1 to access \Windows on drive C. Press **Enter**.

4. Type the Administrator account password, and press **Enter**. What is displayed on the screen?

5. Type **help**, and press **Enter**. What information do you see? Can you run chkdsk? Press the **spacebar** to return to the prompt.

6. Type **help diskpart**. What can you do with this utility? What utility would you use to repair the Master Boot Record? Record your observations.

7. Type **exit** and press **Enter** to leave the Recovery Console, and reboot.

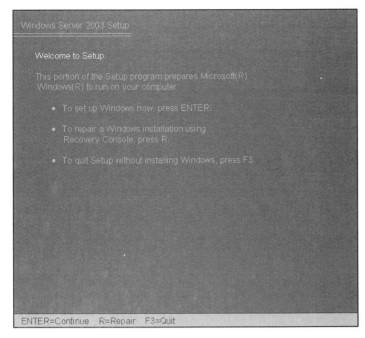

Figure 12-2   Starting Recovery Console

General Tips for Fixing Boot Problems

Using the safe mode, Recovery Console, and other techniques, Tables 12-3 and 12-4 provide tips for fixing boot problems and responding to Stop error messages that may be displayed. A Stop message is an error message displayed when the server experiences a serious problem and then stops functioning.

Table 12-3   Troubleshooting boot problems

Boot Problem	Solutions
A message appears when booting, such as one of the following: Inaccessible Boot Device; Invalid Partition Table; Hard Disk Error; Hard Disk Absent or Failed	1. The boot sector on the NTFS partition is corrupted or the hard drive is damaged. This may be caused by a virus, a corrupted partition table, a BIOS setting change, or a corrupted disk. Check the BIOS setup to make certain it is correct. Correct any improper settings (also make sure the CMOS battery is working).
	2. If there are no BIOS problems, boot the system using the Recovery Console. Insert a virus scanner in drive A:, and attempt to scan the hard disk for viruses. If a virus is found, remove it. Whether or not a virus is found, reboot so you can use the ASR set to replace corrupted files.
	3. If the disk cannot be accessed, determine if the problem is the hard disk, disk controller, or a SCSI adapter; and replace the defective part (make sure to check that a SCSI adapter is properly terminated). If the hard disk must be replaced, reinstall the operating system.
The system hangs when booting	1. Turn the power off and on to the computer to reboot. Try rebooting a couple of times.
	2. If rebooting does not work, check the BIOS settings to be sure they have not changed and that the CMOS battery is working. If many of the BIOS settings are incorrect, replace the battery and restore the proper settings.

12

Table 12-3   Troubleshooting boot problems (continued)

Boot Problem	Solutions
	3. For an SMP computer, the hal.dll file may be corrupted. Boot up so you can use the Recovery Console to reinstall the hal.dll from the manufacturer's disk.
You see the message that there is a nonsystem disk or disk error	1. Remove any disks from drive A: or the CD-ROM drive, and reboot. 2. If Step 1 does not work, boot using the Recovery Console and reinstall the Winboot.ini file from the ASR set, because this file may be corrupted on the system drive. 3. Boot so that you can access the Recovery Console and run fixboot.
Changes were made to the system configuration when last logged on and now the computer does not boot	Stop the boot process immediately and reboot using the Last Known Good Configuration option on the Advanced Menu Options screen (press F8 when you boot the computer). Once logged on, check the configuration and fix any problems, such as a bad or removed device driver.
The screen display goes blank or is jumbled as the computer begins booting into Windows Server 2003	1. Immediately stop the boot process. Restart the computer, accessing the BIOS Setup before starting Windows Server 2003. Check the video BIOS setup to make sure it is correct, and restore any settings that are changed. Reboot the computer. 2. If there are no BIOS problems, reboot using the Enable VGA Mode from the advanced menu options. Once logged on, check and reinstall the display driver.
A driver is missing, but you are not sure which one, or the operating system is having trouble recognizing all hardware components on the computer when it boots	Boot using safe mode, and watch for a problem as the drivers are loaded, or boot using the Enable Boot Logging option from the advanced menu options, and examine the \Windows\ntbtlog.txt file.

Table 12-4   Troubleshooting boot problems associated with stop messages

Stop Message*	Solutions
0x00000023 and the message Fat File System or NTFS File System	1. Boot into safe mode or the Recovery Console, and run chkdsk to repair any damaged files. 2. If you have recently installed a virus scanner or a disk defragmenter that is not from Microsoft or compatible with Windows Server 2003, boot into safe mode or use Last Known Good Configuration, and remove that software.
0x0000001E and the message Kmode_Exception_Not_Handled	1. If you have recently installed a new video system and associated drivers, remove the new hardware, and reboot into the safe mode to remove the new drivers (or boot using Enable VGA Mode). Do the same if you have installed any new drivers. 2. Verify the video setup in the computer's BIOS or install any updated BIOS software offered by the computer vendor. 3. Reboot using safe mode or the Recovery Console, and make sure that you are not out of disk space.
0x000000B4 and the message Video Driver Init Failure	If you have recently installed a new video system and associated drivers, remove the new hardware, and reboot into the safe mode to remove the new drivers (or boot using Enable VGA Mode).

Table 12-4 Troubleshooting boot problems associated with stop messages (continued)

Stop Message*	Solutions
0x0000007B and the message Inaccessible_Boot_Device	1. Boot into safe mode, and check for a virus. 2. Boot into the Recovery Console, and restore the Master Boot Record using the fixmbr command. 3. Boot into the Recovery Console, and run chkdsk to repair any damaged files.
0x0000002E and the message Data Bus Error or 0x0000007F and the message Unexpected Kernel Mode Trap	Boot using the Recovery Console, and run memory test software such as diagnostics that come with your computer or from a memory vendor, and replace any defective memory.
0x0000000A and the message IRQL Not Less or Equal	Suspect a hardware resource conflict caused by a new device or card you have added. If you can boot using the safe mode, check the system log. If you cannot boot into safe mode, remove the new device or devices and boot using Last Known Good Configuration.
0x00000058 and the message Ftdisk Internal Error	Suspect that the main volume in a mirrored set has failed. Boot using the secondary volume, and use the Disk Management tool to attempt to repair the main volume and resynchronize it with the secondary volume. If you cannot repair the volume, use the Disk Management tool to break the mirrored set, replace the damaged disk, and then recreate the mirrored set.
0x000000BE and the message Attempted Write to Readonly Memory	Boot using the Enable Boot Logging option and then boot again into safe mode (or the Recovery Console) so you can examine the \Windows\ntbtlog.txt log for a driver that did not start or that is causing problems, then reinstall or replace the driver using the safe mode or by copying it into the system using the Recovery Console.

* Information in this table is derived from Microsoft's help documentation entitled *Troubleshooting Specific STOP Messages*.

12

BACKING UP AND RESTORING SYSTEM STATE DATA

To protect against a disaster and to provide a way to recover system information, regularly back up the Windows Server 2003 system state data. In Windows Server 2003, the system state data consists of several critical elements:

- System and boot files
- Active Directory
- SYSVOL folder (when the Active Directory is installed)
- Registry
- COM+ Class Registration information
- DNS zones (when DNS is installed)
- Certificate information (when certificate services are installed)
- Server cluster data (when server clustering is used)

All of the system state data is backed up as a group because many of these entities are interrelated. When you back up the system state data, keep in mind that you can only back it up from the local computer, which means that the backup medium, such as a tape drive, must be physically attached to that computer.

When you back up the system state data, also make sure you are backing up the system protected files, which are the startup system files needed by Windows Server 2003. These files include:

- *Ntldr*—Initiates the startup process, operating system selection, and hardware detection
- *Bootsect.dos*—Used for dual-boot systems
- *Boot.ini*—Used by Ntldr to obtain startup information, such as which operating systems are available and their location
- *Ntdetect.com*—Detects the computer's hardware
- *Ntbootdd.sys*—A driver for SCSI adapters, if present
- *Ntoskrnl.exe*—The Windows Server 2003 kernel
- *Hal.dll*—The hardware abstraction layer

All of these files are located in the root of the system partition, except Ntoskrnl.exe and Hal.dll, which are in the \Windows\system32 folder. To ensure that the system protected files are backed up, make sure that System State is selected to be backed up before you click the Start Backup button. When you see the Backup Job Information dialog box before the backup starts, click the Advanced button, and make sure that Automatically backup System Protected Files with the System State is checked.

Activity 12-3: Backing up System State Data and System Protected Files

Time Required: Approximately 10 minutes

Objective: Learn how to back up the system state data and system protected files.

Description: This activity enables you to practice backing up the system state data and system protected files. You do not complete the backup, but simply find out how to include these files with your regular backups or to create a backup of these files. For this activity, you do not need backup media. (You may need to log into the computer after rebooting in Activity 12-2.)

1. Click **Start**, point to **All Programs**, point to **Accessories**, point to **System Tools**, and click **Backup**.
2. When the Backup or Restore Wizard starts, click the link for **Advanced Mode**.
3. Click the **Backup** tab. Click the **System State** check box in the left pane (see Figure 12-3), which enables you to back up the system state data. Note that you can select to back up only this information, or you can combine backing up the system state data with any other folders or files.

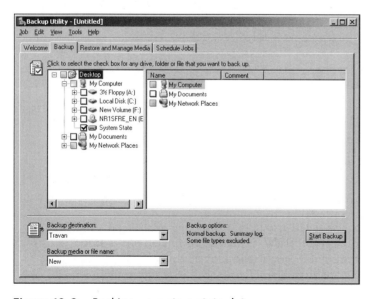

Figure 12-3   Backing up system state data

4. Click **Start Backup**.

5. In the Backup Job Information dialog box, click **Advanced**.

6. Make sure that **Automatically backup System Protected Files with the System State** is selected (see Figure 12-4). This option is checked by default when you select System State in Step 3, otherwise it is deactivated.

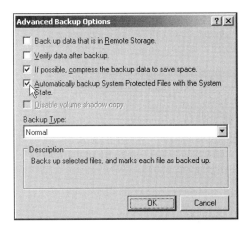

Figure 12-4   Backing up the System Protected Files

7. Click **Cancel** to exit the Advanced Backup Options dialog box.

8. Click **Cancel** in the Backup Job Information dialog box.

9. Close the **Backup Utility** window.

If you need to restore the system state data, remember that all of the data must be restored, not just selected portions such as the registry. To restore the system state data, start the Backup utility, and click the Advanced Mode link. Click the Restore and Manage Media tab, choose and expand the backup media in the left pane, and select the System State box.

RESTORING A FAILED SYSTEM VOLUME

If the drive containing the system volume fails, use the following steps to replace it and restore the information on it using the system state data and system protected files backups, plus your other data file backups:

1. Replace the failed hardware.

2. Install Windows Server 2003, Standard Edition, from the CD-ROM on the new drive.

3. Use the Backup utility to restore the system state data and all other data, using the most recent backup tapes.

If you are using only normal backups, then the restore simply involves using the most current normal backup tape or tapes. If you have designed the backups to combine normal plus differential or incremental backups, then there will be additional steps after restoring from the last normal backup. You need to restore from the appropriate differential or incremental backups.

Sometimes you need to turn to other resources to help you troubleshoot. There are many resources available through the Microsoft Web site (*www.microsoft.com*), such as the Knowledge Base, white papers, and TechNet information. A subscription to the Microsoft TechNet CDs is another reference source. On the Windows Server 2003, Standard Edition, CD-ROM, check the \Support\Tools folder for additional tools you can use to manage your server, such as tools for managing Active Directory and repairing disk problems. The Windows Server 2003 Resource Kit, which includes documentation not found in the manuals, can be purchased from Microsoft.

USING AND CONFIGURING EVENT VIEWER

A valuable tool for diagnosing all kinds of server problems is Event Viewer (see Figure 12-5). There are three principal **event logs** that contain a record of all types of server events: system, security, and application. Also, there are event logs for services that you may have installed, such as the Directory Service, DNS Server, and File Replication Service logs.

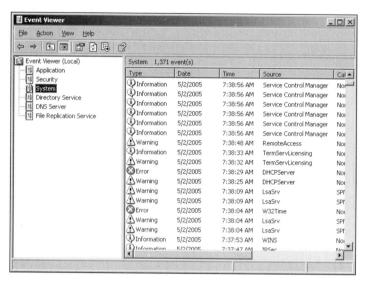

Figure 12-5   Event Viewer

The **system log** records information about system-related events such as hardware errors, driver problems, and hard drive errors. The **security log** records access and security information about logon accesses and file, folder, and system policy changes. If you have auditing set up, for instance, file auditing, use the security log to track each audited event, such as a successful or failed attempt to access a file. If you choose to audit an account or folder, the audit data is recorded in the security log. The **application log** records information about how software applications are performing, if the programmer has designed the software to write information into the log. For example, if a software error occurs, it may be recorded in the log. The **Directory Service log** records events that are associated with Active Directory, such as updates to Active Directory, events related to the Active Directory database, replication events, and startup and shutdown events. The **DNS Server log** provides information about instances in which (1) DNS information is updated, (2) there are problems with the DNS service, and (3) the DNS server has started successfully after booting. File replication activities are recorded through the **File Replication Service log**, which contains information about (1) changes to file replication, (2) when the service has started, and (3) completed replication tasks.

There are several elements related to working with event logs, which are discussed in the next sections:

- Viewing log events
- Creating filters
- Maintaining event logs

Viewing Log Events

Log events are displayed in Event Viewer with an icon that indicates the seriousness of the event. An informational message, such as notification that a service has been started, is prefaced by a blue "i" displayed in a white comment circle; a warning, such as a statement that a CD-ROM is not loaded, is depicted by a black "!" (exclamation point) that appears on a yellow caution symbol; and an error, such as a defective disk adapter, is indicated with a white "x" that appears inside a red circle (see Figure 12-5).

Each log displays descriptive information about individual events, such as the following information provided in the system log:

- Type of event—information, warning, or error

- Date and time of the event

- Source of the event (which is the software application or hardware reporting it)

- Category of event, if one applies, such as a system event or logon event

- Event number, so the event can be tracked if entered into a database (associated events may have the same number)

- User account involved in the event, if applicable

- Name of the computer on which the event took place

Event Viewer is opened by clicking Start, pointing to All Programs, pointing to Administrative Tools, and clicking Event Viewer. Two other ways to access Event Viewer are as an MMC snap-in or from the Computer Management tool, under System Tools in the tree. Event Viewer contains options to view all events or to set a filter so only certain events are viewed, such as only error events.

To view the contents of a log, click that log in the tree under Event Viewer. To view the detailed information about an event, double-click the event (see Figure 12-6). Read the description of the event for more information.

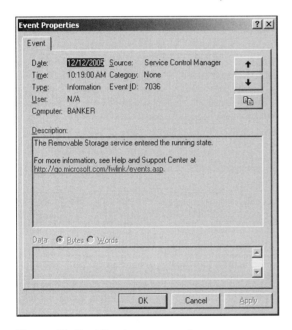

Figure 12-6   Viewing an event

The event logs are a good source of information to help you troubleshoot a software or hardware problem. For example, if Windows Server 2003 crashes unexpectedly, reboot and look at the logs as a first step. A memory allocation or disk problem may be found quickly through the help of the system log. If a software application hangs, check the application log for information.

Using the Event Viewer Filter Option

All of the event logs in Event Viewer have a filter option to help you quickly locate a problem. For example, you can design a filter to show only events associated with the disk drives or only events that occurred on the previous afternoon. The events can be filtered on the basis of the following criteria:

- Event type, such as information, warning, error, success audit (for the security log), failure audit (for the security log)

- Source of the event, such as a particular service, software component, or hardware component

- Category of the event, such as a security change

- Event ID, which is a number assigned by Event Viewer to identify the event

- User associated with the event

- Computer associated with the event

- Date range

- Time of day range

Maintaining Event Logs

The event logs quickly fill with information, and from the beginning you should establish how you want the logs maintained. There are several ways to maintain the logs:

- Size each log to prevent it from filling too quickly.

- Regularly clear each log before it is full.

- Automatically override the oldest events when a log is full.

Some network administrators prefer to save the log contents on a regular basis, such as weekly or monthly. Others prefer to allow the logs to overwrite the oldest events. It is recommended that you develop a maintenance schedule to save the log contents for a designated time period, because the logs contain valuable information about historical server activity.

To tune the event logs, open Event Viewer, and right-click each log you want to tune, one at a time, and click Properties. In the Log size box on the General tab, set the log size in the Maximum log size KB box. Set the maximum log size to match the way you want to handle the logs. The default size is 16,384 KB. For example, if you want to accumulate two weeks of information, set the size to enable that much information to be recorded, for instance 22,000 KB. You need to test this setting for a few weeks to make sure that the size you set is adequate. A common way to make sure that an event log is never completely filled is to use one of these options: Overwrite events as needed or Overwrite events older than *X*(amount of) days. For example, you might set up the log to overwrite events that are older than 14 days, so that you continuously have at least two weeks of information stored in a log.

 If the server is a busy domain controller on which auditing is enabled, even a large security log may contain only enough space to record a few hours of audited events. In this situation, besides setting a large log size, consider auditing only what is necessary for regularly viewing the log for the information you are seeking.

There also are options to save and clear the individual logs. To save a log, right-click the log in the tree, click Save Log File As, enter a name for the log file, and click Save. You can save the log as one of three kinds of files:

- *.evt*—Is saved in event log format

- *.txt*—Is saved as a tab-delimited text file that can be imported into a spreadsheet

- *.csv*—Is saved as a comma-delimited text file that can be imported into a spreadsheet

When you are logged on as Administrator, the event log files are saved by default in the folder \Documents and Settings\Administrator\My Documents. To clear a log, right-click the log in the tree of the Event Viewer, and click Clear all Events.

Activity 12-4: Using Event Viewer

Time Required: Approximately 10 minutes

Objective: Use Event Viewer to view system log events.

Description: In this activity, you use Event Viewer to examine system log events, and you practice building a filter.

1. Click **Start**, point to **All Programs**, point to **Administrative Tools,** and click **Event Viewer**.

2. If no logs appear in the tree, double-click **Event Viewer (local)**. What logs are available? Click each log to view its contents, and record your observations.

3. Click **System in the tree** and briefly scroll through its contents. Are there any errors or warnings reported? If so, find out more about one or two of the errors or warnings by double-clicking the error or warning. Click **OK** after you are finished viewing the error or warning information.

4. Right-click **System in the tree** and click **Properties** to see the dialog box shown in Figure 12-7. Look first at the General tab. Where is the system log stored? What is the maximum size for the log and what happens when the maximum size is reached? Record your observations.

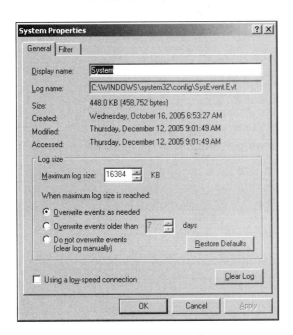

Figure 12-7   System log properties

5. Click **Overwrite events older than** and specify **14** days. Click **Apply**.

6. Click the **Filter** tab.

7. Remove the check marks from all events except **Information**, **Warning**, and **Error**.

8. Click the list arrow in the **Event source** box, and scroll through the options. Record some of the options that you recognize. Select **Netlogon** so that you only view events associated with logon activity (Figure 12-8).

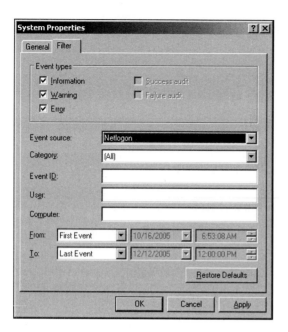

Figure 12-8   Creating a filter

9. Click **OK**. How does using the filter change what you view in the system log? Does this mean that the events you viewed before creating the filter are deleted, or simply not displayed?

10. Close **Event Viewer**.

TROUBLESHOOTING SECURITY USING THE SECURITY CONFIGURATION AND ANALYSIS TOOL

Even though you have been careful about setting up security and security policies, there may still be omissions in the security you have established. Also, as time passes, the security requirements on a server or in a domain may change. Windows Server 2003 offers the Security Configuration and Analysis tool, which is an MMC snap-in, to help you monitor and analyze security. This tool works by creating a database from which to configure a server and perform a security check. For example, if you are setting up the first DC, you can use this tool to configure the server for the default domain security policy. Later, you can use the tool to perform an analysis of the policy, to determine if you need to make modifications on the basis of growth in server use. You can use the tool to import an existing template or to import a new security template that you have created. The database may be built from an existing Group Policy or a security template, or you can construct a database the first time that you run the tool. After a database is in place, as for the domain or for an OU, you should periodically analyze it to see if it meets the system's security recommendations.

Activity 12-5: Using the Security Configuration and Analysis Snap-in

Time Required: Approximately 20 minutes

Objective: Learn how to use the Security Configuration and Analysis Snap-in.

Description: In this activity, you use the Security Configuration and Analysis Snap-in to create a sample security database and then analyze it.

1. Click **Start**, and click **Run**

2. Type **mmc**, and click **OK**.

3. Maximize the console windows, if necessary.

4. Click the **File** menu, and click **Add/Remove Snap-in**.

5. Click the **Add** button, and then double-click **Security Configuration and Analysis**.

6. Click **Close,** and then click **OK**.

7. For this activity, create a practice database by right-clicking **Security Configuration and Analysis** in the tree, and clicking **Open Database**.

8. In the File name box, provide a name for the database that consists of **Domain** plus your initials. Click **Open**.

9. In the Import Template box, click **setup security.inf**, and then click **Open**. Wait a few moments for the system to generate the database. Notice in the right pane that you can now use this tool to configure your server (configure the Group Policies) or to analyze the security settings.

10. For the sake of practice in analyzing settings on a database, right-click **Security Configuration and Analysis** again, and then click **Analyze Computer Now**.

11. Make sure that the error log file location is appropriate, and then click **OK**. The tool displays an Analyzing System Security dialog box to show what it is checking (see Figure 12-9).

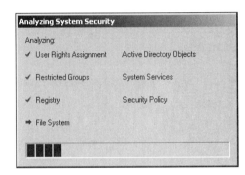

Figure 12-9   Analyzing System Security box

12. Right-click **Security Configuration and Analysis** in the tree, and click **View Log File**.

13. The results written to the log are displayed in the right pane (see Figure 12-10). Scroll through the log file to examine its contents. (Because you generated a sample database for demonstration purposes, your results do not necessarily reflect actual errors on your system.)

14. Close the **Console1** window, and click **No**.

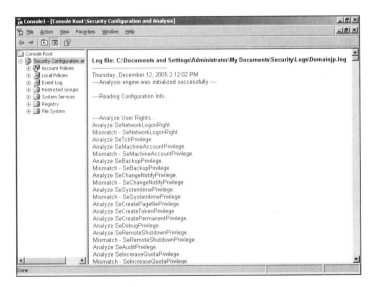

Figure 12-10   Security analysis results

TROUBLESHOOTING CONNECTIVITY

One area that server and network administrators often troubleshoot is TCP/IP connectivity. For example, a common problem is the use of duplicate IP addresses. This can happen in situations where static IP addressing is used, with the network administrator or user typing in the IP address and subnet mask when the computer is set up. If two computers are using the same IP address, one or both will not be able to connect to the network; or both are likely to experience unreliable communications such as sudden disconnections.

Some TCP/IP utilities, such as Telnet, have IP troubleshooting tools built in. The same is true for workstations and servers running TCP/IP-compatible operating systems, such as Windows Server 2003 and Windows XP Professional. You can test the IP address of a Windows client, such as Windows XP, or a Windows 2003 server by opening the Command Prompt window and typing ipconfig to view a dialog box showing the adapter address (MAC or Ethernet), IP address, subnet mask, and other information for that workstation (see Figure 12-11). If the server is using an IP address that is identical to the address used by another networked computer that is turned on, the subnet mask value is 0.0.0.0 when you run one of these utilities.

Figure 12-11   Using ipconfig in Windows Server 2003

Another tool for testing TCP/IP connections is the ping utility. You can poll the presence of another TCP/IP computer from the Windows Server 2003 or Windows XP Professional Command Prompt window by typing ping and the IP address or computer name of the other computer. Many server administrators use ping to quickly test the presence of a server or mainframe from their office when there are reports of connection problems to that computer. Pinging a server on a network in another state or remote location also enables you to quickly test if your Internet connectivity is accessible from your office workstation. Figure 12-12 illustrates the ping utility as used from Windows Server 2003.

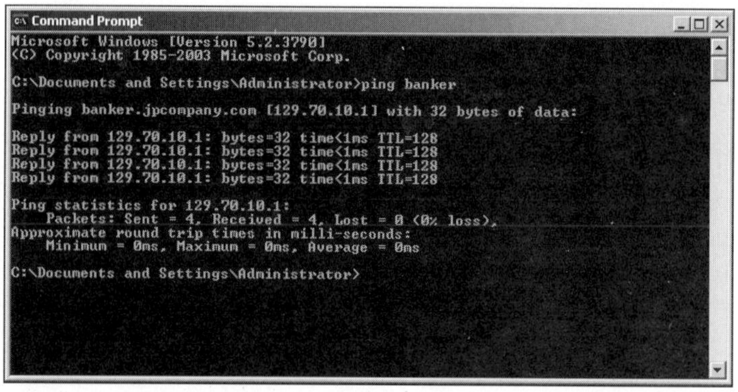

Figure 12-12   Using ping

Netstat is a utility available in Windows Server 2003, Windows XP Professional, Windows 2000, and other Windows operating systems and is a quick way to verify that a workstation or server has established a successful TCP/IP connection. This utility provides information about TCP and UDP connectivity. Sometimes a TCP/IP session to a server or mainframe computer hangs. You can determine this by entering netstat -e from the Command Prompt window at that computer (see Figure 12-13). Two columns of received and sent data are displayed. If these columns contain 0 bytes, it is likely the session is hung. If it is, and the computer is running Windows Server 2003, or Windows XP Professional, use the Network Connections option from Control Panel to disable the computer and then to reconnect. You can do this by opening the Network Connections tool, clicking Local Area Connection, and clicking Disable as shown in Figure 12-14. To reestablish the connection, open the Network Connections tool, and click Local Area Connection. For Windows 2000 computers, use the Network and Dial-up Connections tool to do the same thing. For clients running Windows NT, 98, and 95, reboot the computer and try again. Disabling the connection or rebooting resets the NIC and the TCP/IP connectivity to make sure you have a clean connection.

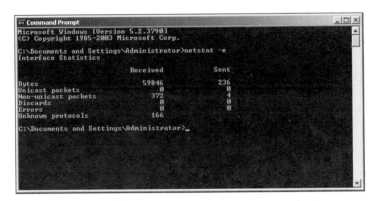

Figure 12-13   Using the netstat –e command in Windows .NET Server 2003

Figure 12-14   Disabling a connection in Windows Server 2003

The netstat -e command also provides a quick indication of the number of transmission errors and discarded packets detected at that computer's NIC. For a more comprehensive listing of communication statistics, type netstat -s. Table 12-5 lists some useful diagnostics available from the Command Prompt windows in Windows Server 2003, Windows XP Professional, and Windows 2000.

Table 12-5   Windows Server 2003, XP, and 2000 diagnostic commands for TCP/IP connectivity

Diagnostic Command	Function
arp	Displays Address Resolution Protocol (ARP) information, such as using the arp -a command to view the arp cache information at a computer (see Chapter 1)
ipconfig	Displays information about the TCP/IP setup at that computer (enter ipconfig /? to view all of the options for this commands)
nslookup	Shows information about DNS servers
pathping	Polls another TCP/IP node showing the path through routers along the way (including packet loss through routers, see Chapter 1)
ping	Polls another TCP/IP node to verify you can communicate with it (enter only ping to view all of the options for this command)
netstat (-a, -e, -s)	Displays information about the TCP/IP session from that computer (enter netstat /? to view all of the options for this command)
nbtstat (-n)	Shows the server and domain NetBIOS names registered to the network (enter only nbtstat to view all of the options for this command)
tracert (server or host name)	Shows the number of hops and other routing information on the path to the specified server or host (enter only tracert to view all of the options for this command)

Activity 12-6: Using TCP/IP Connectivity Troubleshooting Tools

Time Required: Approximately 10 minutes

Objective: Learn how to use nbtstat and netstat.

Description: In this activity, you have an opportunity to use nbtstat to view computers (NetBIOS names) on the network and then netstat to view all connections.

1. Click **Start**, point to **All Programs**, point to **Accessories**, and click **Command Prompt**.

2. At the command prompt, enter **nbtstat −n** and press **Enter**. What information is displayed? Record your observations.

3. Next, type **nbtstat −s** and press **Enter**. What information is displayed by this command? Record your observations.

4. Now type **netstat −a** at the command prompt and press **Enter**. What information is produced by this command? Note your observations.

5. How can you use the ipconfig command to verify your own TCP/IP connection? What is the purpose of the ping command? Try both of these commands (you can ping your own computer, if you do not have the name or IP address of another computer to ping).

6. Close the **Command Prompt** window.

REMOTELY ADMINISTERING A SERVER

In some organizations it is important for server administrators to be able to remotely access a server in order to solve a problem. The remote access may be from another building, from home, or while traveling. There are two ways to remotely access a Windows 2003 server for administration:

- Using Remote Desktop client
- Using Remote Assistance

You can use the Remote Desktop client to remotely access and manage the server, such as through a dial-up line and via a RAS or VPN server. Use the Remote Desktop client at your workstation to log onto your regular account that you use for administration (see Chapter 9). As of this writing, up to two Remote Desktop connections are supported without installing a terminal server.

To enable remote administration through Remote Desktop, ensure that Allow users to connect remotely to your computer is checked in the System Properties on the Remote tab (see Figure 12-15). Also, make sure that you have configured a strong password for the account from which you perform administration. Microsoft defines the following as characteristics of a strong password:

- Contains seven or more characters

- Does not reflect qualities about you that others might guess, such as your name, information about your family, or the name of your organization

- Is not a word that can be found in a dictionary

- Is changed at regular intervals without repeating a previously used password

- Contains a combination of uppercase and lowercase characters, numbers, and symbols

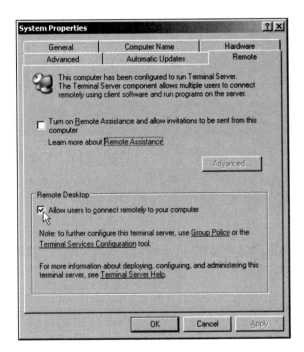

Figure 12-15   System Properties Remote tab

 If Windows Server 2003 is configured as a terminal server, Allow users to connect remotely to your computer is checked by default. If your server is not a terminal server, this option is not checked by default, and you need to configure it to enable Remote Desktop for remotely administering a server.

Another way to remotely access a server is by enabling Remote Assistance. You enable remote assistance on the System Properties Remote tab (see Figure 12-15) by clicking the Turn on Remote Assistance and allow invitations to be sent from this computer option. Also, you need to set up a Group Policy to enable remote assistance. Within a Group Policy, Remote Assistance is enabled or disabled through Computer Configuration, Administrative Templates, System, and Remote Assistance, as shown in Figure 12-16.

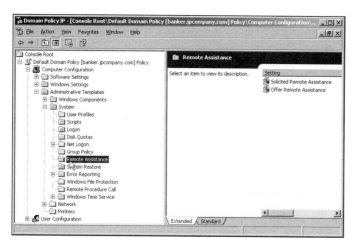

Figure 12-16   Configuring remote assistance in a Group Policy

You must use Windows XP to remotely access the server. The general steps for accessing the server from Windows XP are:

1. Click **Start** and click **Help and Support**.

2. Click **Tools** (click Change View, if necessary to expand the window to view all of the Tools options.)

3. Click **Offer Remote Assistance**.

4. Enter the name of the server, and click **Connect**.

Activity 12-7: Enabling Remote Administration

Time Required: Approximately 5 minutes

Objective: Learn how to enable remote administration in Windows Server 2003.

Description: In this activity, view where to enable Remote Desktop and where to turn on Remote Assistance in Windows Server 2003.

1. Click **Start**, right-click **My Computer**, and click **Properties**.

2. Click the **Remote** tab (see Figure 12-15).

3. Notice that to enable accessing the server using Remote Desktop for administration, you should verify that **Allow users to connect remotely to your computer** is checked. Or to enable access through Remote Assistance, ensure that **Turn on Remote Assistance and allow invitations to be sent from this computer** is checked. What would you do next to configure Remote Assistance?

4. Close the **System Properties** dialog box.

CHAPTER SUMMARY

❏ Before problems occur, develop a problem-solving strategy that includes understanding your server and network, training users to help, step-by-step problem solving, and tracking problems.

❏ There are many sources of boot problems. Fortunately, Windows Server 2003 comes with several tools to address these problems, such as safe mode, the ASR set, and the Recovery Console.

❏ Regularly back up the system state data and system protected files in case of emergencies, such as a failed boot partition or volume.

❑ Understand how to restore a failed volume, including system state data and system protected files, so you are prepared in advance.

❑ Learn to regularly use Event Viewer as a monitoring and troubleshooting tool. Also, configure your event logs to match the needs of your organization.

❑ Use the Security Configuration and Analysis tool to troubleshoot security policy problems.

❑ There are many tools for troubleshooting TCP/IP connectivity problems at the server or on a client, including ipconfig, ping, nbtstat, and netstat.

❑ You can remotely administer a server using Remote Desktop client or Remote Assistance.

KEY TERMS

application log — An event log that records information about how software applications are performing.

Directory Service log — Records events that are associated with Active Directory, such as updates to Active Directory, events related to Active Directory's database, replication events, and startup and shutdown events.

DNS Server log — An event log that provides information about events associated with the DNS server, such as instances in which DNS information is updated, when there are problems with the DNS service, and when the DNS server has started successfully after booting.

event logs — Logs that you can view through Event Viewer that record information about server events, such as errors, warnings, or informational events.

File Replication Service log — An event log that contains information about file replication events such as changes to file replication, when the service has started, and completed replication tasks.

Last Known Good Configuration — The Windows Server 2003 configuration that is stored in the registry and is the configuration in effect prior to making a system, driver, or configuration change since the last time the computer was booted.

Recovery Console — A recovery tool that enables you to access the Windows Server 2003 command line to perform recovery and troubleshooting operations. The Recovery Console can be added as a boot option or started from the Windows Server 2003 CD-ROM.

safe mode — A boot mode that enables Windows Server 2003 to be booted using the most generic default settings, such as for the display, disk drives, and pointing device, plus only those services needed to boot a basic configuration.

security log — An event log that records access and security information about logon accesses, file, folder, and system policy changes.

system log — An event log that records information about system-related events such as hardware errors, driver problems, and hard drive errors.

SYSVOL — A shared folder, which is set up when Active Directory is installed and that contains publicly available files that users and DCs need for domain access. SYSVOL folders are replicated among DCs.

12

REVIEW QUESTIONS

1. You need to troubleshoot a boot problem on a Windows 2003 server, and you want to make sure that you do not have network connectivity while you are troubleshooting (to keep users from logging on). Which of the following advanced boot modes can you use?

   a. Safe Mode

   b. Enable VGA Mode

   c. Safe Mode with Command

   d. all of the above

   e. only a and b

   f. only a and c

2. You walk into the computer room one morning and notice that there is a message at the Windows Server 2003 console that the application log is full. Which of the following might be true? (Choose all that apply.)

    a. The application log is not enabled.

    b. The application log is set to Do not overwrite events.

    c. The application log needs to be set to a larger size.

    d. The application log is not really full, it is just set to use a low-speed connection, and that connection is particularly slow right now.

3. Which of the following can you use to access the Recovery Console?

    a. Use the Recovery Console option on the Administrative Tools menu.

    b. Press Ctrl+F10 from the keyboard while the server is booted into the operating system.

    c. Select the Recovery Console button after pressing Ctrl+Alt+Del.

    d. Insert the Windows Server 2003, Standard Edition, CD-ROM, shut down the system, reboot from the CD-ROM, and press R on the Welcome to Setup screen.

4. The financial auditors at your organization have requested that you audit all successful and failed accesses to the vouchers and payroll files. Where do you look to view the audit results?

    a. System log

    b. Directory Service log

    c. Audit log

    d. Security log

    e. Application log

5. Your diagnosis of a problem that prevents your server from booting is that the Master Boot Record is corrupted. Which of the following tools enable(s) you to access the server so that you can repair it? (Choose all that apply.)

    a. Recovery Console

    b. Master Fix button on the General tab of the System option in Control Panel

    c. Recovery floppy disk automatically created when you install Windows Server 2003

    d. Booting from the Windows Server 2003 CD-ROM and pressing F9.

6. The computer committee on your campus is very concerned about security. One of the members has heard about the Security Configuration and Analysis tool and claims that you should be using it to block intruders, because he claims it can detect accounts that are intruding and then automatically disable those accounts. What is your response?

    a. This is an appropriate tool for the functions he has described.

    b. This tool cannot fulfill his claims, but it can be used to configure security and to later analyze security.

    c. This tool only automatically blocks the accounts that you specify within the tool.

    d. This tool is only capable of analyzing file and folder security.

7. You have made several changes to the monitor display settings by using the Display option in Control Panel. When you reboot into the Windows Server 2003 desktop after making those changes, the monitor just flickers and you see nothing. Which of the following advanced boot options enable you to boot so that you can view the desktop and change the settings back? (Choose all that apply.)

    a. Safe Mode

    b. Enable VGA Mode

    c. Last Known Good Configuration

    d. Start Windows Normally

8. Which of the following is (are) system state data on a Windows 2003 server that has Active Directory installed? (Choose all that apply.)

   a. SYSVOL folder

   b. registry

   c. boot files

   d. system files

9. Your Windows 2003 server is having trouble booting, and you suspect that it is related to a driver or service that is not properly starting. How can you track each of the startup actions of the server so that you can later go back and review each one for problems?

   a. Select Enable Boot Logging from the advanced menu options when you boot.

   b. Use the Net Log command from the Recovery Console.

   c. Select the Debugging Mode from the advanced options when you boot.

   d. Enable Full System Logging as a Group Policy, and then reboot the server.

10. Which of the following might be part of your problem-solving strategy?

   a. Reboot the server once a day to prevent problems and reset all registers.

   b. Regularly check the event logs.

   c. Look for the simple solutions first.

   d. all of the above

   e. only a and b

   f. only b and c

11. The system log contains hundreds of entries, but you only want to look at error events associated with the Workstation Service. How is this possible?

   a. Create a trap.

   b. Turn off recording of the information and warning events.

   c. Set up a filter.

   d. Print out the log so that it is easier to read.

12. The _____ tool keeps a security-related database and enables you to examine existing security settings in one place.

   a. Active Directory Trusts and Domains

   b. Security Configuration and Analysis

   c. Active Directory Database

   d. Security Display

13. When you try to reboot your server, you see the message that there is a nonsystem disk. What should you do first?

   a. You have no choice but to reinstall the Windows Server 2003 operating system.

   b. Use the Recovery Console to boot into the system and run the fixsystem program.

   c. Check the floppy and CD-ROM drives, in case there is a nonsystem disk or disc in one of those drives, remove the disk/disc, and try rebooting.

   d. Press Ctrl+Alt+Shift to directly access the system files from which to boot.

14. When you boot a server, press _____ to access the Advanced Options Menu screen.

   a. Ctrl+F10

   b. F8

   c. Ctrl+A

   d. the spacebar three times

12

15. When you try to boot into your server you see the messages "0x0000002E" and "Data Bus Error." Which of the following might you suspect?

   a. a RAM problem

   b. a disconnected keyboard

   c. a defective NIC

   d. a defective monitor

16. How can you back up system protected files?

   a. In the Backup tool, select to back up these files as part of the list of folders and files you can back up.

   b. Use the Emergency Backup Data option in Control Panel.

   c. In the Backup tool, first select to back up the system state data and then make sure that backing up the system protected files is selected in the advanced backup options.

   d. Use the System option in Control Panel to create a system protected files floppy disk backup.

17. Which of the following are event logs available in Windows Server 2003? (Choose all that apply.)

   a. File Replication Service log

   b. Directory Service log

   c. Audit log

   d. DNS Server log

   e. Application log

18. Which of the following is a file format you can select to save an event log? (Choose all that apply.)

   a. .msi

   b. .sav

   c. .lg

   d. .evt

   e. only a and b

   f. only b and c

19. Ntoskrnl.exe is an example of a(n) _____.

   a. system protected file

   b. SMP computer driver file

   c. disk controller file

   d. operating system security file

20. _____ is the Recovery Console command to view hardware drivers and system services.

   a. dir

   b. listsvc

   c. enable –ls

   d. ls –services

21. The _____ command-line command is used to show the NetBIOS names registered on a network.

   a. arp –a

   b. netbios –names

   c. bios

   d. nbtstat –n

22. Which of the following can be used to remotely administer a Windows 2003 server from Windows XP Professional?

    a. Admin Access tool

    b. Remote Desktop client

    c. Remote Terminal

    d. Server Access tool

23. Which of the following command-line commands enables you to view information about the TCP/IP session at your Windows 2003 server?

    a. netstat

    b. nslookup

    c. route

    d. session

24. Which of the following are characteristics of a strong password? (Choose all that apply.)

    a. consists of seven or more characters

    b. contains a combination of uppercase and lowercase characters, numbers, and symbols

    c. is a word commonly found in the dictionary (so that it is easy to remember)

    d. represents a quality familiar to you, such as your middle name

25. In Windows XP Professional, you can use the Remote Assistance option to remotely access a Windows 2003 server from the _____.

    a. Administrative Tools menu

    b. Remote option in My Computer

    c. Help and Support option on the Start menu

    d. Remote Access option in Control Panel

12

CASE PROJECTS

Case Project Background

Haberdashers is a clothing manufacturer for women and men that specializes in trendy fashions. The main offices of the company are in a building that is fully networked and houses eight Windows 2003 servers. The Management, Customer Service, Marketing, Planning, and Financial Services departments are located in the main offices. All of the servers run 24 hours a day, seven days a week, because the Customer Service Department always has people available to take orders by Web server and by telephone. Customer Service also works to coordinate shipments with the Inventory and Distribution departments that are in five locations in Canada and the United States. The server administrator with the most troubleshooting experience has just resigned to take another job and Haberdashers has hired you through Bayside IT Services as a temporary resident consultant until you can train another server administrator in troubleshooting.

Case Project 12-1: Troubleshooting Strategy

When you first start training the server administrator who will be the main troubleshooter, what recommendations do you have for developing a troubleshooting strategy? Create a short paper to give to the server administrator in training.

Case Project 12-2: Addressing a Server Problem

While you are training the server administrator, one of the servers suddenly crashes. Where would you look first for a clue about what happened and how would you explain to the administrator the steps and tools you would use? Create a set of notes about this to give to the server administrator in training.

Case Project 12-3: Troubleshooting Access and Security Problems

The director of the Marketing Department is working to launch a costly new marketing campaign and is already experiencing a lot of pressure. She calls you because some of her staff cannot log on to the system and access several new folders that have been set up for them. Also, it appears that someone has obtained information from a top-secret folder and provided it to a competing company. Create a report for the director about the tools and techniques you can use to address these problems as quickly as possible.

Case Project 12-4: Solving a Boot Problem

Because of a sudden power surge transferred by a grounding problem in the network cable, the server that has customer service data seems to have several corrupted system files, a corrupted registry, and intermittent problems booting. The administrator that you are training is on the scene first, and now reports that the server either displays a message that there is a nonsystem disk or it hangs while booting. What techniques and tools can you use to troubleshoot and solve this problem? Create a set of notes to record the options you try, for later reference by the server administrator in training.

APPENDIX

A

WINNT AND WINNT32 INSTALLATION SWITCHES

Windows Server 2003, Standard Edition, is installed using one of two installation programs: Winnt or Winnt32. Winnt is typically used when you start an installation from the Windows Server 2003, Standard Edition, CD-ROM or when you upgrade from an earlier version of Windows. Winnt32 is used when upgrading or installing from a 32-bit version of Windows, such as Windows 98 or Windows 2000.

Both Winnt and Winnt32 can be used with a variety of switches to enable you to have more control over how Windows Server 2003, Standard Edition, is installed. The switches for Winnt are shown in Table A-1 and the switches for Winnt32 are provided in Table A-2.

Table A-1 Command-line switches for Winnt

Switch	Purpose
/?	Lists the switches for Winnt
/a	Initiates the accessibility options for those who have visual, hearing, or movement disabilities
/e:command	Executes a command after the Windows portion of the setup, for example to start a program or open Control Panel
/i:initialization filename	Specifies that you are using an initialization file other than the default, Dosnet.inf (this initialization file shows where installation files are located)
/r:foldername	Creates an optional folder of files copied from the Windows Server 2003 CD-ROM (the folder is not deleted after completion of the installation)
/rx:folder	Creates an optional folder of files copied from the Windows Server 2003 CD-ROM (the folder is removed at the completion of the installation)
/s:drive:\folder or /s:\\server\folder	Uses a path for the installation files other than the current path
/t:drive:\folder	Copies the temporary files used by the installation to a specified location (otherwise, they are copied to the target drive of the installation)
/u:script file	Used in an unattended installation to specify the name of the script or answer file containing installation commands and should be used with the /s command
udf:id	Enables a uniqueness database file to be used with an unattended installation as a way to ensure that particular information in the script can be changed, such as the name of the server ("id" specifies the name of the database file, for example, udf:install.dbf)

Table A-2   Command-line switches for Winnt32

Switch	Purpose
/?	Lists the switches for Winnt32
/checkupgradeonly	This option determines your system's compatibility with Windows Server 2003
/cmd:command	Executes a command before the Windows portion of the setup is completed and just after you have provided configuration information
/comdcons	Adds a Recovery Console option to the Boot.ini file so that you can fix problems with an installation
/copydir:\folder	Creates a special subfolder in the final \Windows folder, usually implemented for information specific to that installation, for example, to store specialized drivers (see the note following this table) for use only during the installation; the folder is retained after the installation is completed
/copysource:\folder	Creates a special subfolder in the final \Windows folder, usually implemented for information specific to that installation, for example, to store specialized drivers for use during the installation or to store for later use; the folder is deleted after the installation is completed
/debug level:file	Creates a file to help you debug installation problems on the basis of the level you specify (Winnt32.log is the default if no file is specified; levels are 0 = major errors, 1 = errors, 2 = warnings, 3 = information, 4 = detailed information)
/dudisable	Prevents setup from accessing the Internet to determine if there are newly updated installation files that can be integrated with this particular installation (Windows Server 2003 enables dynamic updating in case one or more of the files on the installation CD-ROM are out of date)
/duprepare:\folder or duprepare:\\server\folder	Enables you to ready a shared drive to hold dynamic update files from Microsoft's Web site
/dushare:\folder or /dushare:\\server\folder	Used in conjunction with duprepare to indicate the name of the folder or share containing dynamic update files that have been obtained already from Microsoft's Web site
/emsport:communications port	Permits you to use the new Windows Server 2003 Emergency Management Services for remote access (over com1 or com2 ports for dial-up access) of a server; to turn this off, use /emsport:off
/emsbaudrate:bps	Enables you to configure the bps rate when /emsport communications are enabled (note that baud rate is generally replaced by bits per second or bps on modems)
/m:\folder	Enables you to install files from the default installation folders on the CD-ROM and from a folder you specify with the /m command; if the installation finds two files of the same name, it uses the file in the folder specified by /m
/makelocalsource	Copies the CD-ROM source files to the same disk that is designated for the Windows folder (enabling you to later install additional services or components from your local hard disk)
/noreboot	Does not automatically reboot after files are copied to the hard disk, enabling you to run a command in the interim, for example, to check the dates on driver files for the most current versions
/s:drive:\folder or /s:\\server\share\folder	Uses a path for the installation files other than the current /s:\\ path. Also enables you to copy files from two or more sources by specifying multiple /s commands
/syspart:drive	Enables you to copy the files used by Windows Setup to a hard drive, remove the hard drive, and install it in another computer (can be used by computer manufacturers, who install the first phase, but leave the second phase of the installation to the purchaser to specify parameters unique to her or his site such as the server name; must be used with /tempdrive)
/tempdrive:drive	Temporary files and the final Windows Server 2003 system files are copied to the drive specified, for example, to drive D: in /tempdrive:D
/unattend	For an unattended installation, enables you to upgrade Windows NT Server 4.0 (Service Pack 5 or above) and Windows 2000 Server to Windows Server 2003, using the parameters already in place for your current version

A

Table A-2   Command-line switches for Winnt32 (continued)

Switch	Purpose
/unattend [seconds]:script file	Used in an unattended installation to specify the name of the script file containing installation commands (the seconds parameter is used to create an interval between the time that the setup files are copied and the time that the computer reboots, so you can interrupt to enter a command)
udf:id	Enables a uniqueness database file to be used with an unattended installation so that particular information in the script can be changed, such as the name of the server ("id" specifies the name of the database file, for example, udf:install.dbf)

The default name of the Windows Server 2003 folder that holds system files is \Windows. Previously, in Windows NT and Windows 2000 (all versions) the default name for this folder was \Winnt.

Glossary

access control list (ACL) — A list of all security descriptors that have been set up for a particular object, such as for a shared folder or a shared printer.

access server — A device that connects several different types of communications devices and telecommunication lines to a network, providing network routing for these types of communications.

Active Directory — A central database of computers, users, shared printers, shared folders, and other network resources, and resource groupings that is used to manage a network and enable users to quickly find a particular resource.

active partition — The partition from which a computer boots.

Address Resolution Protocol (ARP) — A protocol in the TCP/IP suite that enables a sending station to determine the MAC or physical address of another station on a network.

aggregated links — Linking two or more communications channels, such as ISDN channels, so that they appear as one channel, but with the combined speed of all channels in the aggregate.

alert — Provides a warning of a specific Windows Server 2003 system or network event. The warning is sent to designated users.

answer file — A text file that contains a complete set of instructions for automating the installation of Windows Server 2003.

application log — An event log that records information about how software applications are performing.

assigning applications (or software) — Involves configuring a Group Policy so that a particular software application is automatically started through a desktop shortcut, through a menu selection, or by clicking a file that has a specific file extension.

attribute — A characteristic associated with a folder or file used to help manage access and backups.

auditing — In Windows Server 2003, a security capability that tracks activity on an object, such as reading, writing, creating, or deleting a file in a folder.

Automated System Recovery (ASR) set — Backup media, such as CD-Rs and a floppy disk, containing the system files and settings needed to start a system running Windows Server 2003 in the event of a system failure.

Automatic Private IP Addressing (APIPA) — Windows Server 2003 supports Automatic Private IP Addressing (APIPA) to automatically configure the TCP/IP settings for a computer. The computer assigns itself an IP address in the range of 169.254.0.1 to 169.254.255.254 if a DHCP server is not available.

Backup Domain Controller (BDC) — A server that maintains a read-only copy of the user accounts database that is replicated from the PDC.

Bandwidth Allocation Control Protocol (BACP) — Similar to BAP, but is able to select a preferred client when two or more clients vie for the same bandwidth.

Bandwidth Allocation Protocol (BAP) — A protocol that works with Multilink in Windows Server 2003 to enable the bandwidth or speed of a remote connection to be allocated on the basis of the needs of an application, with the maximum allocation equal to the maximum speed of all channels aggregated via Multilink.

base priority class — The initial priority assigned to a program process or thread in the program code.

basic disk — In Windows Server 2003, a partitioned disk that can have up to four partitions and that uses logical drive designations. This type of disk is compatible with MS-DOS, Windows 3.x, Windows 95, Windows 98, Windows NT, Windows 2000, Windows XP, and Windows Server 2003.

basic input/output system (BIOS) — A program on a read-only or flash memory chip that establishes basic communication with components such as the monitor and disk drives. The advantage of a flash chip is that you can update the BIOS.

benchmark (or **baseline**) — A measurement standard for hardware or software used to establish performance baselines under varying loads or circumstances.

bidirectional printing — Ability of a printer connected to a computer's parallel port to conduct two-way communications between the printer and the computer, such as to provide out of paper information; also bidirectional printing supports Plug and Play and enables an operating system to query a printer about its capabilities.

boot partition — Holds the Windows Server 2003 \Windows folder containing the system files.

broadcast — A message sent to all computers on a network segment (but usually blocked to other segments by a router).

Challenge Handshake Authentication Protocol (CHAP) — An encrypted handshake protocol designed for standard IP- or PPP-based exchange of passwords. It provides a reasonably secure, standard, cross-platform method for sender and receiver to negotiate a connection.

CHAP with Microsoft extensions (MS-CHAP) — A Microsoft-enhanced version of CHAP that can negotiate encryption levels and that uses the highly secure RSA RC4 encryption algorithm to encrypt communications between client and host.

CHAP with Microsoft extensions version 2 (MS-CHAP v2) — An enhancement of MS-CHAP that provides better authentication and data encryption and that is especially well suited for VPNs.

client — A computer that accesses resources on another computer via a network or direct cable connection.

client access license (CAL) — A license to enable a workstation to connect to Windows Server 2003 as a client.

clustering — The ability to increase the access to server resources and provide fail-safe services by linking two or more discrete computer systems so they appear to function as though they are one.

community — A group of hosts that share the same SNMP Services.

community name — In SNMP communications, a rudimentary password (name) used by network agents and the network management station (or software) in the same community so that their communications cannot be easily intercepted by an unauthorized workstation or device.

Compressed Serial Line Protocol (CSLIP) — A newer version of SLIP that compresses header information in each packet sent across a remote link.

connection-oriented communication — Also called a connection-oriented service, this service provides several ways to ensure that data is successfully received at the destination, such as requiring an acknowledgement of receipt and using a checksum to make sure the packet or frame contents are accurate.

connectionless communication — Also called a connectionless service, a communication service that provides no checks (or minimal checks) to make sure that data accurately reaches the destination node.

container — An Active Directory object that houses other objects, such as a tree that houses domains or a domain that houses organizational units.

contiguous namespace — A namespace in which every child object has a portion of its name derived from its parent object.

copy backup — Backs up only files or folders that are manually selected for the backup, and the archive attribute is not changed or reset to show the files or folders have been backed up.

counter — Used by System Monitor, this is a measurement technique for an object, as when measuring the processor performance by percentage in use.

counter log — Traces information on System Monitor objects that a server administrator configures, taking a snapshot at specified intervals.

daily backup — Backs up only files that have been changed or updated on the day the backup is performed.

Data Encryption Standard (DES) — A data encryption method developed by IBM and the National Security Agency in cooperation with the National Bureau of Standards as an encryption technique using a secret key between the communicating stations. Triple DES employs three secret keys combined into one long key.

data type — The way in which information is formatted in a print file.

default gateway — The IP address of the router that has a connection to other networks. The default gateway address is used when the host computer you are trying to contact exists on another network.

defragmenting — A software process that rearranges data to fill in the empty spaces that develop on disks and makes data easier to obtain.

DFS cache timeout — The amount of time that a DFS shared folder is retained in the client operating system's cache for fast access.

DFS link — A path that is established between a shared folder in a domain and a DFS root.

DFS root — The main Active Directory container that holds DFS links to shared folders in a domain.

DFS topology — Applies to a domain-based DFS model and encompasses the DFS root, DFS links to the root, and servers on which the DFS structure is replicated.

DHCP relay agent — A server, such as a RAS or a VPN server, or computer that broadcasts IP configuration information between the DHCP server on a network and the client acquiring an address.

differential backup — A backup of new or changed files; the archive attribute is not reset after the file is backed up.

digital subscriber line (DSL) — A technology that uses advanced modulation technologies on regular telephone lines for high-speed networking at speeds of up to 60 Mbps between subscribers and a telecommunications company.

directory service — A large container (database) of network data and resources, such as computers, printers, user accounts, and user groups that enables management and fast access to those resources.

Directory Service Client (DSClient) — Microsoft software for pre-Windows 2000 clients that connect to Windows 2000 Server and Windows Server 2003 and enables those clients to view information published in Active Directory.

Directory Service log — Records events that are associated with Active Directory, such as updates to Active Directory, events related to Active Directory's database, replication events, and startup and shutdown events.

disjointed namespace — A namespace in which the child object name does not resemble the name of its parent object.

disk duplexing — A method of fault tolerance similar to disk mirroring in that it prevents data loss by duplicating data from a main disk to a backup disk; disk duplexing places the backup disk on a different controller or adapter than is used by the main disk.

disk mirroring — A method of fault tolerance that prevents data loss by duplicating data from a main disk to a backup disk. Some operating systems also refer to this as disk shadowing.

disk quota — Allocating a specific amount of disk space to a user or application with the ability to ensure that the user or application cannot use more disk space than is specified in the allocation.

distributability — Dividing complex application program tasks among two or more computers.

Distributed Component Object Model (DCOM) — A standard built upon the Component Object Model (COM) to enable object linking to take place over a network. COM is a standard that allows a software object, such as a graphic, to be linked from one software component to another (such as copying a picture from Microsoft Paint and pasting it in Microsoft Word).

Distributed File System (DFS) — A system that enables folders shared from multiple computers to appear as though they exist in one centralized hierarchy of folders instead of on many different computers.

distribution group — A list of users that enables one e-mail message to be sent to all users on the list. A distribution group is not used for security and thus cannot appear in an ACL.

DNS dynamic update protocol — A protocol that enables information in a DNS server to be automatically updated in coordination with DHCP.

DNS Server log — An event log that provides information about events associated with the DNS server, such as

instances in which DNS information is updated, when there are problems with the DNS service, and when the DNS server has started successfully after booting.

domain — A grouping of resource objects—for example, servers, computers, and user accounts—to enable easier centralized management of these objects. On Windows Server 2003 networks, a domain is contained within Active Directory as a higher-level representation of how a business, school, or government agency is organized.

domain controller (DC) — A Windows 2003 server that contains a full copy of the Active Directory information. You can add a new object to Active Directory via a domain controller, such as a new user account. Also, a Windows 2003 server configured as a domain controller replicates any changes made to its copy of Active Directory to every other domain controller in the same domain.

domain local security group — A group that is used to manage resources—shared folders and printers, for example—in its home domain, and that is primarily used to give global groups access to those resources.

Domain Name System (DNS) — Also called Domain Name Service, a TCP/IP application protocol that enables a DNS server to resolve (translate) domain and computer names to IP addresses, or IP addresses to domain and computer names.

domain-based DFS model — A DFS model that uses Active Directory and is available only to servers and workstations that are members of a particular domain. The domain-based model enables a deep root-based hierarchical arrangement of shared folders that is published in Active Directory. DFS shared folders in the domain-based model can be replicated for fault tolerance and load balancing.

dotted decimal notation — An addressing technique that uses four octets, such as 100000110.11011110. 1100101.00000101, converted to decimal (e.g., 134.22. 101.005) to differentiate individual servers, workstations, and other network devices.

driver — Software that enables a computer to communicate with such devices as network interface cards, printers, monitors, and hard disk drives. Each driver has a specific purpose, such as to handle network communications.

driver signing — A digital signature that Microsoft incorporates into driver and system files as a way to verify the files and to ensure that they are not inappropriately overwritten.

DSL adapter — A digital communications device that links a computer (or sometimes a router) to a DSL telecommunications line.

dynamic addressing — An IP address that is automatically assigned to a client from a general pool of available addresses and that may be assigned each time the client is started or it may be assigned for a period of days, weeks, months, or longer.

dynamic disk — In Windows Server 2003, a disk that does not use traditional partitioning, which means that there is no restriction to the number of volumes that can be set up on one disk or to the ability to extend volumes onto additional physical disks. Dynamic disks are only compatible with Windows Server 2003 and Windows 2000 Server platforms.

Dynamic DNS (DDNS) — A form of DNS that enables client computers to update DNS registration information so that this does not have to be done manually. DDNS is often used with DHCP servers to automatically register IP addresses on a DNS server.

Dynamic Host Configuration Protocol (DHCP) — A network protocol that provides a way for a server to automatically assign an IP address to a workstation on its network.

Encrypting File System (EFS) — Set by an attribute of NTFS, this file system enables a user to encrypt the contents of a folder or a file so that it can only be accessed via private key code by the user who encrypted it. EFS adheres to the Data Encryption Standard's expanded version for data protection.

enhanced metafile (EMF) — A data type for printing used by Windows 95, 98, Me, NT, 2000, XP, and 2003 operating systems. EMF print files offer a distinct advantage in Windows operating system environments because they are very portable from computer to computer.

Ethertype (ETYPE) — A property of an Ethernet frame that includes a two-byte code for the protocol type and is used in Ethernet communications by some vendors, but is not a part of the Ethernet standard.

event logs — Logs that you can view through Event Viewer that record information about server events, such as errors, warnings, or informational events.

extended partition — A partition that is created from unpartitioned free disk space and is linked to a primary partition in order to increase the available disk space.

Extensible Authentication Protocol (EAP) — An authentication protocol employed by network clients that use special security devices such as smart cards, token cards, and others that use certificate authentication.

fault tolerance — Techniques that employ hardware and software to provide assurance against equipment failures, computer service interruptions, and data loss.

File Replication Service log — An event log that contains information about file replication events such as changes to file replication, when the service has started, and completed replication tasks.

File Transfer Protocol (FTP) — Available through the TCP/IP protocol suite, FTP enables files to be transferred across a network or the Internet between computers or servers.

filter — A capacity in network monitoring software that enables a network or server administrator to view only designated protocols, network events, network nodes, or other specialized views of the network.

forest — A grouping of trees that each have contiguous namespaces within their own domain structure, but that have disjointed namespaces between trees. The trees and their domains use the same schema and global catalog.

format — An operation that divides a disk into small sections called tracks and sectors for the storage of files.

formatting — A process that prepares a hard disk partition for a specific file system.

forward lookup zone — A DNS zone or table that maps computer names to IP addresses.

fragmented — A normal and gradual process in which files become spread throughout a disk, and empty pockets of space develop between files.

frame — A unit of data that is transmitted on a network that contains control and address information, but not routing information.

Frame Relay — A WAN communications technology that relies on packet switching and virtual connection techniques to transmit at speeds from 56 Kbps to 45 Mbps.

global catalog — A grand repository for all objects and the most frequently used attributes for each object in all domains. Each forest has a single global catalog that can be replicated onto multiple servers.

global security group — A group that typically contains user accounts from its home domain, and that is a member of domain local groups in the same or other domains, so as to give that global group's member accounts access to the resources defined to the domain local groups.

globally unique identifier (GUID) — A unique number, up to 16 characters long, that is associated with an Active Directory object.

graphics device interface (GDI) — An interface on a Windows network print client that works with a local software application, such as Microsoft Word, and a local printer driver to format a file to be sent to a local printer or a network print server.

Group Policy — A set of policies that govern security, configuration, and a wide range of other settings for objects within containers in Active Directory.

Group Policy object (GPO) — An object in Active Directory that contains Group Policy settings for a site, domain, OU, or local computer.

handle — A resource, such as a file, used by a program that has its own identification so the program is able to access it.

hardware compatibility list (HCL) — A list of computer hardware tested by Microsoft and determined to be supported by a specific Microsoft operating system, such as Windows Server 2003, Standard Edition.

hardware profile — A hardware profile is a set of instructions telling the operating system which devices to start or which device settings to use when your computer starts.

hibernate — A mode in which the computer components are shut down, and information in memory is automatically saved to disk before the disk is powered off. The power supply and CPU remain active to startup all components when you press a key or move the mouse.

hive — A set of related registry keys and subkeys stored as a file.

home directory or **folder** — A server folder that is associated with a user's account and that is a designated workspace for the user to store files.

host address (A) resource record — A record in a DNS forward lookup zone that consists of a computer or domain name correlated to an IPv4 (or 32-bit) address.

hot fix — Ability to automatically "fix" data in areas of a hard disk that have become damaged or corrupted over time, without taking down the computer or operating system. Whenever possible, the operating system moves the data to a reserved good area, without users noticing. The damaged areas of disk are then marked so they are not used again.

hot-add memory — Memory that can be added without shutting down the computer or operating system.

I/O address — The address in memory through which data is transferred between a computer component and the processor.

incremental backup — A backup of new or changed files. The archive attribute is removed once the file is backed up.

inherited permissions — Permissions of a parent object that also apply to child objects of the parent, such as to subfolders within a folder.

inherited rights — User rights that are assigned to a group and that automatically apply to all members of that group.

instance — Used by System Monitor, when there are two or more types of elements to monitor, such as two or more threads or disk drives.

Integrated Services Digital Network (ISDN) — A telecommunications standard for delivering data services over digital telephone lines with a current practical limit of 1.536 Mbps and a theoretical limit of 622 Mbps.

Internet Authentication Service (IAS) — Used to establish and maintain security for RAS, Internet, and VPN dial-in access, and can be employed with RADIUS. IAS can use certificates to authenticate client access.

Internet Information Services (IIS) — A Microsoft Windows Server 2003 component that provides Internet Web, FTP, mail, newsgroup, and other services, and that is particularly offered to set up a Web server.

Internet Printing Protocol (IPP) — A protocol that is encapsulated in HTTP and that is used to print files over the Internet.

Internet Protocol (IP) — Internet Protocol (IP) is the Internet layer protocol responsible for addressing packets so that they are delivered on the local network or across routers to other networks or subnets.

Internet Server Application Programming Interface (ISAPI) — A group of dynamic-link library (DLL) files that consist of applications and filters to enable user customized programs to interface with IIS and to trigger particular programs, such as a specialized security check or a database lookup.

interrupt request (IRQ) line — A hardware line that a computer component, such as a disk drive or serial port, uses to communicate to the processor that it is ready to send or receive information. Intel-based computers have 16 IRQ lines, with 15 of those available for computer components to use.

IP address — A logical address assigned to each host on an IP network. It is used to identify a specific host on a specific network.

IP Security (IPSec) — A set of IP-based secure communications and encryption standards created through the Internet Engineering Task Force (IETF).

IPv6 host address (AAAA) resource record — A record in a DNS forward lookup zone that consists of a computer or domain name mapped to an IPv6 (or 128-bit) address.

Kerberos — A security system developed by the Massachusetts Institute of Technology to enable two parties on an open network to communicate without interception from an intruder, by creating a unique encryption key for each communication session.

Kerberos transitive trust relationship — A set of two-way trusts between two or more domains (or forests in a forest trust) in which Kerberos security is used.

kernel — An essential set of programs and computer code that allows a computer operating system to control processor, disk, memory, and other functions central to its basic operation.

Last Known Good Configuration — The Windows Server 2003 configuration that is stored in the registry and is the configuration in effect prior to making a system, driver, or configuration change since the last time the computer was booted.

Layer Two Tunneling Protocol (L2TP) — A protocol that transports PPP over a VPN, an intranet, or the Internet. L2TP works similarly to PPTP, but unlike PPTP, L2TP uses an additional network communications standard, called Layer Two Forwarding, that enables forwarding on the basis of MAC addressing.

load balancing — On a single server, distributing resources across multiple server disk drives and paths for better server response; on multiple network servers, distributing resources across two or more servers for better server and network performance.

local area network (LAN) — A network of computers in relatively close proximity, such as on the same floor or in the same building.

local print device — A printer, such as a laser printer, physically attached to a port on the local computer.

local security group — A group of user accounts that is used to manage resources on a standalone computer.

local user profile — A desktop setup that is associated with one or more accounts to determine what startup programs are used, additional desktop icons, and other customizations. A user profile is local to the computer in which it is stored.

mandatory user profile — A user profile set up by the server administrator that is loaded from the server to the client each time the user logs on; changes that the user makes to the profile are not saved.

master folder — The main folder that provides master files and folders for a DFS root or link when replication is enabled.

member server — A server that is a member of an existing Windows 2000 Server or Windows Server 2003 domain, but that does not function as a domain controller.

Microsoft Point-to-Point Encryption (MPPE) — An end-to-end encryption technique that uses special encryption keys varying in length from 40 to 128 bits.

mirrored volume — Two dynamic disks that are set up for RAID level 1 so that data on one disk is stored on a redundant disk.

modem — A modulator/demodulator that converts a transmitted digital signal to an analog signal for a telephone line. It also converts a received analog signal to a digital signal for use by a computer.

mounted drive — A physical disk, CD-ROM, or Zip drive that appears as a folder and that is accessed through a path like any other folder.

multicasting — A single message is sent from one location and received at several different locations that are subscribed to receive that message.

Multilink or **Multilink PPP (MPPP)** — A capability of RAS to aggregate multiple data streams into one logical network connection for the purpose of using more than one modem, ISDN channel, or other communications line in a single logical connection.

multimaster replication — In Windows Server 2003, there can be multiple servers, called domain controllers (DC)s, that store Active Directory information and replicate it to each other. Because each DC acts as a master, replication does not stop when one is down, and updates to Active Directory continue, as when creating a new account.

multitasking — The capability of a computer to run two or more programs at the same time.

multithreading — Running several program processes or parts (threads) at the same time.

name resolution — A process used to translate a computer's logical or host name into a network address, such as to a dotted decimal address associated with a computer—and vice versa.

namespace — A logical area on a network that contains directory services and named objects, and that has the ability to perform name resolution.

network — A communications system that enables computer users to share computer equipment, software, and data, voice, and video transmissions.

network address translation (NAT) — Sometime used by firewalls, NAT translates IP addresses on an internal or local network so that the actual IP addresses cannot be determined on the Internet, because the address seen on the Internet is a decoy address used from a pool of decoy addresses.

network interface card (NIC) — An adapter board designed to connect a workstation, server, or other network equipment to a network medium.

Network Monitor — A Windows Server 2003 network monitoring tool that can capture and display network performance data.

Network Monitor Driver — Enables a Microsoft-based server or workstation NIC to gather network performance data for assessment by Network Monitor.

Network News Transfer Protocol (NNTP) — Used over TCP/IP-based networks by NNTP servers to transfer news and informational messages organized and stored in newsgroups.

network operating system (NOS) — Software that enables computers on a network to communicate and to share resources and files.

network print device — A printing device, such as a laser printer, connected to a print server through a network.

normal backup — A backup of an entire system, including all system files, programs, and data files.

object — A network resource, such as a server or a user account, with distinct attributes or properties, that is defined in a domain, and exists in Active Directory.

Open Database Connectivity (ODBC) — A set of database access rules used by Microsoft in its ODBC application programming interface for accessing databases and providing a standard doorway to database data.

organizational unit (OU) — A grouping of objects within a domain that provides a means to establish specific policies for governing those objects and that enables object management to be delegated.

ownership — Having the privilege to change permissions and to fully manipulate an object. The account that creates an object, such as a folder or printer, initially has ownership.

packet — A unit of data that is transmitted on a network that contains control and address information as well routing information.

page fault — This occurs whenever memory pages must be called from disk (from the paging file).

paging — Moving blocks of information, called pages, from RAM to virtual memory (the paging file) on disk.

paging file — Disk space, in the form of a file, for use when memory requirements exceed the available RAM.

partition — A process in which a hard disk section or a complete hard disk is set up for use by an operating system. A disk can be formatted after it is partitioned.

partitioning — Blocking a group of tracks and sectors to be used by a particular file system, such as FAT or NTFS.

Password Authentication Protocol (PAP) — A nonencrypted, plaintext password authentication protocol. This represents the lowest level of security for exchanging passwords via PPP or TCP/IP.

peer-to-peer networking — A network on which any computer can communicate with other networked computers on an equal or peer basis without going through an intermediary, such as a server or host.

per seat licensing — A server software license that requires that there be enough licenses for all network client workstations.

per server licensing — A server software license based on the maximum number of clients that log on to the server at one time.

performance log — Tracks system and network performance information in a log that can be viewed later or imported into a spreadsheet, such as Microsoft Excel.

permissions — In Windows Server 2003, privileges to access and manipulate resource objects, such as folders and printers, or a privilege to read a file or to create a new file.

Plug and Play (PnP) — Ability of added computer hardware, such as an adapter or modem, to identify itself to the computer operating system for installation. PnP also refers to the Intel and Microsoft specifications for automatic device detection and installation. Many operating systems, such as Windows, Macintosh, and UNIX/Linux now support PnP.

Point-to-Point Protocol (PPP) — A widely used remote communications protocol that supports IPX/SPX, NetBEUI, and TCP/IP for point-to-point communication (for example, between a remote PC and a Windows 2003 server on a network).

Point-to-Point Tunneling Protocol (PPTP) — A remote communications protocol that enables connectivity to a network through the Internet and connectivity through intranets and VPNs.

pointer (PTR) resource record — A record in a DNS reverse lookup zone that consists of an IP (version 4 or 6) address correlated to a computer or domain name.

portable operating system interface (POSIX) — Standards set by the Institute of Electrical and Electronics Engineers (IEEE) for portability of applications.

PostScript printer — A printer that has special firmware or cartridges to print using a page-description language (PDL).

preemptive multitasking — Running two or more programs simultaneously so that each program runs in an area of memory separate from areas used by other programs.

primary DNS server — A DNS server that is used as the main server from which zones are administered, as when updating records in a forward lookup zone for a domain. A primary DNS server is also called the authoritative server for that zone.

Primary Domain Controller (PDC) — The server that maintains the master copy of user account information.

primary partition — Partition or portion of a hard disk that is bootable.

print client — Client computer or application that generates a print job.

print queue — A stack or lineup of print jobs, with the first job submitted at the top of the stack and the last job submitted at the bottom, and all of the jobs waiting to be sent from the spooler to the printer.

print server — Network computer or server device that connects printers to the network for sharing and that receives and processes print requests from print clients.

Printer Control Language (PCL) — A printer language used by non-PostScript Hewlett-Packard and compatible laser printers.

printer driver — Contains the device-specific information that Windows Server 2003 requires to control a particular print device, implementing customized printer control codes, font, and style information so that documents are converted into a printer-specific language.

printer pooling — Linking two or more identical printers with one printer setup or printer share.

privileged mode — A protected memory space allocated for the Windows Server 2003 kernel that cannot be directly accessed by software applications.

protocol — A strictly defined set of rules for communication across a network that specifies how networked data is formatted for transmission, how it is transmitted, and how it is interpreted at the receiving end.

publish — Making an object, such as a printer or shared folder, available for users to access when they view Active Directory contents and so that the data associated with the object can be replicated.

publishing applications (or software) — Involves setting up specific software through a Group Policy so that Windows 2000/XP clients install the software from a central distribution server using the Add or Remove Programs or the Add/Remove Programs option in Control Panel.

RAID-5 volume — Three or more dynamic disks that use RAID level 5 fault tolerance through disk striping and creating parity blocks for data recovery.

RAW — A data type often used for printing MS-DOS, Windows 3.x, and UNIX print files.

Recovery Console — A recovery tool that enables you to access the Windows Server 2003 command line to perform recovery and troubleshooting operations. The Recovery Console can be added as a boot option or started from the Windows Server 2003 CD-ROM.

redundant array of inexpensive (or independent) disks (RAID) — A set of standards designed to extend the life of hard disk drives and to prevent data loss from a hard disk failure.

registry — A database used to store information about the configuration, program setup, devices, drivers, and other data important to the setup of Windows operating systems, such as Windows Server 2003.

registry entry — A data parameter in the registry stored as a value in hexadecimal, binary, or text format.

registry key — A category of information contained in the Windows Server 2003 registry, such as hardware settings or software settings.

registry subkey — A key within a registry key, similar to a subfolder under a folder.

Remote Authentication Dial-In User Service (RADIUS) — A protocol and service set up on one RAS or VPN server, as in a domain for example, when there are multiple RAS or VPN servers to coordinate authentication and to keep track of remote dial-in statistics for all RAS and VPN servers.

replica set — A grouping of shared folders in a DFS root that are replicated or copied to all servers that participate in DFS replication. When changes are made to DFS shared folders, all of the participating servers are automatically or manually synchronized so that they have the same copy.

resource — Has two definitions: (1) on a network, this refers to an object such as a shared printer or shared directory that can be accessed by users; and (2) on workstations as well as servers, a resource is an IRQ, I/O address, or memory that is allocated to a computer component, such as a disk drive or communications port.

Resultant Set of Policy (RSoP) — A Windows Server 2003 tool that enables you to produce reports about proposed or current Group Policy settings for the purpose of planning and troubleshooting, when there are multiple Group Policies in use (such as for OUs and domains).

reverse lookup zone — A DNS server zone or table that maps IP addresses to computer or domain names.

roaming profile — Desktop settings that are associated with an account so that the same settings are employed no matter which computer is used to access the account (the profile is downloaded to the client from a server).

root key — Also called a subtree, the highest category of data contained in the registry. There are five root keys.

router — A device that connects networks, is able to read IP addresses, and can route or forward packets of data to designated networks.

Routing and Remote Access Services (RRAS) — Microsoft software services that enable a Windows 2003 server to provide routing capabilities and remote access so that off-site workstations have access to a Windows Server 2003 network through telecommunications lines, the Internet, or intranets.

safe mode — A boot mode that enables Windows Server 2003 to be booted using the most generic default settings, such as for the display, disk drives, and pointing device, plus only those services needed to boot a basic configuration.

scalability — The ability of a network operating system to meet the increased demands and growth of a business.

schema — Elements used in the definition of each object contained in Active Directory, including the object class and its attributes.

scope — A range of IP addresses that a DHCP server can lease to clients.

scope of influence (scope) — The reach of a type of group such as access to resources in a single domain or access to all resources in all domains in a forest (see domain local, global, and universal security groups).

secondary DNS server — A DNS server that is a backup to a primary DNS server and therefore is not authoritative.

Security Account Manager (SAM) database — A database of information about user accounts, groups, and privileges stored in a Windows NT domain.

security group — Used to assign a group of users permission to access network resources.

security log — An event log that records access and security information about logon accesses, file, folder, and system policy changes.

Serial Line Internet Protocol (SLIP) — An older remote communications protocol that is used by some UNIX computers. The modern compressed SLIP (CSLIP) version uses header compression to reduce communications overhead.

server — A single computer that provides extensive multiuser access to network resources.

server-based networking — A model in which access to the network and resources, and the management of resources, is accomplished through one or more servers.

Service Access Point (SAP) — An access point in network communications, which specifies the network process that should accept a frame at the destination, such as TCP/IP,

BPDU (a frame type used by network bridges), and special manufacturers, including Novell (for IPX/SPX).

Service Advertising Protocol (SAP) — An IPX/SPX-compatible protocol that is used by NetWare clients to identify servers and the network services provided by each server.

service pack — An operating system update that provides fixes for known problems and provides product enhancements.

service ticket — In Kerberos security, a permanent ticket good for the duration of a logon session (or for another period of time specified by the server administrator in the account polices) that enables the computer to access network services beginning with the Logon service.

share permissions — Permissions that apply to a particular object that is shared over a network, such as a shared folder or printer.

Simple Mail Transfer Protocol (SMTP) —An e-mail protocol used by systems having TCP/IP network communications.

Simple Network Management Protocol (SNMP) — Used for network management and performance monitoring on TCP/IP-based networks.

simple volume — A portion of a disk or an entire disk that is set up as a dynamic disk.

site — An option in Active Directory to interconnect IP subnets so that the server can determine the fastest route to connect clients for authentication and to connect DCs for replication of Active Directory. Site information also enables Active Directory to create redundant routes for DC replication.

spanned volume — Two or more Windows Server 2003 dynamic disks that are combined to appear as one disk.

spool file — A print file written to disk until it can be transmitted to a printer.

spooler — In the Windows 95, 98, Me, NT, 2000, XP, and 2003 environment, a group of DLLs, information files, and programs that process print jobs for printing.

spooling — A process working in the background to enable several print files to go to a single printer. Each file is placed in temporary storage until its turn comes to be printed.

standalone DFS model — A DFS model in which there is no Active Directory implementation to help manage the shared folders. This model provides only a single or flat level share.

standby — A mode in which the computer components are shut down and information in memory is not written to disk storage. The power supply and CPU remain active, waiting to start up all components when you press a key or move the mouse.

static addressing — An IP address that is assigned to a client and that remains in use until it is manually changed.

streaming — Playing a multimedia audio, video, or combined file received over a network before the entire file is received at the client.

stripe set — Two or more basic disks set up so that files are spread in blocks across the disks.

striped volume — Two or more dynamic disks that use striping so that files are spread in blocks across the disks.

striping — A data storage method that breaks up data files across all volumes of a disk set to minimize wear on a single volume.

subnet mask — Used to distinguish between the network part and the host part of the IP address and to enable networks to be divided into subnets.

subtree — Same as root key.

symmetric multiprocessor (SMP) computer — A type of computer with two or more CPUs that share the processing load.

system environment variables — Variables defined by the operating system and that apply to any user logged onto the computer.

system log — An event log that records information about system-related events such as hardware errors, driver problems, and hard drive errors.

System Monitor — The Windows Server 2003 utility used to track system or application objects. For each object type there are one or more counters that can be logged for later analysis, or tracked in real time for immediate system monitoring.

system partition — Partition that contains boot files, such as Boot.ini and Ntldr in Windows Server 2003.

system policy — A grouping of user account and computer parameters that can be configured in Windows NT 4.0 enabling some control of the desktop environment and specific client configuration settings.

system policy editor — Used to configure system policy settings in Windows NT 4.0 and is also available in Windows 2000 Server, but not in Windows Server 2003.

SYSVOL — A shared folder, which is set up when Active Directory is installed and that contains publicly available files that users and DCs need for domain access. SYSVOL folders are replicated among DCs.

T-carrier — A dedicated leased telephone line that can be used for data communications over multiple channels for speeds of up to 44.736 Mbps.

Telnet — A TCP/IP-based application that provides terminal emulation services for access to a server, such as Windows Server 2003.

terminal — A device that consists of a monitor and keyboard to communicate with host computers that run the programs. The terminal does not have a processor to use for running programs locally.

terminal adapter (TA) — Popularly called a digital modem, links a computer or a fax to an ISDN line.

terminal server — A server configured to offer Terminal Services so that clients can run applications on the server, similar to having clients respond as terminals.

TEXT — A data type used for printing text files formatted using the ANSI standard that employs values between 0 and 255 to represent characters, numbers, and symbols.

thin client — A specialized personal computer or terminal device that has a minimal Windows-based operating system. A thin client is designed to connect to a host computer that does most or all of the processing. The thin client is mainly responsible for providing a graphical user interface and network connectivity.

thread — A block of program code executing within a running process. One process may launch one or more threads.

total cost of ownership (TCO) — The cost of installing and maintaining computers and equipment on a network, which includes hardware, software, maintenance, and support costs.

trace log — Monitors particular events (far fewer than offered through System Monitor) specified by a server administrator, so that the log contains only those instances when the events occur, as when creating a trace to record each time there is disk input/output activity or when there is an Active Directory Kerberos security event.

transitive trust — A trust relationship between two or more domains in a tree in which each domain has access to objects in the others.

Transmission Control Protocol (TCP) — Part of the TCP/IP suite, a protocol that is responsible for the reliable transmission of data on a TCP/IP network. TCP is a connection-oriented protocol ensuring that all packets sent using TCP are delivered successfully and in the right order.

Transmission Control Protocol/Internet Protocol (TCP/IP) — The default protocol suite installed with Windows Server 2003 that enables network communication.

tree — Related domains that use a contiguous namespace, share the same schema, and have two-way transitive trust relationships.

two-way trust — A domain relationship in which both domains are trusted and trusting, enabling one to have access to objects in the other.

unicast — A message that goes from one single computer to another single computer.

Uniform Resource Locator (URL) — An addressing format used to find an Internet Web site or page.

uninterruptible power supply (UPS) — A device built into electrical equipment or a separate device that provides immediate battery power to equipment during a power failure or brownout.

uniqueness database file (UDF) — A text file that contains an answer set of unique instructions for installing Windows Server 2003 in the unattended mode and that is used with an answer file.

universal security group — A group that is used to provide access to resources in any domain within a forest. A common implementation is to make global groups that contain accounts members of a universal group that has access to resources.

User Datagram Protocol (UDP) — A connectionless protocol that can be used with IP, instead of TCP.

user environment variables — Environment variables that are defined on a per user basis.

virtual directory — A URL formatted address that provides an Internet location (virtual location) for an actual physical folder on a Web server that is used to publish Web documents.

virtual memory — Disk storage allocated to link with physical RAM to temporarily hold data when there is not enough free RAM.

virtual private network (VPN) — A private network that is like a tunnel through a larger network—such as the Internet, an enterprise network, or both—that is restricted to designated member clients only.

volume — A basic disk partition that has been formatted for a particular file system, a primary partition, a volume set, an extended volume, a stripe set, a stripe set with parity, or a mirror set. Or a dynamic disk that is set up as a simple volume, spanned volume, striped volume, RAID-5 volume, or mirrored volume.

volume set — Two or more formatted basic disk partitions (volumes) that are combined to look like one volume with a single drive letter.

Windows Internet Naming Service (WINS) — A Windows Server 2003 service that enables the server to convert NetBIOS computer names to IP addresses for network and Internet communications.

Windows NT LAN Manager (NTLM) — An authentication protocol used in Windows NT Server 3.5, 3.51, and 4.0 that is retained in Windows 2000 Server and Windows Server 2003 for backward compatibility for clients that cannot support Kerberos, such as MS-DOS and Windows 3.1x.

workgroup — As used in Microsoft networks, a number of users who share drive and printer resources in an independent peer-to-peer relationship.

workstation — A computer that has its own central processing unit (CPU) and may be used as a stand-alone or network computer for word processing, spreadsheet creation, or other software applications.

X.25 — An older packet-switching protocol for connecting remote networks at speeds up to 2.048 Mbps.

zone — A partition or subtree in a DNS server that contains specific kinds of records in a lookup table, such as a forward lookup zone that contains records in a table for looking up computer and domain names in order to find their associated IP addresses.

Index